The revival of romance as a literary form and the imaginative impact of the French Revolution are acknowledged influences on English Romanticism. But the question of how these seemingly antithetical forces combined has rarely been addressed. In this innovative study of the transformations of a genre, David Duff examines the paradox whereby the unstable visionary world of romance came to provide an apt and accurate language for the representation of revolution, and how this literary form was itself politicised in the period. Drawing on an extensive range of textual and visual sources, he traces the ambivalent ideological overtones of the chivalric revival, the polemical appropriation of the language of romance in the 'pamphlet war' of the 1790s, and the emergence of a radical cult of chivalry among the Hunt–Shelley circle in 1815–17. Central to the book is a detailed analysis of Shelley's neglected revolutionary romances *Queen Mab* and *Laon and Cythna*, flawed but fascinating poems in which the politics of romance is most fully displayed.

CAMBRIDGE STUDIES IN ROMANTICISM 7

ROMANCE AND REVOLUTION

This series aims to foster the best new work in one of the most challenging fields within English literary studies. From the early 1780s to the early 1830s a formidable array of talented men and women took to literary composition, not just in poetry, which some of them famously transformed, but in many modes of writing. The expansion of publishing created new opportunities for writers, and the political stakes of what they wrote were raised again and again by what Wordsworth called those 'great national events' that were 'almost daily taking place': the French Revolution, the Napoleonic and American wars, urbanization, industrialization, religious revival, an expanded empire abroad and the reform movement at home. This was an enormous ambition, even when it pretended otherwise. The relations between science, philosophy, religion and literature were reworked in texts such as *Frankenstein* and *Biographia Literaria*; gender relations in *A Vindication of the Rights of Woman* and *Don Juan*; journalism by Cobbett and Hazlitt: poetic form, content and style by the Lake School and the Cockney School. Outside Shakespeare studies, probably no body of writing has produced such a wealth of response or done so much to shape the responses of modern criticism. This indeed is the period that saw the emergence of those notions of 'literature' and of literary history, especially national literary history, on which modern scholarship in English has been founded.

The categories produced by Romanticism have also been challenged by recent historicist arguments. The task of the series is to engage both with a challenging corpus of Romantic writings and with the changing field of criticism they have helped to shape. As with other literary series published by Cambridge, this one will represent the work of both younger and more established scholars, on either side of the Atlantic and elsewhere.

ROMANCE AND REVOLUTION

Shelley and the Politics of a Genre

David Duff

University of Aberdeen

Published by the Press Syndicate of the University of Cambridge
The Pitt Building, Trumpington Street, Cambridge CB2 1RP
40 West 20th Street, New York, NY 10011–4211 USA
10 Stamford Road, Oakleigh, Melbourne 3166, Australia

First published 1994
Reprinted 1996

Printed in Great Britain at Woolnough Bookbinding Ltd, Irthlingborough, Northants.

A catalogue record for this book is available from the British Library

Library of Congress cataloguing in publication data

Duff, David A. S., 1962–
Romance and revolution : Shelley and the politics of a genre / David Duff.
p.   cm. – (Cambridge studies in romanticism)
Includes bibliographical references (p.   ) and index.
ISBN 0 521 45018 7 (hardback)
1. Shelley, Percy Bysshe, 1792 – Knowledge – Literature.   2. Politics and literature –
England – History – 19th century.   3. Revolutionary poetry, English – History and
criticism.   4. France – History – Revolution, 1789–1799 – Influence.   5. Romances –
Adaptations – History and criticism.   6. Medievalism – England – History – 19th century.
7. English poetry – Frence influences.   8. Chivalry in literature.   9. Romanticism –
England.   10. Literary form.   I. Title.   II. Series
PR544.L5D84   1994
821.7–dc20   93–34648   CIP

ISBN 0 521 45018 7 hardback

TAG

In memory of my father,
Robert Stewart Duff

Contents

Illustrations

x

Acknowledgments

It gives me pleasure to acknowledge, firstly, the assistance of Timothy Webb, who introduced me as an unsuspecting undergraduate to the study of Romanticism, and who was closely involved with this project from the start; also that of John Birtwhistle, whose lucid responses enabled me, at a later stage, to reappraise and refine my ideas about revolutionary romance. To both I am much indebted, as I am to others at the University of York who gave help or encouragement, especially Simon Bainbridge, Bruno Balducci, Chris Bernard, Barbara Couchman, Philip Cox, Anne-Julie Crozier, Jack Donovan, Gary Farnell, Peter Finch, Jean Gregorek, Debbie Grice, Hugh Haughton, Steven Matthews, Tina Moore, Anita Pacheco and Andrea Sullivan. In preparing the work for publication I have benefited greatly from the critical advice and support of Marilyn Butler, and from the many valuable suggestions made by James Chandler, Josie Dixon and the two readers for Cambridge University Press. Helen Lynch has contributed to this book in numerous ways, and several parts of the argument were worked out in collaboration with her. My thanks too, for expert technical assistance, to Jacek Szelożyński and Mirek Jasiński; and to my daughter Koshka, for waiting.

Acknowledgment is also due to the Trustees of the British Museum and to the British Library for permission to reproduce materials from their collections; and to Oxford University Press for making available to me the proofs of the (now published) first volume of *The Prose Works of Percy Bysshe Shelley.*

Abbreviations

KSJ	*Keats–Shelley Journal*
KSMB	*Keats–Shelley Memorial Bulletin*
KSR	*Keats–Shelley Review* (formerly the *Keats–Shelley Memorial Bulletin*)
Letters	*The Letters of Percy Bysshe Shelley*. Ed. Frederick L. Jones. 2 vols. Oxford: Clarendon Press, 1964.
Poems	*The Poems of Shelley*. Ed. Geoffrey Matthews and Kelvin Everest. 1 vol. so far. London: Longman, 1989.
Poetical Works	*Shelley: Poetical Works*. Ed. Thomas Hutchinson, with corrections by Geoffrey Matthews. Oxford University Press, 1970.
Poetry and Prose	*Shelley's Poetry and Prose: Authoritative Texts, Criticism*. Ed. Donald H. Reiman and Sharon B. Powers. New York: Norton, 1977.
Prose	*Shelley's Prose; or, The Trumpet of a Prophecy*. Ed. David Lee Clark. Corrected edn. (1966), with preface by Harold Bloom. London: Fourth Estate, 1988.
Prose Works	*The Prose Works of Percy Bysshe Shelley*. Ed. E. B. Murray. 1 vol. so far. Oxford University Press, 1993.
Shelley and His Circle	*Shelley and His Circle 1773–1822*. An edition of the manuscripts in the Carl H. Pforzheimer Library. 8 vols. Ed. Kenneth Neill Cameron (vols. I–IV) and Donald H. Reiman (vols. V–VIII). Cambridge, Mass.: Harvard University Press, 1961–86.

Introduction

The purpose of this book is to explore a critical phase in the history of romance, and of Romanticism, represented by the persistent conjunction of the theme of revolution with the language and form of romance; to locate the origins of this development in the political prose and verse of the 1790s; and to examine its consequences in the poetry of Shelley, through a close reading of his two revolutionary romances *Queen Mab* and *Laon and Cythna; or, The Revolution of the Golden City* (also known as *The Revolt of Islam*).

Three different kinds of enquiry are brought together here. One is concerned with genre, and the politics of genre; another is about the origins and contexts of Romanticism; the third involves Shelley, and his relation to the literary and political culture of his time. In its investigation of romance, this book proceeds from a number of assumptions and definitions: from Northrop Frye's claim[1] that there is a utopian or 'revolutionary' quality inherent in romance, which results from its 'dialectical' structure and uncompromising idealism, displayed both in the conception of character and 'in the polarizing between two worlds, one desirable and the other hateful'; from Fredric Jameson's important essay on romance,[2] with its rigorous theoretical modelling of the politics of the genre, and its suggestive historical question about 'what, under wholly altered historical conditions, can have been found to replace the constitutive raw materials of magic and otherness which medieval romance found ready to hand in its socioeconomic environment'; from Patricia Parker's analysis of the narrative structure of romance,[3] which shows that its dynamic (and, by extension, its politics) is ambivalent and unstable rather than straightforwardly teleological; from recent work on the sexual politics of romance;[4] and from other theoretical and historical studies, cited in the following pages, which provide clues as to how romance, either in its imaginative structure or in its ideological functioning, might be deemed to have a 'politics' as well as a 'poetics'.

Yet my starting point is the claim that there is something intrinsically paradoxical about the idea of a politics of romance, and about the conjunction of the terms 'romance' and 'revolution'. If one answer (and for my purposes, the most pertinent) to Jameson's question about what replaces magic in the 'magical narratives' of the modern age is politics itself, this is by no means self-evident, for the differences between the two phenomena are more apparent than their similarities. Until recently, romance was most often defined as a genre that had very little to do with the realities of history or politics – as indeed synonomous with pure fiction or fantasy. Nevertheless, the link is now almost taken for granted as one of the central facts in the literary history of English Romanticism, and there is a virtually canonical argument that identifies its two major influences as the revival of romance and the impact of the French Revolution. According to this account, which received its classic formulation in Harold Bloom's essay on 'The Internalization of Quest Romance' (1970),[5] the genre reappears in the mid-eighteenth century, acquires apocalyptic scope as a result of the expectations raised by the French Revolution, and is subsequently internalised to create the paradigmatic Romantic form: the psychological quest romance. Shelley's deployment of the genre is seen to follow a similar pattern in that he begins by writing didactic, utopian romances, and ends up writing internalised, visionary works like *Prometheus Unbound*, *Epipsychidion* and *The Triumph of Life*.

Much of the evidence presented here confirms this account, but it alters the emphasis, and offers a new historical focus. By highlighting, and problematising, the relation between romance and revolution, I seek to recover the paradox concealed in the familiar claim that Romanticism is somehow a combination of the two, and thus to reveal some of the tensions, oppositions and ambivalence that surround the texts – not all of them literary – in which that fusion first takes place. I also attempt to give a more scrupulously historical account of the Romantic transformation of romance by maintaining distinctions between contemporary perceptions of the genre and our own, and by looking in detail at how images, themes, metres and other generic materials were transmitted and modified from one text to another. Above all, my aim is to reassess Shelley's relation to romance, and to Romanticism, by concentrating on two poems –

both largely ignored by modern scholarship – in which much of the work of generic reconstruction is performed, and in which the politics of romance is most fully displayed.

The paradox can be seen in its starkest form in the polemical prose and verse produced during the 'pamphlet war' of the 1790s, where themes and images from romance were repeatedly used, positively or negatively, to describe the extraordinary events of the French Revolution, and the possibilities, or dangers, to which it was seen in England to give rise. This is not quite the point made by Frye when he talks of the revolutionary quality inherent in romance, nor by Gillian Beer[6] when she refers to earlier moments in the history of the genre when the magical and the political became linked. The point here is that, with the French Revolution, history itself seemed to enter the domain of the miraculous, and romance to offer a vivid and accurate language to describe what was happening. And these were not merely isolated allusions. In the writings and speeches of the great counter-revolutionary Edmund Burke, romance imagery is so common as to constitute a kind of myth-making, the figurative narrative that results being both a polemical device to influence his readers and a subliminal encoding of the trauma of revolution. More fragmentary but no less vivid is the revolutionary romance contained in the writings of Burke's opponents, a myth of revolution that often employs the very same metaphors to opposite effect, and that, like Burke's, continued to shape perceptions of the Revolution for generations to come. To explore these two myths, and the confrontation between them, is the aim of the first chapter of this book, which draws on a variety of texts from the 1790s and early 1800s, including polemical tracts, parliamentary speeches, newspaper verses, political cartoons and private letters. The chapter concludes with a discussion of Wordsworth's famous lines on the 'French Revolution, As It Appeared to Enthusiasts at Its Commencement', a text (drafted in 1804) which brilliantly draws together opposing representations of the French Revolution, and in so doing exposes the full ambivalence of the language of revolutionary romance.

Yet it is not just at the level of imagery that we can discern a politics of romance in the literature of this period. In ways that are difficult but possible to determine, political circumstances ultimately affected the literary form itself. While some writers, such as Robert Southey and Walter Scott, wrote mythological or historical romances partly as an escape from the pressure of political affairs and everyday life,

Byron on the other hand may be said in *Childe Harold's Pilgrimage* (1812–18) to have modernised the genre in order to explore the expanded, troubled consciousness of post-revolutionary Europe, a distinctly political project as well as a signal instance of the internalisation of quest romance. It is in the poetry of Shelley, however, that romance received its fullest political development, and underwent its most remarkable formal transformations. Chapter Two is a study of the first of Shelley's revolutionary romances, *Queen Mab* (1813). This, the most radical and outspoken of all his poems, establishes a direct and conscious link with the revolutionary culture of the 1790s, reviving its millenarian language and reasserting many of its themes, while also laying claim to a wider philosophical heritage which extends from Plato to Sir William Drummond. But the audacity of Shelley's 'philosophical poem' lies not just in its radical ideas and inflammatory tone but also in its form, which, together with its Notes, constitutes a remarkable synthesis of diverse elements: eighteenth-century allegory, Miltonic epic, metrical romance, dream vision and revolutionary polemic. Faced with such a heterogeneous work, it is impossible to treat the poem purely as an aesthetic object, and I therefore adopt a more flexible approach, exploring various aspects of its form and content, and invoking a wide range of sources and contexts. My central concern, however, is with Shelley's political exploitation of romance: of the teleological structure and utopian core of the genre; of its traditional, but now potentially subversive theme of virtue; and of archetypal motifs such as the enchantress (in this case Queen Mab herself) and the Bower of Bliss, drawn both from literary sources and from the metaphorical language of other political writings.

One of the images, or themes, that most often resurfaced in the political writing of the time was that of chivalry. Almost all of the original replies to Burke's *Reflections on the Revolution in France* (1790) make some reference to the extraordinary passage in which he identifies the misfortunes of Marie-Antoinette at Versailles with the demise of the 'age of chivalry'. Most of his political antagonists simply ridiculed the passage, more often than not by reference to *Don Quixote*; but there were some who sought to reclaim the notion of chivalry, and to show that the ideals it expressed were closer to those of the Revolution itself than to those of the *ancien régime*. The effect of this dispute was to politicise the whole question of chivalry, with the result that the so-called 'chivalric revival' which took place after the turn of the century – mainly through the influence of Scott, though it had begun earlier – was strongly coloured by politics. Broadly speaking, the chivalric revival was a reactionary phenomenon, its function being to amuse the upper classes and to galvanise patriotic sentiment during the era of the Napoleonic Wars. There were, however, a number of writers of a different political persuasion or social class who sought to continue the polemic with Burke and his successors by adapting the fashionable theme of chivalry to their own purposes, and reinterpreting its codes in terms of a radical or liberal politics. Foremost among these were Leigh Hunt, Thomas Love Peacock, and Shelley himself, who together formed what may be described as a radical cult of chivalry in the years 1815–17. Their endeavours in this regard, in both the private and the public sphere, have passed largely unrecorded in the history of the chivalric revival, and are the subject of my third chapter. The chapter also deals with the example of Byron, whose adoption of the theme in the first two cantos of *Childe Harold's Pilgrimage* anticipates, in its mock-serious tone as much as in its political application of the medieval code, many of the manoeuvres of the Hunt–Shelley circle. In the case of Shelley, whose fictitious ancestor 'Sir Guyon de Shelley' figures in the title of the chapter, I present a more general account of his interest in the theme, giving special attention to his engagement with the ideas of Godwin.

The fourth and final chapter considers Shelley's most ambitious reworking of the chivalric ethos, *Laon and Cythna* (1817). Written 'in the style and for the same object' as *Queen Mab*, this poem has a more obvious claim to the designation 'romance', its dominant idiom being that of romance, and its basic structure consisting of a sequence of quests. Like *Queen Mab*, it seeks to reawaken the political idealism of the early 1790s, and to advance a 'liberal and comprehensive morality' based on Godwin's *Enquiry Concerning Political Justice* (1793); but it does so by subtler means, replacing the naked didacticism of the earlier poem with an affective poetics derived from Spenser and Wordsworth. Described in the Preface as 'an experiment on the temper of the public mind', *Laon and Cythna* is a unique confrontation with its own historical moment, a poetic engagement with the political imagination of early nineteenth-century England which, in Shelley's analysis, was still burdened with traumatic memories of the French Revolution. Crucially, that engagement takes place through the form of romance, so that whilst the inspired but failed revolution that constitutes the central action of the poem is obviously at one level a fictionalised version of the French Revolution, the controlling perspective is a redemptive or transcendent one, and the poem moves according to the dynamic of quest narrative or myth rather than history. Revolutionary both in its subject-matter and in its transformation of generic conventions, *Laon and Cythna* is a fascinating case of the politics of romance, as well as a perfect (if previously unrecognised) example of the internalisation of the genre – one that is of particular interest in that it displays all the stages of the process of internalisation in the course of a single poem.

Two of the chapters, then, are contextual, two textual in emphasis. But the relationship between the former and the latter is more active than such a description might imply. A main contention of this book is that Shelley's revolutionisation of the form of romance is preceded and made possible by the revolutionisation of the language of romance that took place in the political writing of the Revolution debate, and by the existence in the English imagination of the 'revolutionary romance' of the French Revolution itself. *Queen Mab* and *Laon and Cythna*, although written a generation later, directly invoke and engage these contexts, recycling modes of thought and expression from the 1790s, and taking as their point of departure the historical and imaginative experience that Shelley called 'the master theme of the epoch – the French Revolution' (*Letters*, 1, 504). The two poems thus provide a powerful illustration of what has become increasingly apparent to historians and theoreticians of genre: namely, that the development of a genre takes place not only within the confines of literary form, but also through other ideological productions – here visual as well as verbal – with which literary texts interact.[7]

This book begins as an essay in intertextuality and ends as an exercise in practical criticism. One of the most striking things to emerge is the way in which particular phrases and images from romance, or particular statements *about* romance, were almost endlessly repeated and reformulated throughout the period in question (and across the historical divide which separates the first from the second generation of English Romantics), as though those utterances or topoi had become indispensable to the period's awareness of itself. That this is so should not perhaps surprise us, but it is not immediately obvious why, for example, the Spenserian motif of the Bower of Bliss should equally well have served Wordsworth's account of the French Revolution, Shelley's portrayal of the Prince Regent, and Southey's description of a Hindu heaven; or why Burke's pronouncement of the death of chivalry should have given rise not only to countless rejoinders during the 1790s, but also, two decades later, to a diatribe against commerce in *Queen Mab*, a discussion of love in Hazlitt's essay 'On Pedantry', and a comic symposium in Peacock's novel *Melincourt*. To throw some light on these matters is not the least of my aims in the following pages.

CHAPTER I

The French Revolution and the politics of romance

That love of truth and virtue which seems at all times natural to liberal minded youth, was at this time carried to a pitch of enthusiasm, as well by the extraordinary events that had taken place, as by the romantic prospects of ideal excellence which were pictured in the writings of philosophers and poets. A new world was opening to the astonished sight. Scenes, lovely as hope can paint, dawned on the imagination: visions of unsullied bliss lulled the senses, and hid the darkness of surrounding objects, rising in bright succession and endless gradations, like the steps of that ladder which was once set up on the earth, and whose top reached to heaven. Nothing was too mighty for this new-begotten hope: and the path that led to human happiness seemed as plain – as the pictures in the Pilgrim's Progress leading to Paradise. Imagination was unable to keep pace with the gigantic strides of reason, and the strongest faith fell short of the supposed reality.

Hazlitt, *Memoirs of the Late Thomas Holcroft* (1816)

Of all the conceivable ways of describing a political revolution, few would seem more implausible than to compare it to a chivalric romance – especially if the event in question were the French Revolution of 1789, the revolution which sought to do away with all that remained of the feudal system under which the chivalric romances had once flourished. Revolution is characterised by the 'rapid expansion of political consciousness',[1] the interpenetration of 'common, private existence with the perception of historical processes',[2] whereas the essence of romance is 'its legendary, fairy-tale atmosphere', its removal from 'political reality' and 'geographic, economic, and social conditions'.[3] In the eyes of contemporaries, the French Revolution marked the triumph of reason over superstition: it was the Enlightenment in action. A romance, on the other hand, was a 'fabulous narrative' from the 'dark ages', a 'fictitious recital'

8

based upon marvels and miracles.[4] What possible similarity could there be between the two?

Yet the political writing of the Revolutionary period is full of images from romance. Syrens, furies, harpies, giants, spells, trances, magic swords, wicked wizards, chivalric knights, round tables, castles, caves and bowers of bliss: we encounter all of these, as similes or metaphors, in the work of English political writers of the 1790s. Time and time again, the world of old romance was invoked to depict some aspect of the new political culture in France or at home, or to furnish some impression of the great events of the Revolution, or to envision its future prospects. Often the very same images were used by those sympathetic as by those hostile to the Revolution. In the writings of Burke such images form an elaborate figurative subplot which is both a rhetorical device to influence the views of the British public, and the expression of a deep imaginative reaction to the trauma of revolution. It was partly in response to this negative mythology of revolution, as well as in response to events themselves, that another myth of revolution developed in the English political imagination in this period, one whose structure and idiom was also that of romance, but whose politics was fundamentally opposed to Burke's. The confrontation between these two myths – between the counter-revolutionary romance of Burke and the revolutionary romance contained in the writings of his opponents – is one of the most interesting features of the so-called 'pamphlet war' of the 1790s. The aim of the present chapter is to explore this confrontation by examining the contrasting uses of romance themes and images in some of the polemical literature of the Revolutionary decade, and also to trace its extension into some of the poems of the time.

THE STATUS OF ROMANCE IN THE 1790S

Several reasons will emerge to explain why a language which was seemingly so unsuitable for the purpose of describing a political revolution acquired such currency in this context. Two general points need to be made in advance. The first concerns the status of romance.[5] At the end of the eighteenth century, the body of early literature that was then known as 'romantic poetry' (and the word 'romantic' itself) had a very ambiguous reputation. On the one hand, it had been thoroughly discredited by two hundred years of hostile criticism, which included the attacks of the Puritans,[6] who condemned the old romances on moral and religious grounds (viewing them as unfortunate relics from the 'papist' past), and the war of attrition conducted during the Enlightenment,[7] when the romances fell into further disrepute because of their dependence on magic and superstition (they were now seen as products of the 'dark ages', belonging to the infancy of society). In addition there had been Cervantes's brilliant parody of romance and chivalry in *Don Quixote*, a text which exercised a peculiar fascination for eighteenth-century England, and which greatly influenced the development of its major genre, the novel.[8] The adjective 'romantic', coined in the 1650s in order 'to mark the distinction between the truth of nature and the falsehood of romance',[9] soon became what John Foster in 1806 called 'a convenient exploding word',[10] that is, a term of derision and abuse – usually to be found alongside terms like 'chimerical', 'fantastic', 'extravagant', 'unnatural'. Romance, from this perspective, was a language of the absurd.

Since the middle of the eighteenth century, however, a new and more sympathetic attitude to romance had been gaining favour. Largely as a result of the efforts of literary historians like Thomas Percy, Richard Hurd and Thomas Warton, it was no longer universally believed that the literature of the middle ages was superstitious or childish nonsense. The old romances – which now began to be available again in something like their original form – were not just to be considered as grotesque curiosities from the distant past. Chivalry was not necessarily to be thought of as the ludicrous institution to which Cervantes had reduced it, nor should 'romantic' be merely a byword for what is false or unnatural. The earlier view is well represented by David Hume when, in an essay of 1727, he accounts for the 'monstrous Birth' of 'Romantick Chivalry' by pointing out the erratic operation of the mind when imagination takes leave of judgment:

'Tis observable of the human Mind that when it is smit with any Idea of Merit or Perfection beyond what its Faculties can attain, & in the pursuit of which, it uses not Reason and Experience for its Guide, it knows no Mean, but as it gives the Rein & even adds the Spur to every florid Conceit or Fancy, runs in a moment quite wide of Nature. Thus we find when, without Discretion, it indulges its devout Fervors, that, working in such fairy-ground, it quietly burys itself in its own Whimsies & Chimera's, & raises up to itself a new set of Passions, Affections, Desires, Objects, & in short a perfectly new World of its own, inhabited by different Beings, & regulated by different Laws, from this of ours.[11]

Two factors made possible the development of a new attitude to the chivalric romances and to the romantic dimension in later, canonical authors such as Spenser, Shakespeare and Milton. The first was the emergence of a new aesthetic which challenged neoclassical precepts and valuations.[12] Long before the romance revival itself, Joseph Addison's famous papers in *The Spectator* on 'The Pleasures of the Imagination' (1712) articulated the argument that would be echoed and elaborated by all subsequent defenders of 'romantic' literature, namely that the value of such writing – what Dryden had called 'the faerie way of writing' – resides precisely in the fact that the author does *not* follow nature and imitate the real world, since by inventing a world of his own, he thereby demonstrates his creativity and originality, these being the attributes valued by the new poetics.

A second factor that contributed to the revaluation of romance was the development of a historical approach to literary criticism. The growing interest in the literature of the middle ages was nourished by an expanding knowledge of the middle ages themselves.[13] What had previously been thought 'unnatural' in the old romances – notably the institution of chivalry – was now claimed to have an historical foundation in the customs and beliefs that prevailed at the time they were written. At first, this line of argument would appear to run counter to the argument about creativity (a paradox which has not been sufficiently explored in the historiography of Romantic aesthetics), yet the two are often found side by side in the work of the romance revivalists. In his dissertation 'Of the Origin of Romantic Fiction in Europe', affixed to his *History of English Poetry* of 1774, Thomas Warton defines romance as a 'species of fabulous narrative', but talks in the same paragraph of early examples of the genre 'coinciding with the reigning manners'.[14] Richard Hurd ends his *Letters of Chivalry and Romance* (1762) by making a firm distinction between 'historical' and 'poetical truth', and by endorsing the anti-mimetic thesis of Addison, but much of what has gone before is an attempt to show that the code of chivalry as reflected in the old romances (in fact he is usually thinking of Spenser) had actually been practised by medieval noblemen.[15] Likewise in Scott's 'Essay on Romance' (1824), a definition of the genre as 'a fictitious narrative in prose and verse, the interest of which turns upon marvellous and uncommon incidents' is followed by a discussion built on the premise that 'romance and real history have the same common origin'; only latterly has the term romance 'come to be used to distinguish works of pure fiction'. The process by which romance evolved is identified as the embellishing action of the 'love of the marvellous, so natural to the human mind', upon the facts of history, a formulation which appears to reflect contemporary speculation on the nature of myth – and indeed the category of romance is tentatively expanded to embrace 'the mythical and fabulous history of all early nations'.[16]

There were, then, more constructive ways of thinking and writing about romance. It was possible at the end of the eighteenth century to speak approvingly of the 'romantic', to allude meaningfully to the old romances, or even to recreate the form in its entirety by writing a modern romance of chivalry or a 'gothic novel'. But to do so was to invite the disapproval and scorn of those to whom such things remained 'Whimsies and Chimera's'. The coexistence of the two attitudes – the romanticist and the rationalist – meant that the language of romance, whether used for literary purposes or in other contexts, was peculiarly unstable and ambivalent. Its imaginative force was recognised, but its legitimacy not generally accepted. Moreover, it was always susceptible to inversion, its positive associations quickly reducible to negative ones. Even individual writers tend to reflect this ambivalence, using the idiom positively at one moment and negatively at another (it is important to remember that many of the images are *inherently* ambivalent, doubleness being one of the traditional themes of romance). As we shall see, this has interesting consequences in the context of a polemical exchange.

Its ambivalent connotations may help to explain why the language of romance was suitable for the purposes of *satire* in the debate on the French Revolution. But they do not tell us why it should also have served as a more direct metaphorical resource, to convey actual perceptions of the Revolution. To understand this we need to reflect on the nature of the phenomenon to which this language was being applied. For the point is that in 1789 history itself seemed to have taken a 'fabulous' turn. As de Toqueville wrote,[17] the French Revolution 'created the politics of the impossible', and marvels and miracles now seemed like everyday events. 'Few persons but those who lived in it', wrote Robert Southey, looking back from middle age, 'can conceive or comprehend what the memory of the French Revolution was, nor what a visionary world seemed to open upon those who were just entering it. Old things seemed passing away and nothing was dreamt of but the regeneration of the human race.'[18] What better way of describing this dream of perfectibility, the prospect of creating a paradise on earth by an act of transformational will, than by means of a literary genre whose very subject-matter is 'a perfectly new World', one 'inhabited by different Beings, & regulated by different Laws, from this of ours'? This would apply not only to to those who believed that the new world heralded by the French Revolution would be a utopia, an ideal society regulated by reason and the rights of man, and inhabited by perfectly virtuous citizens, but also to those who believed that it would be – indeed, in parts of France, already was – a community of deluded and irrational fanatics, founded on vice and violence. For both, the magical narratives of romance – with their ideal heroes, transformation scenes and earthly paradises, but also their terrifying monsters, and their deceptions, temptations and errors – offered an apt and accurate metaphorical language to write about the extraordinary phenomenon that confronted them.

BURKE'S COUNTER-REVOLUTIONARY ROMANCE

'In the time I have lived to', wrote Edmund Burke in 1797, the final year of his life, 'I always seem to walk on enchanted ground. Everything is new, and, according to the fashionable phrase, revolutionary.'[19] The comment is provoked by the 'striking and peculiar' title of a recent pamphlet on the French war, and forms part of his last, unfinished *Letter on a Regicide Peace*. More remarkable in retrospect than the rubric of that particular pamphlet is Burke's own metaphor of walking on enchanted ground. To epitomise his experience of a world in which everything seemed 'new' and 'revolutionary', Burke adopts a traditional image from old romance. Bunyan's name for one of the scenes in *The Pilgrim's Progress*,[20] Enchanted Ground, had since become a familiar – even fashionable – phrase to describe any territory in romance that was under the spell of a magician; indeed a synecdoche for the whole world of magic and faery found in the old romances.[21] Specifically, Burke's wording seems to echo Addison's memorable description of reading Ovid, where the romantic topos is applied to a classical precursor: 'when we are in the *Metamorphosis*, we are walking on enchanted Ground, and see nothing but Scenes of Magick lying round us'.[22] For Mr Spectator, in 1712, Ovid excels among the classical authors at entertaining us 'with something we never saw before'; he 'has shewn us how the Imagination may be affected by what is Strange'. For

Burke, some eighty years later, that visionary province of poetry has acquired a sinister relevance to the real world of politics. An ancient monarchy metamorphosed into a revolutionary republic is truly something never seen before, a fact as strange as any fiction; and to Burke's distraught imagination, the unprecedented events in France, and their repercussions elsewhere, often do seem frighteningly like 'Scenes of Magick'. Whether or not this precise allusion was intended, Burke's chosen phrase carried such connotations, and their fitness to his theme is not accidental. Burke's metaphor of walking on enchanted ground can also be seen to recall a whole sequence of images in his writings that represent aspects of the French Revolution in terms of magic. An early example from the *Reflections on the Revolution in France* (1790) is when he disparages the obscure, provincial practitioners of law who now predominantly compose the Third Estate of the National Assembly as 'men, suddenly, and, as it were, by enchantment, snatched from the humblest rank of sub-ordination'.[23] If 'enchantment' at first seems a rather extravagant term for the mechanism of democratic election, it certainly communicates the sheer novelty of the notion of popular representation, as well as registering Burke's suspicion and disapproval. Bolder still is the later image in the same work by which we are exhorted to look with horror on the revolutionists as

children of their country who are prompt rashly to hack that aged parent in pieces, and put him into the kettle of magicians, in hopes that by their poisonous weeds, and wild incantations, they may regenerate the paternal constitution, and renovate their father's life.[24]

With hindsight, it is tempting to read this extraordinary passage – which alludes to a macabre anecdote, told by Ovid and others, about the efforts of the daughters of King Pelias to rejuvenate their father in the manner prescribed by Medea – as a prophecy of the execution of Louis XVI (which took place in 1793). In its original context, however, the magicians at the cauldron signify the members of the Constitutive Assembly at work, the 'father' being the state, and the 'paternal constitution' its body of laws. Dismembering the aged parent refers to the dismantling of the old body politic, not the person of the King, and magic basically involves drafting a new constitution.

But this is not simply a rhetorical *tour de force*: there is an underlying imaginative logic. Motivating the whole programme of constitutional – and institutional – renewal in France was the conviction that politics can transform the essential character of a society. This was the audacious and liberating creed that Jean-Jacques Rousseau had preached, the doctrine that after 1789 linked 'revolution' to 'regeneration' and lent such enormous significance both to the renovation of government and to the propagation of a revolutionary culture. From the standpoint of Burke's conservatism, however, this was a radical fallacy in the new philosophy, a claim for a dimension to politics that in reality does not exist. The character of a nation of people is determined by manners, morals and custom; innovation is not reform but perversion of 'the natural order of things'.[25] To Burke's nature, then, the Rousseauist theory was a sort of political supernatural, exposed in practice as being at best chimerical,[26] and at worst violently *un*natural. It is apt and consistent, therefore, for the revolutionary experiment to be represented metaphorically as a piece of wizardry both gruesome and ludicrous. In this light, even the detail of 'wild incantations' can be seen to be pertinent, indicating the vital role of oaths, slogans and individual words – such as 'liberté', 'égalité', 'fraternité', 'citoyen', 'nation', 'patrie' – both in revolutionary practices and in the legislation itself. Even today, analytical historians of the Revolution readily speak of 'magic words' and 'revolutionary incantations'.

Burke continues to use the language of the supernatural in some of his later polemics on the Revolution. An outstanding example is the passage in *A Letter to a Noble Lord* (1796) in which the French revolutionists are pictured as 'harpies':

The French revolutionists complained of everything; they refused to reform anything; and they left nothing, no, nothing at all *unchanged*. The consequences are *before* us, – not in remote history; not in future prognostication: they are about us; they are upon us. They shake the public security; they menace private enjoyment. They dwarf the growth of the young; they break the quiet of the old. If we travel, they stop our way. They infest us in town; they pursue us to the country. Our business is interrupted; our repose is troubled; our pleasures are saddened; our very studies are poisoned and perverted, and knowledge is rendered worse than ignorance, by the enormous evils of this dreadful innovation. The revolution harpies of France, sprung from night and hell, or from that chaotic anarchy, which generates equivocally 'all monstrous, all prodigious things', cuckoo-like, adulterously lay their eggs, and brood over, and hatch them in the nest of every neighbouring state. These obscene harpies, who deck themselves in I know not what divine attributes, but who in reality are foul and ravenous birds of prey, (both mothers and daughters,) flutter over our heads, and souse down upon our tables, and leave nothing unrent, unrifled, unravaged, or unpolluted with the slime of their filthy offal.[27]

There is an unmistakable note of obsession here, evidence of what commentators frequently refer to as a pathological strain in the rhetoric of Burke's final pamphlets.[28] It is not sufficient to account for language such as this by drawing a general correspondence between the increasingly savage course taken by the Revolution, and the increasingly monstrous form of Burke's imagery. In fact, the theme here is not revolutionary violence but – once again – innovation, the paragraph having started with a restatement of his cardinal precept (now offered as nothing less than a 'proverb'), '*to innovate is not to reform*'. To recognise this fact is, on the one hand, to highlight the morbid aspect to the author's imaginative move, the unseemly transformation of the notion of change into that of obscenity and filth. On the other hand, it allows us to locate the direct pressure of meaning within the image, the calculated force with which these infesting, ravening, mythological creatures are made to encode the pervasive and relentless desire of the revolutionists to make things new. The analogy, though exorbitant, is exact. The details and emphases of the final sentence repeat metaphorically the progression of antitheses in the first part of the paragraph which form a literal survey of 'the enormous evils of this dreadful innovation'; and the penultimate sentence plays cleverly upon the idea of 'anarchy' whilst envisioning an infernal provenance for the 'revolution harpies' adequate to such enormities.

The imagery here originally derives not from Ovid, of course, but from Virgil, whose lines on the harpies from Book III of the *Aeneid* are quoted in a footnote, with an appended comment to the effect that the 'horrid and disgusting' reality of 'the revolutionists and constitutionalists of France' surpasses even the imaginary monstrosity that Virgil struggled to express.[29] As used by Burke, the harpies acquire a further significance. He elaborates upon Virgil's 'Virginei volucrum vultus' with his own breed of 'revolution harpies', 'who deck themselves in I know not what divine attributes, but who in reality are foul and ravenous birds of prey'. While it serves primarily, if (as the footnote maintains) inadequately, to evoke the actual 'horror of the times', the image also incorporates their apparent attractions, the 'divine attributes' of the harpies symbolising the utopian promises of the revolutionists. The Revolution is characterised as all the more vicious for its false appearance of virtue.

The notion of illusion, or false attraction, is a recurrent theme in Burke's commentaries on the revolutionary ideology. Liberty, the supreme ideal of the French Revolution, he personifies as 'that seductive *Circean* liberty',[30] alluding to the famous enchantress in Homer's *Odyssey*. In an earlier passage in the *Reflections* he refers contemptuously to 'the delusive plausibilites, of moral politicians'.[31] Most telling of all, though, are his remarks about Rousseau, whose writings were the greatest single influence on the moral politics of the National Assembly. The charge of being a romantic visionary rather than a political theorist was one that had often been made against Rousseau. Burke's criticism – he argues here on the authority of Hume, who 'had from Rousseau himself the secret of his principles of composition' – is more shrewd:

> That acute, though eccentric, observer had perceived, that to strike and interest the public, the marvellous must be produced; that the marvellous of the heathen mythology had long since lost its effect; that giants, magicians, fairies, and heroes of romance which succeeded, had exhausted the portion of credulity which belonged to their age; that now nothing was left to a writer but that species of the marvellous, which might still be produced, and with as great an effect as ever, though in another way; that is, the marvellous in life, in manners, in characters, and in extraordinary situations, giving rise to new and unlooked-for strokes in politics and morals.[32]

Since no one still believed in the supernatural, Rousseau had contrived to 'strike and interest' the public by reproducing the effects of the 'marvellous' in the domain of 'politics and morals'. The revolutionary legislators, however, had taken him literally. Rousseau's chimeras and paradoxes had 'become with them serious grounds of action, upon which they proceed in regulating the most important concerns of the state'. Burke, instinctively mistrustful of abstract reasoning, had warned in his very first published work, *A Vindication of Natural Society* (1756), of the ingenious charms, pleasing sophistries and dazzling falsehoods of 'the fairyland of philosophy'. It was no wonder that happenings in France seemed to him to have a disturbing, magical quality, like scenes of enchantment from a romance, because the fairyland of philosophy was now the world in which the people of that country breathed and moved. As Burke's friend and fellow MP William Windham exclaimed in the House of Commons in March 1790, 'it would seem as if the ideal world were about to overrun the real'.[33]

Yet Burke too is consciously using the resources of the 'marvellous'. The supernatural beings of the 'heathen mythology' may have lost their credibility; 'giants, magicians, and fairies' may no longer be supposed to exist. These creatures are nevertheless much in evidence in his own writings, not as real entities, but as metaphors. Because no one still believed in the 'marvellous', such metaphors were very well suited for the purposes of satire, to ridicule the specious claims of the Revolution. But there was more to it than that. Ovid, Virgil and Homer – let alone Spenser – would hold little interest for us now if it were not possible for us to be affected by things in which we did not literally believe: by creatures of the imagination, as Addison would say. Burke, then, uses the 'marvellous' in order to shock as well as to mock. Many of his images are intended more to frighten the English public than to ridicule the French Revolution: in terms of his own aesthetic categories as interpreted recently by Ronald Paulson, they derive from 'the terrible of his sublime'.[34] To appreciate how effective these figurative devices proved, one need only glance at some of the political caricature of subsequent years. Burke's sinister fairyland of magicians, syrens and harpies immediately entered into general circulation as a vivid and versatile satirical iconography, inspiring such celebrated cartoons as Thomas Rowlandson's 'A Charm for Democracy, Reviewed, Analysed & Destroyed', published in the *Anti-Jacobin Review* on 1 February 1799 (plate 5). Its continued presence in the English political imagination for at least another generation is illustrated by the publication twenty years later of political magazines with titles like *The Black Dwarf*, *The White Dwarf* and *The Gorgon* (two of these were radical journals,[35] but the authors' personae – in each case an ambiguous creature of the supernatural – ultimately derive from Burke's political imagery, or from the visual iconography to which it gave rise[36]).

An even clearer illustration of Burke's influence on anti-Jacobin satire is provided by Mary Burges's popular work *The Progress of the Pilgrim Good-Intent, in Jacobinical Times* (1800), an ingenious if rather laboured rewriting of Bunyan's allegory designed to expose the 'false terms' and 'false ideas' by which the proponents of 'PHILOSOPHISM' had sought to seduce the unwary 'into a participation in their crimes'.[37] Though the author does not acknowledge it, her obvious inspiration is the work of Burke, 'the perversion of language' – that is, the sleight-of-hand by which 'the name of every moral virtue is assigned to its opposite vice' – having been a constant theme of his polemics against the revolutionary philosophy.[38] Indeed his writings furnish not just the theme but the literary model for the allegory, the whole narrative being a kind of sustained Burkean metaphor. A good example is the episode of the Enchanted Ground (as in Bunyan's original allegory, this is the plain which lies between the Delectable Mountains and the Celestial City). In the midst of the plain, which is shrouded in mist and darkness and has the attribute of inducing drowsiness in those who pass over it, stands 'a vast and gloomy edifice, adorned on all sides with sepulchral emblems, with sculls, and bones and implements of death'. This is nothing other than the entrance to hell, though its doorway bears the inscription '*Eternal Sleep*', and it is described by the pilgrim's guide (who calls himself 'HOPE' but whose 'ghastly visage' reveals him to be 'the demon DESPAIR') as a 'vast dormitory' erected on the orders of 'Mr. PHILOSOPHY' by 'the mighty power of ATHEISM' as 'a refuge from the tyranny of SUPERSTITION, and...the terrors of ETERNITY' (pp. 184–87). GOOD-INTENT is not fooled by this description, however, and at the mention of the name of ATHEISM he runs away from the dismal mansion and proceeds without further delay towards the Celestial City. The book ends a few pages later with an apocalyptic scene in which the dormitory collapses into ruins at the sound of a heavenly trumpet and its awakened occupants are devoured by fire, all observed with great satisfaction from the far bank of the river of immortality by GOOD-INTENT. Burke too would surely have been satisfied, and Burges's extension of the metaphor of 'walking on enchanted ground' is perfectly consistent with both the logic and the language of Burke's many descriptions of the dangers posed by the atheistical philosophy of France.

The enchanters and monsters, however, form only part of Burke's political fairyland. He has too his 'heroes of romance'. Even more conspicuous than the supernatural imagery representing the forces of revolution is the chivalric terminology he uses to represent the forces of reaction. In a well-known passage in the *Reflections*, Burke contrasts the present misfortunes of Marie-Antoinette at the hands of the revolutionaries with his 'delightful vision' of her during his last visit to France:

It is now sixteen or seventeen years since I saw the queen of France, then the dauphiness, at Versailles; and surely never lighted on this orb, which she hardly seemed to touch, a more delightful vision. I saw her just above the horizon, decorating and cheering the elevated sphere she just began to move in, – glittering like the morning-star, full of life, and splendor, and joy. Oh! What a revolution! and what an heart must I have, to contemplate without emotion that elevation and that fall! Little did I dream when she added titles of veneration to those of enthusiastic, distant, respectful love, that she should ever be obliged to carry the sharp antidote against disgrace concealed in that bosom; little did I dream that I should have lived to see such disasters fallen upon her in a nation of gallant men, in a nation of men of honour and of cavaliers. I thought ten thousand swords must have leaped from their scabbards to avenge even a look that threatened her with insult. – But the age of chivalry is gone. – That of sophisters, oeconomists, and calculators, has succeeded; and the glory of Europe is extinguished for ever. Never, never more, shall we behold that generous loyalty to rank and sex, that proud submission, that dignified obedience, that subordination of the heart, which kept alive, even in servitude itself, the spirit of an exalted freedom. The unbought grace of life, the cheap defence of nations, the nurse of manly sentiment and heroic enterprize is gone! It is gone, that sensibility of principle, that chastity of honour, which felt a stain like a wound, which inspired courage whilst it mitigated ferocity, which ennobled whatever it touched, and under which vice itself lost half its evil, by losing all its grossness.[39]

James Boulton, in his account of Burke's political language, identifies this 'apostrophe' to the French Queen as 'the centrepiece of the *Reflections*', not least because 'it is the most memorable passage – a fact of vital importance in a piece of persuasive writing'.[40] That this was so will be amply demonstrated in the remainder of this chapter, and in later parts of this book. At present, though, the point I want to make is that while recording the death of chivalry Burke gives us a singularly vivid picture of it. His complaint is that ten thousand swords did *not* leap from their scabbards to defend the person or pride of Marie-Antoinette – but what remains with us is surely the compelling impression that here, as metaphor at least, they *did*. In the realm of the reader's imagination, the chivalric glory of France – and England – is rather immortalised than made extinct. Aristocratic sentiments are marshalled as they are mourned.

Burke, moreover, is now the defender of 'pleasing illusions', of 'super-added ideas, furnished from the wardrobe of a moral imagination'.[41] His description of the dauphiness is an exercise in the language of enchantment (she is both chivalric queen and beautiful enchantress), and it is as *dis*enchanters, or annihilators of romance, that the revolutionists are pictured (all is to be 'dissolved by the conquering empire of light and reason'). He pleads for hierarchy and the Crown in the very terms in which elsewhere he castigates the 'marvellous' politics of equality. And indeed, his own prescription for political power (by explicit analogy with a traditional principle of aesthetic composition) is precisely that it must strike and interest the public:

> The precept given by a wise man, as well as a great critic, for the construction of poems, is equally true as to states. *Non satis est pulchra esse poemata, dulcia sunto.*[42]

In the light of our other examples, all this seems somewhat ironic. But the irony is not Burke's: the views put forward here are serious ones. His contrast between the 'glory' of the 'age of chivalry' and the emptiness of a modern society of 'sophisters, oeconomists, and calculators', is central to Burke's whole political argument.[43] There is no satire in his description of pre-revolutionary France as 'a generous and gallant nation', the preserve, even to its own disadvantage, of 'high and romantic sentiments of fidelity, honour, and loyalty'. Here Burke is quite happy, as Marx put it, to 'play the romanticist'.[44] That is, when used to propound his own nostalgic conservatism, his own vision of an ideal society, the language of romance no longer partakes of the ironic depreciation we have seen him exploit so effectively at other moments. On the contrary, he speaks at these moments in the tradition of writers like Thomas Percy and Richard Hurd, whose scholarly lament for a lost world of romance and chivalry (Hurd talks of the 'great revolution in modern taste', and of 'the magic of the old Romances' having been 'perfectly dissolved'[45]) he transforms into a political lament for the *ancien régime* in France: a lament which in both cases was designed to bring about a revival – or rather a counter-revolution.

ANTITHESISING BURKE: PAINE, GODWIN, MACKINTOSH

Having invoked the Enlightenment critique of the 'marvellous', and then proceeded to couch his own political argument in the language of romance and chivalry, Burke had supplied his opponents with obvious weapons with which to come back at him. The opportunities were not missed. Of over seventy replies[46] to the *Reflections on the Revolution in France*, most were hostile and many used Burke's own devices and phrases to criticise him. Among the earliest replies was Thomas Christie's *Letters on the Revolution in France* (Part I, 1791), which accused Burke of varnishing over 'the deformity of folly and oppression':

> With majestic grace, worthy of a nobler office, he conducts us to the Temple of Superstition, and the magic of his language soothes our hearts into holy

reverence and sacred awe. But…we turn with disgust from the false splendor of the mansion of Idolatry, and hasten with chearful steps to the humble abode of unadorned Truth, to bow before her august presence, and receive from her the simple and salutary instructions of eternal wisdom.[47]

Burke, at once the defender of the 'pleasing illusions' of the institutions of Church and State and the scourge of the 'wizards' of democracy, is caricatured as a minister of superstition and idolatry, using the 'magic' of his language to lull his readers into a state of 'holy reverence' for the false grandeur of the *ancien régime*. Samuel Parr, in his *Sequel to the Printed Paper lately Circulated in Warwickshire by the Revd. Chas. Carter* (1792) also testifies to the 'magic force' of the *Reflections*:

Upon the first perusal of Mr. Burke's book, I felt, like many other men, its magic force; and, like many other men, I was at last delivered from the illusions which had 'cheated my reason', and borne me on from admiration to assent. But though the dazzling spell be now dissolved, I still remember with pleasure the gay and celestial visions, when 'my mind in sweet madness was robbed of itself'. I still look back, with a mixture of piety and holy awe, to the wizard himself, who, having lately broken his wand, in a start of frenzy, has shortened the term of his sorceries; and of drugs so potent, as 'to bathe the spirits in delight', I must still acknowledge that many were culled from the choicest and 'most virtuous plants of paradise itself'.[48]

The allusions are to *Comus* and *The Tempest*, but again the imagery of spells and sorcery has probably been suggested by Burke himself, though it is now turned against him. What Parr is referring to when he talks of Burke 'having lately broken his wand' is not entirely clear (it may be a reference to the 'sentence of retirement' passed upon Burke by members of the Whig party in consequence of his quarrel with Fox[49]), but it is not difficult to see from this passage how Parr, like some others we shall mention, ended up a supporter of Burke's cause. J. Sharpe, the radical author of *A Rhapsody to E ---- B ---- Esq.* (1792), was evidently less susceptible to the charms of the *Reflections*:

> when penetrating sages
> Expect to read polemic pages
> And find no argument appears,
> But every jaunty passage wears
> The tinsel'd garb that fancy wrought,
> And from her fairy regions brought,
> To deck romance her darling guest,
> And rival fact when simply drest;
> The insult sense disdains to brook,
> And to the shelf confines the book.[50]

These couplets comment upon Burke's style rather than his argument (the allegation being that he is *all* style and no argument), but the same opposition is there, between unadorned truth and the 'tinsel'd garb' of fancy, with 'fairy' and 'romance' in their familiar role as exploding words. For Mary Wollstonecraft, whose *Vindication of the Rights of Men* appeared within three weeks of the *Reflections*, it is bogus sentiment that is the real target. When she accuses Burke of simultaneously being the dupe of his 'romantic enthusiasm' and of manipulating a current fashion for romance, she makes it clear that she has been led 'to confine the term romantic to one definition – false, or rather artificial, feelings'. Not that Burke is devoid of genuine feeling, but 'There appears to be such a mixture of real sensibility and cherished romance in your composition, that the present crisis carries you out of yourself; and since you could not be one of the grand movers, the next *best* thing that dazzled your imagination was to be a conspicuous opposer'[51] (here Wollstonecraft introduces her critique of the 'specious homage' of women – epitomised by Burke's idealisation of Marie-Antoinette – that is to be developed with such acumen in *A Vindication of the Rights of Woman*).

It is Tom Paine, though, who makes the strongest assault upon Burke's tendentious romanticism. By far the most influential reply to the *Reflections* (the second part also answers Burke's *Appeal From the New to the Old Whigs*), Paine's trenchant, levelling polemic *Rights of Man* (1791–92) confronts Burke both on what he says and how he says it. Within two or three pages, Paine is dismantling Burke's arguments in the exact terms in which Burke himself had sought to discredit Rousseau. Burke's denial of the existence of political rights, and the confidence he expresses that the people of England utterly disclaim them too – and indeed would risk their lives and fortunes to defend that point (i.e. 'to maintain they have *not* rights', as Paine puts it), are dubbed 'strange and marvellous ... and suited to the paradoxical genius of Mr Burke'. His whole method of reasoning, Paine observes, 'is of the same marvellous and monstrous kind', with its superstitious appeals to the past and its mystification of the nature of society.[52] 'Marvellous' here signifies 'ridiculous', Paine's rationalistic discourse epitomising the scepticism and scorn of the Enlightenment for the supernatural and all things 'romantic'. Paine's is a rhetoric of disenchantment. Burke had mourned for the romance of the *ancien régime*, and regretted that its magic had been dissolved by 'the conquering empire of light and reason'. For Paine, this was a cause for celebration. Revolution meant freedom from the enchantment of the past, and he saw France as trying to rid itself of the horrors and follies that had bound it to the 'gothic' middle ages. Like others, he interpreted the destruction of the Bastille as the perfect symbol of the downfall of feudal despotism, the two being 'as figuratively united as Bunyan's Doubting Castle and Giant Despair'.[53] Other anachronistic institutions appeared to be going the same way. By abolishing the law of primogeniture, the French constitution had sought 'to exterminate the monster Aristocracy'. So too 'the folly of titles', which 'are like circles drawn by the magician's wand, to contract the sphere of man's felicity'. Paine believed that man had now broken that magic circle, and come to its senses: 'It has put down the dwarf, to set up the man.'[54]

Not surprisingly, the part of the *Reflections* that provoked the most vigorous responses was the passage about Marie-Antoinette and the 'age of chivalry'. Almost all of the replies make some reference to this passage. John Thelwall refers to it mockingly as 'Burke's sentimental romance of Antoinetta, the falling star of chivalry, or royalty in the suds'.[55] For Paine, it was the ultimate proof of the speciousness of Burke's thesis, and to make the point he invokes a figure which Burke had used to ridicule the claims of the Revolution: Don Quixote. Burke had made a satirical connection between the liberation of France and the deliverance of the condemned criminals by 'the metaphysic Knight of the Sorrowful Countenance'.[56] Paine alludes to Quixote to parody Burke himself:

When we see a man dramatically lamenting in a publication intended to be believed, that, '*The age of chivalry is gone!*' that '*The glory of Europe is extinguished for ever!*' that '*The unbought grace of life*' (if any one knows what it is), '*the cheap defence of nations, the nurse of manly sentiment and heroic enterprise, is gone!*' and all because the Quixote age of chivalry nonsense is gone, what opinion can we form of his judgement, or what regard can we pay to his facts? In the rhapsody of his imagination, he has discovered a world of windmills, and his sorrows are, that there are no Quixotes to attack them.[57]

Paine employs his usual tactics, breaking up his quotations, punctuating (and puncturing) them with pointed asides, paraphrasing and finally making a nonsense of them. *Don Quixote* provided a ready-made critique of chivalry, and Paine applies it to good effect, surrounding Burke's 'age of chivalry' with 'Quixote…nonsense', and using the famous episode of the windmills to satirise his opponent's deluded imagination. Burke is even more the fool in that *his* sorrows are 'that there are no Quixotes to attack them' – except himself.[58]

Another parodic attack on Burke's 'eloquent Nonsense' is made by Samuel Taylor Coleridge in the printed version of his political lectures of 1795, the *Conciones ad Populum, or Addresses to the People*. One of the themes of the lectures – calculated to appeal to his audience mainly of dissenters – was the complicity of the Church of England in what he saw as an unjust and unholy war against France, a complicity that had recently been demonstrated in the House of Lords by the almost unanimous backing given by the bishops to a motion supporting the continuance of the war. Allowing that the Anglican bishops might be right in deeming 'the fate of their Religion to be involved in the contest', he mischievously argues that this is a cause for celebration rather than alarm, emphasising the point in a footnote by rewriting Burke's 'age of chivalry' passage as an ironic prophecy of the extinction of a form of organised religion now indistinguishable, in its perversion of doctrine and corruption of practice, from Roman Catholicism:

The age of Priesthood will soon be no more – that of Philosophers and Christians will succeed, and the torch of Superstition be extinguished for ever. Never, never more shall we behold that generous Loyalty to rank, which is prodigal of its own virtue and its own happiness to invest a few with unholy Splendors; – that subordination of the Heart, which keeps alive the spirit of Servitude amid the empty forms of boasted Liberty! This dear-bought Grace of Cathedrals, this costly defence of Despotism, this nurse of grovelling sentiment and cold-hearted Lip-worship, will be gone – it will be gone, that sensibility to Interest, that jealous tenacity of Honors, which suspects in every argument a mortal wound; which inspires Oppression, while it prompts Servility; – which stains indelibly whatever it touches; and under which supple Dullness loses half its shame by wearing a Mitre where reason would have placed a Fool's-Cap! The age of Priesthood will be no more – Peace to its departing spirit! With delighted ears should I listen to some fierce Orator from St. Omers or from Bedlam, who should weep over its Pageantries rent and faded, and pour forth eloquent Nonsense in a funeral Oration.[59]

The 'fierce Orator from St. Omers' is of course Burke himself, an allusion to the familiar rumour that he was secretly a Jesuit, trained at the seminary of St Omer in France.

William Godwin takes a more serious approach. Though not a polemical piece of writing in the sense that the *Rights of Man* is, Godwin's *Enquiry Concerning Political Justice* (1793) also takes issue with some of Burke's statements, and twice addresses the subject of chivalry. The first mention of it occurs during the discussion of aristocracy in Book v. The criterion by which Godwin judges the value of a particular institution is its tendency to create virtue. Alongside the many reasons which he gives for finding fault with the aristocratic system, he makes the limited concession that there once existed a 'gallant kind of virtue that, by irresistibly seizing the senses, seemed to communicate extensively, to young men of birth, the mixed and equivocal accomplishments of chivalry'. Godwin does not elaborate this remark, except to observe that 'flattery' and 'effeminate indulgence' were two of the less wholesome tendencies of chivalry, and to claim that in more recent times 'the energies of intellect' have replaced 'personal prowess' as the primary object 'of moral emulation'.[60] In Book VIII he takes a rather different tack. Having previously implied that chivalry was something of the past, an institution rendered obsolete by the development of commerce and learning, he now argues that the 'feudal spirit' – that is, the spirit of 'servility' and 'dependence' – had, on the contrary, been perpetuated by the unequal distribution of property and wealth:

Observe the pauper fawning with abject vileness upon his rich benefactor, speechless with sensations of gratitude, for having received that which he ought to have claimed, not indeed with arrogance, or a dictatorial spirit and overbearing temper, but with the spirit of a man discussing with a man, and resting his cause only on the justice of his claim. Observe the servants that follow in a rich man's train, watchful of his looks, anticipating his commands, not daring to reply to his insolence, all their time and their efforts under the direction of his caprice. Observe the tradesman, how he studies the passions of his customers, not to correct, but to pamper them, the vileness of his flattery and the systematical constancy with which he exaggerates the merit of his commodities. Observe the practices of a popular election, where the great mass are purchased by obsequiousness, by intemperance and bribery, or driven by unmanly threats of poverty and persecution. Indeed 'the age of chivalry is' not 'gone'! The feudal spirit still survives that reduced the great mass of mankind to the rank of slaves and cattle for the service of a few.[61]

Viewed unsentimentally, and in the context of society as a whole rather than just of the privileged classes, this is the 'feudal and chivalrous spirit' that Burke had sought to uphold, the 'generous loyalty to rank', the 'proud submission', 'dignified obedience' and 'subordination of the heart'. Godwin has often been criticised for the abstract and visionary nature of his politics, but here it is observation not theory that carries his argument. Indeed one can only make proper sense of his commitment to the principle of total human independence – the principle which his egalitarian, anarchist utopia would seek to realise – if one appreciates the strength of his aversion to the 'hourly corruption' and domestic oppression that result from existing social arrangements, and make up the present 'spectacle of injustice'.

Godwin responds to Burke's announcement of the death of chivalry by demonstrating that its spirit had survived, and that its influence was a wholly malign one. The response of James Mackintosh, in his *Vindiciae Gallicae* (1791), is also both to demystify and then quarrel with Burke's statement, in this case by reminding his readers that 'chivalry' is another term for the aristocracy, and warning them that the French aristocracy was at present far from defunct:

Crusades were an effervescence of chivalry, and the modern St. Francis has a knight for the conduct of these crusaders, who will convince Mr. Burke that the age of chivalry is not past, nor the glory of Europe gone for ever. The Comte d'Artois, that scyon worthy of Henry the Great, the rival of the Bayards and Sidneys, the new model of French Knighthood, is to issue from Turin with ten thousand cavaliers for the delivery of the peerless and immaculate Antonietta of Austria from the durance vile in which she has so long been immured in the Thuilleries, from the swords of the discourteous knights of Paris, and the spells of the sable wizards of democracy.[62]

The point Mackintosh is making here is that Burke's imaginary scene of the Queen being rescued from her indignity is actually all too plausible. The Comte d'Artois (brother of Louis XVI), having emigrated soon after the fall of the Bastille and the break-up of the Court party, was presently urging the Austrian Emperor Leopold II (brother of Marie-Antoinette) to intervene against the Revolution and restore the French monarchy, with his own forces assisted by exiled French nobles. Just such an attempt was made, unsuccessfully, in the late summer of 1792, when the Duke of Brunswick invaded France with a large army of Austro-Prussian regulars and *émigré* 'legions'. Mackintosh, then, is absolutely right to point to this threat as it existed in 1791, and it is a brilliant polemical move on his part to identify the literal prospect of an aristocratic intervention with Burke's chivalric metaphor of ten thousand swords leaping to the defence of Marie-Antoinette. This both annuls Burke's immediate point – the age of chivalry is *not* past – and illustrates what he has just revealed to be the fundamental purpose of the *Reflections*: 'It is the manifesto of a Counter Revolution.'[63]

Of course, the passage also functions as parody. Rather than merely asserting that Burke is being 'romantic', Mackintosh brings this home to us by borrowing the chivalric idiom of the original, and rewriting the whole scene as though it were an episode from a chivalric romance, with the Comte d'Artois as the hero, and Marie-Antoinette as a damsel-in-distress being rescued from her captivity at the hands of 'the sable wizards of democracy'. Indeed, this is hardly an exaggeration of Burke's original description. All Mackintosh has done is join together a number of Burke's own images from the *Reflections*, and attached them all to a single episode. This has the effect of rendering the scene instantly ridiculous (without the need for further comment on the 'nonsense' of chivalry), and also of suggesting that Burke's view of the French Revolution is governed by literary models rather than by facts and logic.

Another way of putting this is to say that Mackintosh lays bare Burke's mythology of revolution. Firstly, he demonstrates the connection between Burke's chivalric idealisation of the French monarchy and his vilification of the wizards of democracy. This itself affords a significant insight into the imaginative organisation and subliminal rhetoric of Burke's text. But Mackintosh goes further, by identifying Burke himself as the hero of his own counter-revolutionary romance, using the power of the written word to mobilise the aggrieved parties of Europe to his 'philanthropic crusade'. The 'obvious object' of the *Reflections*, Mackintosh writes,

is to inflame every passion and interest, real or supposed, that has received any shock in the establishment of freedom. He probes the bleeding wounds of the princes, the nobility, the priesthood, and the great judicial aristocracy. He adjures one body by its dignity degraded, another by its inheritance plundered, and a third by its authority destroyed, to repair to the holy banner of his philanthropic crusade. Confident in the protection of all the Monarchs of Europe, whom he alarms for the security of their thrones, and having insured the moderation of the fanatical rabble, by giving out among them the savage *war-whoop* of atheism, he already fancies himself in full march to Paris, not there to re-instate the deposed despotism (he disclaims the purpose, and who would not trust such virtuous disavowals) but at the head of this army of priests, nobles, mercenaries, and fanatics, to dictate as the tutelar genius of France, the establishment, without commotion or carnage, of a just and temperate freedom, equally hostile to the views of kingly or popular tyrants.[64]

Once again there is a mixture of levity and seriousness here, but the important point is that it identifies the heroic dimension in the romanticism of the *Reflections*: that is, Burke's image of himself as defender of the political faith and brave crusader against the dark forces of revolution.

Confirmation that this was indeed the role in which Burke saw himself (though by the end of his life he had come to regard it as an increasingly lonely and desperate crusade) can be found in a conversation that is reported to have taken place during Mackintosh's visit to Burke's home at Beaconsfield at Christmas 1796. The subject is again 'that mother of all evil, the French Revolution', and the significance of the exchange is that Burke is handing over the role of 'faithful knight of the romance' to Mackintosh himself:

I never think of that plague-spot in the history of mankind without shuddering. It is an evil spirit that is always before me. There is not a mischief by which the moral world can be afflicted that it has not let loose upon it. It reminds me of the accursed things that crawled in and out of the mouth of the vile hag in Spenser's Cave of Error ... You, Mr. Mackintosh, are in vigorous manhood; your intellect is in its freshest prime, and you are a powerful writer; you shall be the faithful knight of the romance; the brightness of your sword will flash destruction on the filthy progeny.[65]

To revert to the quotation with which we began, it is apparent that it was not as a passive spectator but as an active hero of romance that Burke imagined himself 'walking on enchanted ground'. As for Mackintosh, he obviously accepted the commission as Burke's successor. 'Regarding his visit', wrote Thomas Green, 'Mackintosh was in the habit of saying that in a half hour Burke overturned the reflections of a whole life.'

As a postscript to this, it is interesting that Green himself was assigned the role of revolutionary dragon-killer in an anonymous verse satire entitled 'Modern Philosophy, and the Godwynian System', published in the *Christian Observer* in 1803.[66] As a footnote explains, Green had earned the respect of the Evangelicals with his *Examination of the Leading Principles of the New System of Morals ... as Set Forth by Mr. Godwin in his Enquiry Concerning Political Justice* (1798), and he is accordingly figured in the final lines of the poem as a St George unmasking the false-seeming goddess of the Modern Philosophy (an idolatrous creed of which 'Godwyn' is the 'arch-priest' and 'hierophant'):

> With truth and logic arm'd, lo, Green prepares
> To trace her wiles, unfold her secret snares,
> Strips off the gorgeous covering which conceals
> Her bloated form, her shapeless limbs reveal;
> The gazing eye, with horror fix'd beholds
> A fiend with angel's face, and dragon folds.   (lines 51–56)

One of a number of satires directed against Godwin around the turn of the century (*The Progress of the Pilgrim Good-Intent* is another, and we shall encounter further examples in the next chapter), the poem, in its conjunction of anti-Jacobin polemic with Spenserian imagery, is yet another illustration of the counter-revolutionary romance which Burke installed in the English political imagination.

THE THEME OF CHIVALRY

The power of metaphor alone does not account for the extraordinary impression that Burke's elegy for the 'age of chivalry' made on contemporary readers. Part of its force derives from the inherent attraction of the notion of chivalry. That appeal may be appreciated by glancing at some of the accounts of chivalry that were currently in circulation. 'Though commonly looked upon as a barbarous sport, or extravagant amusement of the dark ages', the institution of chivalry 'was the school of fortitude, honour, and affability', wrote Thomas Warton in his Postscript to the second edition of his *Observations on the Faery Queen* (1762):

> Its exercises, like the grecian games, habituated the youth to fatigue and enterprise, and inspired the noblest sentiments of heroism. It taught gallantry and civility to a savage and ignorant people, and humanised the native ferocity of the northern nations. It conduced to refine the manners of the combatants, by exciting an emulation in the devices and accoutrements, the splendour and parade, of their tilts and tournaments: while its magnificent festivals, thronged with noble dames and courteous knights, produced the first effusions of wit and fancy.[67]

Richard Hurd's account of chivalry, largely based on the work of the French scholar Sainte-Palaye, is even more admiring. Among the characteristics which he assigns to 'the singular profession' of the chivalric knights are

> Their romantic ideas of justice; their passion for adventures; their eagerness to run to the succour of the distressed; and the pride they took in redressing wrongs and removing grievances ... [68]

Once the prejudice against the 'dark ages' began to fall away, it is not surprising that the intrinsic appeal of the idea of chivalry, and the validity of many of the ideals which the chivalric code expressed, began once more to be recognised. This was already happening in England at the time Burke wrote the *Reflections*; and in the decades that followed, the revival of chivalry – carried forward by a new generation of scholars, as well as by the remarkable success of the modern romances of chivalry written by Walter Scott and others, was to assume the status almost of a cult. The *Reflections* themselves undoubtedly contributed to this process, but Burke's real achievement was to recognise the political connotations of the chivalric ideal, not so much in its original context as in its bearing on more recent historical events. By attributing to pre-revolutionary France the vaunted characteristics of the 'age of chivalry' – prowess, generosity, gallantry and religion – Burke channels into his aristocratic polemic all the energy and appeal of the Romantic revival. By the same token, his intervention has the effect of politicising the debate on the significance of chivalry and the chivalric legacy, and of extending its terms of reference from the past to the present.

Burke's political appropriation of the theme of chivalry created problems for his opponents. To dismiss his chivalric idealisation of the *ancien régime* was to run the risk of dismissing the chivalric ideals themselves, some of which (generosity and justice, for example) would clearly merit a place in any theory of private or public virtue. Alternatively, in drawing attention to the idea of chivalry for the purposes of satire, there was the danger that its intrinsic appeal would prove too strong to demolish. A skilful polemicist like Paine is able to avoid these pitfalls by consistently rejecting anything that savoured of the 'romantic', while at the same time resting his own claims to the ideals of justice and generosity on the basis of straightforward political logic. Or there is the tactic used by Catherine Graham in her *Observations on the Reflections* (1790), which is to concede the value of chivalry as a response to the historical situation in which it arose (it was 'indeed a proper remedy to the evils arising from *ferocity, slavery, barbarism,* and *ignorance*'), but to reject Burke's account of its long-term influence by pointing out that all that remained of the original ideals were '*false* notions of honour' typified by the practice of duelling – which she felicitously defines as '*methodized sentimental barbarism*'.[69] On the other hand, the anonymous pamphlet entitled *Temperate Comments upon Intemperate Reflections* (1791) illustrates how the attempt to satirise Burke's use of the language of chivalry can prove self-defeating. Like Paine, the author of the pamphlet aims to poke fun at Burke by alluding to *Don Quixote*, but in this case the ploy fails because his description of his antagonist as a chivalrous hero soon ceases to operate as parody, so positive are the suggestions it contains about 'the blessings of chivalry'. Having quoted in full Burke's lament for the age of chivalry, he continues as follows:

This sublime and beautiful exclamation would not have done discredit to the mirror of knighthood, that valorous champion whose admirable gallantry and noble achievements are famed in history by Cervantes. Its effect was so powerful, that we almost expected to find our author sallying forth in armour upon another Rosinante, to punish the corruption of manners, the degeneracy of virtue, the contempt of honour, the absence of humanity, the shameful inattention to beauty, – in a word, to correct the enormous depravity of the times, by restoring to a grateful and admiring world, the blessings of chivalry.[70]

Simply to mention the names of Cervantes and Rosinante is not sufficient to turn these images of chivalry into satire, and there is nothing else in the passage to alert us to its ironic purpose. Rather than demolishing, it serves to reinforce the claims of the original, and indeed unwittingly highlights the personal myth which helps to give such force to Burke's polemic.

Mackintosh engages in a similar strategy but succeeds where the author of *Temperate Comments* fails because he is fully conscious of Burke's own rhetorical strategies. When Mackintosh depicts Burke in the guise of a crusading knight ('in full march to Paris') the effect is genuinely ludicrous, even though his primary intention is to warn us to take seriously the threat of a 'chivalric' counter-revolution. However, he does not let the matter rest there: as he goes on to say, the subject of chivalry is 'fertile in reflexions of a different kind'.[71] Although parodied in the Introduction to *Vindiciae Gallicae*, the theme receives earnest historical attention in the main body of the text, where he disputes Burke's claims in a less polemical fashion. Without going into details, he admits that chivalry, or rather the 'system of manners of which chivalry was more properly the effusion than the source' (the distinction, unimportant to his argument, is supposed to indicate that his concern for historical accuracy is greater than Burke's) 'is without doubt one of the most interesting and peculiar appearances in human affairs'. As Burke had maintained – and this was a standard view at the time, developed by the historians of the Scottish Enlightenment[72] – the chivalric system had 'contributed to polish and soften Europe'. It had created 'mildness in the midst of a barbarous age'. It had paved the way for the 'diffusion of knowledge' and the 'extension of commerce'. Its influence was thus still discernible, but only indirectly. Where Burke had erred was in supposing that chivalry itself, as a system of manners and sentiments, had outlived the circumstances which gave it birth (i.e. the 'age of chivalry' was gone long before the French Revolution):

> Commerce and diffused knowledge have, in fact, so completely assumed the ascendant in polished nations, that it will be difficult to discover any relics of *Gothic manners*, but in a fantastic exterior, which has survived the generous illusions that made these manners splendid and seductive.[73]

Yet even as he makes this point about the irrelevance of '*Gothic manners*' in modern European culture, Mackintosh betrays a lingering fascination with the romance of chivalry: 'splendid and seductive' manners, 'generous illusions' – the very words reveal its continued attraction for him. Nowhere does he mention the chivalric ideals – that would presumably be too risky a move – but even so, the inherent attractions of the theme threaten to overwhelm his historical critique of Burke.

The case of Godwin illustrates the dilemma in rather different ways. His treatment of chivalry in the *Enquiry Concerning Political Justice* has already been discussed, and we have noted the strength of his reaction against Burke's idealisation of the chivalric legacy. Yet these are by no means his final words on the subject. As we shall discover later, Godwin considerably revised his views on the 'age of chivalry' and its aftermath. One reason why he may have been disposed to do so is suggested by *Political Justice* itself. For in certain respects the 'exalted morality' which Godwin expounds there is very similar to the one enshrined in the ancient code of chivalry. Both are systems of 'personal virtue' that centre on the principle of 'justice'. Both extol what Hurd called 'disinterested valour' (for Godwin, the equivalent is 'disinterested benevolence'). Both place great value on personal freedom, and emphasise the obligation to maintain and defend it in others as well as oneself. Both stress man's position as an independent moral agent. Of course, there are many other things that separate them – not the least being that one is essentially military and religious, the other strictly pacifist and secular – but the similarities are striking. In *Political Justice* itself, the analogy remains implicit, although it almost comes to the surface when the image of the Garden of Armida from Tasso's *Gerusalemme Liberata* is used to dramatise the dangers of intellectual imitation.[74] But the connection is made explicit eight years later in Godwin's *Thoughts Occasioned by the Perusal of Dr. Parr's Spital Sermon* (1801). Itself an impressive display of the author's own independence of mind, this is a detailed reply to the attacks made upon Godwin by erstwhile liberals –

including Samuel Parr and James Mackintosh – who had changed political camps during the 1790s while he himself had remained true to his original principles. More than that, it is an attempt 'to delineate the history of apostacy'; and after having analysed the 'tergiversation' of the Jacobin generation in England, he reflects upon it in what will now be familiar terms:

The intercourse of the world has a powerful tendency to blunt in us the sentiments of enthusiasm, and the spirit of romance; and, whatever truth we may suppose there to be in the progressive nature of man, it is so far remote from the transactions of ordinary life, and the feelings which impel us in such transactions to bend to the routine of circumscribed and unspeculative men, that it can with difficulty preserve its authority in the midst of so strong a contagion.[75]

In the preceding paragraph he has defended the doctrines of *Political Justice* in quasi-chivalric terms such as generosity, disinterestedness, and 'nobleness of nature'. Here he expressly identifies his radical idealism with 'the spirit of romance', lamenting its tendency to be eroded by the parochial and reactionary pressures of 'ordinary life'. This is a highly significant move, tending to invert the whole rhetoric of romantic conservatism, and to reclaim, for positive rather than satirical purposes, the mode of expression that had been so successfully appropriated by Burke. In so doing, it also looks forward to the revolutionary romanticism of Shelley, whose poetry is pervaded by the Godwinian 'spirit of romance'.

THE REVOLUTIONARY ROMANCE OF THE ENGLISH RADICALS

Among the next generation, there were to be more sustained attempts to reclaim the notion of chivalry for the liberal or radical cause, by writers like Hunt, Hazlitt, Peacock and Shelley: these will be the subject of a later chapter. Even among Godwin's generation, though, there were other 'friends of liberty' who realised that its idiom could be used for purposes other than that of satirising Burke, or who discerned in the literature of romance and chivalry a political dimension answering to their own ideals. Robert Southey's poem 'Romance' (1794), a progress ode outlining the fortunes of romance from ancient to modern times, hints at this radical application of the theme with its description of the Knights of the Round Table as 'prompt for innocence to fight, / Or to quell the pride of proud oppression's might'.[76] Significantly, it is not personal gallantry but

the struggle against 'oppression' that Southey identifies as the
essence of chivalry, a levelling sentiment that is reinforced in the last
stanza by his enthusiastic nomination of Jean-Jacques Rousseau, the
modern embodiment of revolutionary romance, as his 'guardian
sprite'.

Other writers made more direct connections between romance and
revolutionary politics by using the language of romance to glamorise
the ideas and actions of the French Revolution itself, as in Helen
Maria Williams's description, in the second of her *Letters from France*
(1790), of what happened on the former site of the Bastille: 'The
ruins of that execrable fortress were suddenly transformed, as if with
the wand of necromancy, into a scene of beauty and pleasure.'[77] If
the prison of the Bastille was a ready-made symbol of the gothic
world of the *ancien régime*, what better metaphor could there be for
what became of it (the site 'was covered with fresh clods of grass' and
planted with liberty trees) than that of a pastoral metamorphosis?
This is like Burke in reverse, testifying to the almost magical manner
in which the Revolution altered the nature of things, but presenting
it as a force of good rather than evil.

In the same way, Liberty was personified by radicals not as the
wicked enchantress, as in Burke, but the chivalric queen or heroine of
romance,[78] or the passionate lover whose charms are to be embraced
rather than resisted. All three images are brought together in George
Dyer's ode 'On Liberty' (1792), which was publicly recited in the
French fashion at a celebration in Belfast to mark the third
anniversary of the fall of the Bastille, and subsequently reprinted in
the *Morning Chronicle*:

> Hail! more refulgent than the morning star,
> Gay queen of bliss, fair daughter of the sky,
> I woo thee, Freedom! May I hope from far
> To catch the brightness of thy raptur'd eye?
> While not unseemly streams thy zoneless vest,
> Thy wild locks dancing to the frolic wind;
> And borne on flying feet, thou scorn'st to rest,
> Save where meek truth her modest seat may find.
> Hail! radiant form divine, blest Liberty!
> Wher'er thou deign'st to rove, oh! let me rove with thee.[79]

Drawing on French revolutionary iconography as well as English
sources, Dyer's portrayal of Freedom as a sexually liberated but
benevolent 'queen of bliss' suggests how the Revolution has altered

the sexual politics of romance, as though Spenser's Acrasia had been freed from the confines of her Bower, and permitted to 'rove' without fear of moral censure or destruction. Yet some of the ambiguity of the underlying image perhaps remains, in that, even while celebrating the pleasures of liberty, Dyer feels the need to circumscribe them, revealing by denying his anxiety that the forces unleashed may be 'unseemly' and even uncontrollable.

Similar apprehensions are expressed, in almost identical language, in Coleridge's 'To a Young Lady, With a Poem on the French Revolution' (1796), the personification of Liberty merging here with the person of the young lady to whom the poem is addressed, with Coleridge himself in chivalric guise as the exultant (but subsequently guilty) warrior-lover who 'shook the lance, / And strode in joy the reeking plains of France' (25–26).[80] In his 'France: An Ode' (1798) the emotional dynamic becomes even more complex, as Coleridge attempts to reaffirm his commitment to the (now carefully plato-nised) ideal of Liberty while also confessing his complicity in the crimes that had been committed in her name. Originally entitled 'The Recantation: An Ode', the poem ends by renouncing his belief in all earthly manifestations of 'The spirit of divinest Liberty', and it has therefore rightly been seen as part of the literature of rev-olutionary disenchantment. Yet it is interesting that where Coleridge actually uses the image of disenchantment, in the phrase (later borrowed by Shelley[81]) 'a disenchanted nation', it is to signify the liberation of France from the enchantment of the *ancien régime*. In Coleridge's recasting of the revolutionary romance, it is the revo-lutionists who wield the 'tyrant-quelling lance', and the monarchs of Europe who are 'Like fiends embattled by a wizard's wand' (28–37), just as in his sonnet to Burke (1794) it is Burke himself who is the enchanter, 'Blasting with wizard spell' the 'laurell'd fame' of Freedom.

For Wordsworth, the link between chivalric romance and rev-olutionary politics was suggested by the historical fact that some of the revolutionaries in France were actually members of the nobility, notably his friend Michel Beaupuis. The well-known description of Beaupuis in Book IX of *The Prelude* makes much of this, presenting him as a nobleman who has democratised the idea of chivalric 'service' by binding himself 'unto the poor / Among mankind', to whom he 'Transferred a courtesy which had no air / Of condescension, but did rather seem / A passion and a gallantry' (IX, 310–20).[82] Thomas de

Quincey, recollecting this description many years later in a biographical article on Wordsworth in *Tait's Edinburgh Magazine* (1839),
highlights this imaginative link when he writes how, at the outbreak
of the Revolution, 'the gallant Beaupuis put on the garb of chivalry;
it was a chivalry the noblest in the world, which opened his ear to the
Pariah and the oppressed all over his mis-organized country'.[83] In
The Prelude, however, the analogy is taken even further in that
Wordsworth attributes the chivalric ideals not just to Beaupuis but
also to the common people of France, 'a people risen up / Fresh as the
morning star':

> Elate we looked
> Upon their virtues, saw in rudest men
> Self-sacrifice the firmest, generous love
> And continence of mind, and sense of right
> Uppermost in the midst of fiercest strife.   (IX, lines 392–96)

For Wordsworth, the Revolution, in its early days, appeared to mark
not the end but the beginning of an 'age of chivalry' – a new kind of
chivalry based not on aristocratic exclusivity but on a common
democratic commitment to the virtues of generosity, temperance and
justice.

The whole description is of course highly idealised, as Wordsworth
plainly indicates when he remarks how he and Beaupuis 'wandered'
'through the events / Of that great change' 'As through a book, an
old romance, or tale / Of Fairy' (IX, 305–8). But the literary analogy
is a problematic one. Several recent commentators have argued that
Wordsworth's invocation of romance is as much a warning note as an
attempt to recapture the hopes and pleasures of his stay in France.[84]
As at earlier moments in *The Prelude* when the notion of romance is
foregrounded in this way, the implication seems to be that, for all his
'chivalrous delight' (IX, 503), Wordsworth had wandered from his
natural course and succumbed to some form of temptation or
illusion; or at least that a crisis of some kind was impending. However
we interpret Wordsworth's literary signals, the fact remains that by
the end of Book IX Wordsworth's 'revered companion' is dead, and
the chivalric romance of the Beaupuis episode has been superseded
by the 'tragic Tale' of Vaudracour and Julia, which encodes,
obscurely, the story of his broken relationship with Annette Vallon,
while also foreshadowing the political and personal conflicts of Books
x and xi.

The historian Lynn Hunt claims to have detected a similar

transition, from romance to tragedy, in the language of the French politicians themselves.[85] In an intriguing account of what she calls the 'poetics of power' in the French Revolution, she applies Frye's 'generic plots' or *mythoi* to define the narrative structures that underlie and inform revolutionary rhetoric at different stages of the Revolution. The transition from comedy to romance and then to tragedy reflects increasing uncertainty about the course of the Revolution, and the growing obsession with conspiracy.[86] Romance begins to replace comedy in 1792, as the 'family harmony' of constitutional monarchy breaks up, and the Revolution came to be seen 'more like a quest, in which the heroes were the brothers of the revolutionary fraternity, who faced a series of life-and-death struggles with the demonic forces of counterrevolution'. The ascendancy of Robespierre and the Republic of Virtue marks both the extreme expression of romance and the shift to tragedy.

Properly to examine these claims, which suggest fascinating parallels between the self-representations of the French revolutionaries and the figurative encoding of the Revolution by English observers, is beyond the scope of the present enquiry. But an immediate illustration both of Hunt's argument about French revolutionary rhetoric and of the parallel with English revolutionary writing can be found in Coleridge and Southey's historical drama *The Fall of Robespierre* (1794), the 'sole aim' of which, according to Coleridge's Dedication, was 'to imitate the empassioned and highly figurative language of the French orators',[87] and which was based on accounts in English newspapers of speeches delivered in the National Assembly in the week leading up to Robespierre's death on 28 July 1794.[88] Here, for example, is Robespierre's address to the Convention at the beginning of Act II (written by Southey), where he stands accused of having betrayed the Revolution and of being a 'self-will'd dictator':

> Once more befits it that the voice of Truth,
> Fearless in innocence, though leaguered round
> By Envy and her hateful brood of hell,
> Be heard amid this hall; once more befits
> The patriot whose prophetic eye so oft
> Has pierced thro' faction's veil, to flash on crimes
> Of deadliest import. Mouldering in the grave
> Sleeps Capet's caitiff corse; my daring hand
> Levelled to earth his blood-cemented throne,
> My voice declared his guilt, and stirred up France

To call for vengeance. I too dug the grave
Where sleep the Girondists, detested band!
Long with the shew of freedom they abused
Her ardent sons. Long time the well-turn'd phrase,
The high-fraught sentence and the lofty tone
Of declamation, thunder'd in this hall,
Till reason midst a labyrinth of words
Perplex'd, in silence seem'd to yield assent.
I durst oppose. Soul of my honoured friend,
Spirit of Marat, upon thee I call –
Thou know'st me faithful, know'st with what warm zeal
I urg'd the cause of justice, stripp'd the mask
From faction's deadly visage, and destroy'd
Her traitor brood. Whose patriot arm hurl'd down
Hébert and Rousin, and the villain friends
Of Danton, foul apostate! those, who long
Mask'd treason's form in liberty's fair garb,
Long deluged France with blood, and durst defy
Omnipotence! but I it seems am false!
I am a traitor too! I – Robespierre!
I – at whose name the dastard despot brood
Should murmur? who shall speak?

Robespierre's metaphors narrate a romance in miniature, featuring himself as the intrepid and incorruptible hero Truth, embattled against political Envy and the monstrous forces of counter-revolution (for Robespierre, vice *is* the counter-revolution), advancing 'the cause of justice' and exposing the evil duplicity of opposing factions. The world of revolutionary politics is one of villains and verbal labyrinths, in which only he has remained faithful to the revolutionary cause, undeluded and undeflected from his quest, and able with his sword-like eye to pierce through to the true nature of things. It is an impressive piece of oratory, drawing in part on the rhetoric of that other great political orator, Milton's Satan (a source which helps alert us to the element of self-deception in the speeches). But Robespierre's 'wild eloquence' does not save him, and the play ends with Barrère's damning judgment, like one of Milton's disenchanting asides ('So spake the fiend ... '[89]), upon the 'cool ferocity that persuaded murder / Even whilst it spake of mercy!' (III, 201–2). The Miltonic analogy is particularly apt since *Paradise Lost* too charts a trajectory from romance to tragedy brought about by the agency of its most accomplished orator.

What is missing from *The Fall of Robespierre* – and this is a sure sign that the romance is turning into a tragedy – is any real sense of the original ideals of the French Revolution: it has become a quest without a goal, a narrative of unending conflict. In its earlier phase, the revolutionary romance had a much more pronounced teleology, far more emphasis being placed on the ultimate objectives of the Revolution. Indeed it was in the representation of these goals that English revolutionary writing was at its most 'romantic', not only in the sense that it frequently became, like romance, a form of wish-fulfilment, but also in that the wishes themselves were often drawn directly from literary sources. In the words of Thomas Spence, from his tract *The Rights of Infants* (1796):

> Yes, all that prophets e'er of bliss foretold,
> And all that poets ever feign'd of old,
> As yielding joy to man, shall now be seen,
> And ever flourish like an evergreen.[90]

The late eighteenth century was not the first era to harbour such expectations, nor the first to attempt to translate the prophecies of Scripture, the speculations of philosophers, or the fantasies of poets, into political action; but it was an age in which the prospect of a totally new order acquired unprecedented intensity and immediacy, the French Revolution being interpreted throughout Europe as 'the portent of universal felicity'.[91] On the first page of his tract *Common Sense* (1776), Paine had written that 'Government, like dress, is the badge of lost innocence; the palaces of kings are built on the ruins of the bowers of paradise.'[92] With the dismantling of the monarchy in France, it seemed to the likes of Paine and Spence that the 'bowers of paradise' would now be restored.

If, as I am suggesting, the radical version of revolutionary romance incorporates both the utopian vision of the Revolution and the conflict necessary to realise it, then perhaps the most complete illustration of this paradigm is Joel Barlow's poem *The Conspiracy of Kings*. Published in London in October 1792, it was written at a moment of high confidence among British radical circles, when, as Gwyn Williams writes, 'a new expression of the British libertarian tradition and a new French democratic republic were not merely related, they were identified'.[93] This identity of purpose is reflected in the style of the poem, which reproduces many of the characteristics of French revolutionary rhetoric (beginning with the theme of conspiracy) while at the same time displaying the apocalyptic frame of reference which is so marked a feature of English revolutionary

writing. What makes it of further interest in the present context is
that it is also another satirical reply to Burke's *Reflections*, which
means that while promoting its own mythology of revolution, it
simultaneously contrives to unmask and discredit that of Burke.

'Addressed to the Inhabitants of Europe, from Another Quarter of
the World' (i.e. Barlow's native America), the poem opens with an
invocation to 'Eternal Truth' to leave 'that far shore / Where justice
reigns, and tyrants tread no more', and to assist the author to 'tell the
bliss that Freedom sheds abroad, / The rights of nature and the gift
of God'. The reference to God is somewhat misleading, since this is an
aggressively secular production, and Barlow launches immediately
into a prolonged invective against the 'Drones of the Church and
harpies of the State' whose 'impious arts' and 'magic spells' have
been used 'To rob, to scourge, and brutalize mankind' (22). He then
turns to his title theme, rejecting out of hand the suggestion that a
'conspiracy of kings' could possibly succeed, and ridiculing one by
one the 'sceptred horde' of Europe to whom the drones and harpies
look to save their 'sinking cause'. Last but not least among these is
Burke, the 'sordid sovereign of the letter'd world', whom Barlow calls
on to explain his motives for abandoning the cause of liberty and
joining the conspiracy:

> Oh Burke, degenerate slave! with grief and shame
> The Muse indignant must repeat thy name.
> Strange man, declare, – since, at creation's birth,
> From crumbling Chaos sprang this heav'n and earth
> Since wrecks and outcast relics still remain,
> Whirl'd ceaseless round Confusion's dreary reign,
> Declare, from all these fragments, whence you stole
> That genius wild, that monstrous mass of soul,
> Where spreads the widest waste of all extremes,
> Full darkness frowns, and heav'n's own splendour beams;
> Truth, Error, Falsehood, Rhetoric's raging tide,
> And Pomp and Meanness, Prejudice and Pride,
> Strain to an endless clang thy voice of fire,
> Thy thoughts bewilder and thy audience tire.   (lines 105–18)

In answer to his own question ('whence you stole / That genius wild,
that monstrous mass of soul'), Barlow alludes to the myth of Phaeton,
combining it with the fall of Lucifer and the Miltonic war in Heaven
to create an allegory of political apostasy and moral self-betrayal:

> Like Phoebus' son, we see thee wing thy way,
> Snatch the loose reins, and mount the car of day,

To earth now plunging plough thy wasting course,
The great Sublime of weakness and of force.
But while the world's keen eye, with generous glance,
Thy faults could pardon and thy worth enhance,
When foes were hush'd, when Justice dar'd commend,
And e'en fond Freedom claim'd thee as a friend,
Why in a gulph of baseness sink forlorn,
And change pure praise for infamy and scorn?
And didst thou hope, by thy infuriate quill
To rouse mankind the blood of realms to spill?
Then to restore, on death-devoted plains,
Their scourge to tyrants, and to man his chains?
To swell their souls with thy own bigot rage?
First stretch thy arm, and, with less impious might,
Wipe out the stars, and quench the solar light;
'*For heav'n and earth*,' the voice of God ordains,
'*Shall pass and perish, but my word remains*,'
Th' eternal Word, which gave, in spite of thee,
Reason to man, that bids man be free.   (lines 119–39)

Barlow appeals to Burke's unstable aesthetic of the sublime to hint at the deep psychological compulsions that led to his transformation from a son of light into a prince of darkness. The horrors he sees in the French Revolution are thus in fact the horrors of his own corrupted soul.

Here, then, are the forces of counter-revolution. In their own eyes they are the defenders of the old glory of Europe, embarked on a 'wild crusade' to restore the pomp and splendour of monarchical government. Thus far are we permitted access to Burke's counter-revolutionary mythology. But in Barlow's eyes – that is, in the dominant mythology of the poem – they represent the forces of evil: 'harpies', 'villains', 'vampires', 'all the hell that springs / From those prolific monsters, Courts and Kings' (207–8). Defending the new republic against this assortment of miscreants is Man, the hero of Barlow's revolutionary romance, who is armed only with the voice of Reason. In the first half of the poem, Man's role is a combative one: to expose the tyrants and defeat the conspiracy. But in the second half, the ultimate goal of his quest becomes apparent, as Barlow envisions a renovated world in which mankind will unite in a 'fraternal family divine':

From Orders, Slaves and Kings,
To thee, O Man, my heart rebounding springs.
Behold th' ascending bliss that waits your call,

Heav'n's own bequest, the heritage of all.
Awake to wisdom, seize the proffer'd prize;
From shade to light, from grief to glory rise.
Freedom at last, with Reason in her train,
Extends o'er earth her ever-lasting reign;
See Gallia's sons, so late the tyrant's sport,
Machines in war and sycophants in court,
Start into men, expand their well-taught mind,
Lords of themselves and leaders of mankind.
On equal rights their base of empire lies,
On walls of wisdom see the structure rise;
Wide o'er the gazing world it towers sublime,
A modell'd form for each surrounding clime.
To useful toils they bend their noblest aim,
Make patriot views and moral views the same,
Renounce the wish of war, bid conquest cease,
Invite all men to happiness and peace,
To faith and justice rear the youthful race,
With strength exalt them and with science grace,
Till Truth's blest banners, o'er the regions hurl'd,
Shake tyrants from their thrones, and cheer the waking world
In northern climes, where feudal shades of late
Chill'd every heart and palsied every State ...   (lines 243–68)

Here, in effect, is Barlow's counter-vision to Burke's 'age of chivalry'. In a polemical move which will be repeated many times in the poetry of Shelley, Barlow reclaims the language of kingship and empire to describe a polity which is liberated from precisely those things: a 'reign' of Freedom, an 'empire' of rights, men 'Lords of themselves'. But he also uses the imagery of romance, and if *The Fall of Robespierre* is, in its figurative language, a romance without a goal, *The Conspiracy of Kings* carries the generic plot beyond the *agon* to the 'ascending bliss' of a restored paradise. The sublime structure that rises before us in these lines is Barlow's metaphor for a reconstructed France, yet it is also a naturalised version of the Celestial City of the Book of Revelation. 'Heav'n's own bequest' has become 'the heritage of all', and it is situated not in the next world but in this one, for as the author insists, 'tis the present world that prompts the song, / The world we see, the world that feels the wrong, / The world of men' (31–4).

THE WORDSWORTHIAN SYNTHESIS

It is easy to see that the polarity inherent in romance made it an obvious vehicle for polemic. Many of the previous examples demonstrate this. By the same token (that is, by their very contrariety), they suggest too that romance has a profoundly ambiguous language. Romantic metaphors always seem susceptible to reversal. In one sense, to remark upon this is merely to restate a central theme within the genre, that of doubleness, and to recall the original signification of many of its images. What is perhaps surprising, on the other hand, is the extent to which, in the present context, the writers themselves seem not to recognise the persistently ambivalent status of the language they are employing. Ironies abound, but are only partially comprehended at any one time: the relevant connections are often not made until the next ironic reply. One notable exception to this, which can also be seen to draw together much of what has been discussed here, is the famous passage from Book x of *The Prelude* which was first published in *The Friend* on 26 October 1809, and then reprinted with slight variations in Wordsworth's *Poems* of 1815 under the title 'French Revolution, As It Appeared to Enthusiasts at Its Commencement' (I quote the passage in full as it was first printed in *The Friend*):

> Oh! pleasant exercise of hope and joy!
> For mighty were the auxiliars, which then stood
> Upon our side, we who were strong in love!
> Bliss was it in that dawn to be alive,
> But to be young was very heaven! oh! times,
> In which the meagre stale forbidding ways
> Of custom, law, and statute, took at once
> The attraction of a country in Romance!
> When Reason seem'd the most to assert her rights,
> When most intent on making of herself
> A prime Enchanter to assist the work,
> Which then was going forward in her name!
> Not favour'd spots alone, but the whole earth
> The beauty wore of promise – that which sets
> (To take an image which was felt no doubt
> Among the bowers of Paradise itself)
> The budding rose above the rose full blown,
> What temper at the prospect did not wake
> To happiness unthought of? The inert
> Were rous'd, and lively natures rapt away!
> They who had fed their childhood upon dreams,

The play-fellows of fancy, who had made
All powers of swiftness, subtilty, and strength
Their ministers, used to stir in lordly wise
Among the grandest objects of the sense
And deal with whatsoever they found there
As if they had within some lurking right
To wield it; – they too, who of gentle mood
Had watch'd all gentle motions, and to these
Had fitted their own thoughts, schemers more mild
And in the region of their peaceful selves; –
Now was it that both found, the Meek and Lofty
Did both find helpers to their heart's desire
And stuff at hand, plastic as they could wish! –
Were call'd upon to exercise their skill
Not in Utopia, subterraneous fields,
Or some secreted island, heaven knows where!
But in the very world, which is the world
Of all of us, the place where in the end
We find our happiness, or not at all![94]

Reading this, our initial impression, like that of the 'enthusiasts', is of the overwhelming excitement and optimism, the 'hope and joy', of the revolutionary scene. Wordsworth's description epitomises, almost *summarises*, the revolutionary romance. Here is Barlow's 'ascending bliss'. Here are Paine's 'bowers of paradise' risen from the ruins of the palaces of kings. Here are the buds which at the close of *Rights of Man* presage the 'political summer'. For these were times in which even abstruse theories of government 'took at once the attraction of a country in Romance'. The 'meagre stale forbidding ways / Of custom, law, and statute' – the very political map of what had been and what had held it there – dissolved into a series of enticing avenues of exploration, now that theories had at last the power to redraw the map. The 'ways' were instantly transformed into the pathways of a romance landcape, drawing the quester. Reason, traditionally the agent of disenchantment, herself sought the role of a 'prime Enchanter', presiding over the magical terrain. Previously an exercise of the imagination, the task of fashioning an earthly paradise was now a serious practicality: there was 'stuff at hand' in the real world and 'helpers to [the] heart's desire'. In the great work of re-creation, all were called on to participate, and the prospect of transformation encompassed 'Not favour'd spots alone, but the whole earth'.

In his evocation of the idealistic mood of the early years of the

French Revolution, particularly for those of his generation who were young and 'strong in love', Wordsworth captures perfectly the 'spirit of romance' of which Godwin had written in his *Reply to Parr*. In the context of *The Prelude*, the passage relates specifically to the period of Wordsworth's own stay in France in 1792, as recollected in Book IX. It was with Beaupuis that he first began to take a real interest in revolutionary politics, 'To think with fervour upon management / Of nations' (x, 685–86), and to investigate the ways of 'custom, law and statute':

> Oft in solitude
> With him did I discourse about the end
> Of civil government, and its wisest forms,
> Of ancient prejudice and chartered rights,
> Allegiance, faith, and laws by time matured,
> Custom and habit, novelty and change ...   (IX, lines 328–33)

It was then that Wordsworth felt most strongly that elation – a mixture of political zeal and 'chivalrous delight' – to which the passage from Book x gives such eloquent expression. In his account of the effects of the French Revolution upon two different sorts of temperament, the 'Lofty' and the 'Meek', he perhaps has in mind himself and Beaupuis, the latter having been described as 'Meek, though enthusiastic to the height / Of highest expectation' (IX, 300–1). Of Annette Vallon there is still no mention, but it is striking nevertheless that the whole revolutionary experience is couched in the language of love: arousal and rapture, 'beauty' and 'desire', the symbolism of the 'budding rose'. There are even echoes of Shakespeare's *Antony and Cleopatra*. 'O times!', declares Cleopatra – as if the phrase encapsulated everything – recalling the heyday of their love now Antony is gone. It is Antony who boasts to Caesar of his 'strength of love'. For nature to have imagined such a man as Antony, says Cleopatra, is to have outdone anything that fancy could create:

> It's past the size of dreaming: nature wants stuff
> To vie strange forms with fancy, yet t' imagine
> An Antony were nature's piece 'gainst fancy,
> Condemning shadows quite.   (v, ii, lines 94–97)[95]

So too did nature exceed fancy in creating the French Revolution: or rather, as Wordsworth tells us, those who had been 'The playfellows of fancy' now found 'stuff at hand, plastic as they could wish'. For

Wordsworth, as for Coleridge and Dyer, the 'joy' of the Revolutionary 'dawn' was almost erotic in its intensity, and the 'hope' nothing less than apocalyptic. Here, then, is the romantic myth writ large, a celebration of the Revolution which surpasses even that of Barlow in its exultant and universal optimism.

Yet all is not as straightforward as it first appears. For what exactly is 'the attraction of a country in romance'? Is it not something we should resist? Judging from what we have learned about 'enchanted ground', it is an attraction which may well be fraught with illusion. The 'ways' of romance as often as not lead to places of temptation, deception and error. Is this magical domain, this would-be paradise, in actuality but Burke's 'fairyland of philosophy'? There is something disturbing too about the idea of Reason seeking to make herself into an 'Enchanter' (again, one is reminded of Burke's phrase 'that seductive *Circean* liberty'). Enchanters usually belong to the dark strain in romance: the assistance they give is, to say the least, equivocal. Moreover, if 'the work ... was going forward in her name', should it have outstripped Reason, as is perhaps implied? Does this mean that what was going forward in the name of Reason was not altogether rational (as in Madame Roland's famous cry 'O Liberty, what crimes are committed in thy name!'[96])? Did the Revolution forge ahead, as it were, while she tried to catch up, to assert her rights, having in order to do so to make herself an enchanter and 'assist'? Where she did not 'assist', had she no rights, and was she ignored? The more one examines the syntax of Wordsworth's statement, the more one suspects that all was not as it 'seem'd'. Similarly, his presentation of 'that which sets / ... The budding rose above the rose full blown' speaks of a hierarchy relation based on judgment. One can therefore question: *is it right* that the beauty of the bud should be set above that of the rose full-blown? In contrast to the absence of doubt 'Among the bowers of Paradise itself', a suspicion may be sown.

Even the word 'Bliss', in Wordsworth's celebrated line, could be taken as a note of warning. Is this, like that of Acrasia in Spenser's Bower of Bliss, 'nam'd amis', a bliss which was 'turn'd to balefulnesse'?[97] Acrasia's Bower in Book II of *The Faerie Queene* is figured as an illusion of bliss wrought by enchantment, a parody of the true pleasure and happiness to be found only in heaven. Within the illusory paradise lurk wild beasts that were once men, youthful lovers whose liquid spirits have been sucked from their slumbering eyes. It is not just the conjunction of the word bliss with the image of bowers of paradise that suggests the analogy. Like Spenser's, Wordsworth's earthly paradise is a scene of enchantment and seduction. It is a place, or a time, when youthful lovers under the spell of a 'prime Enchanter' (in the 1815 version this reads 'prime Enchantress', strengthening the Spenserian analogy) were 'rouzed' and 'rapt' away, following 'their heart's desire'. The preference for 'The budding rose above the rose full blown' among the 'bowers of Paradise' also powerfully recalls the ethos of Spenser's Bower, with its deceptive *carpe florem* lay:

> Ah see the Virgin Rose, how sweetly shee
> Doth first peepe forth with bashful modestee,
> That fairer seemes, the lesse ye see her may;
> Lo see soone after, how more bold and free
> Her bared bosome she doth broad display;
> Loe see soone after, how she fades, and falles away.
> So passeth, in the passing of a day,
> Of mortall life the leafe, the bud, the flowre,
> Ne more doth flourish after first decay,
> That earst was sought to decke both bed and bowre,
> Of many a Ladie, and many a Paramowre:
> Gather therefore the Rose, whilest yet is prime,
> For soone cames age, that will her pride deflowre:
> Gather the Rose of loue, whilest yet is time,
> Whilest louing thou mayst loued be with equall crime.
>
> (II, xii, stanzas 74–75)[98]

It is a principle of the Bower's seduction that, like the enfolded buds of the Virgin Rose, that which is half-hidden beguiles the more. As with the two bathing girls encountered by Guyon, what is glimpsed or concealed increases desire, in which the very covering partakes. Though theirs parodies the appeal of true virgin modesty, that which 'wears' 'the beauty ... of promise' still further entices. Acrasia's veil but discovers and heightens her allure. She herself lies 'Upon a bed of Roses' in a garden enjoying perpetual Summer, where storm and frost never violate the 'tender buds or leaves', and Spring and Autumn, with their renewal and fruition, never come. As soon as we become aware of a possible analogy with the 'fond favourites' of the 'false enchauntresse' Acrasia, Wordsworth's description of the 'pleasant exercise' of the 'enthusiasts' in the Revolutionary dawn becomes a deeply worrying one. The example of Cleopatra – another enchantress in the tradition of Circe and the fairy mistress of Celtic myth and medieval romance – although more ambivalent, is hardly more reassuring. Loss of judgment for love of an enchantress brings a catastrophe whose global proportions are constantly stressed.

> Age cannot wither her, nor custom stale
> Her infinite variety: other women cloy
> The appetites they feed, but she makes hungry,
> Where most she satisfies. For vilest things
> Become themselves in her, that the holy priests
> Bless her, when she is riggish.   (II, iii, lines 235–40)

Is this the character of the attraction which Wordsworth detects in the Revolutionary enchantment? Cleopatra also invokes in more down-to-earth fashion the image of the rose central to the Bower of Bliss: 'What, no more ceremony?', she cries, at the abrupt arrival of Caesar's messenger:

> See my women,
> Against the blown rose may they stop their nose,
> That knelt unto the buds.   (III, xiii, lines 38–40)

If Wordsworth had it in mind, this would certainly apply to many of the erstwhile enthusiasts of the Revolution at the time of writing his retrospective piece. He himself appears eager to give full acknowledgment to the 'buds', and yet the whole passage, it seems, is open to an interpretation opposite in tendency to the one first presented.

If we return the poem to its original context in *The Prelude*, this interpretation can be supported by other passages where the metaphor of enchantment is associated with false consciousness or delusion. For example, William Pitt, whom Wordsworth heard speaking in the House of Commons during his residence in London in 1791, is credited with the power to enchant his audience with his remarkable oratory (specifically, the image is that of a 'hero in romance' blowing a magical horn[99]), but it is an 'enchantment' that proves ultimately spurious, for 'Words follow words' but 'sense' only *seems* 'to follow sense'; and the 'Marvellous' 'strain', 'Transcendent, superhuman as it is, / Grows tedious even in a young man's ear' (VII, 536–43). Similarly, when later under the sway of Godwinian rationalism in the period leading up to his crisis of 1796, Wordsworth compares himself to a 'wizard' who, 'by simple waving of a wand', 'instantaneously dissolves / Palace or grove' (the allusion is to Prospero's 'rough magic' speech in *The Tempest*[100]):

> even so did I unsoul
> As readily by syllogistic words
> (Some charm of logic, ever within reach)
> Those mysteries of passion which have made,
> And shall continue evermore to make –
> In spite of all that reason hath performed,
> And shall perform, to exalt and to refine –
> One brotherhood of all the human race … (XI, lines 80–87)

If the mention of unsouling the mysteries of passion does not make it sufficiently clear that this 'charm of logic' is a specious or an undesirable one, earlier references to Godwin's system as 'the philosophy / That promised to abstract the hopes of man / Out of his feelings' (X, 806–8), and as 'materials for a work / Of false imagination, placed beyond / The limits of experience and of truth' (X, 846–48), put the matter beyond doubt.

The very title of the 'Bliss' fragment, added by Wordsworth in 1815 and retained in subsequent editions of his works, contains qualifying or distancing signals. Lest his description of the hope and joy of those times be mistaken for a statement of his present attitude to the Revolution, or for an objective assessment of its character, the title specifies that the poem is about the 'French Revolution' not as it was, but 'As It Appeared' – not to him alone, or to the impartial spectator, but 'to Enthusiasts' (a term that usually carried derogatory connotations,[101] suggesting excessive or misdirected zeal); and only 'at Its Commencement'. The title also deprives the French Revolution of its definite article, as though to deny its uniqueness as an historical event, or otherwise undermine its dignity.

Although some readers still fail to appreciate the ironies that the passage affords, and treat it as though it were an example rather than an analysis of liberal illusions about the French Revolution, a number of critics have recently sought to expose the dark underside of Wordsworth's passage, pointing to the negative associations of certain of its literary images, or stressing the parallels between Wordsworth's metaphorical language and Burke's.[102] Yet there is a danger of overstating the ironic interpretation. By 1804, the utopian promise of the early 1790s may have seemed to Wordsworth like a false dawn – a grand illusion fostered by what, in Burkean fashion, he would call in *The Convention of Cintra* (1808) 'the pestilential philosophism of France' – but he nowhere suggests, as does Burke at every available opportunity, that the Revolution was inherently evil.

A similar objection might be made to the reading that claims that the point of Wordsworth's allusion to the Bower of Bliss, here and in the earlier Cambridge episode, is that, like the Bowers of Acrasia and Phaedria, they are *false* paradises encountered by the poet *en route* to the true paradise, only to be found (in Wordsworth's case) in 'the everyday workings of Nature'.[103] The 'prospect' of universal happiness opened by the French Revolution may have turned out to be an illusory one – when Wordsworth was writing, that was a matter of historical record – but Wordsworth does not say that to have entertained those hopes and to have tasted that 'bliss' was to have been guilty of intemperance. Indeed, just twenty lines later, he makes a rather different judgment on his own moral condition at this time (we need to remember that the passage above relates to the period before England declared war on France in February 1793, the event which was to change everything for Wordsworth):

> I moved among mankind
> With genial feelings still predominant,
> When erring, erring on the better side,
> And in the kinder spirit...

> In brief, a child of Nature, as at first,
> Diffusing only those affections wider
> That from the cradle had grown up with me,
> And losing, in no other way than light
> Is lost in light, the weak in the more strong.

> (x, lines 738–41, 752–6)

This confirms the many suggestions in the 'Bliss' passage itself that Wordsworth was acting in accordance with nature rather than in defiance of it; and while noticing the undercurrent of irony, we should not ignore the 'mighty auxiliars' which then stood *upon his side*. If, then, to have participated in the revolutionary enthusiasm was to have erred, it was, in Shelley's phrase, a 'generous error',[104] and Wordsworth was strengthened rather than diminished by it. Coleridge makes much the same judgment on his own youthful 'Jacobinism' in the essay in *The Friend* to which the extract from *The Prelude* was appended: 'My feelings...and imagination did not remain unkindled in this general conflagration; and I confess I should be more inclined to be ashamed than proud of myself, if they had!'[105]

To isolate any particular line of influence, or to infer that Wordsworth's meanings are dictated by a single source, therefore, may be to falsify the poem and underestimate Wordsworth's achievement. The evidence of this chapter suggests that both Barlow *and* Burke, and a whole political literature, lie behind this passage;[106] and that Wordsworth has in fact recognised and drawn together both the positive *and* negative versions of the revolutionary romance. It is remarkable, moreover, how closely interwoven are Wordsworth's images from political writing and those from literary romance. Because he is fully aware of the literary origins of the figurative devices that had been used to such powerful and varied effect by political authors of the period, he is able both to speak the language of revolution (to present the French Revolution 'As It Appeared' to contemporaries) and to use that language in a more subtle and complex way. The result is an extraordinary synthesis, in which Paine's 'bowers of paradise', Barlow's 'ascending bliss' and Burke's 'enchanted ground' are united in the allusion to Spenser's Bower of Bliss, itself a composite image that draws together many different motifs in Spenserian romance. One aspect of Acrasia's Bower is brought out very clearly in Edward Young's sorrowful meditation on 'sublunary Bliss' in the first of his *Night Thoughts* (1742), another literary text with which Wordsworth was certainly familiar:

> Bliss! sublunary Bliss! proud words and vain:
> Implicit treason to divine Decree!
> A bold Invasion of the rights of Heaven!
> I clasp'd the Phantoms, and I found them Air.
>
> (lines 198–201)[107]

The opposition here is with heavenly bliss, 'A perpetuity of bliss'. That emphasis is crucial for Young, a poet whose torment is transience; but the basic opposition underlies Spenser's original allegory, which not only encodes specific temptations to intemperance, but also sets a general limit on the amount of earthly satisfaction that can be expected or permitted under a Christian dispensation. A similar implication lurks beneath the 'Bliss' of Wordsworth's Revolutionary dawn: that the rights of man, or the rights of Reason, may, by their very nature, constitute an 'Invasion of the rights of Heaven' – an implication readily discerned by Shelley when he remarks, somewhat ironically, on the 'demonical' notion expressed by the final lines of Wordsworth's poem (*Letters*, II, 406–7).

Yet Wordsworth's poem is genuinely ambivalent, rather than merely ironic. It is informed rather than controlled by the allusion to the Bower of Bliss, and there are many elements in Wordsworth's description that resist the analogy, and are therefore not reducible to irony. The stress it places on the mental energy and activity (the 'exercise') of the enthusiasts, for example, is in marked contrast to the passivity of Acrasia's lovers; and in the context of *The Prelude* as a whole, it is only later, and under altered circumstances, that the enchantment of Reason takes the more ominous form of a 'charm of logic' by which to 'unsoul the mysteries of passion'. It is because Wordsworth does not conceive of his poetic account as an exercise in apostasy, however subtle, that Cleopatra rather than Acrasia may be nearer to the presiding enchantress of the Revolution. Though an enchantress, Cleopatra, in all her 'infinite variety', is a more ambivalent and sympathetic figure than Acrasia. Her attractions lead to disaster, to tragedy, but not to hell. Antony is not a youthful lover, and Cleopatra definitely a 'blown rose'. If there is some form of subtextual dialogue taking place between Shakespeare's play and Wordsworth's account, this enables the latter to presuppose and juxtapose age (or experience) even while it speaks of youth – rather as the poem itself presupposes hindsight and the 'maturer mind'. Unlike that of Acrasia and her victims, the love between Antony and Cleopatra is not judged by its consequences alone, and Cleopatra herself makes the point, crucial to the theme both of Shakespeare's play and of Wordsworth's poem, that although the 'times' are over they live in the retelling.[108]

CHAPTER 2

Romance and revolution in Queen Mab

The genius of Philosophy is walking abroad, and with the touch of Ithuriel's spear is trying the establishments of the earth. The various forms of Prejudice, Superstition and Servility start up in their true shapes, which had long imposed upon the world under the revered semblances of Honour, Faith and Loyalty.

> Anne Laetitia Barbauld, *An Address to the Opposers of the Corporation and Test Acts* (1790)

Those who believe that Heaven is, what earth has been, a monopoly in the hands of a favoured few, would do well to reconsider their opinion: if they find that it came from their priest or their grandmother, they could not do better than reject it.

> Shelley, *Declaration of Rights* (1812), article 16.

For decades after his death, the macabre imagery of Burke's anti-Jacobin polemic continued to haunt the English political imagination. In 1821 this found expression in Robert Southey's feverish attack on the 'Satanic School' in the Preface to his official tribute to the late King George III, *A Vision of Judgment*. The poem is now chiefly remembered as the occasion for Byron's composition of the same name, a stinging reply to the 'magnanimous Laureate' and sometime author of *Wat Tyler*, in the form of a travesty of his crudely sycophantic dream vision. We can take it that the creator of *Don Juan* was very much in mind in Southey's diatribe against 'those monstrous combinations of horrors and mockery, lewdness and impiety, with which English poetry has, in our day, … been polluted'.[1] But so too, no doubt, was Shelley, for 1821 was also the year which saw the publication – without the author's consent – of that most impious of poems, *Queen Mab*. Written some ten years previously, *Queen Mab* had originally been printed for private circulation as long ago as 1813; a version of the first two cantos, and an extract from the sixth, had appeared in Shelley's *Alastor* volume of 1816; and two of the long notes to the poem, on atheism and on 'natural diet', had previously been issued as separate pamphlets. Only now, though, was *Queen Mab* available to the public in its entirety, in the pirated editions of William Clark and Richard Carlisle.[2]

Confirmation of Shelley's supposed membership of the 'Satanic School' came in a review of *Queen Mab* in the *Literary Gazette and Journal of Belles Lettres* of 19 May 1821. Noting that certain parts of the poem had already been published separately, the reviewer elaborates upon the Satanic theme in order to condemn the whole and vilify the author:

Though the hellish ingredients, therefore, are now for the first time brought together into one cauldron, they have, like those of the evil beings in Macbeth, previously disgusted the world in forms of separate obsceneness.

We have spoken of Shelley's genius, and it is doubtless of a high order; but when we look at the purposes to which it is directed, and contemplate the infernal character of all its efforts, our souls revolt at the tenfold horror of the energy it exhibits, and we feel as if one of the darkest of the fiends had been clothed with a human body, to enable him to gratify his enmity against the human race, and as if the supernatural atrocity of his hate were only heightened by his power to do injury. So strongly has this impression dwelt upon our minds that we absolutely asked a friend who had seen this individual, to describe him to us – as if a cloven foot, or horn, or flames from the mouth, must have marked the external appearance of so bitter an enemy to mankind.[3]

It is not only blasphemy, and a Satanic 'enmity against the human race', of which Shelley stands accused, but also personal immorality – a charge which soon becomes explicit when the reviewer turns from the 'outward semblance' to the 'inner man', and openly denounces him in a footnote as an 'incestuous wretch'. This is probably intended to hint at Shelley's alleged relations with Claire Clairmont, or at current rumours about the association of Byron, the Shelleys and Claire at Geneva in 1816 – and the very notion of a 'Satanic School' has more to do with biographical scandal of this kind than it does with literary criticism.

It has also, of course, to do with politics, and the *Literary Gazette* is quite right to see the 'raving atheism' of *Queen Mab* as an integral part of its political polemic. For the purpose of the poem is indeed to expose 'the depravity of the existing system' and to shape out a new world 'in millennial perspective'. The portrayal of Shelley as a Satan

QUEEN MAB;

A

PHILOSOPHICAL POEM:

WITH NOTES.

BY

PERCY BYSSHE SHELLEY.

ECRASEZ L'INFAME!
Correspondance de Voltaire.

Avia Pieridum peragro loca, nullius ante
Trita solo; juvat integros accedere fonteis;
Atque haurire: juratque novos decerpere flores.
*   *   *   *   *   *   *
Unde prius nulli velarint tempora musæ.
Primum quod magnis doceo de rebus; et arctis
Religionum animos nodis exsolvere pergo.
Lucret. lib. iv.

Δος πυ ςῶ, καὶ κοσμον κινησω.
Archimedes.

LONDON:

PRINTED BY P. B. SHELLEY,

23, Chapel Street, Grosvenor Square.

1813.

Figure 1. Title page to *Queen Mab*, June 1813. 'A small neat Quarto, on fine paper & so as to catch the aristocrats: They will not read it, but their sons & daughters may' (*Letters*, 1, 361).

let loose upon the public mind is fully in keeping with the poem's own apocalyptic imagery, and it is no accident that such accusations of Satanism recall the style of Burke, since *Queen Mab*, with its relentless libertarianism and audacious promise of an earthly paradise, raises once again the spectre of Jacobinism that Burke so much opposed.

It is all the more striking that the poem was written in 1811–13, a time when the ideological debates of the Revolutionary decade had very much receded from public view. The millenarian enthusiasm of the early 1790s seemed to most a thing of the past; and repression of the English radicals active in the 1790s had been so thorough that, of those who had not actually altered their allegiances, all but a few had been forced into silence or exile. The fact that Shelley, in 1812, was unaware that William Godwin was still alive is a measure of how far such figures had fallen from prominence, as is the fact that the death in 1809 of the greatest of all the radicals, Tom Paine, passed almost totally unnoticed in England – or indeed America, to where he had returned in 1802. In the midst of the Napoleonic Wars, with attention fixed on foreign affairs, British radicalism was definitely at a low ebb. Even the parliamentary reformers, claiming not the 'Rights of Man' but the ancient constitutional rights of Englishmen, were hard-pressed for support in these years, such that in 1812 the London branch of Major Cartwright's Union for Parliamentary Reform could not even enlist the necessary one hundred sponsors (although outside London, and among the working class, reformist sentiment seems to have remained stronger).[4]

Like Blake, then, the young Shelley takes it upon himself to keep the divine vision in time of trouble, the 'divine vision' in the latter case being the dream of a secular millennium founded on the principles of the Enlightenment. The fact that Shelley, through this singular act of intellectual independence and imaginative retrieval, attempts a revival of the revolutionary mood of the early 1790s has long been recognised, but the significance of *Queen Mab* as a link between the political and literary culture of the late eighteenth century and that of the second decade of the nineteenth has not been fully explored, nor have the exact terms of that imaginative engagement. In particular, there has been confusion about the poem's genre or form, concerning which a large number of more or less contradictory claims have been made. There is also continuing disagreement over the ideological content of the poem, notably as to the extent of Shelley's adherence to the political doctrines of Godwin, and his use of French political sources. While most critics would agree that *Queen Mab* is Shelley's most radical poem, it is not altogether clear whether the author's apparent allegiance to Godwinian precepts is compatible with the assertion that it is also a 'revolutionary' text.

The aim of the present chapter is to resolve some of these questions, and to reassess both the politics and the poetics of Shelley's 'philosophical poem'. This will involve a careful scrutiny of the poem's ideological sources and generic contexts, and a detailed analysis of the poem itself. Central to my argument is the claim that *Queen Mab* is, in fact, another 'revolutionary romance', a text that gives belated expression to the utopian aspirations engendered by the French Revolution, and subsequently modified by writers like Godwin; and one that, in so doing, recreates at the level of form the fusion of romance and revolution which existed in the imagery of the 1790s. The result is a crude but powerful exploitation of the politics of romance, marking a crucial stage both in Shelley's own deployment of the genre, and in the larger development of this extraordinarily versatile literary form.

THE TITLE PAGE

Queen Mab. At first glance, nothing could have seemed more innocuous. The last major publication to carry that title was a popular collection of French fairy stories 'designed for the innocent Amusement of Children'.[5] Mab had also been the subject of light verses by Ben Jonson, Robert Herrick and Michael Drayton, and, more recently, Charlotte Dacre.[6] The most famous portrayal of this intriguing character out of English folklore, however, is in Mercutio's speech in *Romeo and Juliet* (i, iv, 53–94), and it is more than likely that this was the passage from Shakespeare which Shelley originally intended to use as a motto for his own composition (*Letters*, i, 361). Yet *Queen Mab* is only part of his title. The full title is *Queen Mab; A Philosophical Poem: With Notes*.[7] The name, with all its associations of magical lore, flights of fancy and elfish dreams, is immediately contrasted with a generic designation which promises quite the opposite: high seriousness and intellectual rigour – altogether guaranteed by the prospect of 'Notes'.

In 1813, or 1821, the irony would not have been quite so serene. Firstly, the generic classification was unusual. In the past hundred

years there had been countless 'didactic poems' and 'poetical essays',
but only a handful of works which had described themselves as
'philosophical poems'.[8] Of these, at least three could more properly
be termed 'anti-philosophical poems', since their manifest purpose
was to attack any form of knowledge that challenged the authority of
biblical dogma. Sir Richard Blackmore's *The Creation: A Philosophical
Poem* (1712) purports to contain a positive proof of the proposition
that 'THERE IS A GOD', but mostly consists of laboured attempts to
refute the arguments of 'atheistical' and 'irreligious' philosophers
such as Lucretius, whose poem *De Rerum Natura* had evidently
supplied his literary model. Perhaps inspired by the success of
Blackmore's *Creation* (which had been praised by Addison in *The
Spectator* as 'one of the most useful and noble Productions in our
English verse'[9]), William Dawson wrote a poem eleven years later
with the title, *The Atheist: A Philosophical Poem, Representing and
Confuting the Arguments Brought in Favour of their Tenets* (1723). A much
more recent precedent, no less pious in its intentions but more private
in the manner of its philosophising, was Thomas Heming's *Themes of
Admiration: A Philosophical Poem* (1812). This also appears to have
been inspired by Blackmore's *Creation*, though it also shows the
influence of Pope's *Essay on Man* (1734) and Young's *Night Thoughts*
(1741–46), two very different works which may serve to remind us of
the range of eighteenth-century 'philosophical' poetry – though
neither carries that generic denomination.

What the author of *Themes of Admiration* seemingly did not realise
is that the word 'philosophical' had acquired a rather different
connotation in recent years. In 1801 the essayist John Foster
described philosophy as 'a term that would be venerable, if it could
be rescued from the misfortune of being hackneyed into cant, and
from serving the impiety which substitutes human ability for divine
power'.[10] The 'vain demigods of an hour' to whom Foster goes on to
attribute blame for this linguistic aberration are the ideological
leaders of the French Revolution, but in effect he is registering and
rejecting the shift that had already occurred in the meaning of the
term as a result of the secularising philosophy of the Enlightenment
(a reminder of this shift is the specific meaning that still attaches to
the French word *philosophe*).

Yet it was neither the 'reformers' nor the 'projecting visionaries'
who had turned 'philosophy' into a cant term – not in England, at
least. It was the *opponents* of reform, the *counter*-revolutionaries, who

had transformed that 'venerable' term into one of abuse. Primary responsibility here lies with Burke, for whom the delusions and menaces of philosophy had been a constant theme of attack (the later French tracts are aptly described by one commentator[11] – by analogy with Pope's *Dunciad* – as Burke's *Philosophiad*). The propagandist Hannah More delivered the same message to 'mechanics, journeymen and day labourers' in the following exchange between Jack Anvil the Blacksmith and Tom Hod the Mason from her tract *Village Politics* (1793):

TOM. What is *Philosophy*, that Tim Standish talks so much about?
JACK. To believe that there's neither God, nor devil, nor heaven, nor hell.
    – To dig up a wicked old fellow's [i.e. Voltaire's] rotten bones, whose books, Sir John says, have been the ruin of thousands; and to set his figure up in a church and worship him.[12]

By the end of the 1790s, the word 'philosophy' had become almost synonomous with the phrase 'the New [or Modern] Philosophy', and both were part of the regular jargon of anti-Jacobinism. Thus, Elizabeth Hamilton's *Memoirs of the Modern Philosophers* (1800) is not, as might now appear from its title, a set of biographical sketches of the leading thinkers of the day, but a satirical novel about Godwin, avowedly written 'in opposition to the opinions generally known by the name of the *New Philosophy*'. Similarly, in Mary Burges's allegory *The Progress of the Pilgrim Good-Intent, in Jacobinical Times* (1800), the character called 'Mr Philosophy' is not the dignified old sage whom well-meaning pilgrims expect to find when they stop at the Palace of Wisdom, but a fast-talking sophist (dressed in classical garb to disguise his youth) who turns out to be an evil magician. This hardly comes as a surprise to the reader, who has already been told in the Preface that the author considers it her solemn duty to exert her utmost efforts 'in resisting the attacks, and exposing the wiles, of our arch-enemy, PHILOSOPHISM' (p. vii).

It was not just the *word* 'philosophy' that had been discredited. The subject itself appeared to have suffered the same fate. That, at least, was the conclusion of Sir William Drummond, who wrote in the Preface to his *Academical Questions* (1805) of 'the general distaste, which has existed of late years in this country for all speculative and metaphysical reasoning', and of 'the silly clamour which mistaken zeal has raised against philosophy'.[13] Mr Flosky, the romantic metaphysician in Peacock's novel *Nightmare Abbey* (1818), makes the point more plainly when he says that 'the French Revolution made us shrink from the name of philosophy'.[14] It took a long time for its name to be cleared. In 1826 people no longer produced works with titles like *Modern Philosophy and Barbarism* (one of the more outspoken attacks on Godwin's theories,[15] published in 1798) or 'Drinking versus Thinking, or A Song Against the New Philosophy'[16] (Coleridge's contribution to the 'silly clamour', from 1801), but Hazlitt could still write that 'Reason has become a sort of by-word, and philosophy has, "fallen first into a fasting, then into a sadness, then into a decline, and last, into the dissolution of which we all complain!"'[17] The comment (with its allusion to *Hamlet*) occurs in Hazlitt's essay on Godwin from *The Spirit of the Age*, a biographical sketch which is also a personal reflection on philosophy's decline by a writer whose own intellectual career began with a metaphysical treatise published in the year 1805.

Given the negative associations that had become attached to the name of philosophy, it is hardly surprising that neither of the two new translations of Lucretius's *De Rerum Natura* that were published during this period announces itself as a 'philosophical poem', the former (1805) preferring the neutral designation 'A Didactic Poem', and the latter (1813) resorting to the cumbersome phrase 'A Didascalic Poem'[18] – a generic label singular enough to earn a place in the *OED*. If these are cases where an author has avoided the term 'philosophical' because of its adverse political connotations, there is an interesting example in the *Anti-Jacobin* of a poem to which that term *was* applied for the very same reason. 'The Loves of the Triangles', which appeared in three instalments during April and May of 1798, is one of the best known poems of the *Anti-Jacobin*, a wide-ranging satire (written by divers hands) in the form of an elaborate parody of Erasmus Darwin's highly successful poem *The Loves of the Plants* (1789). Its subtitle is 'A Mathematical and Philosophical Poem', a classification which is itself parodic, comically encapsulating Darwin's stated ambition 'to enlist Imagination under the banner of Science',[19] and implicitly mocking the very idea of a poem 'with Philosophical Notes'.[20] But this is only part of the point of the satire. The reason why Erasmus Darwin became a target for the *Anti-Jacobin* was not just that he had attempted to mix poetry with science, but because he had once expressed support for the French Revolution, in a long invocation to Liberty in another of his poems, *The Economy of Vegetation* (1791). The true motive behind the

parody is political not aesthetic, and at its centre is an ironic song of
praise to a 'regenerate' France

> Where TASTE with RAPINE saunters hand in hand;
> Where nursed in seats of innocence and bliss,
> REFORM greets TERROR with fraternal kiss;
> Where mild PHILOSOPHY first taught to scan
> The wrongs of Providence, and the *rights* of MAN;
> Where MEMORY broods o'er FREEDOM's earlier scene,
> The *Lantern* bright, and brighter *Guillotine* ...   (lines 131–37)[21]

As always with the *Anti-Jacobin*, the logic is one of guilt by association,
and it is no accident that for the purposes of the satire Darwin is
identified with that other 'Jacobin' philosopher William Godwin, of
whom the fictitious author 'Mr Higgins' is an obvious caricature.

Whether or not Shelley was familiar with the precedents for his
'philosophical poem',[22] he is unlikely to have been unaware of the
connotations of that term. His choice of generic subtitle was, I
suggest, a calculated rhetorical signal: a deliberate invocation of the
polemical manner of the 1790s, and a confident reassertion of the
radical tradition of philosophical enquiry represented by Darwin,
Godwin and Drummond. The conjunction of the phrase 'A
Philosophical Poem' with the name of Queen Mab reinforces this
impression, re-enacting precisely that fusion of the magical and the
political found so often in earlier revolutionary literature. Mab is
indeed the revolutionary spirit personified, like the 'queen of Bliss' in
George Dyer's ode 'On Liberty' (1792), or the 'prime Enchanter'
Reason in Wordsworth's lines on the French Revolution. Burke had
once warned of 'the fairyland of philosophy', and spoken of his
experience of revolution as like 'walking on enchanted ground'. In
Shelley's philosophical poem, the Queen of the Fairies makes a
triumphant return, and takes us right inside her palace of enchantment. The 'fairies' midwife' of *Romeo and Juliet* is redeployed to
practise what Paul Ricoeur, following Plato, calls the 'intellectual
midwifery' of the utopian educator.[23] 'With Notes', that is with
revolutionary spells spelt out in common prose, now sounds like sheer
provocation.

So much for the title. I have mentioned that Shelley planned to
introduce a motto from Shakespeare. None appears in the printed
version. Mercutio's line 'O then I see Queen Mab hath been with
you' does, however, turn up a few years later as an epigraph to a very
different political publication. In 1819, amidst the social crisis –

particularly acute in Scotland – prompted by the 'Peterloo' mass-acre, Walter Scott wrote three articles under the pseudonym SOMNAMBULUS for the *Edinburgh Weekly Journal*, in which, using the literary device of a dream vision, he attacked the proposals and aspirations of the radicals. The first vision was prompted by an editorial in the *Scotsman* on 13 November 1819 which had called for a union of all opposition groups in order to bring down the government. The second attacks 'the insane idea of the equalization of property', and is targeted in particular at the Spencean philan-thropists. In the third, Scott treats 'with scorn and derision' the subject of 'Radical Reform and Universal Suffrage'. The articles were immediately republished as a pamphlet entitled *The Visionary*,[24] which uses the Queen Mab motto to signify the futility of the radical projects of social and political change ('Begot of nothing but vain fantasy', as Mercutio says of dreams to his friend Romeo). There is no evidence that Scott knew of Shelley's poem, but the contrasting use of the Queen Mab motif illustrates the currency, and continuing instability, of this political iconography.

Shelley also intended to write a Preface, which has not come to light. What do appear on the title page are three epigraphs, which, like the title itself, are important preliminary signals. The famous slogan from Voltaire, 'ECRASEZ L'INFAME!', immediately inscribes the poem into the Enlightenment, and heralds Shelley's own vigorous assault upon Christian revelation.[25] The lines from *De Rerum Natura*, as well as proclaiming deliverance from religious superstition, emphasise the novelty and boldness of Shelley's venture, somewhat ironically in the sense that he is actually following Lucretius into 'the Pieran realm', or the genre of the philosophical poem.[26] Underlining his encyclopaedic ambitions in *Queen Mab*, Shelley's third epigraph is taken from the Greek of Archimedes. John Foster, in the essay quoted above,[27] complains that political reformers 'are for ever introducing the story of Archimedes, who was to have moved the world if he could have found any second place on which to plant his engines'; and indeed, like the phrase from Voltaire, this epigraph functions here as a formula, linking Shelley's poem to other projects for reforming the world (the most important precedent is Paine's *Rights of Man*, the second part of which opens with the declaration: 'What Archimedes said of the mechanical powers, may be applied to Reason and Liberty: "*Had we*", said he, "*a place to stand upon, we might raise the world*"'). If the citation of Lucretius expresses Shelley's philosophical aspirations, that of Archimedes stresses the urge for practical realisation. Together with the title, the three epigraphs act as a coded manifesto, simultaneously revealing and concealing the purpose of the poem.

Queen Mab is therefore both philosophical and polemical, a meditation 'on the nature of things' and a declamation against 'things as they are'. But is it really a *revolutionary* poem, as is often claimed? Mab could hardly be more different from that other folk figure who became, as the persona of the radical journalist Jacques-René Hébert during the early years of the French Revolution, the very symbol of popular revolution: Le Père Duchesne. Where Mab is stately and imperious, Père Duchesne is a rough-mannered, pipe-smoking old artisan.[28] Both have their *grandes colères* and their *grandes joies* (the 'changing glows' of Mab's 'burning speech'), but where every issue of *Le Père Duchesne* is sprinkled with swear-words, with *bougres* and *foutres*, *Queen Mab* maintains an aristocratic refinement of diction, being full of words like 'pure', 'eminent', 'lofty' and 'noble'. If the voice of the urban *sans-culottes* is the one true voice of revolution, and the obscenities of Hébert's news-sheet the only authentic signification of a revolutionary situation, *Queen Mab* cannot really be called a 'revolutionary' text. Comparing Shelley's version of Queen Mab with Shakespeare's, Shelley even seems to have discarded those characteristics that made her a genuinely subversive figure in the popular imagination (Shelley's mischievous 'Witch of Atlas' is arguably closer in spirit to the Queen Mab of folk tradition).

But Hébert's verbal shock tactics were not the only manifestation of what Roland Barthes calls the 'revolutionary mode of writing'.[29] Even during the heyday of *Le Père Duchesne*, in 1793, the dominant mode of revolutionary writing and speech was the elevated classical rhetoric of Robespierre. Although Shelley would not have relished the comparison, there are occasions when Queen Mab does indeed sound like 'the Incorruptible'. When the polemic is at its most intense, the language of the poem has just that mixture of purity and violence that we associate with Robespierre and the so-called 'Republic of Virtue'. It is significant, then, that one of the most discerning analysts of the oratory of the French Revolution has defined the atmosphere of Robespierre's later speeches as compounded out of Volney's *Les Ruines; ou Méditations sur les Révolutions des*

Empires (1791) and Condorcet's *Esquisse d'un Tableau Historique des Progrès de l'Esprit Humain* (1794), since these same works are also known to have shaped the language and form of *Queen Mab*. The atmosphere is that of a 'mysterious, Gothic-novel world of veiled conspiracy, avowed traitors, assassins, and tyrants, in which a mysterious Titan, larger than life size, asserts his superior understanding of France and of the world'; the personality displayed is 'alternately that of a martyr and a conqueror'.[30] There are elements here that are not found in *Queen Mab*, such as the paranoia and the personal will to power, but the mood of the poem does indeed have much in common with Robespierre's speeches, not least in what one critic has called, somewhat unsympathetically, its 'lurid melo-drama'[31] – a feature that reminds us that Shelley, unlike Robespierre, had actually written gothic novels in his youth. The fact that the poem also deals in philosophical abstractions does not invalidate the comparison, since this was itself one of the defining characteristics of French revolutionary rhetoric.[32] The same can be said of the strongly metaphorical quality of the poem's political language, a feature that it shares with what Coleridge, in the the Preface to *The Fall of Robespierre*, called the 'highly figurative' language of the French revolutionaries.[33] *Queen Mab* is not a formal imitation of the oratory of the French Revolution, but both in its messianic fervour and in the ferocity of its polemic, no less than in its potent blend of politics and philosophy, and of abstract and figurative language, it bears unmistakable traces of the French revolutionary style.

Of course there are native influences too, but it is to the 1790s that we must look for these rather than the political writings of Shelley's own day. If the poem does not openly speak of revolution (the word is mentioned only once, inconsequentially, and Mab is explicit in her commitment to *gradual* – albeit *total* – change), it is certainly not written in the language of 'moderate' or even 'radical reform'. *Queen Mab* has little in common with the speeches of Sir Francis Burdett or the pamphlets of Major Cartwright; less still with the populist rhetoric of agitators such as Henry 'Orator' Hunt, whom Shelley regarded with deep suspicion. On the other hand, the poem is manifestly indebted to Godwin's *Enquiry Concerning Political Justice* and the militant republicanism of the *Rights of Man*;[34] while its nearest poetical equivalent is probably Joel Barlow's metrical broadside *The Conspiracy of Kings* (1792).

Both in substance and style, however, Shelley's is a far more extreme political statement than any of these precursors. An illustration of this is his attack on commerce in Canto v. It is sometimes claimed that Shelley has here simply turned into verse Book VIII of *Political Justice*. Yet Godwin only once touches on the subject, and then it is to repeat the standard view of the Whig historians that commerce had played a vital role 'in the progress of modern Europe from barbarism to refinement' by breaking down the barriers between the social classes, and permitting people of humble origin to rise to positions of wealth alongside 'those who were cased in mail'.[35] Paine, in his chapter on 'Ways and Means of Improving the Condition of Europe', gives an even stronger endorsement of the principle of commerce, claiming that if it 'were permitted to act to the universal extent it is capable, it would extirpate the system of war, and produce a revolution in the uncivilized state of governments'.[36] Barlow, too, in his epic *The Columbiad* (1807), envisions a millennial future in which commerce will vie with science to be the 'aspiring genius' of an age of peace and plenty:

> Gay streamers lengthen round the seas and skies
> The countless nations open all their stores,
> Load every wave and crowd the lively shores;
> Bright sails in mingling mazes streak the air,
> And commerce triumphs o'er the rage of war. (x, lines 156–60)

Here, by contrast, is *Queen Mab* on the subject:

> Commerce has set the mark of selfishness,
> The signet of its all-enslaving power
> Upon a shining ore, and called it gold:
> Before whose image bow the vulgar great,
> The vainly rich, the miserable proud,
> The mob of peasants, nobles, priests, and kings,
> And with blind feelings reverence the power
> That grinds them to the dust of misery.
> But in the temple of their hireling hearts
> Gold is a living god, and rules in scorn
> All living things but virtue.
>
> Since tyrants, by the sale of human life,
> Heap luxuries to their sensualism, and fame
> To their wide-wasting and insatiate pride,
> Success has sanctioned to a credulous world
> The ruin, the disgrace, the woe of war …
>
> The harmony and happiness of man
> Yields to the wealth of nations; that which lifts

His nature to the heaven of its pride,
Is bartered for the poison of his soul;
The weight that drags to earth his towering hopes,
Blighting all prospect but of selfish gain,
Withering all passion but of slavish fear,
Extinguishing all free and generous love
Of enterprise and daring, even the pulse
That fancy kindles in the beating heart
To mingle with sensation, it destroys, –
Leaving nothing but the sordid lust of self,
The grovelling hope of interest and gold,
Unqualified, unmingled, unredeemed
Even by hypocrisy.   (v, lines 38–43, 53–68, 79–93)

We should not automatically conclude that Shelley's is the more 'radical' position. In Shelley's diatribe, there is a definite element of snobbery – of aristocratic contempt for trade and mercantile wealth. Only a man with a private income could accuse the 'mob of peasants' who need to trade in order to survive of being motivated by the same blind reverence for gold as the 'vulgar great' and the 'vainly rich'. His own social position is betrayed even more starkly in a letter to Elizabeth Hitchener, when he states that 'Vile as aristocracy is, commerce, purse-proud ignorance & illiterateness is more contemptible' (*Letters*, I, 151). Even if we leave aside the question of class prejudice, it remains true that Shelley's attitude to commerce was more commonly associated with conservative than with radical politics.[37]

In fact, one of the most interesting and unexpected features of Shelley's polemic against commerce is his appropriation of Burke's lament for the 'age of chivalry' from the *Reflections on the Revolution in France*. The parallel seems highly improbable until we realise that Shelley, like Burke, is contrasting a condition of society in which man's virtuous propensities are fulfilled and one in which they are denied or destroyed. In so doing, Shelley borrows Burke's controlling metaphor of elevation and fall, and, more importantly, such key words from Burke's chivalric lexicon as 'pride', 'generous', 'love', and 'enterprise'.[38] Shelley's conception of what it was that constituted the lost glory of Europe (or the 'harmony and happiness of man') does not in every respect agree with Burke's, but both authors make the point – and with a comparable degree of rhetorical intensity – that it has been, or is being, 'extinguished'. What is remarkable, moreover, is that in recycling Burke's opposition between the 'age of chivalry' and that 'of sophisters, oeconomists and calculators', Shelley reveals that part of its original force lay in the fact that it gave expression to profound (and on Burke's part, probably unconscious) anxieties about the advance of capitalism. Burke's ostensible theme was the 'revolution in manners' associated with the rise of democratic politics, exemplified by the disrespectful treatment of Marie-Antoinette at Versailles, but the climax of the passage, with its contrast between the two 'ages', suggests that Burke may really have been more worried about the 'great revolution' described by Adam Smith in *The Wealth of Nations* (1776), and echoed by Paine – the transformation of the social order brought about by 'the silent and insensible operation of foreign commerce and manufactures'.[39]

This commercial revolution is exactly the target of Shelley's polemic, and it is no coincidence that the passage quoted above directly alludes to Smith's treatise. With Shelley's dictum that 'The harmony and happiness of man / Yields to the wealth of nations', what remained implicit and ambiguous in the *Reflections* thus becomes explicit and unequivocal: namely, that the capitalist ethic which Burke elsewhere defended and celebrated[40] was in reality destructive of those very ideals which Burke wished to preserve. The same message is stated even more bluntly in Shelley's Notes to the poem (and the following can be taken as confirmation that the passage from the *Reflections* is active in *Queen Mab*):

Let it be remembered, that it [commerce] is a foe to everything of real worth and excellence in the human character. The odious and disgusting aristocracy of wealth is built upon the ruins of all that is good in chivalry and republicanism; and luxury is the forerunner of a barbarism scarce capable of cure. (*Poems*, I, 418)

In this case, it is not only Burke whom Shelley is echoing. As if to underline his polemical appropriation of Burke's lament for the 'age of chivalry', the Burkean opposition between chivalry and commerce (here reformulated as a contrast between two different forms of 'aristocracy'), is combined with Paine's famous pronouncement in *Common Sense* that 'the palaces of kings are built upon the ruins of the bowers of paradise',[41] thereby transforming the aristocratic sentiments of the *Reflections* into a radical indictment of the *status quo*. Four years later, Burke and Paine are combined to similar polemical effect in Shelley's *Address to the People on the Death of the Princess Charlotte* (1817), where Paine's memorable comment on the Marie-Antoinette passage, 'he pities the plumage but forgets the dying bird', is taken as a motto for Shelley's own argument that public sentiment over the death of the Prince Regent's daughter would be better directed at the more deserving cases of the three 'Luddites' executed in the same year.

Shelley's charge against commerce is that it is by nature corrupting, both of society as a whole and of the individual. It is in this sense that the poor man's life is infected by the same poison as the rich man's; the one by choice, the other by compulsion barters his 'harmony and happiness' for material gain, and instead of 'free and generous love' practises 'the sordid lust of self'. Intriguingly, this last phrase is derived from the introductory epistle to Walter Scott's poem *Marmion* (1808) where, in his well-known elegy, he had praised Pitt for having 'Spurn'd at the sordid lust of pelf, / And serv'd his Albion for herself'.[42] Another instance of the crude but highly purposeful imitation that is so characteristic of *Queen Mab*, Shelley commandeers Scott's phrase in order to use it to precisely the opposite effect: to condemn the 'sordid' values which Pitt, as long-standing prime minister of England, had done so much to instil in the land of 'Albion'. That Shelley has altered 'pelf' to 'self' reinforces his point that what is degrading about the 'sordid lust of pelf', the fetishistic desire for 'interest and gold' induced by the capitalist system, is that it *is* also a 'lust of self', rapacious selfishness being all that remains of man's drive for betterment when all his generous instincts have been blighted or extinguished.

Shelley was not alone among English radicals in his opposition to the principle of commerce, or in his adaptation of the conservative argument about the incompatibility of virtue and commerce. John Thelwall, for instance, had argued in his *Rights of Nature* (1796) that, far from being the solution to the problem of war, the commercial system – that is, international trade – 'furnishes the pretence and means of war'.[43] The luxury trade in particular was often attacked by radicals on the grounds that it widened the gap between rich and poor. There was also a widespread fear that the expansion of commerce would lead to a decay of the social fabric, a view expressed, for instance, in Anne Laetitia Barbauld's poem *Eighteen Hundred and Eleven* (1812),[44] and deliberately exploited in Shelley's polemic. What distinguishes *Queen Mab*, however, is the totality and intensity of its attack on the commercial system, and on the rationale of political economy. It is for reasons such as these that Shelley's poem, together with its Notes, has justly been said to constitute 'the most revolutionary document of the age in England'.[45]

'Revolutionary' in a political sense, that is. Kenneth Cameron makes no such claim with regard to the poem's aesthetic character. Olwen Campbell makes that distinction more bluntly, readily conceding the seditious nature of Shelley's opinions, but adding that the mixture of 'revolutionary war-cries' and 'mincing eighteenth-century verse' seems almost to be a contradiction in terms.[46] Were this description valid, the contradiction need not surprise us. Then as now, most poetry that was revolutionary in its content was conservative in its form, a paradox that has been explored by the French critic Michel Beaujour,[47] who argues that 'political revolution' and 'poetic revolution' are inherently incompatible. From a linguistic point of view, what distinguishes the revolutionary poem from the rallying cry or slogan is 'its multiple meanings, its flight from specificity, the distance which it keeps from the referent'. Yet from a political viewpoint, 'no poetry, to the extent that it turns away from history and communication, is revolutionary'.

This argument has immediate bearing on the question of di-dacticism, a feature of Shelley's 'philosophical poem' that presents major obstacles to modern readers. Post-romantic criticism has tended to accept De Quincey's view (itself an elaboration of Wordsworthian tenets) that 'didactic poetry' is a *contradictio in adjecto*, involving a 'collision between two purposes – the purpose of use in mere teaching, and the purpose of poetic delight'; it arises out of a misconception of the nature of poetry, and of the manner in which poetry can be said to teach.[48] Furthermore, there is direct evidence that Shelley himself, as he grew older, found didactic poetry – including his own youthful *Queen Mab* – increasingly abhorrent. Like De Quincey, he came to believe that the morality of poetry consists not in making direct statements about right and wrong, but in stimulating and strengthening 'that faculty which is the organ of the moral nature of man' – the imagination.[49]

And yet, *as* a didactic poem, history has judged *Queen Mab* to have been a remarkable success, ultimately achieving positively *dogmatic* status as the 'gospel' of the Owenites, and later the 'Chartists'

Bible'.[50] Had he known this, one wonders whether the author would still have maintained, as he did in a letter to the *Examiner* in 1821, that the poem was 'better fitted to injure than to serve the cause of freedom'.[51] For one could very plausibly argue that it was precisely those features which, in Shelley's later view, made it 'worthless' as poetry – its prescriptive character, its directness, its didacticism – that made *Queen Mab* valuable in a political context. Part of its appeal and prestige undoubtedly lay in the fact of its being poetry rather than prose (a fact disputed by at least one of the early reviewers), but what made the poem *useful* to the Owenites and the Chartists was not its literary quality but its effectiveness as propaganda. At any rate, there have been many critics who have been content both to affirm its importance as part of the radical culture of the nineteenth century, and at the same time to deny that it has any artistic merit whatsoever.

However, 'mincing eighteenth-century verse' will not do as a description of the form of *Queen Mab*. The poem uses a combination of two verse forms, neither of which can justly be termed 'eighteenth-century'. One of them is blank verse, a measure that had rarely been used in didactic poems, almost all of which, from the time of Dryden to Erasmus Darwin, had been written in rhyming couplets. In breaking with this convention, Shelley follows the example of Milton, who, in *Paradise Lost*, had also rejected rhyme in favour of blank verse.[52] For Milton, this choice was a *political* as well as an aesthetic decision – indeed the two could not be separated. Eschewing the 'jingling sound of like endings' and the 'smoothnesse' admired in the Restoration, and its ideological counterparts (Milton felt such verse as operating through easy and fulfilled expectations, lulling the political and poetical senses at the expense of sense, inducing passivity, acceptance), he sought to recover 'ancient liberty' for the heroic poem by liberating it from 'the troublesome and modern bondage of rhyming'.[53] Blank verse was for Milton associated with notions of truly public utterance, and therefore with oratory, and it is to the example of the learned ancients that he appeals to redeem the 'barbarous age'. It is easy to see how the connection between poetry and oratory, explicitly stated by Milton in his note on 'The Verse' of *Paradise Lost*, would appeal to Shelley in *Queen Mab*.

I want to concentrate here, though, on Shelley's other choice of metre: what he refers to in a letter as 'blank lyrical measure'. Here too there is a Miltonic precedent, as Shelley acknowledges when he cites 'in support of this singularity' *Samson Agonistes*, the choruses of

Greek tragedy, and Southey's metrical romance *Thalaba the Destroyer* (*Letters*, I, 352). As far as contemporary readers were concerned, however, it was simply 'the Thalaba style',[54] and there can be no doubt that Southey's poem (published in 1801) was indeed Shelley's primary model, for there are numerous similarities between the two works, beginning with their opening lines. Having been often remarked in the early reviews, the close relationship between *Queen Mab* and *Thalaba* is now taken for granted by Shelley's critics. But there are important questions that have not been asked. After all, the affinity between a 'philosophical poem' and a 'metrical romance' is not an immediately obvious one. Why did Shelley choose to imitate Southey? Was it simply that his poetic style afforded a fashionable sweetener for *Mab*'s political wormwood? Or were there other factors affecting this choice of literary model? And what exactly was 'the Thalaba style'?

To answer these questions, we need to know something about the background to Southey's poem, its place in the history of the genre to which it belongs, and its public reception. Stuart Curran has suggested that the originality of *Thalaba* lies in its prolific myth-making (the narrative is based on the episode of the Domdaniel in the *Arabian Tales*, but this story is extensively elaborated by Southey), and in the fact that it was the first romance of the Romantic period to focus on an individual quest.[55] To contemporaries, however, its most conspicuous innovations were in style rather than subject-matter. Southey's experiment was to adapt for the purposes of narrative a method of presentation derived from the lyric; so that the story is told not 'directly' as in an epic, but 'by implication' as in an ode or ballad.[56] The 'lyrical' metre is an integral part of the experiment. Instead of composing in blank verse, or in the stanzaic form of *The Faerie Queene*, or in an alliterative metre of the kind that was used in medieval romances (these being the three measures that had most commonly been adopted in modern metrical romances), Southey chose an irregular, unrhymed verse form that he claimed to have learned from Dr Sayers's *Dramatic Sketches of the Northern Mythology* (1790). Although Southey was aware that other English poets had experimented with a rhymeless lyrical measure, it was only Sayers, in his view, who had succeeded in this difficult verse form. Here, then, is the origin of 'the Thalaba style'. Transferred to another genre and another mythology, the flexible verse form and lyrical technique of Sayers's dramatic choruses become the impassioned, odic, 'Arabesque' style of Southey's Arabian tale – a metrical romance with a compulsively episodic plot and a metre in continuous transition.

The fact that Southey did not actually invent the lyrical verse form of *Thalaba* does not detract from the originality of his application of that measure. Nor did it qualify the criticisms levelled at Southey when the poem was published. The *Dramatic Sketches* of Sayers had been quite favourably received, but Southey's poetical innovations did not please the literary reviewers, nor did the poem achieve any great popularity with the reading public. A typical response was that of the *British Critic*, which dismissed Southey's experiment as a 'complete monument of vile and depraved taste', its irregular lyricism 'unlike verse or sense'.[57] Even Southey's friends expressed reservations, believing that he had departed too far from conventional practice. Landor, for instance, whose own romance *Gebir* (1798) was acknowledged by Southey as an important influence on *Thalaba*, later made the following comments on Southey's unusual metres:

> Are we not a little too fond of novelty and experiment, and is it not reasonable to prefer those kinds of versification which the best poets have adopted and the best judges have cherished for the longest time?... Poetry is intended to soothe and flatter our prepossessions; not to wound or irritate or contradict them. We are at liberty to choose the best modifications, we are not at liberty to change or subvert. We are going too far from our great luminaries.[58]

William Taylor, another friend and fellow romance-writer who was involved to the extent of personally advising Southey during the composition of *Thalaba*, reviewed the poem in 1803 for the *Critical Review*, and while defending it – with great subtlety and skill – against previous criticism, also felt compelled to register his own objections. According to Taylor, the problem is not so much the unconventionality of the poem as its lack of cohesion, the bewildering combination of an 'abrupt and lyrical' form of narration and a 'wild and rambling' march of event.[59]

Southey was surprised and disappointed by the poor sales of *Thalaba*, and – temporarily at least – discouraged by the criticisms it received. But these feelings were overshadowed by the bitterness and anger he felt at the treatment meted out to the poem in the very first issue of the *Edinburgh Review*, in October 1802. Francis Jeffrey's anonymous review has since become famous for its pioneering

account of the 'new school of poetry' that had arisen in England in
recent years, subsequently known as the 'Lake School' (though
Jeffrey does not actually use that phrase here). Although Southey
later rejected[60] the alleged resemblance between his own poetry and
that of the other 'Lake' poets (a disclaimer with which modern
scholarship has generally concurred), the fact remains that the first
recognisable analysis of what is now known as the 'Romantic
revolution' in English poetry took *Thalaba the Destroyer* as its text.

   Jeffrey's review is a devastating critique of the 'new school', and of
Thalaba in particular. If *Thalaba* is comparatively sparing in its use of
the 'language of the vulgar' (which Jeffrey regards as one of the most
intolerable features of the new system of poetry), it is by no means free
of it. The subject 'is almost as ill chosen as the diction', consisting 'of
the most wild and extravagant fictions', and openly setting 'nature
and probability at defiance'. Southey's stylistic experiment earns
similar disapproval, 'the conduct of the fable' being 'as disorderly as
the versification', and the author's attempt to imitate Oriental
imagery marred by numerous instances 'of disproportioned and
injudicious ornaments'.[61] In part, this can be read as a restatement of
traditional objections to romance, a genre that from the beginning
had attracted censure for its errancy and extravagance.[62] Indeed,
Southey's Arabian tale was a perfect target for such criticism, since
those very features of the genre were often believed at the time to have
derived from what Warton in his *History of English Poetry* (1774) called
'that fantastic and brilliant imagery which composes the system of
Arabian imagination'[63] – that is, from what were supposedly the
Arabic origins of romance. The review is also notable as an attempt
by an unreconstructed neoclassicist to resist the encroachments of the
phenomenon of Romanticism. But Jeffrey's aesthetic criteria are
ultimately inseparable from political ones. This is made clear at the
start in his disparaging remarks on the doctrines and sentiments of
the 'new school', a 'sect of dissenters' whose primary sources of
inspiration include the 'antisocial principles, and distempered
sensibility of Rousseau – his discontent with the present constitution
of society ... and his perpetual hankering after some unattainable
state of voluptuous virtue and perfection'. Implicitly, politics
continues to inform Jeffrey's whole analysis of Southey's poem, the
language of the critique implying a straightforward connection
between Southey's anti-establishment politics and his unruly and
irregular verses, between his unreasonable political aspirations and

his irrational poetic fictions, between libertarian principles and the 'unbounded license' of metre. Seen from this perspective, the 'Thalaba style' is the embodiment in poetry of the politics of freedom and innovation.[64]

Given that the year in which *Thalaba* was published, 1801, was also the year in which Southey accepted a British government appointment as private secretary to the Chancellor of the Irish Exchequer,[65] this argument may strike us as somewhat ironic; more so, when we consider Southey's reuse of that style – or a variation upon it – in his 'Indian Tale' *The Curse of Kehama* (1810), by which time the author was, amongst other things, an established contributor to the aggressively conservative *Quarterly Review*. The irony does not escape Hazlitt, whose portrait of Southey in *The Spirit of the Age* focuses on the tension between his essentially 'revolutionary' temperament and his latterly acquired role as 'poet-laureate and courtier'. In *Thalaba*, in *Kehama*, indeed in all of his poems, Southey is a 'poetic libertine': experimental, irregular, digressive, extreme. Even in *A Vision of Judgement* (1821), Hazlitt sees Southey's nature breaking out in spite of himself:

Does he not dedicate to his present Majesty that extraordinary poem on the death of his father, called *The Vision of Judgement*, as a specimen of what might be done in English hexameters? In a court-poem all should be trite and on an approved model. He might as well have presented himself at the levee in a fancy or masquerade dress.[66]

As in Blake's 'Satanic' reading of Milton, Hazlitt's claim is that Southey continued to belong to the devil's party without knowing it. One thing, however, that neither Hazlitt nor Jeffrey mentions about *Thalaba* are the dues paid on the opposite side – namely to God. For all its structural licence, and the Islamic context of its fiction, the poem is carefully grounded in Christian ethics, something it is content to share with its nearest narrative (as distinct from stylistic) model, *The Faerie Queene*.

Comparing Southey's *Joan of Arc* (1793) with *Thalaba*, the same point is made by the shift from political epic to moral romance. There is an obvious element of escapism in this move, the use of romance as a retreat from the pressure of contemporary affairs. In Scott's romances a similar development takes place, into the recesses of history rather than the timeless realms of mythology (although in both cases, as we shall see, the political resonance is not entirely absent[67]). In *Queen Mab*, on the other hand, Shelley is employing the genre in an overtly political context. It has been argued that Shelley's object in 'using the measure that Southey had made famous', and in 'beginning his poem as though it were to be a typical Southey narrative', was 'to ease his readers by degrees into the radical propaganda which forms the core of the poem'.[68] This is undoubtedly part of the explanation, but in light of what we have been discussing, Shelley's choice of stylistic model in *Queen Mab* seems rather more purposeful. What I suggest is that by linking it with revolutionary subject-matter, Shelley was consciously reclaiming the politics of the 'Thalaba style'.

Two years previously it would not have been a question of reclamation. It is a matter of record that Southey's poetry was one of Shelley's earliest enthusiasms, and an important factor in this was clearly the belief that Southey was a *radical* poet. Admiration for his poetry went hand in hand with admiration for his politics; and the young Shelley apparently saw no split between the poet of the 'Botany Bay Eclogues' and the poet of *Thalaba* or *Kehama*, since he freely borrowed from both when writing his own political poems. A good example is the 'Fragment. Supposed to be an Epithalamion of Francis Ravaillac and Charlotte Cordé' from *The Posthumous Fragments of Margaret Nicholson* (1810), which is distinctly unSouth-eyan in its frank sexuality but takes its political cue from Southey's poem on Charlotte Cordé,[69] besides making use of the visionary machinery and lyrical verse form of *Thalaba*. It is also significant that when placing an advertisement for his (now lost) *Poetical Essay on the Existing State of Things* in the *Oxford University and City Herald* in February 1811, Shelley chose as an epigraph four lines from *The Curse of Kehama* which describe the effects of an appalling famine, as though Southey's Oriental romance could be read as some sort of political allegory of contemporary England.

It seems that it was not until Shelley was about to meet Southey in Keswick in December 1811 that he realised that his revered author had become a confirmed Tory, presumably by reading or hearing about some of Southey's actual opinions on the 'existing estab-lishments'. The shock of this discovery is apparent from his furious letter to Elizabeth Hitchener of 15 December:

Southey has changed. I shall see him soon, and I shall reproach him of [for] his tergiversation – He to whom Bigotry Tyranny and Law was hateful has become the votary of these Idols, in a form the most disgusting. – The

Church of England it's Hell and all has become the subject of his panegyric.
– the war in Spain that prodigal waste of human blood to aggrandise the
fame of Statesmen is his delight, the constitution of England with its
Wellesley its Paget & its Prince are inflated with the prostituted exertions of
his Pen. I feel a sickening distrust when I see all that I had considered good
great & imitable fall around me into the gulph of error. (*Letters*, I, 208)

Shelley's estimation of Southey somewhat improved after conversation with him, but the distrust remained – to emerge on a number
of subsequent occasions.[70]

   Yet clearly Shelley still considered Southey's poetry 'imitable'
because he decided to make use of the 'Thalaba style' in *Queen Mab*.
Is this because Shelley, like Hazlitt, recognised the inherently
'revolutionary' quality of Southey's style, and therefore still regarded
it as a suitable model for a radical poem irrespective of Southey's
actual politics? Or was Shelley deliberately trying, as it were, to
subvert his source? The answer is probably both. There is no trace of
irony in Shelley's handling of the free lyrical measure and rapid
narrative manner he borrowed from *Thalaba*; and these definitely
contribute to the revolutionary spirit of *Queen Mab*. To this extent,
Shelley can be said to have identified a revolutionary quality in
Southey's poem, and to have harnessed its energies for an expressly
political purpose – to attack those very institutions which Southey
was now explicitly defending.

   But there is another sense in which Shelley was in effect subverting
his source, by deliberately playing his poem off against Southey's.
This can be demonstrated by straightforward comparison. Take, for
instance, the opening lines of *Thalaba*:

> How beautiful is night!
> A dewy freshness fills the silent air;
> No mist obscures, nor cloud, nor speck, nor stain,
> Breaks the serene of heaven;
> In full-orb'd glory yonder Moon divine
> Rolls through the dark blue depths.[71]

The similarity with the opening of *Queen Mab* has already been noted.
Now observe also the beginning of Canto IV of Shelley's poem:

> How beautiful this night! the balmiest sigh,
> Which vernal zephyrs breathe in evening's ear,
> Were discord to the speaking quietude
> That wraps this moveless scene. Heaven's ebon vault,
> Studded with stars unutterably bright,

> Through which the moon's unclouded grandeur rolls,
> Seems like a canopy which love had spread
> To curtain her sleeping world.

The passage is in blank verse rather than lyrical measure, but the wording, and the scene itself, again recall Southey's opening lines. In *Queen Mab*, however, this gentle night-piece is rapidly contrasted with a shocking description of battle. The nocturnal landscape is succeeded by another picture of beauty and tranquillity, a sunset 'o'er ocean's waveless field', which is suddenly transformed into a scene of storm and shipwreck. This in turn is interrupted by what contemporaries would probably have recognised as an image of the bloody winter warfare of Napoleon's Russian campaign – specifically the burning of Moscow, reports of which were reaching England as Shelley composed the poem:

> Ah! whence yon glare
> That fires the arch of Heaven? – that dark red smoke
> Blotting the silver moon? The stars are quenched
> In darkness, and the pure and spangling snow
> Gleams faintly through the gloom that gathers round!
> Hark to that roar, whose swift and deaf'ning peals
> In countless echoes through the mountains ring,
> Startling pale Midnight on her starry throne!
> Now swells the intermingling din; the jar
> Frequent and frightful of the bursting bomb;
> The falling beam, the shriek, the groan, the shout,
> The ceaseless danger, and the rush of men
> Inebriate with rage ...   (IV, lines 33–45)

The technique of abrupt transition and contrast has in fact been learned from Southey, this being one of the hallmarks of his style (derived ultimately from the Pindaric ode). But whereas in *Thalaba* or *Kehama* this technique is simply a way of creating surprise and excitement in the narrative, in *Queen Mab* it serves an ulterior purpose: to startle the reader into political consciousness. The particular effect here is to impress upon us, by re-enacting in the movement of the poetry itself, the destructiveness of war – the rest of the canto consisting of a diatribe against those Shelley considered reponsible for causing wars: 'Kings, priests, and statemen'.

   According to one modern commentator, it is features such as these that explain why *Queen Mab* subsequently found favour among working-class radicals:

Its passionate zeal, utmost sincerity and iconoclastic sweep create a rhythm that goes straight to the heart, but then at the very moment of such a profound effect comes the jerking movement which jolts the reader rather badly, thus annihilating the aesthetic effect it was trying to create ... For the sophisticated reader it is a defect which prejudices him against the poem ... But in the case of the unsophisticated reader, the passionate sweep of the rhythm, as well as its shoddy, jerky quality are a virtue. It keeps his mind alive, since it does administer the badly needed jolts. It enlightens him, inspires him and moves him to action.[72]

The suggestion here is that the poem works by deliberately undermining its aesthetic effect in order to achieve a political effect. Such an argument would perhaps be hard to sustain over the poem as a whole, but it certainly holds for individual passages like the one above. And on these occasions it is Southey's poem *Thalaba the Destroyer* which provides Shelley's 'aesthetic' counter-model, while at the same time furnishing the basis of *Queen Mab*'s disruptive lyrical style.

THE BOWER OF BLISS MOTIF

In its bold synthesis of the form of *Thalaba* with the subject-matter of a 'philosophical poem', *Queen Mab* represents a decisive moment in the revival of romance. A genre which had usually functioned as a means of escape from the harsh world of politics and current affairs became, in Shelley's hands, the medium for a revolutionary polemic. Reviewing George Crabbe's *The Borough* in the *Quarterly Review* in 1810, one contemporary critic had spoken of the need for readers of romance 'to take shelter from the realities of life in the paradise of fancy',[73] an escapist formula perfectly reflected in the title of John Hamilton Reynolds's poem *The Eden of Imagination* (1814). For Shelley, however, pandering to such needs amounted to an abnegation of the poet's responsibilities, his view at that time being 'that all poetical beauty ought to be subordinate to the inculcated moral – that metaphorical language ought to be a vehicle for useful & momentous instruction' (*Letters*, I, 98).

Applied to romance, this didactic imperative would seem to point back to an earlier conception of the genre, as moral allegory. It has been argued that *Queen Mab* is precisely that – a belated example of eighteenth-century moral allegory, a literary form that had once been very popular, and specimens of which were still appearing in Shelley's lifetime.[74] Earlier examples of the genre include William

Thompson's *Sickness* (1745–46), James Thomson's *The Castle of Indolence* (1748), Gilbert West's *Education* (1751), Thomas Denton's *The House of Superstition* (1762), William Mickle's *The Concubine* (1767), Sir William Jones's 'The Palace of Fortune' (1772), Leigh Hunt's 'The Palace of Pleasure' (1801) and Erasmus Darwin's *The Temple of Nature* (1803).

There are indeed generic affinities between these poems and *Queen Mab*, and Carlos Baker performs a valuable service in making us aware of Shelley's debt to this largely forgotten tradition. But the similarities should not be exaggerated. Most of the works that comprise this tradition are didactic poems concerned with the reformation of morals; *Queen Mab*, on the other hand, is a polemical poem whose burden is revolutionary political change. Although there are parallels between some of the institutions and crimes attacked, Shelley at every point raises the stakes, and politicises the argument. Baker, for instance, equates Shelley's condemnation of 'custom' in the third canto of *Queen Mab* with the allegory of the 'monstrous giant' named Custom in West's *Education*. But West's 'moral thesis' (his own phrase) is about reforming the curriculum, not about reforming the government; about the 'despotic sway' of outmoded pedagogical practices, not about the arbitrary power of despotic kings. The massive difference between the two texts can be illustrated immediately by a comparison between Paedia's polite appeal to the 'noble, opulent, and great' in Canto I of West's poem, and Mab's angry address to 'priest, conqueror, or prince' in Canto IV of Shelley's. The former reads as follows:

> To you, ye noble, opulent, and great!
> With friendly voice I call, and honest zeal;
> Upon your vital influences wait
> The health and sickness of the commonweal;
> The maladies you cause, yourselves must heal.
> In vain to the unthinking harden'd crowd
> Will Truth and Reason make their just appeal;
> In vain will sacred Wisdom cry aloud;
> And Justice drench in vain her vengeful sword in blood.

> With you must reformation first take place:
> You are the head, the intellectual mind
> Of this vast body politic; whose base
> And vulgar limbs, to drudgery consign'd,
> All the rich stores of science have resign'd
> To you, that by the craftsman's various toil,

> The sea-worn mariner, and sweating hind,
> In peace and affluence maintain'd, the while
> You, for yourselves and them, may dress the mental soil.[75]

In *Queen Mab*, we get this:

> Look to thyself, priest, conqueror, or prince!
> Whether thy trade is falsehood, and thy lusts
> Deep wallow in the earnings of the poor,
> With whom thy master was: – or thou delight'st
> In numbering o'er the myriads of thy slain,
> All misery weighing nothing in the scale
> Against thy short-lived fame: or thou dost load
> With cowardice and crime the groaning land,
> A pomp-fed king. Look to thy wretched self!
> Aye, art thou not the veriest slave that e'er
> Crawled on the loathing earth? Are not thy days
> Days of unsatisfying listlessness?
> Dost thou not cry, ere night's long rack is o'er,
> 'When will the morning come?' Is not thy youth
> A vain and feverish dream of sensualism?
> Thy manhood blighted with unripe disease?
> Are not thy views of unregretted death
> Drear, comfortless, and horrible? Thy mind,
> Is it not morbid as thy nerveless frame,
> Incapable of judgment, hope or love?
> And dost thou wish the errors to survive
> That bar thee from all sympathies of good,
> After the miserable interest
> Thou hold'st in their protraction? When the grave
> Has swallowed up thy memory and thyself,
> Dost thou desire the bane that poisons earth
> To twine its roots around thy coffined clay,
> Spring from thy bones, and blossom on thy tomb,
> That of its fruit thy babes may eat and die?   (IV, lines 237–65)

The subject-matter is not dissimilar – both speeches call upon England's rulers to take the initiative in social reform, and thus safeguard the future well-being of the community – but in their message and tone the two could hardly be less alike. Where West's educator speaks with 'friendly voice' and 'honest zeal', and merely hints at the 'maladies' which may be caused in the body politic by a failure to respond to his appeal, Shelley's dispenses with all civilities and condemns the rulers of the country as corrupt and corrupting. In

Shelley's eyes, the poor are not guided but exploited; and instead of euphemistic 'maladies', we are told of the 'sensualism' and 'disease', the 'cowardice' and 'crime' of those who profit by their labour. In a sequence of rhetorical questions, Shelley combines the Delphic injunction to 'know thyself' with a stark warning to the oppressor to 'watch thyself', ending with a macabre allegory of the consequences of a failure to do so (the final image combines the forbidden tree of the Garden of Eden with the mythical poison-tree, a plant whose exhalations killed all things that lived under its shade). Whatever affinities *Queen Mab* has with poems such as West's, there is no equivalent to this gothic language of denunciation in the moral allegories of Augustan England.

There *is* some sort of equivalent, however, in Constantin Volney's *Les Ruines* (1791), a French prose work which manifestly does not belong to the above genre, yet which shares a very similar narrative structure. The resemblances between *Queen Mab* and *Les Ruines* were pointed out in at least two of the early reviews, and the fact that one of these was the highly favourable notice published in 1815 in the *Theological Inquirer* – a review probably written in collaboration with Shelley himself[76] – may be taken as confirmation of an intentional link between these two works. By imitating Volney, Shelley was deliberately associating his poem with one of the most famous philosophical tracts of the Revolutionary period in France, which had been translated into English almost immediately and since become a key text of the English radical movement.[77] The fictional device of a supernatural figure surveying the 'grand & comprehensive topics' of past, present and future (*Letters*, I, 324) was thus a tried and tested vehicle for a revolutionary vision – though Shelley, while adopting Volney's general plan, omits any specific reference to the French Revolution or to Volney's projected 'assemblée générale des peuples'.[78] As we shall see, the 'paradise of peace' envisioned in *Queen Mab* represents a transcendence even more complete.

There is, however, another element in the generic tradition of the moral allegory which connects *Queen Mab* much more closely with some of the poems Baker cites, and also with a variety of other texts, including Southey's *Thalaba* and *The Curse of Kehama*. It is an allegorical theme we have already encountered several times in the political poetry and prose of the 1790s, and one that will reappear, in a number of different guises, in *Laon and Cythna*. I propose to examine this topos in some detail not only because it reveals unexpected, and previously undiscovered, associations between these various texts, but also because it offers a new way of looking at *Queen Mab* itself, highlighting a romance structure that extends beyond the visionary frame, and provides a focus for much of the revolutionary thought of the poem. The theme in question is the Spenserian motif of the Bower of Bliss.

At least three of the moral allegories cited by Baker are, in part at least, direct imitations of Spenser's Bower of Bliss, which warns of the dangers of sensual excess and of the potential conflict between desire and duty. Leigh Hunt's 'Palace of Pleasure', from his *Juvenilia* (1801),[79] is the most straightforward, simply substituting the name of Pleasure for that of Acrasia, and situating the scene in a 'gorgeous palace' rather than a bower (Spenser himself features a 'Pallace brave' amidst the scenery of the Bower of Bliss, and in an earlier speech of Belphoebe's compares the perilous and painful road to the 'happie mansion' of 'honor' with the 'easie' way and 'passage plaine' to 'pleasures pallace'[80]). Hunt tells us in advance the moral to be drawn from his tale: it 'endeavours to correct the vices of the age, by showing the frightful landscape that terminates the alluring path of sinful Pleasure'. But the hint is not necessary, since the allegory is plain enough, and similar moral conclusions are voiced within the poem itself. Yet the final note that Hunt strikes is a political rather than a moral one. Having been rescued from the clutches of Pleasure by the 'Angel figure' of Religion, a chastened Sir Guyon is sent on his way with a fighting song from Glory:

> 'Go', sung she, striking her exalted lyre,
> 'Go, lift th'oppress'd, and beat th'oppressor low;
> 'Go where sad Justice sees her sons expire,
> 'And tyranny quaffs down the tears of woe!'

As in Southey's early poem 'Romance', the notion of 'virtue' is equated here with that of political justice, and Hunt expresses the chivalric ethos in a specifically political vocabulary of 'oppressor' and 'oppress'd', 'tyranny' and levelling.

The Fairy Queen in Sir William Jones's 'Palace of Fortune'[81] is called Fortune, and in *her* 'gorgeous palace' (evidently a stock phrase) she, like Queen Mab, is a benevolent instructress rather than a malevolent enchantress. But the poem, in rhyming couplets, includes an episode directly based on Spenser's Bower of Bliss. A 'lovely stripling' named Pleasure steps before the queen and asks for

'beds of dewy flowers', 'sparkling wine' and a 'willing damsel' with
whom to gather-he-rosebuds-while-he-may. The Fairy Queen grants
this request, and her pupil Maia (a prototype of Shelley's Ianthe)
looks into a magic mirror and sees a beautiful bower in which
Pleasure and the mistress he desired sport in 'amorous play'.
Bashfully she looks away. Then she looks again,

> and sees, with sad surprise,
> On the clear glass far different scenes arise:
> The bower, which late outshone the rosy morn,
> O'erhung with weeds she saw, and rough with thorn;
> With sting of asps the leafless plants were wreath'd;
> And curling adders gales of venom breath'd: –
> Low sat the stripling on the faded ground;
> And, in a mournful knot, his arms were bound...

Instead of pleasure, there is 'Despair, and grief, remorse, and raging
pain'. Again, the moral is delivered quite explicitly:

> Take sage example from this moral scene;
> See! how vain pleasures sting the lips they kiss,
> How asps are hid beneath the bowers of bliss!

Yet in this poem it is not Glory who has the final word. A figure
named 'Glory' does indeed appear in the next scene, a knight in
shining armour with 'quiv'ring lance' and 'princely mien'. But no
sooner does he lie down to rest from the toils of war and dream of new
foes and new conquests, than his 'faithless page' puts a dagger
through his breast with the words 'The tyrant dies; oppression is no
more.' In Jones's version, Glory himself is an oppressor, and Spenser's
chivalric militarism has been converted into something like pacifism.

   The most sophisticated of the Spenserian allegories cited by Baker,
Thomson's *Castle of Indolence*,[82] is also closely modelled on Spenser's
Bower of Bliss, and on the related episode of Phaedria's Bower from
earlier in Book II of *The Faerie Queene*. Like the Bowers of Phaedria and
Acrasia, the Castle of Indolence, with its surrounding vale, seems at
first to be a place of 'perfect ease' and tranquillity, a pre-lapsarian
world where 'nought but candour reigns', and 'Good-natured
lounging' is all the business of the day. But it turns out to be another
false paradise, an illusory landscape created by 'that most enchanting
wizard' Indolence. The reality of the vale is revealed in the final
stanzas, when the hero of the story confronts the wizard and waves his
own 'anti-magic wand':

Sudden the landskip sinks on every hand;
The pure quick streams are marshy puddles found;
On baleful heaths the groves all blackened stand;
And, o'er the weedy foul abhorred ground,
Snakes, adders, toads, each loathly creature crawls around.

(II, stanza lxvii)

Thomson's message would appear to be an alarmingly simple one: 'Who does not act is dead; absorbed entire / In miry sloth, no pride, no joy he hath' (II, liv).

The attractions of the vale, however, seem curiously in excess of the requirements of the allegory, this being a place not only of private ease but also of social harmony, a land from which 'interest, envy, and strife are banished' (I, xv), and where 'freedom reigned with no alloy' (I, xxxv). It is not just the work ethic to which Indolence is opposed and from which he offers a refuge, but also the profit motive – the 'savage thirst of gain' (I, xi; a phrase that may well be the source for Scott's 'sordid lust of pelf'). Spenser's Phaedria also offers a sanctuary from worldliness, and the reader of romance knows to be suspicious of such descriptions, coming as they do from the mouth of the 'wicked enchanter'; but are we really more convinced by the good bard Philomela's counter-claim that the 'toiling swain' – in other words, the rural labourer of 1748 – is 'the happiest of the sons of men' (II, lv)? Having heard of the land 'where solitude and perfect silence reigned (I, xxix), would we really rather listen to songs of war, 'the hero's ire', 'the patriot's noble rage' (I, xxxii)? In Spenser's version of the allegory, the recommendations of 'knightly exercize' as opposed to luxurious ease are self-evident: they are the essence of the chivalric ideal. In *The Castle of Indolence*, on the other hand, the appeal of the active life is not so clear; and by the end of Canto I we are left with serious doubts about the wisdom of destroying the pastoral world which has been opened to our view.

Thomson attempts to resolve these uncertainties by introducing in Canto II the figure of the 'Knight of Arts and Industry', whose mission it is to overthrow the Castle of Indolence, and the 'barbarous world to civilize'. Again, though, he is a strangely unconvincing hero. It seems a little suspicious that this champion of urban civilisation, having 'quickened' the towns with his 'mechanic arts' (II, xx), should then choose to go and live in the country – not indeed spurning the 'cares of rural industry' (II, xxvii), but leading a life remote from the 'social commerce' and 'renowned marts' of the

'fervent city' (II, xx). It is worrying too, as the narrator himself points
out, that the Knight of Arts and Industry should take so long to get
around to cultivating the fine arts (II, xxii). For all his 'atchievements
fair', it is hard to dispel the impression that this enterprising hero is
not all he is cracked up to be; and that his arguments, or his motives,
for wanting to transform a land of ease into one of industry are not
altogether to be trusted. In short, the poem seems less than wholly
convinced by its own moral thesis.

If this ambivalence reveals, as Patricia Parker claims,[83] a lurking
suggestion in the poem that the 'soul-dissolving' charms of indolence
'are the charms of the tradition of romancing itself' (an imaginatively
subversive notion later taken up by Coleridge and Keats), it may also
reflect Thomson's feelings about the social realities to which the poem
alludes. To call *The Castle of Indolence* an allegory of the Industrial
Revolution would be to state the matter too bluntly (and we must
remember that the term 'industry', in 1748, did not yet carry all its
modern connotations[84]); but there can be little doubt that Thomson
is using the Spenserian motif of the Bower, and of *destroying* the Bower,
partly in order to comment on the massive social and economic
changes which – as a result of the spread of commerce and industry
– were already a visible fact in most of the towns and villages of
England. The hesitations and ambiguities that mark the poem's
progress can therefore be said to express deep anxieties – conscious or
otherwise – about the consequences of those changes, both for the
fortunes of poetry and for society as a whole.

Although Southey's verse narratives are very different in style and
structure from the static allegories of the previous century, they are
ultimately derived from the same Spenserian model, and both
Thalaba and *The Curse of Kehama* include Bower of Bliss episodes.
Closest in spirit and narrative outline to Spenser's original is the
version that we meet in Book VI of *Thalaba*.[85] Having emerged from
the 'dreadful cave' of the giant Zohak, the eponymous hero is guided
by a meteor to a secret, idyllic vale on the top of a mountain, to which
he gains admission, in the time-honoured fashion of romance, by
blowing the ivory horn that hangs beside the gate (it 'breathed a
sweet and thrilling melody'). Once inside, he is called upon to 'taste
/ The joys of Paradise'. Those alone 'for lofty deeds / Mark'd' are

> permitted thus
> A foretaste of the full beatitude,
> That in heroic acts they may go on

> More ardent, eager to return and reap
> Endless enjoyment her, their destined meed.
>
> (vi, lines 234–38)

Surrounded by 'glittering tents', 'odorous groves' and 'gorgeous palaces', Thalaba at first stood in silent astonishment,

> And passively received
> The mingled joy which flow'd on every sense …
>
> (vi, lines 244–45)

'Full of the bliss, yet still awake / To wonder', he then entered a banquet room; but did not succumb, like the other guests, to 'the delicious juice / Of Shiraz' golden grape', a beverage expressly forbidden by the Prophet; nor was tempted by the 'troop of females' in 'Transparent garments' who performed the cabaret. To be sure, he 'gazed',

> But in his heart he bore a talisman,
> Whose blessed alchemy to virtuous thoughts refined
> The loose suggestions of the scene impure. (vi, lines 370–73)

That talisman the reader now knows to be 'Faith' (Thalaba having cast aside the magical ring of Abdaldar in the previous episode), as a result of whose 'blessed alchemy' the spectacle brings to mind instead his own 'Arabian maid', the long-lost Oneiza. Thus, with tears running down his cheek, he heads for the nearest exit, arriving at the grove on the other side of the bridge just in time to rescue his beloved from an unknown assailant. Like Spenser's Sir Guyon, and true to his own title 'the Destroyer', Thalaba then proceeds in Book vii to demolish the whole bower, now identified as 'The Paradise of Sin' and the enchanted playground of the evil sorcerer Aloadin.

The one significant difference between this episode and Spenser's lies in the substitution of a male for a female enchanter. Aloadin, or Aloadine, was the name given by Marco Polo to the 'old man of the Mountayne', a fascinating figure from Persian folklore who is sometimes identified with the Islamic heretic Hasan as-Sabbah, founder of the sinister community known as the Assassins. As portrayed in *Purchas His Pilgrims*, which Southey cites in his footnote to this scene, Aloadin was not so much a magician as a political despot, a 'Tyrant, feared in all those parts'; his method of exercising power was through a handful of men, whose fanatical allegiance he secured by the trick of exposing them to an illusory paradise which he had contrived, to which their return was assured if they obeyed his orders. The faithful, or 'fedayeen', were then required to execute his policy of assassinating his enemies. Idealised, the story was to form the subject of Shelley's unfinished prose romance *The Assassins* (1814). Southey highlights the figure of Aloadin himself, a detail which, in the age of Robespierre and Napoleon, contained an obvious topical allusion to the continuing danger posed by gifted tyrants – a point Southey was to make again in his characterisation of the despotic Kehama. Indeed the Arabian legend of the 'Domda-niel', with which Southey combines the story of Aloadin, had already been used as an allegorical device in the *Anti-Jacobin* poem 'The Loves of the Triangles' (line 87) to represent the evils of the French Revolution. And the image of Napoleon as evil enchanter was soon to become a very familiar one in the literature of the period, perhaps most forcefully illustrated in Leigh Hunt's masque *The Descent of Liberty* (1815), an allegorical celebration of Napoleon's defeat.

Although seemingly far removed from the world of politics and current affairs, the topos of the Bower of Bliss – with its constituent elements of earthly paradise, wicked enchanter, and chivalric hero, and its themes of seduction and destruction – was thus one that readily lent itself to political allegory. Long before Wordsworth used the motif to signify the instability and deceptiveness of the utopian expectations aroused by the French Revolution, it had served a variety of other writers as a metaphorical resource for the rep-resentation of social change, and by 1813 Shelley could have found many examples of the political application of the motif. None, however, is more striking than Shelley's own deployment of the Bower in *Queen Mab*, where it appears on no fewer than three separate occasions, in each case making a vital contribution to the rev-olutionary dynamic of the poem.

Again, its presence in this context at first seems implausible, even paradoxical. The Christian morality of Spenser's Bower of Bliss seems utterly alien to Shelley's 'philosophical poem', the last two cantos of which explicitly deny the distinction between earthly and heavenly fulfilment on which the original allegory is founded. Yet notice how closely the landscape of Shelley's concluding 'paradise of peace' resembles that of the traditional Bower of Bliss, with its 'garden-isles', its 'fertile valleys, resonant with bliss', and its bower-like woods that 'overcanopy the wave' (IX, 102–4). 'The habitable earth is full of bliss' (VIII, 58), says Mab of this glorious future; and indeed the word 'bliss' itself is repeated in almost every paragraph, encapsulating the condition of utopian felicity towards which the whole poem has been moving. Shelley, though, has borrowed the language of the Bower only to reclaim it, for here 'bliss' carries no ironic resonance, no suggestion of indulgence or deception, the point being that this is a *true* not a false paradise. It is also, amongst other things, a *sexual* paradise, in which

> The kindred sympathies of human souls
> Needed no fetters of tyrannic law:
> Those delicate and timid impulses
> In nature's primal modesty arose,
> And with undoubted confidence disclosed
> The growing longings of its dawning love,
> Unchecked by dull and selfish chastity,
> The virtue of the cheaply virtuous,
> Who pride themselves in senselessness and frost.
>
> (IX, lines 76–84)

In flagrant defiance of the repressive conventions of the Bower of Bliss, Shelley's 'sweet place of bliss' (IX, 15) is presented as a *vindication* of pleasure, not a repudiation of it. It is a paradise of the id not of the ego, an expression of confidence in the 'primal modesty' of nature (IX, 79) rather than the artificial modesty of society; or in what Shelley, in an important phrase from the Notes, terms 'natural temperance'.[86]

Shelley also openly defies the institution of marriage. Marriage is the 'tyrannic law' to which the lines above refer, and of all the 'deep pollutions and horrid blasphemies' of the poem, it is Shelley's apparent advocacy of what has since been called free love which provoked the most outrage among contemporaries. A typical reaction was that of the *Literary Gazette*, which could hardly dare to stain its pages by thinking about the sexual arrangements in Shelley's 'new moral, or rather immoral world',[87] though happy to repeat the slander about Shelley's supposedly incestuous personal life. Yet despite the common charge that the millennium in *Queen Mab* was a manifesto for promiscuity, there is an ethical dimension to Shelley's erotic projections which links the poem once again to the allegories we have been discussing. In *Queen Mab* liberation of the senses is ultimately linked to the liberation of man's moral and intellectual nature. Like the chaste Hindu heaven in *The Curse of Kehama* (from where Shelley directly borrows the phrase[88]), Shelley's sexual paradise is 'Of purest spirits, [a] pure dwelling-place' (IX, 8), where 'virtue, love, and pleasure' go 'hand in hand' (IX, 75). For every

mention of 'bliss' in the closing cantos of the poem, there are several
of 'virtue':

> Here now the human being stands adorning
> This loveliest earth with taintless body and mind;
> Blest from his birth with all bland impulses,
> Which gently in his noble bosom wake
> All kindly passions and all pure desires.
> Him, still from hope to hope the bliss pursuing
> Which from the exhaustless lore of human weal
> Dawns on the virtuous mind ...   (VIII, lines 198–205)

Shelley did not believe that man is at present 'taintless', or that he
would immediately become so by the removal of existing social
constraints. His celebration of human desire unbridled by the 'fetters
of tyrannic law' refers to a millennial future and explicitly assumes a
prior regeneration of man's whole being.

This conception of bliss, predicated upon 'the virtuous mind',
should be compared with a passage from Canto II, soon after the
arrival of Ianthe and Mab at the Hall of Spells. The scenery, of
golden clouds and crimson mists 'Floating to strains of thrilling
melody' which 'Yielded to every movement of the will', symbolises a
state of mind which seems not unlike the one described in Cantos VII
and IX:

> Upon their passive swell the Spirit leaned,
> And, for the varied bliss that pressed around,
> Used not the glorious privilege
> Of virtue and of wisdom.   (II, lines 40–44)

Ianthe, her soul newly delivered from her bodily frame and the 'stain
of earthliness' (I, 135), experiences a 'varied bliss' that seems not
dissimilar to the one portrayed above. But here there is the vital
qualification that Ianthe 'Used not the glorious privilege / Of virtue
and of wisdom'. Mab offers the following commentary:

> 'Spirit!' the Fairy said,
> And pointed to the gorgeous dome,
> 'This is a wondrous sight
> And mocks all human grandeur;
> But, were it virtue's only meed, to dwell
> In a celestial palace, all resigned
> To pleasurable impulses, immured
> Within the prison of itself, the will
> Of changeless nature would be unfulfilled.
> Learn to make others happy. Spirit, come!

> This is thine high reward: – the past shall rise;
> Thou shalt behold the present; I will teach
>   The secrets of the future.'   (II, lines 55–67)

By way of explanation, we are given what is quite clearly a condensed version of the allegory of the Bower of Bliss or Palace of Pleasure. Mab begins by making the Aristotelian point that complete resignation to 'pleasurable impulses' leads to an imprisonment of the self: the classical definition of 'intemperance' that is the basis of Spenser's allegory, and of later imitations such as Hunt's and Southey's. Shelley's modifies this conclusion, however, in that the moral which Mab goes on to draw is not about the sinfulness or illusoriness of pleasure, but about the neglect of social responsibility entailed by the pursuit of merely private pleasure. Virtue, Shelley implies, can only finally be fulfilled in the *public* sphere; and 'the will / Of changeless nature' is, so to speak, a *general* will. Hence the injunction: 'Learn to make others happy'.

There are further parallels with Southey's poem. Quite apart from the close verbal similarities (the phrase 'thrilling melody' is a direct borrowing), the mental state of Ianthe as she enters the Hall of Spells almost exactly reproduces that of Thalaba as he enters the blissful vale of Aloadin. The scenery is different, but the psychological content is much the same, both passages being about a passive state of pleasurable sensation. Thalaba's passivity is directly stated (VI, 244–45), Ianthe's symbolised by the flaccid consistency and 'passive swell' of the clouds and mists. The interesting thing is that in each case this state of mind is being *criticised*, as a form of entrancement. In *Thalaba* we realise this only later in the scene when we learn that the paradise is a false one – although to an alert reader the very mention of passivity should itself be a warning signal, since the temptation to passivity (and thus to an abandonment of the heroic quest) was one of the traditional hazards of enchanted ground.[89] In *Queen Mab* the danger is spelt out immediately in Mab's commentary.

In Canto III we are confronted once again with the spectacle of a 'gorgeous palace'. Like the one in Hunt's poem, it is a scene of indolence, wealth and gluttony, where there is 'gold, / Gleaming around, and numerous viands culled / From every clime' (III, 46–48). And, sure enough, these pleasures prove to be illusory, and the revelry 'unjoyous'. Excess has dulled the senses, and 'stubborn vice' has converted all its food 'to deadliest venom'. Having dragged his 'palled, unwilling appetite' to another feast of 'silence, grandeur,

and excess', the occupant of the palace collapses in a stupor on the
couch, but is soon wakened by the torturous pangs of his conscience:

> his fevered brain
> Reels giddily awhile: but ah! too soon
> The slumber of intemperance subsides,
> And conscience, that undying serpent, calls
> Her venomous brood to their nocturnal task.

(III, lines 58–62)

Although there is no wicked enchanter present, this is clearly another
allegorical Palace of Pleasure, and its occupant represents an extreme
case of intemperance, of the man who has fallen victim to the specious
charms of gluttony and indolence, and the 'sordid lust of pelf/self'.
Despite being able to indulge his every wish, the king's appetite is
spoiled by satiety, and instead of pleasure he can feel only pain.

Where this particular use of the motif differs from previous
examples is that it is no longer merely an allegory. In recreating the
archetype of the pleasure palace, Shelley does not forget that there
are also *real* palaces and *real* monarchs. 'Gorgeous palace' is a poetic
convention, but George's palace is a royal residence in central
London. The occupant of Shelley's palace is not just a personification
of Pleasure but an impersonation of the King, a composite caricature
of George III and the Prince Regent. The former, by 1813
irremediably insane, is unmistakable as 'the fool / Whom courtiers
nickname monarch' (III, 31–32), the king with the 'fevered brain'
and the 'frenzied eye' (III, 58, 63). The latter was notorious for his
love of luxury and his gluttony, and his sumptuous residence at
Carlton House had been the scene of some of the worst displays of
royal extravagance in English history, an extravagance that stood in
shameful contrast, as it does in the poem, to the destitution of much
of the labouring population (Shelley had already written a satire,
now lost, on the occasion of one of these gaudy fêtes, and his early
letters are full of anger at the appalling excesses and 'ludicrous
magnificence' of the Prince Regent[90]). The fact that the episode
works at both levels – as an allegorical representation of the hazards
of greed and luxury, and as a literal denunciation of the corruption
of the royal household – illustrates both Shelley's dependence on and
his departure from the conventions of allegorical romance: his ability
to use its existing codes, but also to generate overtly *political* meaning
out of what had been a largely moralistic genre.

The joyless palace of the King is immediately contrasted with the metaphorical palace of 'the virtuous heart' (III, 74), and with an extended portrait of 'The virtuous man'. It is here that Ianthe begins to learn what it is that is missing from the amorphous paradise in the Hall of Spells, and what it is that separates the degraded pleasures of the King's palace from the 'kindly passions' and 'pure desires' of the final cantos. In a sense, the whole meaning of the poem is revealed by the contrasting uses of the Bower of Bliss or Palace of Pleasure motif – by the difference between the 'varied bliss' that 'Used not the glorious privilege / Of virtue and of wisdom' and the bliss which 'Dawns on the virtuous mind'. It is, after all, in order to teach Ianthe to be virtuous and wise that Mab shares with her the secrets of the past, present and future; Mab's magical visions can therefore be said to perform a function precisely equivalent to that of the episodes in Spenserian romance (a single episode in the case of many eighteenth-century imitations) whereby the inexperienced hero or heroine discovers the true nature of virtue. The difference is that where, say, Guyon or Thalaba learn by experience, by trial and error, Ianthe learns by direct instruction. As a result, we do not really see her develop as a character. We deduce rather than witness her transformation from a woman of considerable virtue into one of consummate virtue. This may deprive the poem of what Mary Shelley called 'human interest'; it may also represent one of the defects that Shelley sought to remedy when he went on to write *Laon and Cythna* 'in the style and for the same object as "Queen Mab"', but interwoven with a story of human passion' (*Letters*, I, 557). It should not, however, obscure the centrality in *Queen Mab* of the idea of virtue itself, which now requires close examination.

SHELLEY'S THEORY OF VIRTUE

In the context of works like *The Faerie Queene*, 'The Palace of Fortune' and *Thalaba the Destroyer*, Shelley's poem does not seem at all unusual in its concern with the theme of virtue. Virtue was a traditional preoccupation of romance, a genre that became characterised by its polarisation of good and evil, and by its tendency to idealise the ethical qualities of its heroes and heroines. When Spenser, in his famous letter to Raleigh, defined the purpose of his allegory as being 'to fashion a gentleman or noble person in vertuous and gentle discipline', and proposed to devote one book to each of the twelve 'moral vertues', he was merely making explicit one of the accepted functions of romance, and trying to be systematic rather than impressionistic in his presentation of how to be 'vertuous'. That subsequent writers of moral allegories or metrical romances shared Spenser's aims – albeit on a more modest scale – has already been amply demonstrated here.

Yet when we consider that *Queen Mab* is a poem that expressly challenges the authority of Christian revelation, that specifically rejects at least three of Spenser's moral virtues (holiness, chastity and courtesy), and radically alters the definition of two of the others (temperance and justice), it is not quite so obvious why Shelley should have wanted to retain, and indeed highlight, the idea of virtuousness. One expects to find Southey, a church-going Anglican for most of his life, writing poems about virtuous heroes and heavenly rewards. It comes as something of a surprise in a 'philosophical poem' written by a thoroughgoing atheist – in a romance which is also a revolutionary polemic.

To make sense of this paradox we need to examine what Shelley actually says about virtue, and to consider the *political* context, and purpose, of the poem. By his own account,[91] 'Devotion to Virtue' was Shelley's 'Religion' in his youth, but it was not the religious idea of virtue to which he was devoted. More often than not, when he spoke of 'virtue' he was thinking not of God but of Godwin. The book that taught Shelley how to 'think & feel' was *An Enquiry Concerning Political Justice*, a work whose main theme, as Edmund Blunden has justly remarked, 'might almost be given in one word … Virtue'.[92] The conception of virtue that is presented in *Queen Mab* is, first and foremost, a Godwinian one. The alliance of virtue and wisdom, the interdependence of virtue and justice, the primacy of sincerity, the necessity of universal benevolence, the notion that virtue is the only true road to happiness: all these ideas are derived from *Political Justice*. Shelley's dictum 'The man / Of virtuous soul commands not nor obeys' (III, 174–75) is an aphoristic summary of Godwin's doctrine of rational anarchy. The pivotal lines in Canto VI where Mab reassures the despairing Ianthe that virtue shall ultimately prevail:

> Some eminent in virtue shall start up
> Even in perversest time:
> The truths of their pure lips, that never die,
> Shall bind the scorpion falsehood with a wreath
> Of ever-living flame,
> Until the monster sting itself to death.   (VI, lines 33–38)

bring together two of the fundamental tenets of *Political Justice*:[93] first, that 'a powerful understanding is inseparable from eminent virtue' (p. 305); and second, 'the tendency of truth to the improvement of our political institutions' (p. 302). At the same time, they echo an important passage from the essay 'Of the Utility of Talents' in *The Enquirer* (1797) where Godwin makes a bold appeal for other enquirers to do as he has done – to make themselves heard:

> The affairs of man in society are not of so simple a texture that they require only common talents to guide them. Tyranny grows up by a kind of necessity of nature; oppression discovers itself; poverty, fraud, violence, murder, and a thousand evils follow in the rear. These cannot be extirpated without great discernment and great energies. Men of genius must rise up, to show their brethren that these evils, though familiar, are not therefore less dreadful, to analyse the machine of human society, to demonstrate how the parts are connected together, to explain the immense chain of events and consequences, to point out the defects and the remedy. It is only thus that important reforms can be produced.[94]

Godwin's notion of 'eminent virtue' (a recurrent phrase in *Political Justice*), his belief in the political efficacy of truth-telling, and his exhortation to 'Men of genius' to 'rise up', are fused together in Mab's prophecy, which ends with the characteristic Shelleyan metaphor of 'the scorpion falsehood' stinging itself to death. Moreover, *Queen Mab* itself is a response to Godwin's call, and an enactment of its own theme: a defence of virtue, an exposure of tyranny, an analysis of 'the machine of human society', a pointer to 'the defects and the remedy'.

Yet what exactly is the remedy for political corruption? The question is of course as old as the science of politics. Godwin was not the first philosopher to argue that the remedy lay in the hands of men of virtue and genius. It was an established belief in the republican tradition that in dark times it falls to an elect, especially gifted individual, or group of individuals, to perform acts of virtue on behalf of a corrupt society. Thus Machiavelli, in *The Discourses*:

> For, as I have just said, it is clear that, if in a state which is on the decline owing to the corruption of its material a renaissance is ever to be brought about, it will be by virtue of some one person who is then living, not by virtue of the public as a whole, that good institutions are kept up ... [95]

'Virtue' here renders the Italian *virtù* which is strictly untranslatable, since, as Bernard Crick remarks,[96] it has very little to do with the Christian concept of virtue and virtuousness, and always implies a *political* morality. In the political writings of Rousseau, however, the republican notion of civic virtue underwent a profound modification, and became linked to personal sincerity, transparency and goodness of heart. The civic renaissance, or 'regeneration', that Rousseau deemed possible through the agency of a providential legislator involved nothing less than a transformation of human nature: Rousseau's was above all a *moral* politics.[97]

Although Rousseau is rightly regarded as its major intellectual influence, the phenomenon of the French Revolution provided an entirely new answer to the age-old question: the remedy of revolution itself. What Lynn Hunt calls 'the unexpected invention of revolutionary politics'[98] appeared to offer a total solution to the problem of creating freedom out of servitude and corruption. In the event things went terribly wrong, and revolutionary politics aberrated into 'le despotisme de la liberté contre la tyrannie' (Robespierre's fateful words[99]), and government by guillotine. Hannah Arendt argues that the pervasive mood of suspicion throughout the Revolution, the obsession with conspiracy and hypocrisy which 'transformed Robespierre's dictatorship into the Reign of Terror', was an inevitable consequence of the carrying-over into politics of Rousseau's *âme déchirée*, arising directly out of a 'misplaced emphasis on the heart as the source of political virtue, on *le coeur, une âme droite, un caractère moral*'.[100]

How Godwin's theories would have translated into practice we shall never know. Godwin too affirms the importance of sincerity, even going so far as to criticise Rousseau for his advocacy of 'religious imposture'.[101] But Godwin's touchstone is reason rather than feeling, the head rather than the heart. Central to his theory of political justice is the right (and duty) of private judgment, and its concomitant is a conception of 'personal virtue' which *is* now analogous in certain respects to that of Christian virtuousness, but linked to reason and understanding rather than to grace. Where Godwin diverges furthest from the republican tradition, however, is in his account of what the eminently virtuous must *do* in order to redeem a nation from vice and corruption. On the face of things, his answer appears to be: nothing. The only good government is no government, and there is no place in Godwin's scheme either for the Machiavellian deliverer or the Rousseauist legislator. Even before the outbreak of the Terror, Godwin had already rejected the methods – though not the ideals – of the French Revolution. Neither resistance, revolutions, political associations nor tyrannicide are, we are told, acceptable means of political melioration; instead 'everything may be trusted to the tranquil and wholesome progress of knowledge'.[102] Godwin's is a political philosophy that promised to abstract the hopes of man not only out of his feelings, but also out of his actions.

It is easy to ridicule Godwin on this count. In his own day he was censured by many of his fellow radicals for his 'lukewarmness' in face of the revolutionary experiment in France.[103] Others were simply baffled. John Thelwall voiced the consternation of many readers of *Political Justice* when he wrote:

[I]n the midst of the singularities with which that valuable work abounds, nothing is perhaps more remarkable than that it should at once recommend the most extensive plan of freedom and innovation ever discussed by any writer in the English language, and reprobate every measure from which even the most moderate reform can rationally be expected.[104]

Yet we should not underestimate the cogency of Godwin's insights, or the boldness of his intervention in the British debate on the French Revolution. In the England of 1793, the 'progress of knowledge' and the liberty of discussion were things that could no longer be taken for granted. The project of the Enlightenment was now inescapably associated with the possibility of revolution. 'Terror was the order of the day', wrote Godwin in 1795, explaining why the original preface of his novel *Caleb Williams* (1794), had been suppressed; 'and it was feared that even a humble novelist might be shown to be constructively a traitor'.[105] The prosecution of Paine in 1792 for seditious libel in Part II of *Rights of Man*, the first of many such trials in England and Scotland during the period of the French Revolution,[106] had already proved Godwin's point that the 'cultivation of truth', under present circumstances, was itself a political act. However exaggerated his claims seem to us now, the British government of the time certainly agreed with Godwin's estimate in *Political Justice* of the power of 'opinion' – hence their ruthless determination to control it. The fate of the word 'philosophy', discussed earlier, demonstrates very clearly just how dangerous even *this* method of political reformation was then considered to be. So too does the trajectory of the term 'enquiry' after the publication of Godwin's famous book, as is revealed by a fascinating entry from Charles Pigott's *Political Dictionary* (1795):

Enquiry, – according to the modern construction, signifies Sedition. In the old English dictionary, it was held a CONSTITUTIONAL PRIVILEGE, derived from MAGNA CHARTA and the BILL OF RIGHTS, for the people to *enquire* into the conduct of Kings or Ministers, and into the errors of their government; but all things now seem in a state of revolution, and, according to Mr. Pitt's new code, which is implicitly adopted by all the legal courts through the three kingdoms, *enquiry* implies disloyalty, sedition, or treason, and they who are *audacious* enough to claim this ancient *obsolete* privilege, expose themselves to the penalties of fine, pillory, or imprisonment, and if in Scotland, of transportation for fourteen years to BOTANY BAY. The people, however, begin to murmur at the revolution that the word has undergone, and to *think* that this is not altogether a FREE country.

That the word still carried at least some of this subversive political charge in 1815 is suggested by the full title of the journal which published the first and most favourable review of *Queen Mab*: the *Theological Inquirer, or Polemical Magazine.*

Godwin referred to *Political Justice* as 'the child of the French revolution'.[107] The real weakness of the book is not that he fails to support the French Revolution, but that he makes no attempt to come to terms with it. While entrusting everything to the progress of knowledge, he overlooks the glaring fact that the French Revolution was – as most of his contemporaries agreed – the actual historical result of the dissemination of progressive ideas. Shelley does not neglect this, nor the pessimistic conclusion that more and more people had drawn from it as the situation in France worsened: namely, that the ultimate tendency of progressive ideas was not virtue but 'bloodshed, vice, and slavery'. According to the argument of Shelley's *Proposals for an Association of Philanthropists* (1812), what is proved by the murders that were committed during the period of the French Revolution, and by 'the despotism which has since been established', is 'that the doctrines of philanthropy and freedom were but shallowly understood'. However, progress had been made since then, and Godwin's own writings, Shelley believed, represented a decisive advance over the pre-Revolutionary philosophers. Had Godwin's work not been 'totally devoid of influence' on the course of events in France, and had there been more such men of genius during the Revolution, that country 'would not now be a beacon to warn us of the hazard and horror of Revolutions, but a pattern of society, rapidly advancing to a state of perfection, and holding out an example for the gradual and peaceful regeneration of the world' (*Prose Works*, I, 52).

Judging from the descriptions in his letters, Shelley's lost novel *Hubert Cauvin* (composed 1811–12) would also have delivered what Godwin himself had declined to produce: a Godwinian analysis of the French Revolution. Shelley informed Godwin that the novel was 'an inquiry into the causes of the failure of the French Revolution to benefit mankind' (*Letters*, I, 229); and he told Elizabeth Hitchener that not least among those causes was '*expediency, insincerity,* and *mystery*' (*Letters*, I, 223), terms which strongly suggest a Godwinian frame of reference. Yet oddly enough, 'expediency' was an error which Shelley at one point imputed to Godwin himself. This might seem to be the last thing that the author of *Political Justice* could be accused of, but Shelley makes precisely that charge in his letter to Thomas Jefferson Hogg of 9 May 1811:

> What constitutes real virtue motive or consequence? surely the former ... I have left the proof to Aristotle – shall we take Godwin's criterion, expediency – oh surely not. (*Letters*, I, 81)

In fact Godwin nowhere mentions 'expediency' in his discussions of virtue, and Shelley's criticism is incomprehensible until we realise that by 'expediency' he means 'utility'. Godwin's ethical system is undoubtedly a *utilitarian* one, as may be shown at once by his definition of morality in *Political Justice* as 'that system of conduct which is determined by a consideration of the greatest general good: he is entitled to the highest moral approbation whose conduct is, in the greatest number of instances or in the most momentous instances, governed by views of benevolence, and made subservient to public utility' (pp. 165–66).

At times, Shelley appears to accept this definition: in one of the Notes to *Queen Mab*, for instance, he states that 'utility is morality; that which is incapable of producing happiness is useless' (*Poems*, I, 379). Yet whenever he addresses the specific question of the nature of a virtuous action or agent, he ends up taking a non-utilitarian position, rejecting the consequentialist argument in favour of an intentionalist one. This is shown most explicitly in his *Treatise on Morals*, whose date is uncertain but which was probably composed some time between 1812 and 1816. In it we find clear internal evidence that Shelley was working out his ideas on the nature of virtue in direct response to Godwin's.[108] In *Political Justice* we read:

> Morality, as has already been frequently observed, consists entirely in an estimate of consequences; he is the truly virtuous man who produces the

greatest portion of benefit his situation will admit. The most exalted morality indeed, that in which the heart reposes with the most unmingled satisfaction, relates to the inherent and indefeasible tendencies of actions. But we shall be by no means excusable if we overlook, in our system of conduct, the arbitrary awards of other men. Nothing can be more certain than that an action, suppose of inferior moment or utility, which for its own sake might be right to be performed, it may become my duty to neglect if I know that by performing it I shall incur the penalty of death. (p. 241)

Shelley argues as follows:

The character of actions, as virtuous or vicious, would by no means be determined alone by the personal advantage or disadvantage of each moral agent individually considered. Indeed, an action is often virtuous in proportion to the greatness of the personal calamity which the author willingly draws upon himself by daring to perform it. It is because an action produces an overbalance of pleasure or pain to sentient beings, and not merely because its consequences are beneficent or injurious to the author of that action that it is good or evil. Nay, this latter consideration has a tendency to pollute the purity of virtue, inasmuch as it consists in the motive rather than in the consequences of an action ...

  My neighbor presuming on his strength may direct me to perform or to refrain from a particular action indicating a certain arbitrary penalty in the event of disobedience within his power to inflict. My action if modified by his menaces can in no degree participate in virtue. He has afforded me no criterion as to what is right or wrong. A king, or an assembly of men, may publish a proclamation affixing any penalty to any particular action, [but that is not immoral because such penalty is affixed]. Nothing is more evident than that the epithet of virtue is inapplicable to the refraining from that action on account of the evil arbitrarily attached to it. If the action is in itself beneficial, virtue would rather consist in not refraining from it, but in firmly defying the personal consequences attached to its performance. (*Prose*, p. 191)

Godwin claims that 'morality consists entirely in an estimate of consequences'; Shelley, that 'it consists in the motive rather than the consequence of an action'. The one maintains that 'we shall be by no means excusable if we overlook, in our system of conduct, the arbitrary awards of other men'. The other holds that we 'can in no degree participate in virtue' if we modify our action because of the threat of an 'arbitrary penalty' attending to that action. 'Nothing can be more certain' for Godwin than that 'it may become my duty to neglect' a particular action 'if we know that by performing it I shall incur the penalty of death'. 'Nothing is more evident' to Shelley 'than that the epithet of virtue is inapplicable to the refraining from that action on account of the evil arbitrarily attaching to it'; indeed that 'an action is often virtuous in proportion to the greatness of the personal calamity which the author willingly draws upon himself by daring to perform it'.

It is clear that what Godwin calls the 'most exalted morality' is for Shelley the *only* morality. Godwin allows for different degrees of virtue, but for Shelley only the purest kind is worthy of the name, the rest being mere 'expediency'. At first Shelley appears to be arguing as a consequentialist – the criterion of whether an action is good or evil, he says, is decided by the quantity of pleasure or pain which it produces; but so concerned is he to avoid admitting anything that smacks of 'expediency' into his system that he is soon forced to exclude altogether from his calculations the pleasure or pain that results for the moral agent. The discussion begins with the principle of utility and ends, in effect, with a 'theory of self-sacrifice' – a phrase that actually appears elsewhere in the *Treatise* (*Prose*, p. 189).

Returning to *Queen Mab*, this alerts us to several important modifications of the Godwinian idea of virtue. Firstly, on the question of martyrdom, Mab proclaims:

> There is a nobler glory, which survives
> Until our being fades, and, solacing
> All human care, accompanies its change;
> Deserts not virtue in the dungeon's gloom,
> And, in the precincts of the palace, guides
> Its footsteps through that labyrinth of crime;
> Imbues his lineaments with dauntlessness,
> Even when, from power's avenging hand, he takes
> Its sweetest, last and noblest title – death;   (v, lines 214–22).

Unremarkable in themselves, these lines strike a note which never quite disappears from Shelley's poetry, and it is important to realise that it is not a Godwinian one. Godwin treats martyrdom as a species of suicide, but in *Queen Mab* (and to an even greater extent in *Laon and Cythna*) it is presented as the ultimate form of virtue, the most exalted moral action of all.

If these lines show the putative man of virtue in *Queen Mab* to be more dauntless than his counterpart in *Political Justice*, there are other statements which show him to be more rebellious too. I have said that Shelley's aphorism 'The man / Of virtuous soul commands not nor obeys' epitomises the doctrine of rational anarchy, Godwin's notion that each man should act in accordance with the dictates of his own judgment. In certain respects, however, the resulting formulation is very unGodwinian, as we can see if we turn to the passage in *Political Justice* with which Shelley establishes his disagreement in the *Treatise on Morals*, which is from Godwin's chapter entitled 'Of Obedience'. Godwin's hypothetical example of the man who refrains from performing a virtuous action because of the penalty it would incur, serves in its context[109] to illustrate the third of three different kinds of obedience between which Godwin wants to distinguish, the first and 'purest kind' being 'where an action flows from the independent conviction of our private judgement', the second being where the moral agent defers to the judgment of someone else whom he believes to have a 'superiority of intellect or information' (i.e. on the basis of 'confidence'), and the third being 'where I do that which is not prescribed to me by my private judgement, merely on account of the mischievous consequences that I foresee will be annexed to my omission by the arbitrary authority of some voluntary being'. In this 'scale of obedience', Godwin holds the third kind to be less impure – 'less a source of degradation and depravity' – than the second kind, because 'a man who yields it may reserve, in its most essential sense, his independence' (pp. 239–41).

As we have seen in the *Treatise on Morals*, Shelley proceeds to overturn this argument by refusing to acknowledge as virtuous any action which is modified by the arbitrary menaces of another person. Right from the start, though, he has excluded any suggestion of a connection between virtue and obedience: even the 'purest kind' of obedience has nothing to do with Shelley's idea of virtue. In *Queen Mab* we are told why:

> obedience,
> Bane of all genius, virtue, freedom, truth,
> Makes slaves of men, and, of the human frame,
> A mechanized automaton.　　　　　　　(III, lines 177–80)

The very word 'obedience' is clearly anathema to Shelley,[110] which may reflect his temperamental aversion to all forms of constraint (especially those enforced by orthodox Christianity), but which probably expresses too his feelings about the sycophancy of the aristocracy – one of the major themes of the third canto – and the subservience, or servility, of the disempowered majority.

Godwin himself talks in *Political Justice* of 'the tyranny of command' and of 'the spirit of servility' that results from the unequal distribution of property and wealth (pp. 726, 732). No one who reads to the end of that book can seriously doubt that Godwin was motivated, in part at least, by similar feelings of indignation at the injustices of George III's England. But when the question arises of how it is possible to be virtuous in a corrupt society, Godwin takes a very cautious path. We have already established that the virtuous man in Godwin's system is not an active rebel; rather than engaging in political action, he assists in the propagation of political knowledge, and waits for institutional change to result from the alteration of public opinion. In the meantime, he must live under a government with which he is in complete disagreement, and the chapter 'Of Obedience' explains exactly how he should behave. In other words, it is essentially about *political* obedience. According to Godwin, 'the best advice that could be given to a person in a state of subjection' is:

Comply, where the necessity of the case demands it; but criticize while you comply. Obey the unjust mandates of your governors; for this prudence and a consideration of the common safety may require; but treat them with no false lenity, regard them with no indulgence. Obey; this may be right; but beware of reverence. Reverence nothing but wisdom and skill: government may be vested in the fittest persons; then they are entitled to reverence, because they are wise, and not because they are governors: and it may be vested in the worst. Obedience will occasionally be right in both cases: you may run south, to avoid a wild beast advancing in that direction, though you want to go north. But be upon your guard against confounding things so totally unconnected with each other as a purely political obedience and respect. Government is nothing but regulated force; force is its appropriate claim upon your attention. It is the business of individuals to persuade; the tendency of concentrated strength is only to give consistency and per-manence to an influence more compendious than persuasion. (p. 242)

And the corresponding advice to the government is as follows:

It is yours to shackle the body, and restrain our external actions; that is a restraint we understand. Announce your penalties; and we will make our election of submission or suffering. But do not seek to enslave our minds. Exhibit your force in its plainest form, for that is your province; but seek not to inveigle and mislead us. Obedience and external submission is all you are entitled to claim; you can have no right to extort our deference, and command us not to see, and disapprove of, your errors. (pp. 246–47)

Comparing these statements with the lines quoted above from *Queen Mab*, we may say that the Shelleyan 'man / Of virtuous soul' is indeed a more rebellious figure than his Godwinian neighbour. Both are resolute anarchists, but where one believes that it is his duty to be obedient to unjust authority, the other believes it is his duty to be insubordinate. Both believing that public opinion not action is the means of change, Godwin's man of virtue does nothing; Shelley's, not even what he is told. The one complies and criticises; the other, it would seem, practises civil disobedience.

Whether this makes Shelley's man of virtue a more plausible redeemer than Godwin's is hard to say. It is still difficult to see how such a person or persons will bring about a political transformation simply by the act of speaking the truth. Everything is still entrusted to the 'tranquil and wholesome progress of knowledge' – and of course the 'law of Necessity'. Unlike Godwin, however, Shelley does not lay down rules about what should or should not be done by those whose consciousness has been raised by the 'men of genius'. He does not reprove every practical measure by which political reform might reasonably be put into effect. Once the people are enlightened, they are not expressly forbidden to resist or revolt against their oppressors, nor are they barred from political association. On these matters Shelley's poem is silent, its 'philosophical' rationale being merely to free the mind of confusions which prevent clear thought and action, as explained later in his essay 'On Life':

Philosophy, impatient as it may be to build, has much work yet remaining as pioneer for the overgrowth of ages. It makes one step towards this object; it destroys error and the roots of error. It leaves, what is too often the duty of the reformer in political and ethical questions to leave, a vacancy. (*Poetry and Prose*, p. 477)

A POST-GODWINIAN UTOPIA

About the ultimate goal of the political reformer, the poem is less reticent. In the last two cantos Mab looks beyond 'the sweeping storm of time' (VI, 220) and conjures up a grand vision of the regenerated world that will result from the eventual triumph of virtue over vice and falsehood. Here again there are both strong similarities and marked differences between Shelley's thinking and Godwin's. In the closing chapters of *Political Justice* Godwin speculates about a future in which 'mind will one day become omnipotent over matter', and human life will be capable of being indefinitely prolonged:

Other improvements may be expected to keep pace with those of health and longevity. There will be no war, no crimes, no administration of justice, as it is called, and no government. Beside this, there will be neither disease, anguish, melancholy, nor resentment. Every man will seek, with ineffable ardour, the good of all. Mind will be active and eager, yet never disappointed. Men will see the progressive advancement of virtue and good, and feel that, if things occasionally happen contrary to their hopes, the miscarriage itself was a necessary part of that progress. (pp. 776–77)

Mab too speaks of 'the omnipotence of mind' (VII, 236), of a time when man shall be 'Immortal upon earth' (VIII, 211):

> The deadly germs of languor and disease
> Died in the human frame, and purity
> Blest with all her gifts her earthly worshippers.
> How vigorous then the athletic form of age!
> How clear its open and unwrinckled brow!
> Where neither avarice, cunning, pride, or care,
> Had stamped the seal of grey deformity
> On all the mingling lineaments of time.   (IX, lines 63–70)

Indeed, in Shelley's 'paradise of peace' every single one of Godwin's predictions are fulfilled.

Not just fulfilled, but exceeded. Godwin, to be sure, sets few limits to the perfectibility of man and society; but the regenerated world depicted in the final cantos of *Queen Mab* is a transcendence still more complete. Not only man, but nature itself is regenerated:

> All things are recreated, and the flame
> Of consentaneous love inspires all life:
> The fertile bosom of the earth gives suck
> To myriads, who still grow beneath her care,
> Rewarding her with their pure perfectness:
> The balmy breathings of the wind inhale
> Her virtues, and diffuse them all abroad:
> Health floats amid the gentle atmosphere,
> Glows in the fruits, and mantles on the stream:
> No storms deform the beaming brow of heaven,
> Nor scatter in the freshness of its pride
> The foliage of the ever verdant trees;
> But fruits are ever ripe, flowers ever fair,
> And autumn proudly bears her matron grace,
> Kindling a flush on the fair cheek of spring,
> Whose virgin bloom beneath the ruddy fruit
> Reflects its tint, and blushes into love.   (VIII, lines 107–23)

In Shelley's recreated world, the principle of equality – the foundation of Godwin's ideal human society – is extended even to the animal kingdom, for now 'man has lost / His terrible prerogative, and stands / An equal amidst equals' (VIII, 225–27). So too is the principle of benevolence, for 'The lion now forgets to thirst for blood' (VII, 124), and man no longer 'slays the lamb that looks him in the face, / And horribly devours his mangled flesh' (VIII, 213–14). Even the deadly nightshade has lost its deadliness, and 'Poisons no more the pleasure it bestows' (VIII, 130). Godwin is only interested in the relations between people. Shelley is interested too in the relationship between man and his environment; and a typical metaphor for the pastoral harmony he foresees is Mab's description of how the sound of ocean waves upon the sand 'is wakened into echoings sweet / To murmur through the heaven-breathing groves / And melodize with man's blest nature there' (VIII, 67–69).

Where Shelley expressly disagrees with Godwin is in the importance that he assigns to 'passion'. Peter Marshall has sought to defend Godwin against the charge of being an unfeeling rationalist,[111] a charge most forcefully made by Hazlitt when he remarked that 'Mr Godwin's definition of morals was the same as the admired one of law, *reason without passion.*'[112] This comment 'is the result of a superficial reading', Marshall retorts, pointing to several places where Godwin emphasises the essential role of desire and love in man's moral nature. Yet Godwin himself conceded that he had undervalued the 'domestic and private affections' in the original version of *Political Justice*, an imbalance he aimed to redress in the second edition and in his novels.[113] On the question of sex, Godwin did not alter his original claim in *Political Justice* that the inhabitants of a perfect society would no longer be interested in what he calls 'the mere animal function'. Men and women 'will probably cease to propagate', not because 'the earth will refuse itself to a more extended population', but because it is the tendency 'of a cultivated and virtuous mind ... to diminish our eagernesss for the gratifications of the senses' (p. 776). Despite the prospect of virtual immortality, there will be no population problem in the Godwinian utopia because there will be no more copulation.

In Shelley's utopia, by comparison, the union of body and mind, of 'soul' and 'sense', is a central feature. 'Reason and passion cease to combat there', says Mab; not because the former finally gains hegemony over the latter, but because these traditional enemies are reconciled, so that 'each unfettered o'er the earth extend / Their all-subduing energies, and wield / The sceptre of a vast dominion there' (VIII, 231–34). Nor is this a mere partnership of compromise. Freed from the false constraints of society, passion and reason are natural allies, the one a 'sportive child', the other her 'meek and sober' elder sister:

> Reason was free; and wild though passion went
> Through tangled glens and wood-embosomed meads,
> Gathering a garland of the strangest flowers,
> Yet like the bee returning to her queen,
> She bound the sweetest on her sister's brow,
> Who meek and sober kissed the sportive child,
> No longer trembling at the broken rod.   (IX, lines 50–56)

The 'broken rod' is an image of abandoned authority, in this case the repressive, intimidating authority of orthodox morality over human energy. That it is the energy of *physical* passion – of the libido – that Shelley especially wishes to liberate, has already been demonstrated.

In this respect, it may remind us more of the 'New Amorous World' of Charles Fourier[114] than of Godwin's rationalist utopia. It is unlikely that Shelley was acquainted with the writings of his French contemporary (Fourier's work was largely unknown in England until the 1830s), but there are genuine and interesting correspondences between their ideas, both authors combining a vision of a sexually liberated society with a radical critique of commercial civilisation (in Fourier's case, of civilisation altogether). Politically the two are far apart – Fourier was as much the enemy of republican virtue and the principles of 1789 as he was of orthodox Christian morality and the values of nineteenth-century France – but the comparison makes clear that Shelley, in his prescriptions for a regenerated world, has gone far beyond the terms of the Enlightenment. It also makes the point that *Queen Mab*, though partially modelled on the utopian writings of the Revolutionary period (Godwin, Volney, Condorcet), really belongs to a later, post-Revolutionary generation of utopias; and a historian of ideas would not deem it coincidental that the poem was issued in the same year as Robert Owen's *A New View of Society*, and one year before Saint-Simon's *De la Réorganisation de la Société Européene*. Shelley's 'philosophical poem', then, is both a reassertion of the millenarian hopes of the 1790s and the product of a new phase in the European political imagination in the aftermath of the French Revolution.

The French Revolution itself had of course drastically altered the significance of utopian discourse. In the eighteenth century there had been a vast body of utopian literature,[115] but this was mostly of a purely speculative nature. With the advent of the French Revolution, what had previously been a conceptual exercise entered the realm of concrete possibility. As George Steiner puts it, 'The eternal "tomorrow" of utopian political vision became, as it were, Monday morning.'[116] This is the 'dizzying sense of total possibility' which received its most eloquent (although not, as we know, most unequivocal) expression in Wordsworth's poem on the French Revolution; the same dream expressed by Mary Wollstonecraft in her *Vindication of the Rights of Men*, by Joel Barlow in *The Conspiracy of Kings*, by Thomas Spence in *The Rights of Infants*, and by a host of other English writers of the 1790s. For, as Hazlitt recalled, this was a time when utopian schemes 'were spoken on the house-tops, were whispered in secret, were published in quarto and duodecimo, in political treatises, in plays, poems, songs and romances – made their way to the bar, crept into the church, ascended the rostrum, thinned the classes of the universities ... got into the hearts of poets and the brains of metphysicians, took possession of the fancies of boys and women, and turned the heads of almost the whole kingdom'.[117]

If we are looking for literary analogues for the last two cantos of *Queen Mab*, it is to this context that we must attend, rather than to such poems as Pope's *Messiah*, which has often been cited as the principal source for Shelley's vision of a perfect world. *Mab* certainly resembles *The Messiah* in the way it blends images of the classical Golden Age with apocalyptic motifs from the Bible, but this was also a very common tactic in the poetry and prose of the 1790s. By applying those images to a vision of political or secular redemption, Shelley is closer to Spence than to Pope, although this is not to deny that the latter may also have influenced *Queen Mab*. In fact what is most striking about Shelley's poem is the sheer multiplicity of the materials that it assimilates. To describe his earthly paradise, Shelley is not content to combine ideas from Isaiah and Revelation with hints from Virgil's fourth eclogue: he incorporates elements from a large range of other sources – political, philosophical, religious and literary. Many of these are mentioned in his letters, which reveal an almost encyclopaedic interest in the theme of the earthly paradise. It is 'the favourite idea of all religions,' he tells Elizabeth Hitchener in October 1811, 'the thesis on which the impassioned & benevolent have delighted to dwell' (*Letters*, 1, 152). In the same letter, he explicitly equates the notion of the 'golden age' – of *his* golden age, 'when the present potence [of mind] will become omnipotence' –

with that of 'the millennium of Xtians "when the lion shall lay down with the lamb"'. Two months later he announces to her that he is contemplating two poems, the first 'a picture of the manners, simplicities, and delights of a perfect state of society; tho' still earthly', and the second 'a picture of *Heaven*' (*Letters*, I, 201). *Queen Mab* is a synthesis of all four themes, one that collapses the distinction between earth and heaven, and describes a future state which will be the fulfilment of all man's dreams of plenitude, whether past or future, religious or political. 'Genius has seen thee in her passionate dreams', says Mab,

> And dim forebodings of thy loveliness
> Haunting the human heart, have there entwined
> Those rooted hopes of some sweet place of bliss
> Where friends and lovers meet to part no more.
> Thou art the end of all desire and will,
> The product of all action; and the souls
> That by the paths of an aspiring change
> Have reached thy haven of perpetual peace,
> There rest from the eternity of toil
> That framed the fabric of thy perfectness.　(IX, lines 12–22)

Heaven, Utopia, Golden Age, Millennium: Shelley's 'paradise of peace' is all these things, and the important point is not that 'this favourite theme of all bards is treated in a manner which covers former descriptions with insignificance' (as the *Theological Inquirer* generously asserted[118]), but that it is treated in the (secular) spirit of comparative mythology, as an archetype that expresses a universal wish for a better condition of being.

When Shelley returns to this theme in the final chorus of *Hellas* (1822), he cites the 'great names' of Isaiah and Virgil in a footnote as his 'authority' and 'excuse' for so doing (*Poetical Works*, pp. 479–80). But in his letter to Hitchener he is adamant that the advent (or return) of an earthly paradise will *not* be accomplished 'to complete a prophecy, or by the intervention of a *miracle*' (*Letters*, I, 152). One distinctive feature of *Queen Mab* is Shelley's attempt to suggest a *scientific* justification for his vision of a regenerated world. Rather than simply reporting the altered conditions on earth, he relates a sequence of geographical events which will bring about such changes. Central to his explanation of the transition from imperfection to perfection is his adoption of the age-old theory that the earth is slowly returning to its proper perpendicular axis, an idea which had been discounted by most contemporary scientists, but which still found occasional adherents in Shelley's day (as Cameron notes,[119] it was probably John Frank Newton who persuaded Shelley to champion the theory). Everything follows on from this hypothesis: when the perpendicular axis is regained, the perpetual spring will be restored, the ice-caps will melt and irrigate the deserts, the earth will become abundant and fertile, animals will no longer need to kill for food, man will no longer need to eat animals, disease and violence will cease ... and so on. In this way Shelley is able to confirm the factual truth of classical myth and biblical revelation by appealing to natural law and the logic of cause and effect. It is not superstition but science, not Providence but Necessity, that will transform the earth into a 'sweet scene' of pleasure and profusion.

The question of human agency remains. As we have seen, Shelley keeps silent on the issue of what the virtuous man must do in order to assist or initiate the regeneration of society. He does not openly advocate political revolution, but neither does he expressly forbid it; and his insistence on a *physical* as well as a *mental* transformation of the world means that 'virtue's meed' will not be achieved by internal means alone. This, as has often been pointed out, was a dilemma that Shelley never fully resolved. Even in *A Philosophical View of Reform* (1819), his most considered treatment of the topic, he leaves a vacancy – literally a gap in the manuscript – at the crucial point at which he turns to the question of how the people are to obtain 'the victory over their oppressors' which will free them from 'moral and political degradation'.[120] However, one telling detail in *Queen Mab* may be the fate of the King's palace – the 'palace of the monarch-slave'. In Canto III it was a symbol of injustice and corruption; in Canto IX it is a 'heap of crumbling ruins'. Paine had written that 'the palaces of kings are built on the ruins of the bowers of paradise', a statement that was interpreted by history as an injunction to *renovate* 'the bowers of paradise'. Shelley's reworking of the theme contains the unavoidable implication that renovating paradise means *destroying* 'the palaces of kings'. More selective than his royalist counterpart in *The Faerie Queene*, Shelley's revolutionary Sir Guyon (the absent hero of *Queen Mab*) has demolished the palace in order to redeem the bower; for out of the ruins of the King's palace, 'wide scattered o'er the globe' like the stones of the Bastille, 'happier shapes were moulded, and became / Ministrant to all blissful impulses' (IX, 131–32).

CONCLUSION

'To describe such a performance is not an easy task', wrote Tom Wooler in 1821, reviewing *Queen Mab* for his *Gazette*.[121] Shelley's poem has since been described as many things, including 'an "Essay on Men", in contrast to Pope's "Essay on Man"', a generic reconstruction of Young's *Night Thoughts*, a 'poetical imitation' of Volney's *Ruines*, and a 'Romantic epic'.[122] What one early reviewer praised as its 'divine philosophy', another branded as 'hideous blasphemy'.[123] To George Bernard Shaw, *Queen Mab* was 'a perfectly original poem on a great subject'; to most of his fellow members of the Shelley Society in 1886, it was something of an embarrassment.[124] Even Shelley could describe the poem on one occasion as 'a sincere overflowing of the heart & mind', and on another as 'villainous trash' (*Letters*, I, 566; II, 298).

Most of the judgments about Shelley's 'performance' have not been impartial because they have been affected by political prejudice of one kind or another. This is hardly surprising when we consider the nature of *Queen Mab*. It is a poem whose ideological content is impossible to ignore, being one of the most daring political statements ever to appear in English verse. Confronted with such a text, it is impossible to make a judgment on purely aesthetic grounds because to do so would be to misconceive its very nature, to risk committing what philosophers call a 'category error'. In these circumstances, the critic needs to find other criteria to deal with the object 'as it really is'. Yet it does not follow that we must confuse those different criteria, and run together the question of Shelley's art with that of his politics. In the account which has been given in the preceding pages, I have therefore endeavoured to reveal rather than to resist the design which the poem has upon its readers, and to understand rather than to undermine the principles on which it is constructed.

Several factors have led me to the conclusion that romance is the generic term that best defines Shelley's composition, although to my knowledge it has only once been applied to the poem.[125] Firstly, I believe that its strongest literary affiliations are with the metrical romances of Southey: the relationship is not the superficial one which it has often been taken to be, and it extends beyond the narrative passages at the opening of *Queen Mab*. Secondly, the poem's affinities with eighteenth-century allegory also involve a connection with romance, since the Augustan genre is ultimately derived from the same source as Southey's metrical romances, namely *The Faerie Queene*. A third reason is that the poem constantly draws on a political iconography which is itself a manifestation of romance, beginning with the fusion of magical and political in its very title. In its 'polarizing between two worlds, one desirable and the other hateful',[126] Shelley's entire *political* vision in *Queen Mab* is structured as a romance, being dialectical, teleological, and concerned with the fulfilment of desires. Even the idea of virtue, though a predominantly *political* one for Shelley, and derived more from Godwin than from Spenser, can be accommodated to the notion of romance, since the theme of virtue's progress is as much a part of *The Faerie Queene* as it is of *Political Justice*. Shelley's poem has often been criticised for its lack of a 'vital mythic structure',[127] but it is perhaps not quite so deficient at this level as has been supposed. There is no fundamental difference between the deep imaginative structure of *Queen Mab* and that of *Prometheus Unbound*, and the mythos in question is that of romance.

Yet to think of the poem in this way is to risk losing sight of its distinctive character, and committing the same mistake as those who reduce the whole issue to one of political ideology. While recognising its archetypal contours, it is important to remember too its more specific formal characteristics. There is no question of Shelley having 'worked within' a fixed genre: *Queen Mab* is modelled upon a number of very different works, not all of them literary. Moreover, Shelley himself never used the term romance for his own works, except in the case of his gothic novels *Zastrozzi* (1810) and *St Irvyne* (1811); and by 1812 he had declared himself 'no longer the votary of Romance' (*Letters*, I, 227). Mary Shelley points out in her editorial note on *Queen Mab* that Shelley 'was a lover of the wonderful and wild in literature, but had not fostered these tastes at their genuine sources – the romances and chivalry of the middle ages – but in the perusal of such German works as were current in those days' (*Poetical Works*, p. 837). More will be said in the next chapter about Shelley's attitude to chivalry. As far as *Queen Mab* is concerned, it is certainly true that the poem bears little relation to the romances of the middle ages. It has none of their polyphonic and digressive character. Though it moves towards a goal, there is not what one could really call a quest. Nor indeed is there a hero: Shelley's 'man of virtue' exists in the abstract, and he is not subjected to the usual vicissitudes of a hero of romance. The trip to the stars, and the magical education that ensues, are an

adventure for Ianthe, but this constitutes only the most rudimentary
of plots, and we learn little of her reactions to Mab's visions and
speeches. The outer narrative lacks human tension, and the plot is
mostly static.

These points can easily be made into criticisms of the poem.
Undoubtedly they indicate the extent to which the literary potential
of the genre remains unfulfilled in *Queen Mab*. A similar comment
might be made about the language of the poem, which lacks the
doubleness that is so richly characteristic of romance – the ambivalence developed so cunningly by medieval practitioners of the
genre and systematically exploited in Spenser's great allegory. In the
previous chapter, we saw that the ambivalence of this language had
persisted in the contrasting uses of romance imagery by political
writers of the Revolutionary age. But *Queen Mab*, while making
repeated use of such terms and images, in general seeks to close
ambiguities, to permit one meaning at a time and maintain a tight
control of the process of signification. There are perhaps exceptions to
this, but it is true to say that for all its metaphoric ingenuity, the poem
rarely privileges the signifier over the signified, aesthetic play over
political communication.

However, when Stuart Curran states that 'the outstanding flaw in
Queen Mab' is the abruptness of the transition from a corrupt present
to a perfect future',[128] he is mainly commenting upon the *inner*
narrative, the plot of human destiny which unfolds within the
didactic core of the poem. His objection therefore concerns in the first
instance the political theory rather than the literary form. The same
criticism, as to the ease if not the abruptness of that transition, might
be made of *Political Justice*, and so too of Volney's *Ruines* or
Condorcet's *Esquisse*. In the foregoing discussion, some consideration
has already been given to this crux as it relates to Godwin and
Shelley. But ultimately what we are confronting is the general
problem of utopianism. It was partly because 'utopian socialists' like
Godwin, Owen and Fourier had so little to say about political means
as distinct from idealistic ends that Marx and Engels tried so hard to
distinguish their own 'scientific socialism' from these ineffectual
precursors, and why there has been such a strong tradition of hostility
to utopias in Marxism.[129] In fact in Marx himself, and certainly in
Engels, the attitude to utopianism is not as consistently unsympathetic as has sometimes been thought. Even *The Communist
Manifesto*, which condemns as bourgeois and reactionary the 'fan-

tastic pictures of future society' painted by the utopian socialists, with their 'systematic pedantry, and … their fanatical and superstitious belief in the miraculous effects of their social science', distinguishes between the constructive and the critical element in many utopias, and finds value in such publications in that 'they attack every principle of existing society' and hence 'are full of the most valuable materials for the enlightenment of the working class'.[130]

Shelley did not intend that *Queen Mab* should assist in the enlightenment of the working class, but that appears to have been its destiny. The author's intention was to alter the political consciousness of his own class: he gave instructions for the poem to be printed – for private distribution – as 'A small neat Quarto, on fine paper, & so as to catch the aristocrats: They will not read it, but their sons & daughters may' (*Letters*, I, 361). But it was not until the cheap pirated editions began to appear in May 1821 that *Queen Mab* found its true readership among self-taught working-class radicals. Within a matter of weeks, the poem had acquired sufficient notoriety as part of this unruly political culture for its title to be featured in Isaac Cruikshank's satirical cartoon 'The Revolutionary Association' (plate 8), where, not inappropriately, Shelley's generic subtitle is replaced with the name of Edward Sexby's infamous regicide tract, *Killing No Murder* (1657). For there is no mistaking the critical element in Shelley's vision, or the thrill of polemicism in his unsparing attack upon those he held responsible for the corruption and injustice of contemporary society. One test of whether a utopian text is also a revolutionary one is whether the critical element unleashes more energy than the constructive element can contain. By this measure, Shelley's utopian romance[131] is indeed a revolutionary work, despite Mab's final directive about 'The gradual paths of an aspiring change' (IX, 148), and despite the author's apparent adherence to the utopian illusion that truth, reason and justice will prevail merely by virtue of their rightness. After all, what is revolution if not an abrupt transition of the kind Curran describes?

Plate 1. 'The Knight of the Woful Countenance Going to Extirpate the National Assembly'. Engraving, 15 November 1790. Burke as Don Quixote, wearing a medallion portrait of Marie-Antoinette, emerges from the door of his publisher. The ass has the head of Pope Pius VI, alluding to Burke's rumoured association with the Jesuits.

Plate 2. 'Don Dismallo, After an Absence of Sixteen Years, Embracing His Beautiful Vision!'. Engraving, 18 November 1790, companion print to plate 1. Burke as Don Quixote reunited with Marie-Antoinette, who addresses him as the 'God of Chivalry'. Mrs Burke looks on, weeping.

Plate 3. 'The Aristocratic Crusade: or, Chivalry Revived in Don Quixote de St Omer and His friend Sancho'. Engraving by Isaac Cruikshank, 31 January 1791.

St GEORGE and the DRAGON or the GLORIOUS Aera of 1798.

Plate 4. 'St George and the Dragon or the Glorious Aera of 1798'. Engraving by Isaac Cruikshank, 5 December 1798. Pitt as St George, mounted on a 'John Bull', pierces a dragon with the heads of three political adversaries: Tierney, Sheridan, Fox (severed). Meanwhile, the bull tramples cocks representing Britain's enemies in the Revolutionary War. The cartoon reflects British counter-revolutionary confidence after Nelson's victory at the Battle of the Nile, and the success of the anti-Jacobin campaign at home.

A CHARM FOR A DEMOCRACY, REVIEWED, ANALYSED, & DESTROYED Jany 1st 1799 TO THE CONFUSION OF ITS AFFILIATED FRIENDS.

Plate 5. 'A Charm for a Democracy, Reviewed, Analysed, & Destroyed Jany 1st 1799 To the Confusion of Its Affiliated Friends'. Engraving by Thomas Rowlandson, frontispiece to the *Anti-Jacobin Review*, 2 (1 February 1799). An attack on the radical press and Opposition, elaborating Burke's image of the revolutionary 'kettle of magicians' (*Reflections*, p. 194), and Mackintosh's 'sable wizards of democracy' (*Vindiciae Gallicae*, p. xiii). Crouching to feed the fire with assorted seditious pamphlets is Horne Tooke; standing behind the wizards (right to left) are Lord Derby, Norfolk, Bedford, Tierney, Erskine, Fox, Burdett and Thelwall.

Plate 6. 'Carrying Coals to Newcastle!!'. Engraving, 16 February 1821. The Brass-founders' procession to Brandenburgh House.

Plate 7. 'The Rival Champion!! or Little Wadd Preparing for the One-Eyed Coronation'. Engraving attributed to Isaac Cruikshank, June 1821.

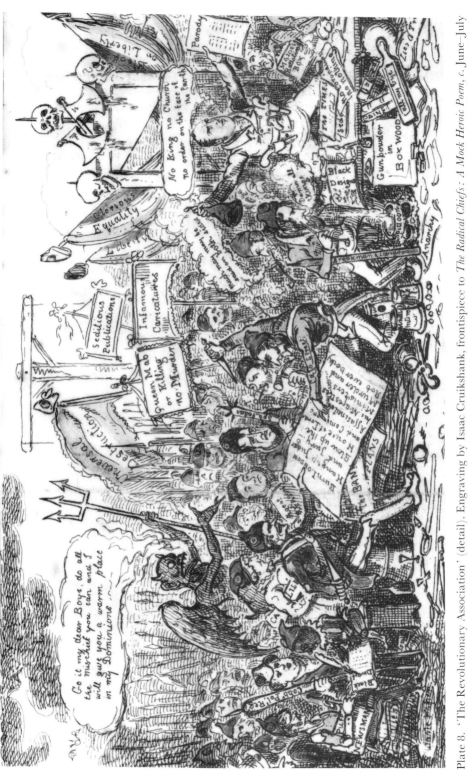

Plate 8. 'The Revolutionary Association' (detail). Engraving by Isaac Cruikshank, frontispiece to *The Radical Chiefs: A Mock Heroic Poem*, c. June–July 1821. A comprehensive attack on current radical tendencies, including the Cato Street gang, Carlile (holding Paine's *Age of Reason*), Wooler (as a Black Dwarf), Henry Hunt ('Spa Fields') and Shelley's *Queen Mab*, linked here with Edward Sexby's regicide tract *Killing No Murder* (1657).

CHAPTER 3

Sir Guyon de Shelley and friends: new light on the chivalric revival

'Feathernest, what is the spirit of the age of chivalry?'

Mr Feathernest was taken by surprise. Since his profitable metamorphosis into an *ami du prince*, he had never dreamed of such a question. It burst upon him like the spectre of his youthful integrity, and he mumbled a half-intelligible reply, about truth and liberty – disinterested benevolence – self-oblivion – heroic devotion to love and honour – protection of the feeble, and subversion of tyranny.

'All the ingredients of a rank Jacobin, Feathernest, 'pon honour!' exclaimed his Lordship.

Thomas Love Peacock, *Melincourt* (1817)

Mab was not the only Queen before the public gaze in 1821. The publication of Shelley's poem in May of that year falls in the midst of the Queen Caroline affair, the controversy occasioned by the Prince Regent's plan to divorce his wife, and subsequently to be crowned without her (the so-called 'one-eyed' coronation). Popular sentiment was outraged, expressing itself in a series of processions, demonstrations, and deputations to the Queen, and support for the 'uncrowned, calumniated and persecuted wife'[1] quickly became a radical cause. A striking cartoon, attributed to Isaac Cruikshank, which appeared in June of that year, features Samuel Waddington ('Little Wadd'), a London shoemaker and well-known radical, dressed as a knight on horseback presenting himself as the Queen's 'Champion', surrounded by revolutionary icons including a shield displaying the motto 'Rights of Man' and pennons bearing revolutionary slogans and liberty caps (plate 7). This is an ironic portrayal, of course, and reminiscent of earlier representations of Burke as Don Quixote. Here, though, the chivalric politics are reversed. The champion is defending not Marie-Antoinette against the mob, but Caroline, an ill-used wife, against her unjust husband, an unjust king – this equation permitting a string of radical demands for justice and reform (duly satirised in the cartoon as, for example, 'Porter 3 Pence Per Pot'). Supporters of Queen Caroline were accused of exploiting the affair for political purposes, which naturally they were.

Where satire of Burke as a chivalric knight was inspired by a literary allusion, the 'age of chivalry' passage in his own *Reflections on the Revolution in France*, this portrayal of Waddington and his followers draws on an actual event. In January 1821 a procession of about eighteen hundred artisans marched through the centre of London to present a loyal address to Queen Caroline in defiance of her husband. Most spectacular of the many deputations prompted by the Queen Caroline affair, this by the Brass Founders and Braziers included eight people dressed as medieval knights, travelling on horseback in full armour, attended by squires or attendants wearing half armour. The Brass Founders and Braziers Company (formerly the Armourers) traditionally provided a suit of armour to be worn at the annual Lord Mayor's Procession, but their contribution to this unauthorised display was far more elaborate.

This bizarre episode in the history of plebeian radicalism is also the source of another satirical cartoon, entitled 'Carrying Coals to Newcastle!!', which depicts spurred and half-armoured marchers with brass kettles and coal scuttles for hats, bearing standards, blowing trumpets and beating with a ladle upon their Hum Drum (plate 6). The braziers did indeed wear brass hats and brandish rods, warming pans and other implements as tokens of their handiwork – ironically, since as Byron points out in an unpublished epigram on the event: 'They'll find, where they're going, much more than they carry.'[2] Yet the irony inherent in the situation of Waddington the radical as monarchical champion is so considerable that the cartoons' extension of it (notably in the 'speech' of the trumpet 'Irony' in Cruikshank's engraving) all but overloads it. The elements of the fantastical, of burlesque and self-parody, present in the staging of the actual march conspire to outreach satire and to render such cartoons almost celebratory even as they deride.

For Mark Girouard, in his book *The Return to Camelot: Chivalry and the English Gentleman*, the Brass Founders' Procession signals an important departure in the history of the chivalric revival: the point at which the notion of chivalry was for the first time employed for radical rather than reactionary purposes, and by commoners rather than aristocrats.[3] Yet we have already seen that Burke's political appropriation of the theme of chivalry in the debate on the French Revolution met with strong resistance from some of his opponents, and that, even in the 1790s, there were liberal or radical writers who claimed to find in the ancient institution of chivalry a moral ethos which echoed their own political ideals. Among the next generation, there were to be more sustained attempts to reclaim the idea of chivalry for the democratic cause. It is these that are the subject of the present chapter, which considers the ideological exploitation of this theme by a number of literary intellectuals in the first two decades of the nineteenth century, beginning with a comparison between Scott and Byron. Central to my argument is the claim that there existed among the Hunt–Shelley circle in the years 1815–17 a self-conscious, politically radical cult of chivalry, conceived in deliberate opposition to the dominant ideology of the chivalric revival, and manifested in a range of public and private writings, including poems, essays, novels, biographies and personal letters. The initial focus of this literary activity was Leigh Hunt, whose 'Round Table' series in the *Examiner* made explicit the notion of a chivalrous coterie dedicated to progressive political ends. It was Shelley, though, who took the concept of chivalry furthest, reinventing the theme in numerous ways and drawing on a wide variety of literary, political and philosophical sources. What I am offering, then, is not only new information about the nature and context of Shelley's ventures into the politics of romance, but also a missing chapter in the story of the chivalric revival, and in the larger topic of Romantic medievalism.

SCOTT, BYRON AND THE POLITICS OF CHIVALRY

As most authors on the subject have noted,[4] there were political overtones to the chivalric revival from the start. This is hardly surprising when we recall that the word 'chivalry' was still in the eighteenth century a common synonym for 'aristocracy', and that the concept had originated as part of the ideology of feudalism, involving complex notions of hierarchy and social obligation, as well as abstract universal ideals such as generosity, justice and courage. At first, these notions were only partially understood by the literary historians and poets who sought to rescue the concept of chivalry from the obscurity and disrepute into which it had fallen, but the political significance of the topic was by no means overlooked, and the chivalric revival quickly acquired ideological functions of its own. These were more varied than might be supposed, for while it is reasonably obvious how the revaluation of chivalry could, indirectly at least, serve the interests of the aristocracy and monarchy, it is not immediately clear why the pioneers of the chivalric revival should have been, in many cases, people of liberal or progressive tendencies. In fact, the rehabilitation of chivalry was, in part at least, the result of a larger enquiry, conducted by the great Whig historians of the late eighteenth century, into the origins and development of civil society. From this historical perspective, the chivalric system, previously discredited as a 'gothic' absurdity, came to be seen as an important stage in the transition from the barbarism of the 'dark ages' to the civilised manners of modern times.[5]

Extending, but ultimately challenging, this progressive, 'enlightened' account was another, more conservative view of the subject whose ideological tendency was, potentially (and paradoxically), more subversive. Chivalric revivalism was, for some, a symptom of unease about the cultural consequences of the Enlightenment itself. Even before Burke's *Reflections*, nostalgia for the middle ages, and for the conception of private and public virtue embodied in the ancient code of chivalry, was frequently associated with an attitude of distrust or dislike towards the secular, mercantile world of Georgian England, and with the belief that the supersession of 'chivalry' by 'commerce' of which the Whig historians of civil society so approvingly spoke, did not in every sense constitute 'progress'. What had been lost in the transition from 'gothic' to 'modern' was not just 'a world of fine fabling' – a culture peculiarly suited, as Richard Hurd[6] explained, 'to the views of a genius, and to the ends of poetry', but a world which, for all its darkness and superstition, may have been more ordered and more harmonious than the one which replaced it.

Burke, as we have seen, moves through all three positions in his treatment of chivalry in the *Reflections*. In one sense, he is clearly writing in the tradition of William Robertson, Adam Ferguson and the Whig historians of the Scottish Enlightenment, whose historical arguments he turns to the overtly political purpose of attacking the French Revolution. In so doing, however, he establishes another, more polemical form of chivalric revivalism, in which chivalry functions as an ideological defence of the principle of monarchy and aristocracy against the threat of revolutionary democracy. Yet he also betrays, in the great Marie-Antoinette passage, an attitude of nostalgia for chivalry, and of hostility to what replaced it, that appears to extend his indictment of Revolutionary France into a condemnation of modernity itself, and to imply an outright opposition, where for the Whig historians there had been continuity, between the values of the 'age of chivalry' and those of the modern capitalist world of 'sophisters, oeconomists, and calculators'.

The publication of Burke's *Reflections* in 1790 gave a new impetus to the chivalric revival, but the political legacy of the book, in this as in other respects, was an ambivalent one, for Burke opened up the subject in more ways than he intended. After his death, however, there were other developments which seemed to secure chivalry as the ideological property of the ruling class. The first of these was the adoption of the theme by the King.[7] Royal interest in the chivalric revival dates back at least as far as 1787, when George III commissioned for the King's Audience Chamber at Windsor Castle a series of historical paintings, several of which treat chivalric motifs, including the centrepiece entitled 'St George and the Dragon'. But it was not until 1802 that royal patronage of chivalry reached its peak, when the King ordered the construction of a pseudo-medieval castle at Kew Gardens, a building (begun but never completed, and demolished in 1827–28) that one observer later compared to the castles 'in which Ariosto or Spenser depicted captive Princesses detained by Giants or Enchanters'.[8] Between 1800 and 1814, large sums of money were also spent gothicising the state apartments at Windsor Castle, including a commission for a second series of paintings depicting the twenty-eight founding Knights of the Garter intended to decorate the medieval chapter house in St George's Chapel. Moreover, the Order of the Garter was itself revived. On St George's Day 1805, twenty-five Knights of the Garter were installed at Windsor, in a magnificent ceremony expressly designed, as one contemporary source remarked, 'to cherish that chivalrous spirit ... which burned in the breasts of our ancestors'.[9]

George III's motives for building a neo-Gothic castle at Kew were primarily aesthetic, but the radicals of the time were quick to recognise its political significance, promptly nicknaming it 'The Bastille'. The revival of the Order of the Garter, on the other hand, was plainly intended as a propaganda tool in the Napoleonic War – 'to fan the flame of loyalty and patriotism', as one contemporary observer put it.[10] And of course chivalric revivalism served the cause of the monarchy itself, re-activating an extensive symbolism of

monarchical authority and tradition. The most spectacular display of
this symbolism was at the coronation of George IV in 1821, at which
everyone from the Privy Councillors to the waiters and ushers wore
specially designed pseudo-Elizabethan costumes. The event culminated in a gigantic mock-medieval banquet in Westminster Hall, the
climax of which occurred when a knight in armour – Dymoke, the
real 'King's Champion' – rode into the hall to re-enact the ceremony
of the Challenge.[11] Here, then, was the official version of the chivalric
revival – patriotic, hierarchical, counter-revolutionary.

If George III and IV were the most lavish patrons of the chivalric
revival, undoubtedly the most influential was Sir Walter Scott. In the
eyes of contemporaries, it was the author of *The Lay of the Last Minstrel*
(1805) and *Marmion* (1808) who was reponsible for bringing chivalry
not just into favour but into fashion. Reviewing *Marmion* for the
Edinburgh Review, Francis Jeffrey observed:

Fine ladies and gentlemen now talk, indeed, of donjons, keeps, tabards,
scutcheons, tressures, caps of maintenance, portcullises, wimples, and we
know not what besides; just as they did, in the days of Dr. Darwin's
popularity, of gnomes, sylphs, oxygen, gossamer, polygynia and poly-
andria.[12]

The popularity of Scott's metrical romances was indeed unprecedented. At a time when the sale of five hundred copies of a poem
would have been counted a modest success, *The Lay of the Last Minstrel*
sold twenty-one thousand copies; *Marmion* was even more popular;
and Scott's third metrical romance, *The Lady of the Lake* (1810), sold
over twenty thousand copies in its first year alone.[13] Despite Jeffrey's
efforts 'to stop the insurrection', Scott also attracted a 'herd of rivals
and imitators', including Margaret Holford's *Wallace; or, the Flight
from Falkirk* (1809), William Stewart Rose's *The Crusade of St. Lewis*
(1810), William Sotheby's *Constance de Castile* (1810), Margaret
Harvey's *The Lay of the Minstrel's Daughter* (1814), and James Hogg's
The Queen's Wake (1814).

That Scott himself was aware of his pre-eminence is made clear in
the introductory epistle to the first canto of *Marmion*, where, in effect,
he addresses the public as a spokesman for the chivalric revival. After
remarking that such illustrious precursors as Spenser, Milton and
Dryden had not scorned the old legends of romance and chivalry, he
defends the attempt of his own generation to revive 'the legendary
lay', in his case by treating the matter of the North:

Warm'd by such names, well may we then,
Though dwindled sons of little men,
Essay to break a feeble lance
In the fair fields of old romance;
Or seek the moated castle's cell,
Where long through talisman and spell,
While tyrants rul'd, and damsels wept,
Thy Genius, Chivalry, hath slept:
There sound the harpings of the North,
Till he awake and sally forth,
On venturous quest to prick again,
In all his arms, with all his train,
Shield, lance, and brand, and plume, and scarf,
Fay, giant, dragon, squire, and dwarf,
And wizard with his wand of might,
And errant maid on palfrey white.
Around the Genius weave their spells,
Pure Love, who scarce his passion tells;
Mystery, half veil'd and half reveal'd;
And Honour, with his spotless shield;
Attention, with fix'd eye; and Fear,
That loves the tale she shrinks to hear;
And gentle Courtesy; and Faith,
Unchallenged by sufferings, time, or death;
And Valour, lion-mettled lord,
Leaning upon his own good sword.

Notwithstanding Scott's admission of the poetic inferiority of his own age ('dwindled sons of little men' etc.), the passage demonstrates, in its fluent adaptation of the idiom of romance and its attractive catalogue of all the themes and formulas of romantic chivalry, just those features that made his poems so popular with the public, and so powerful an influence on the chivalric revival. Scott was not the first modern poet to try to 'break a feeble lance / In the fair fields of old romance', but no one had previously been able to recapture to anything like the same degree the pace and pageantry of medieval chivalric narrative.[14]

Again, the ideological load was considerable. Although Scott denied that his romances were politically motivated, and attempted to disguise his zealous support for the Tory party by adopting the supposedly impartial persona of the 'Border Minstrel', it would be hard to miss what Marlon Ross[15] calls the 'barely submerged' political agenda of *Marmion*, which is to mobilise his British readership for the contemporary war against France, not only by arousing military sentiments with the many descriptions of battle, but also, through the story of the traitorous Marmion, by warning of the dangers resulting from an abandonment of chivalric standards and patriotic loyalties. The connection between chivalry and modern politics is indeed made explicit in the prefatory epistles,[16] where, in a sequence of well-known elegies, he portrays such illustrious war-heroes as Nelson and the Duke of Brunswick in specifically chivalric terms, with the Napoleonic War an exercise in dragon-slaying, consisting not of battles but a sequence of single combats in which each 'champion' pits himself against the 'dragon' Bonaparte. Pitt, too, is commemorated not as a politician but as a modern-day hero of romance, who, in the service of 'Albion' (feminised here as his Queen), perfectly embodied the chivalric virtues of devotion, personal integrity and complete selflessness – an analogy perhaps suggested by Cruikshank's cartoon 'St George and the Dragon or the Glorious Aera of 1798', which depicts Pitt in his prime, seated upon a 'John Bull', triumphing over a three-headed monster representing his political adversaries (plate 4). In Scott's version there is no dragon, but 'pelf', or public money, figures as a temptress whose corrupting charms Pitt has spurned; besides which, he is credited with having successfully deflected the revolutionary energies of the British people (the 'wild mood' of the 'frantic crowd') into the counter-revolutionary war against France, an act of political management which Scott, extending the metaphor of the *preux chevalier*, compares to the controlling of a wild horse.

Yet if the tactical use of such imagery clearly marks a continuation of Burke's anti-Jacobin romance, there are also more complex strategies involved in Scott's recreation of medieval romance, and the political bearing of Scott's conception of chivalry is more ambiguous than it seems. Jeffrey draws attention to this in the review already quoted, when he objects to *Marmion* on the ground that it betrayed the chivalric principle of 'aristocratic superiority' by constantly interrupting the accounts of knightly combat with elaborate descriptions of such things as 'servants' liveries', as if to suggest that the institution of chivalry were not the exclusive preserve of the nobility, but a military culture to which all classes in some way contributed. Such democratic signals may well provide a clue to Scott's enormous popularity as a poet, his achievement having been precisely to tailor the aristocratic genre of romance for a mass readership. As Ross points out, Scott's 'chivalric pose' is thus fraught with ambivalence, in that it reaffirms the 'the mythic harmony and stability of feudal relations' while at the same time subliminally endorsing the altered status of the common man, and expresses the author's 'upper-class nostalgia for patronage' while concealing his actual dependence on a new, specifically bourgeois literary market, one that his own commercial success as a metrical romancer had very much helped to consolidate.[17]

Whether or not this last fact justifies Byron's claim, in 'English Bards and Scotch Reviewers' (1809), that Scott wrote 'for lucre, not for fame', it makes the point that there is an economics as well as a politics of romance in this period, and that the ideology of the chivalric revival is shaped by both. The historical irony of Byron's charge against Scott is, of course, that Byron himself went on to achieve even greater commercial success on 'the fair fields of old romance',[18] beginning with the overnight sensation of the first two cantos of *Childe Harold's Pilgrimage: A Romaunt* (1812). Yet Byron's conception of the genre was in many respects antithetical to Scott's,[19] and his chivalric pose as 'Childe Harold' is a deliberate subversion of the sentimental and prudish idealisations of the chivalric revivalists,[20] and indeed of the original ideals of chivalry. That, at least, is the impression given by the 'Addition to the Preface' to *Childe Harold's Pilgrimage* which Byron wrote in 1813, where he takes issue with criticisms made by George Ellis in a review of the first two cantos which had appeared in the *Quarterly Review*.[21] Ellis had complained that Byron's errant hero was a total anachronism, and a complete stranger to the 'noble spirit of gallantry' inspired by the ancient code of chivalry. On the contrary, Byron replies, the chivalric middle ages 'were the most profligate of all possible centuries', by which standards his own Childe Harold behaved with quite as much 'gallantry' as other knights. Citing (somewhat selectively) the French scholar Sainte-Palaye,[22] he declares that 'The vows of chivalry were no better kept than any vows whatsoever', and mentions Sir Tristrem and Sir Lancelot as examples of celebrated knights who were *sans peur* without being *sans reproche*. Spotless neither, in Byron's eyes, were the courtly ladies 'in whose honour lances were shivered, and knights unhorsed'. In short, chivalry was a sham, one of the 'monstrous mummeries of the middle ages'; and 'Burke need not have regretted that its days are over'.

A rather different impression of the subject is given by the poem itself. The sin-soaked character of Childe Harold is certainly an anti-hero of sorts, but the effect of the characterisation is not simply to debunk the whole chivalric ideal in the manner suggested by Byron's 'Addition to the Preface'. The manifest discrepancies between past and present, ideal and actual, are registered in different ways at different points in the poem, but raw satire is relatively uncommon. A more common feature is nostalgia, and Harold's – later the narrator's – habitual melancholy, insofar as it is not purely con-stitutional, is precisely the result of his thwarted aspirations to the heroic. Moreover, alongside Byron's engaging portrait of dispos-session and disquietude, what also begins to emerge in the course of the poem is a redefined notion of chivalry, in which the old ideals of justice, generosity and compassion for the distressed, have been seriously – if not always successfully – applied to the modern political world. Like the real Lord Byron, whose aristocratic status is mirrored in the persona of the 'Childe', and whose own experiences furnished the outline and many of the details of the poem, Harold practises chivalry in this modern sense through his concern for political justice, his hatred of tyranny, and his willingness to offer support and sympathy for the oppressed peoples of the countries he visits.

Byron's most famous such intervention was of course on behalf of the Greeks, and although the poet's active involvement dates from a later period, it was *Childe Harold's Pilgrimage* that was initially responsible for creating a romantic aura around the cause of Greek nationalism,[23] a fact that will be of great importance when we come to consider Shelley's treatment of the theme in *Laon and Cythna*. Byron's description of the modern Greeks is actually not a very flattering one (he contrasts their degeneracy and apathy under Turkish rule with the 'sublime record' of their classical ancestors), but what appears to have captured the imagination of his readers is Harold's passionate appeal to the 'gallant spirit' of Freedom (II, 73–76), a plea for political self-determination and moral recovery which is partly couched in chivalric terms.

Where the idea of chivalry is explicitly raised in the poem, however, is in connection with the 'romantic Land' of Spain, and it is interesting to observe how this theme is brought to bear upon the complicated political situation of that country around the time the first canto was composed (1809–11). The Spanish episode in *Childe Harold* begins with a stirring evocation of the noble struggles of their Christian ancestors against the Muslims, the centuries of conflict between Cross and Crescent which culminated in the expulsion of the Moors from Granada in 1492. Having resisted the temptation merely to dwell on the 'glorious tale' of past achievements, Harold then turns his gaze to the present situation, the Spanish revolt against the occupying forces of the French which had broken out in 1808 in response to Napoleon's ill-fated decision to replace the Spanish royal family with his brother Joseph Bonaparte. Sheridan had hailed this as the first example of an oppressed nation turning the principles of the Revolution against the French themselves.[24] Byron greets it as a reappearance of the 'ancient goddess' of Chivalry:

> Awake, ye sons of Spain! awake! advance!
> Lo! Chivalry, your ancient goddess, cries,
> But wields not, as of old, her thirsty lance,
> Nor shakes her crimson plumage in the skies:
> Now on the smoke of blazing bolts she flies,
> And speaks in thunder through yon engine's roar:
> In every peal she calls – 'Awake! arise!'
> Say, is her voice more feeble than of yore,
> When her war-song was heard on Andalusia's shore?
>
> (1, stanza 37)

Where Scott and Southey had applied the notion of chivalry to the *British* role in Spain, Byron refers it to the political struggle of the Spaniards themselves: to a nationalist crusade which Byron, like Sheridan, perceived as having been inspired by the libertarian principles of the French Revolution (see, for example, the allusion to the liberty tree at 1, 110, 8).

There is, however, a note of uncertainty expressed in the final lines, which question whether, for all its ardour and fire-power, this recent manifestation of the spirit of chivalry might not be 'more feeble than of yore'. The question is perhaps rhetorical, but there appears to be some doubt as to whether chivalry has really survived the transition from 'thirsty lance' and 'crimson plumage' to 'blazing bolts' and 'engine's roar' – in other words, whether it really has any place at all in the conditions of modern warfare. What follows would seem to confirm this doubt: the goddess of Chivalry is promptly superseded by a grim personification of War, as Byron launches into a diatribe against the empty splendour and destructiveness of battle. The Spanish revolt had rapidly escalated, after the intervention of the British under Wellington, into a full-scale war, and in the poem Harold witnesses the Battle of Talavera, where the 'three potent

nations' met in July 1809. Harold's sympathies of course lie with the
Spanish and (to a lesser extent) the British, but the distinctions
between 'The foe, the victim, and the fond ally' are soon lost in his
macabre sketch of the scene of battle, and his passionate condemnation of the 'Vain Sophistry' of military gain (symptomatically,
this particular conflict was won by the allies, but Wellington was
afterwards unable to face the superior numbers of the French and so
had to retreat to Portugal):

> Three hosts combine to offer sacrifice;
> Three tongues prefer strange orisons on high;
> Three gaudy standards flout the pale blue skies;
> The shouts are France, Spain, Albion, Victory!
> The foe, the victim, and the fond ally
> That fights for all, but ever fights in vain,
> Are met – as if at home they could not die –
> To feed the crow on Talavera's plain,
> And fertilize the field that each pretends to gain.
>
> There shall they rot – Ambition's honour'd fools!
> Yes, Honour decks the turf that wraps their clay!
> Vain Sophistry! in these behold the tools,
> The broken tools, that tyrants cast away
> By myriads, when they dare to pave their way
> With human hearts – to what? – a dream alone.
> Can despots compass aught that hails their sway?
> Or call with truth one span of earth their own,
> Save that wherein at last they crumble bone by bone?
>
> (I, stanzas 41–43)

'Talavera's plain', or the 'glorious field of grief' at Albuera (his next
stop), seem to Harold to represent not just the bloody outcome of
tyrants' ambitions, but also the bloody consequence of the mili-
tarisation of chivalry – whether that of Spain, or of the 'fond ally'
that intervened on its behalf. 'Honour' hardly compensates when
'thousands fall' (I, 44, 4).

Chivalry comes under scrutiny once more when Byron introduces
a distinction between the performance against the French of the
Spanish nobility, and that of the peasantry. As he observes in a
footnote, it was to the treacherous opportunism of Manuel de Godoy,
former prime minister and latterly the Duke of Alcudia (thanks to the
adulterous favouritism of the Queen), that 'the Spaniards universally

impute the ruin of their country'. Nor was this the only example of
'gore-faced Treason' by the aristocracy (I, 48, 8). In Cadiz, the
Marquis of Solano had been killed by the people after refusing to
obey an order to attack the French fleet in May 1808, an act of
treason all the more infamous because Cadiz had been the first city
freed from the Moors and the last to be subdued by the French:
'fallen Chivalry' Byron calls this, in a phrase denoting the betrayal
by the nobility both of its own ancient ideals, and of the modern
chivalric programme of militant nationalism.

Childe Harold, then, can not be read simply as a satire on chivalry.
Even in *Don Juan*, which claims to have turned 'what once was
romantic to burlesque' (IV, 3, 8), we find Byron expressing regret that
his great precursor Cervantes had ridiculed the 'noblest views' of
chivalry, making them 'for mere Fancy's sport a theme creative, / A
jest, a riddle'. Byron's interpretation of chivalry still has a familiar
political resonance:

> Redressing injury, revenging wrong,
>   To aid the damsel and destroy the caitiff,
> Opposing singly the united strong,
>   From foreign yoke to free the helpless native.
>
> (XIII, 10, lines 1–4)

And he may be alluding to the historical events we have been
discussing when he charges Cervantes with having 'demolish'd the
right arm / Of his own country' when he made a nonsense of
'Spain's chivalry' (XIII, 11). However seriously we take this charge (it
was in fact a commonplace by the time Byron was writing[25]), Byron's
treatment of chivalry is neither dismissive nor escapist. Both when
lamenting its historical decline, and when seeking to apply it to a
modern context, he generally affirms the ideal of chivalry, and in so
doing offers an interpretation of its political implications or ob-
ligations which is opposite to that of Burke and Scott.

LEIGH HUNT AND THE ROUND TABLE

Given the British involvement on the Spanish Peninsula, it would not
have been too difficult for contemporary readers of *Childe Harold's
Pilgrimage* to mistake Byron's expressions of support for the Spanish
cause, which were essentially libertarian and democratic in nature,
for patriotic endorsements of the role of the British against the

French. At any rate the political tendencies of the poem did not prevent it from winning celebrity and critical acclaim among that very class of readers whose assumptions and allegiances it implicitly questioned. Those who did detect the democratic note were perhaps reassured by the fact that it was written by an aristocrat; certainly, his social status spared him from the sort of criticisms that were inflicted on other liberal or radical writers of the time. No such indulgence was granted to Leigh Hunt, the son of a lawyer-turned-clergyman, and joint-editor of the liberal journal the *Examiner*. Hunt is an important figure in the revival of romance both for his own contributions to the genre and for his advocacy – as scholar, critic, translator, impresario, or personal friend – of other romancers of the past and present. Of most relevance here, however, is Hunt's adoption of the theme of chivalry in the group of writings known as 'The Round Table'. This was originally a series of essays which appeared under that rubric in the *Examiner* between January 1815 and January 1817, some of which were written by Hunt and some by Hazlitt. The series, with various deletions and additions, was then published in book form under Hazlitt's name, with the same title *The Round Table* (1817).[26]

The collection covers a very wide range of topics, and includes a number of Hazlitt's most famous essays; but it is in some of the early pieces by Leigh Hunt that the chivalric analogy which provides the theme of the series is most fully displayed. In the introductory essay, Hunt informs readers of the magazine 'that we are, literally speaking, a small party of friends, who meet once a week at a Round Table to discuss the merits of a leg of mutton, and of the subjects upon which we are to write'.[27] The impression of ease, connoisseurship and conviviality which this conveys (contrasted by Hunt with the 'solitary and dictatorial manner' of previous essayists) accurately sets the tone for many of his future contributions to the series, and points to a conception of the familiar essay epitomised by a later piece such as 'A Day by the Fire'. At this fanciful domestic reconstruction of the Round Table, Hunt explains that he is to play King Arthur, and recalling a favourite passage from Lydgate, he admits:

I can hardly help fancying that I am putting a triumphant finish to the old prophecy, and feeling in me, under an unexpected but more useful character, the revived spirit of that great British Monarch, who was to return again to light from his subterraneous exile, and repair the Round Table in all its glory ...

Although Hunt is here being characteristically whimsical, or 'facetious' as he preferred to call it, in imagining himself to be the reincarnation of the legendary 'King ycrownid in Fairie', Keats for one came to believe that there was an element of self-delusion in these posturings, commenting in a letter to Benjamin Haydon in May 1817 that 'There is no greater Sin after the 7 deadly than to flatter oneself into an idea of being a great Poet – or one of those beings who are privileged to live out their lives in pursuit of Honour.'[28] A more malicious comment upon Hunt's chivalrous role-playing was made publicly in John Gibson Lockhart's famous article 'On the Cockney School of Poetry' which appeared in the October 1817 issue of *Blackwood's Edinburgh Magazine*. The focus of the attack is not so much Hunt's self-delusion as his presumptuousness, the sheer effrontery of his impersonation of the illustrious King Arthur. That a mere commoner, and moreover the purveyor of a type of poetry that many considered coarse and licentious, should associate himself with the pure aristocratic code of chivalry, was a provocation too great to ignore; and quoting Hunt's introductory remarks on the 'Round Table', Lockhart scornfully reminds his readers of the low origins and parochialism of this new pretender to chivalry, describing him as a 'vulgar man ... perpetually labouring to be genteel'.[29]

Yet whether it was self-delusion, insubordination, or mere playfulness that impelled Hunt to adopt the persona of King Arthur, his interpretation of the chivalric character was not linked exclusively to the notion of personal honour. He explains in the 'Introduction' that in the course of the following essays, the idea of the Round Table, 'and that long train of romantic associations and inspired works connected with it', will sometimes inform not just 'our poetical moments' but also 'our philosophical ... speculations':

for what have the most chivalrous persons been from the earliest ages, but so many moral reformers, who encountered error and corruption with various weapons, who brought down brute force, however gigantic, who carried light into darkness, and liberty among the imprisoned, and dissipated, with some charm or other about them, the illusions of pleasure?[30]

Here Hunt defines the role of 'chivalrous persons' as a public and a political one. While careful – for reasons that will become apparent – to speak only of *moral* reform, it is clear that his agenda is also *political* (for Hunt, as for Shelley, the two are inseparable), for readers of the *Examiner* would have been well aware that 'error and corruption', the use of 'brute force' and of imprisonment, were affairs of state, not merely of individual lives. The timeless themes of chivalric romance to which Hunt alludes, in essence the conflict between right and might, thus become inextricably associated with the long historical struggle for freedom and justice in which the reform movement in Regency England was one more episode. The analogy signals, then, both a political interpretation of the principles of chivalry (and the romance literature connected with it) and a 'chivalrous', or 'romantic', interpretation of the political cause which Leigh Hunt and the *Examiner* were seeking to advance. It is political resistance to this cause, as well as social snobbery, that motivates the attack on Hunt in *Blackwood's*, with its denunciation of the 'extreme moral depravity of the Cockney School'.

I do not intend to trace in detail the application of the chivalric theme in the 'Round Table' essays. In a series of this kind, written over the course of two years, one obviously does not expect rigid consistency of tone or purpose, and it is not surprising to find that many of the essays have very little concern either with chivalry or with moral or political reform. Moreover, major differences of attitude emerge between the two contributors, Hazlitt at one point diverging so far as to take a Burkean line in maintaining that the ideal of chivalry is antithetical to modern notions of intellectual and sexual equality:

The age of chivalry is gone with the improvements in the art of war, which superseded the exercise of personal courage; and the character of a gentleman must disappear with those general refinements in manners, which render the advantages of rank and situation accessible to everyone...

The spirit of chivalrous and romantic love proceeded on the same exclusive principle. It was an enthusiastic adoration, an idolatrous worship paid to sex and beauty. This, even in its blindest excess, was better than the cold indifference and prostituted gallantry of this philosophic age.[31]

Although Hazlitt elsewhere in the 'Round Table' makes clear his political opposition to the author of the *Reflections*, this direct echo of Burke, with its elaboration of Burke's arguments about the incompatibility of chivalry and modern civilisation, hardly assists the project begun by Hunt, of reinterpreting the chivalric code and establishing its moral and political relevance. Likewise, Hazlitt clashes with Hunt over the question of 'the poetical character', Hunt setting store by the fact that the majority of the English poets have displayed 'a feeling for independence' and two of the greatest 'were unequivocally on the side of freedom', Hazlitt remaining deeply sceptical about the psychological origins and political significance of the 'ideal world' or 'perpetual Utopia' inhabited by poets.[32]

The circumstances in which Hunt wrote the first few articles for the 'Round Table' put this whole matter in an intriguing perspective, for the series was started whilst Hunt was in prison serving a two-year sentence for libelling the Prince Regent. Since 3 February, 1813 Hunt had been editing the *Examiner* from inside Horsemonger Lane Gaol, and it was not until 3 February 1815 that he was to obtain his release. Despite the severity of the sentence (which additionally included a fine of a thousand pounds), the fact that he was permitted to continue his journalistic activities indicates the relative leniency of the treatment he received from his gaolers. As we learn from the entertaining account of his imprisonment in his *Autobiography* (1850),[33] arrangements were also made, after an application to the magistrates, for his wife and children to move in with him. Moreover, following his transfer to the prison infirmary, Hunt was provided – to his surprise – not just with his own 'ward' of rooms which he was able to furnish exactly as he wished, but also with a small private garden *en suite*. In the room adjoining the garden he therefore took the opportunity of creating what was at once a pastoral bower and a 'noble room', with its walls papered with a trellis of roses, 'the ceiling painted with clouds and sky', Venetian blinds, bookcases adorned with busts, cut flowers, and a pianoforte: 'Charles Lamb declared that there was no other such room, except in a fairy tale.' Here, or in the garden (a 'miniature piece of horticulture' in which he contrived to have a plot of grass, an abundance of flowers, trellises, and even an apple tree), Hunt received his visitors, read, and wrote – amongst other things, the first few essays of the 'Round Table'.

The conversion of prison to bower (especially once the lover has gained admission) is a familiar motif in romance.[34] Hunt's response to actual captivity incorporates this in a genuine feat of imaginative escapism which eloquently testifies to his ability to inhabit an 'ideal world'. Keats too bears witness to that achievement in his sonnet 'Written on the Day that Mr. Leigh Hunt left Prison'. Reworking Lovelace's famous lines about how 'Stone walls do not a prison make / Nor iron bars a cage', Keats dismisses the suggestion that while shut in prison Hunt 'naught but prison walls did see':

> Ah, no! far happier, nobler was his fate!
> In Spenser's halls he strayed, and bowers fair,
>   Culling enchanted flowers; and he flew
> With daring Milton through the fields of air:
>   To regions of his own his genius true
> Took happy flights.[35]

Keats did not in fact meet Hunt until October 1816, but the allusions to 'bowers fair' and 'enchanted flowers' suggest very strongly that he knew (possibly through Charles Cowden Clarke, a mutual friend) of the fairytale surroundings in which Hunt had served his sentence. At that time strongly under the influence of Hunt's poetry, Keats would also have been keenly aware of Hunt's liking for Spenser[36] and 'daring Milton', predilections which he shared, and which he retained long after outgrowing the kind of romantic verse written by Hunt.

At one level, the idea of 'The Round Table' is simply an extension of the fantasy world created by Hunt during his captivity. In the fifth article in the series he makes the cross-reference himself when he reminds the eager and rather smug correspondent who has offered his services to their noble order that 'by a fortune of war not uncommon to the most powerful Knights of old, the chief of our Round Table has for some time been in the Castle of Dolorous Guard'.[37] Again the tone is playful, but the point of the allegory is that he actually was in prison for pursuing his ideals, 'for showing truth to flattered state'. The article for which Hunt was imprisoned, with its sober truths about the drunken libertine passed off by his flatterers as the 'Glory of the people', was a very real attempt to challenge the dominion of vice and to dissipate the illusions of pleasure (compare *Queen Mab* on 'the fool / Whom courtiers nickname monarch'). As a journalist campaigning for reform against a repressive political establishment, Hunt had indeed carried light into darkness, exposing error and challenging the gigantic force of the state. Quite literally too he had encountered corruption, in the form of two attempts that were made to bribe him to refrain from casting further aspersions on the behaviour of the Prince Regent, the first with the promise of exemption from the prison sentence, the second with the inducement of avoiding the fine. As he records in the *Autobiography*, he declined both, rejecting too an ingenious plan devised by a sympathetic Whig editor of the *Morning Chronicle* which might also have spared him from prison, but would have involved an act of deception, a '*ruse de guerre*', that he was unwilling on principle to commit. Whatever criticisms can be made of Hunt's personal or literary idiosyncrasies, he certainly proved in his capacity as moral and political reformer to have at least some of the traditional attributes of the *preux chevalier*: courage, integrity, and (in Richard Hurd's phrase) 'romantic ideas of justice'.[38]

With Hunt's interpretation of the chivalric character, of what it means to be 'romantic',[39] we have come a long way from Burke, or indeed from Byron. Hunt's adoption of the language of chivalry – again, in deliberate defiance of the reactionary associations it had acquired in other contexts – might also be said to distance him, politically, from the popular radicalism of the time (if no longer an aristocracy, Hunt's new order of chivalry was still obviously the preserve of an educated *élite*). Yet it is worth noting that in an issue of *The Black Dwarf* in 1817 the radical journalist Tom Wooler reaches for the very same metaphor when describing his own arrest and imprisonment on a similar charge of seditious libel. In answer to a letter from 'the Yellow Bonze at Japan', the Black Dwarf ponders the unexpected fame his adventures have brought him, and, abandoning his ordinary persona, proudly declares 'I shall become as notorious as some ancient hero of romance.'[40] The image is not developed, but the fact that one finds such an allusion in one of the most militant popular journals of the time is a measure of the extent to which the language of romance and chivalry had penetrated the political idiom of Regency England. That it remained a fundamentally *unstable* language – a polemical tool that was always susceptible to ironic reversal – is well illustrated by one of the many replies to *The Black Dwarf*, a satirical pamphlet entitled *The Political Quixote; or, The Adventures of the Renowned Don Blackibo Dwarfino, and His Trusty Squire Seditiono; A Romance, in which are Introduced many Popular and Celebrated Political Characters of the Present Day* (1820).[41] Prompted, according to the epigraph on the title page, by 'one of Wooler's *Castles in the Air*, viz. – "The penny subscription is the lever by which the country must be moved and moved effectually"' (another interesting use of the Archimedean formula), George Buxton's 'Romance' turns once again to the theme of Don Quixote in order to mock the crusading idealism of his political opponent and to discredit 'the renowned faction of the Radical Reformers'.

SHELLEY AND CHIVALRY

Shelley was sixteen when *Marmion* was published, and nineteen in the year that saw the first appearance of *Childe Harold's Pilgrimage*. Beginning seriously to read and write at the time when the chivalric revival was at its height, the young Shelley would have encountered the theme in any number of poems, novels, magazines and textbooks – not to mention the *boudoirs* and drawing-rooms of 'fine ladies and gentlemen'. In fact, though, his interest in chivalry appears to date from 1812, and his early correspondence with William Godwin. It is here that we find his first direct references to 'the chivalric age',[42] in each case in response to remarks by Godwin. On both occasions, Shelley confesses his ignorance of the subject but states his earnest intention of making this an area for future enquiry. In his letter of 11 June 1812, he explains in more detail:

I yet know little of the chivalric age, the ancient romances in which are depicted the manners of those times never fell in my way. I have read Southeys Amadis of Gaul & Palmerin of England, but at a time when I was little disposed to philosophize on the manners they describe. – I have also read his Chronicle of the Cid. It is written in a simple & impressive style, & surprised me by the extent of accurate reading evinced by the references. But I read it hastily & and it did not please me so much as it will on a reperusal seasoned by your authority & opinion. (*Letters*, I, 307).

Mary Shelley's editorial note on *Queen Mab*, quoted in the previous chapter, likewise asserts that Shelley was unacquainted at this time with 'the romances and chivalry of the middle ages'; however, he was undoubtedly familiar with the metrical romances of Scott, and the works by Southey that he cites above would have afforded him a detailed impression of the chivalric middle ages.

But it is not difficult to understand why Shelley might have been 'little disposed to philosophize on the manners they describe'. Like many of those who challenged Burke's glorification of the 'age of chivalry' in the 1790s, it is probable that at this point in his life Shelley simply equated 'chivalry' with 'aristocracy', an institution which he professed to find 'vile' in both its ancient and modern forms (*Letters*, I, 151). Of Scott, he wrote that 'the aristocratical tone which his writings assume does not prepossess me in his favour' (*Letters*, I, 98); and he would have known from personal experience the truth of Godwin's claim in *Political Justice* (p. 726) that, far from being a thing of the past, the feudal spirit of the 'age of chivalry' was still manifest in the 'servility' and 'dependence' that continued to mark the relations beteen the social classes, particularly in rural areas such as the one in which Shelley grew up. Writing to Thomas Jefferson Hogg in 1811, he made clear (in Godwinian terms) his belief that the poisonous spirit of deference – or 'obedience' – was inherent in the chivalric code itself: 'I am no admirer of knights their obedience was not founded on reason' (*Letters*, 1, 81). A further reason why Shelley might have resisted the idea of chivalry can be deduced from his critique of the heroic ethos of the classical age (*Letters*, 1, 317), since the argument he uses there about the corrupting effect and destructive consequences of putting 'Honor' before 'virtue' could equally well be applied to the medieval code of honour.

Godwin's opinion on chivalry, however, had altered since the time of *Political Justice*. Always an enthusiastic student of history, in 1803 Godwin had produced a *Life of Geoffrey Chaucer* which presents a surprisingly sympathetic view of the chivalric age. While still condemning the hierarchical and militaristic aspects of the feudal system, he welcomes its decentralisation of power from the state to the family, and acknowledges that one effect of the 'great chain of subordination in the feudal law' is that it 'has generated among and entailed upon us a continual respect to the combinations and affections which bind man to man, and neighbour to neighbour':

The feudal system was the nurse of chivalry, and the parent of romance; and out of these have sprung the principle of modern honour in the best sense of that term, the generosity of disinterested adventure, and the more persevering and successful cultivation of the private affections.[43]

Godwin had conceded in the Preface to *St Leon* (1799) that he had undervalued the 'domestic and private affections' in his original *Enquiry Concerning Political Justice* (1793), an imbalance which he had aimed to redress in the second edition of 1796, and in *St Leon* itself. He now combines the principle of the 'successful cultivation of the private affections' with that of 'the generosity of disinterested adventure' to yield a definition of 'modern honour' that means something other than the mere regard to public appearances, or reputation. It is 'honour' in the latter sense which had been so strikingly exemplified, with disastrous consequences, by the character of Falkland in *Caleb Williams* (1794);[44] and it is the exclusion of that element which helps to explain the shift from his portrayal of 'the poison of chivalry' in *Caleb* to the highly approving account of the legacy of chivalry in the *Life of Chaucer*.

An equally favourable view of chivalry is advanced in an unfinished novel written by Godwin in 1810, in which he celebrates 'the "splendid feelings" which chivalry nourishes beyond any institution ever conceived'.[45] Eight years later, in his *Letter of Advice to a Young American* (1818), Godwin again calls attention to the age of chivalry as a suitable subject of study for a young man learning to be 'independent and generous'. Describing the chivalric period as 'a generous age, though of a very different cast from the best period of ancient history', he recommends by way of introduction Sainte-Palaye's *Mémoires sur l'Ancienne Chevalerie*, Southey's extensively annotated translation of the *Chronicle of the Cid* (1808) and 'Cervantes's admirable romance of Don Quixote'.[46] Chivalry gains further approval later in the work when Godwin turns from the topic of history to that of poetry, and states that 'the great characteristics which distinguish ancient from modern poetry' originate 'in the institutions of chivalry', notably in the importance they assign 'to the female sex'.[47]

Most of Godwin's private letters of advice to the young Shelley have unfortunately been lost, but a passage in his surviving letter of 4 March 1812 shows him – as one would expect – communicating his revised opinion of the chivalric age. Shelley had sent Godwin a copy of his *Address to the Irish People* (1812), and much of the letter is highly critical of the inflammatory tone of the pamphlet, and of Shelley's hasty prescriptions for social change:

One principle that I believe is wanting in you, and in all our too fervent and impetuous reformers, is the thought that almost every institution and form of society is good in its place and in the period of time to which it belongs. How many beautiful and admirable effects grew out of Popery and the monastic institutions in the period when they were in their genuine health and vigour. To them we owe almost all our logic and literature. What excellent effects do we reap, even at this day, from the feudal system and from chivalry![48]

Combining a tribute to chivalry with a plea for restraint, Godwin indeed sounds 'More Burkean than ever', as Peter Marshall comments.[49] Godwin, however, is not setting himself in opposition to political change, but rather reaffirming his belief in the need for *gradual* change. The point of this brief lesson in historical value and social evolution is to overcome Shelley's dismissive, impatient attitude to the past: an attitude, typical of 'fervent and impetuous reformers', which Godwin had always sought to check. On the specific question of chivalry, Godwin's view – as we have seen – is of more recent date, but it results not so much from a revaluation of Burke as from his own further reflections on the theories expounded in *Political Justice*. The passage suggests how much there now is in common between Burke and Godwin on this issue, but it fails to show what separates them – differences which emerge clearly enough from, say, the *Life of Chaucer*. We can of course only conjecture how far Godwin pursued the theme in the lost part of his correspondence with Shelley.

Shelley's wife Harriet believed that Godwin had changed after all, that he had 'grown old and unimpassioned',[50] and lost his political enthusiasm – the 'spirit of romance' he had referred to eleven years previously in his *Thoughts Occasioned by the Perusal of Dr. Parr's Spital Sermon*. Shelley himself was certainly surprised by Godwin's criticisms of his *Address* and the objections to his radical plan for an 'association of philanthropists'. The letters demonstrate that Shelley in turn did not hesitate to argue where he disagreed, nor was he dissuaded by Godwin from continuing with his Irish mission. Yet he did follow Godwin's advice on certain matters, particularly as regards further reading and useful areas of knowledge. One of these areas is 'the chivalric age', references to which almost immediately enter Shelley's writing. Both for the reasons stated by Godwin, and for additional ones to do with his own situation and temperament, chivalry rapidly became a very important theme for Shelley.

The first indication that Shelley had responded to Godwin's comments comes in a letter he wrote to Thomas Hookham on 3 December 1812, from Tanyrallt in North Wales, in which he complains that the gentry in Cambria 'have all the ferocity & despotism of the ancient barons without their dignity & chivalric disdain of shame and danger' (*Letters*, I, 334). Although the judgment he was passing on his Welsh peers was an entirely negative one, what is interesting here is the concession he makes to 'the ancient barons', suggesting that, at the very least, Godwin's comments had alerted him to the beneficial aspects of the institution of chivalry. In another letter sent that same day to Hogg, Shelley writes 'I am clearly aware that the noblest feelings might conduct some few reflecting minds to aristocracy and episcopacy' (*Letters*, I, 335). He cites Hume and Locke as examples, but again it seems to have been Godwin's remarks about the 'excellent effects' of chivalry and 'Popery' which had enabled him to appreciate the positive motives which might lead to such opinions. Without owning to those opinions himself, the fact that Shelley tolerantly cites them here is intended to demonstrate to Hogg the difference between his own political feelings and 'the bigotry of commonplace republicanism, or the violence of faction'.

Shelley picks up this subject with Hogg two months later in his letter of 7 February 1813. Not for the first time in their relationship, Hogg appears to have earned his friend's disapproval by defending a kind of pride which Shelley deemed unreasonable and unworthy:

> The species of Pride which you love to encourage appears to me incapable of bearing the test of Reason. Now do not tell me that Reason is a cold & insensible arbiter. Reason is only an assemblage of our better feelings, passion considered under a peculiar mode of its operation. – This chivalric pride altho of excellent use in an age of vandalism & brutality is unworthy of the nineteenth century. A more elevated spirit has begun to diffuse itself which without deducting from the warmth of love or the constancy of friendship reconciles all private feelings to public utility, & scarce suffers true Passion & true Reason to continue at war. Pride mistakes a desire of being esteemed for that of being really estimable ... Perhaps you will say that my republicanism is proud. it certainly is far removed from pothouse democracy, & knows with what smile to hear the servile applauses of an inconsistent mob. – but tho its cheeks could feel without a blush the hand of insult strike, its soul would shrink neither from the scaffold nor the stake, nor from those deeds & habits which are obnoxious to slaves in power. My republicanism it is true would bear with an aristocracy of chivalry, & refinement, before an aristocracy of commerce & vulgarity, not however from pride but because the one I consider as approaching most nearly to what man ought to be. (*Letters*, I, 352)

There are several important points here. Firstly, in his censure of Hogg's 'chivalric pride' – that which 'mistakes a desire of being esteemed for that of being really estimable' – Shelley in effect applies to chivalry the distinction between honour and virtue which he had earlier made in his remarks to Godwin on the subject of the classical heroism. In this case, though, he strengthens the distinction by introducing on the one hand the word 'pride', and on the other hand (referring to the 'more elevated spirit' which has evolved out of chivalry) the vital phrase: 'reconciles all private feelings to public utility'.

This in itself is a highly significant step because it creates a direct philosophical link – only intimated by Godwin himself – between the utilitarian principle of rational altruism expounded in *Political Justice* and the 'best sense' of the term 'modern honour' as defined above in the *Life of Chaucer*: 'the generosity of disinterested adventure, and the more persevering and successful cultivation of the private affections'. Shelley, however, goes further than this. He talks of an 'aristocracy of chivalry, & refinement…approaching most nearly to what man ought to be'. It is not clear from the context whether by 'aristocracy' Shelley means here a system of political power or simply an *élite* group of men; but in either case the emphasis falls on the notion of 'chivalry, & refinement' as a model of how men 'ought to be'. What is important here is the connection he is making between the political theory of republicanism and the ethical principles of chivalry: between public and private systems of virtue. Having first distinguished what is of genuine value in the idea of chivalry, he has now incorporated it into his own vision of a perfect society.

The theme of the two aristocracies also occurs elsewhere in Shelley's work. The notion that 'aristocracy', though 'vile', is nevertheless preferable to 'commerce', can be found in a number of his early letters. However, it is not until he writes his essay *A Vindication of Natural Diet*, probably in November of 1812, that he begins to speak of commerce as a second form of 'aristocracy' (previously he has tended to think of the matter the other way round, describing 'hereditary accumulation' and 'commercial aggrandizement' as two forms of 'monopoly', neither of which 'can be used as an antidote for the poison of the other'[51]). The passage in which he does so is incorporated virtually unaltered into the Notes to *Queen Mab*, where it serves, as we have seen, to extend his comments in Canto v about the destructive effects of commerce:

Let it ever be remembered, that it is the direct influence of commerce to make the interval between the richest and the poorest man wider and more unconquerable. Let it be remembered, that it is a foe to everything of real worth and excellence in the human character. The odious and disgusting aristocracy of wealth is built upon the ruins of all that is good in chivalry or republicanism (*Poems*, I, 418; compare *Prose Works*, I, 85–86).

Five years later he develops this opposition in his *Address to the People on the Death of the Princess Charlotte* (1817). Here Shelley's argument about the new aristocracy of wealth grows out of a discussion of the national debt,[52] and its effect in producing economic inequality and social division:

It creates a double aristocracy, instead of one which was sufficiently burthensome before, and gives twice as many people the liberty of living in luxury and idleness, on the produce of the industrious and the poor. And it does not give them this because they are more wise and meritorious than the rest, or because their leisure is spent in schemes of public good, or in those exercises of the intellect and the imagination, whose creations ennoble or adorn a country. They are not like the old aristocracy men of pride and honour, *sans peur et sans tache*, but petty piddling slaves who have gained a right to the title of public creditors, either by gambling in the funds, or by subserviency to government, or some other villainous trade. (*Prose Works*, I, 235–36)

This is a passage which has provoked widely divergent reactions among commentators, some regarding it as an example of Shelley at his most irredeemably aristocratic despite his attempt to speak out on behalf of the labouring class, others citing it as proof of his advanced political understanding of contemporary society. Michael Scrivener,[53] for example, finds Shelley's comments on the 'old aristocracy', as distinct from the *nouveaux riches*, both sentimental and inaccurate, claiming that it is mere 'rhetorical duplicity' to heap all the blame for the workers' suffering on the national debt (as William Cobbett had also done). Richard Holmes,[54] on the other hand, maintains that Shelley here identifies the root cause of political oppression, the economic exploitation of the working class by a new, capitalist class who had taken advantage of the growing system of stocks and loans generated by the national debt: it is thus, claims Holmes, 'one of the earliest examples of recognizably "pre-Marxist" analysis to be found in English'.

These positions are not altogether incompatible. Both recognise the fundamentally anti-bourgeois thrust of Shelley's polemic, and Marx himself wrote about the alliance of interests which develops between the workers and the aristocracy at this stage in history, and which gives rise to some of the most vociferous – though ultimately ineffectual – attacks on capitalism. But in considering whether Shelley here falls into Marx's category of 'Feudal Socialist', or speaks as what Donald Reiman calls[55] an 'agrarian reactionary', it is important to realise that the 'old aristocracy' with which he compares the new is not meant to be an historical one. It misses the point to protest that the 'old aristocracy' was probably as immoral as the new: the former point of reference is an idealised one, specifically the ideal expressed in the notion of chivalry. Shelley does not omit to mention that even before the advent of a second aristocracy, the original one was 'sufficiently burthensome', comprised of people 'living in luxury and idleness, on the produce of the industrious and poor'. Those 'men of pride and honour, *sans peur et sans tache*' against whom Shelley measures the 'petty piddling slaves' who form the new capitalist aristocracy, come straight from the pages of Sainte-Palaye and 'the fair fields of old romance'. Far from merely lapsing into sentiment and expressing nostalgia for an aristocratic world that never existed, Shelley is consciously using literary artifice to intensify his attack on the class of people which he correctly identified as the real enemy of social justice. That this is an elaboration not of Godwin's thoughts on the subject, but of *Burke*'s, is a further measure of the complexity of Shelley's response to chivalry, and the artfulness of his polemic.

Shelley returns to the theme of the double aristocracy in *A Philosophical View of Reform* (1819). Although this is plainly a reworking of the earlier passage, there are important differences. The basic contrast is retained, again with the effect of deprecating the financial aristocrats, but his reference to the nobility is now to an historical rather than an ideal one. He states precisely the grounds and limits of his toleration of 'the old aristocracy', which 'has its basis in force' whereas the new one 'has its basis in fraud'. In his depiction of the values and manners connected with the old aristocracy, allusions to chivalry remain, but these too do not pass unqualified:

Instead of one aristocracy, the condition [to] which, in the present state of human affairs, the friends of justice and liberty are willing to subscribe as to an inevitable evil, they [the modern rulers of England] have supplied us with two aristocracies: the one, consisting [of] great land proprietors and merchants who receive and interchange the produce of this country with the produce of other countries; in this, because all other great communities have as yet acquiesced in it, we acquiesce. Connected with the members of [it] is a certain generosity and refinement of manners and opinion which, although neither philosophy nor virtue, has been that acknowledged substitute for them, which at least is a religion which makes respected those venerable names. The other is an aristocracy of attorneys and excisemen and directors and government pensioners, usurers, stockjobbers, country bankers, with their dependents and descendants. These are a set of pelting wretches in whose employment there is nothing to exercise, even to their distortion, the more majestic faculties of the soul. Though at the bottom it is all trick, there is something frank and magnificent in the chivalrous disdain of infamy connected with a gentleman. (*Prose*, p. 245)

If Shelley himself must still be said to speak as one of the landed gentry, he can no longer be accused of being deluded by sentiment as to the true nature and origin of that class. Even the ideals of chivalry to which he alludes as its redeeming feature (insofar as the two are really connected), are now subjected to criticism. This is manifest in his remark about 'the chivalrous disdain of infamy', that 'at the bottom it is all trick' (a comment which recalls his original objections to 'Honor' and 'chivalric pride'). But he expresses reservations too about that 'certain generosity and refinement of manners and opinion' which are also typically defined as 'chivalrous' attributes. While acknowledging their value as a compromise, or 'substitute', these are, he says, 'neither philosophy nor virtue': an exclusion which has some force for Shelley, as *Queen Mab* testifies.

A third area in which Shelley's opinion of chivalry changed concerned its historical influence on the status of women. As we have seen, it was a commonplace of late eighteenth-century historians – reiterated by Burke, Mackintosh and Godwin alike – that the institution of chivalry had 'softened' and 'civilised' the manners and sentiments of the European nations, and helped to distinguish 'the modern from the ancient world'. In his earliest references to chivalry, Shelley appears to reject this view, speaking instead of the 'ferocity and despotism of the ancient barons' and of the 'pride' that the institution fostered. However, by the time he wrote his *Discourse on the Manners of the Ancient Greeks Relative to the Subject of Love* in 1818, he had adopted a much more sympathetic position, on the grounds that the institution of chivalry had raised the status of women, and benefited relations between the sexes:

One of the chief distinctions between the manners of ancient Greece and modern Europe consisted in the regulations and sentiments respecting sexual intercourse. Whether this difference arises from some imperfect influence of the doctrines of Jesus Christ, who alleges the absolute and unconditional equality of all human beings, or from the institutions of chivalry, or from a certain fundamental difference of physical nature existing in the Celts, or from a combination of all or any of these causes acting on each other is a question worthy of investigation. The fact is that the modern Europeans have in this circumstance and in the abolition of slavery made an improvement the most decisive in the regulation of human society; and all the virtue and the wisdom of the Periclean age arose under other institutions in spite of the diminution which personal slavery and the inferiority of women, recognized by law and by opinion, must have produced in the delicacy, the strength, the comprehensiveness, and the accuracy of their conceptions in moral, political, and metaphysical science and perhaps in every other art and science. (*Prose*, pp. 219–20)

Shelley has clearly come a long way from his original position. Yet he has not adopted the view of the Whig historians, for his argument here in fact derives from Schlegel's *Lectures on Dramatic Art and Literature*, which Shelley read in March of 1818. Three years later, in *A Defence of Poetry*, he makes a more complex case:

It was not until the eleventh century that the effects of the poetry of the Christian and Chivalric systems began to manifest themselves...The incorporation of the Celtic nations with the exhausted population of the South, impressed upon it the figure of the poetry existing in their mythology and institutions. The result was a sum of the action and reaction of all the causes included in it; for it may be assumed as a maxim that no nation or religion can supersede any other without incorporating into itself a portion of that which it supersedes. The abolition of personal and domestic slavery, and the emancipation of women from a great part of the degrading restraints of antiquity were among the consequences of these events. (*Poetry and Prose*, p. 496)

Shelley's point about the historical influence of chivalry is reformulated in accordance with one of his main theses in the *Defence* about the effects of the poetry of the 'Celtic nations' (i.e. those north of the Mediterranean) on the 'exhausted population of the South'. He is talking here of 'poetry in its most extended sense', 'the poetry existing in their mythology and institutions'; and his assertion that it contributed to the emancipation of women, and to the abolition of slavery, rests on his prior claim that the poetic principle is the ultimate seed of moral and political renovation. The argument is completed when he goes on to speak of the celebration of love, of 'sexual love' especially, by some of the greatest writers of the 'renovated world':

The true relation borne to each other by the sexes into which the human kind is distributed has become less misunderstood; and if the error which confounded diversity with inequality of the powers of the two sexes has become partially recognized in the opinions and institutions of modern Europe, we owe this great benefit to the worship of which Chivalry was the law, and poets the prophets. (*Poetry and Prose*, pp. 498–99)

Notwithstanding the evils it produced, which he acknowledges but does not discuss, chivalry is finally hailed by Shelley as the 'law' that has governed what he calls the 'religion of love'. At cultural and psychological levels deeper than those examined by eighteenth-century historians, the system of chivalry is seen to have rescued Europe from 'anarchy and darkness', and to have helped to shape the character of the modern world.

We have seen that the notion of chivalry entered into Shelley's thinking on a variety of political, philosophical and literary topics. Yet the idea clearly had a strong personal attraction for him too. This is apparent in the 1813 letter to Hogg already quoted, where the point of Shelley's remark about feeling 'without a blush the hand of insult strike' is not that he lacks a sense of honour – what he elsewhere referred to as 'chivalric disdain of shame' – but rather that he is chivalrous in the best sense, being *sans tache* and therefore impervious to insult. To seek to defend himself in the circumstances described would be to follow the spurious code of honour founded on 'chivalric pride'. On the other hand, Shelley clearly believes himself to be *sans peur*, declaring of his own brand of republicanism that 'its soul would shrink neither from the scaffold nor the stake, nor from those deeds which are obnoxious to slaves in power'. At once an extreme expression of chivalric disdain of danger, and a vow of commitment to the task of making trouble for the government, this nicely captures both the Godwinian 'spirit of romance' which lies at the heart of Shelley's visionary radicalism, and an unGodwinian relish for polemic and political action. It expresses too that urge for martyrdom that we have already encountered in *Queen Mab* and which we shall meet again in *Laon and Cythna*, an interpretation of the chivalric ethos that receives explicit articulation in Shelley's fragmentary 'Treatise on Morals' (? 1816–21), where he states that chivalry was 'founded on the theory of self-sacrifice' (*Prose*, p. 189).

It was not only in his capacity as political reformer, but also in the act of writing itself, that Shelley sometimes liked to think of himself as a modern equivalent of a *preux chevalier*. A good example of this is his letter to Peacock of 15 February 1821, where Shelley adopts the imagery of chivalric combat to announce his intention of composing a reply to *The Four Ages of Poetry*, a copy of which had recently reached him in Pisa:

your anathemas against poetry itself excited me to a sacred rage, or *caloëthes scribendi* of vindicating the insulted Muses. I had the greatest possible desire to break a lance with you, within the lists of a magazine, in honour of my mistress Urania; but God willed that I should be too lazy, and wrested the victory from your hope; since having first unhorsed poetry, and the universal sense of the wisest in all ages, an easy conquest would have remained to you in me, the knight of the shield of shadow and the lance of gossamere. (*Letters*, ɪɪ, 261)

In a colourful figurative application of the conventions of chivalry, Shelley's pictures himself as the Muses' champion, singled out to protect the honour of poetry by entering into a critical duel with Peacock, but compelled to admit that his own indolence, and Quixotic ineffectiveness, would have ensured that the victory go to Peacock. Nonetheless, the reply to Peacock did – very soon – get written, and the idiom of chivalric combat is carried over into Shelley's title: *A Defence of Poetry*. It reappears too, with all the metaphorical inventiveness and humour of the letter, in the passage in the *Defence* where Shelley singles out as the weak spot in Peacock's argument – the omission of 'the effect of the Drama upon life and manners':

For, if I know the knight by the device of his shield, I have only to inscribe Philoctetes or Agamemnon or Othello upon mine to put to flight the giant sophisms which have enchanted him, as the mirror of intolerable light, though on the arm of one of the weakest of the Paladins, could blind and scatter whole armies of necromancers and pagans. (*Poetry and Prose*, p. 490)

Although it makes Shelley's point, this passage stands out stylistically in the *Defence* as a highly coded private joke amidst a public argument. But the imagery itself is very characteristic of Shelley, and there are many other occasions on which he applies chivalric metaphors to the act of creative or critical writing, notably when he adopts the pseudonym 'Elfin Knight' in submitting his 'Hymn to Intellectual Beauty' to the *Examiner* in 1816 (in this case, the *nom de plume* was almost certainly prompted by Hunt's 'Round Table' series, though the poem was eventually published under Shelley's own name); or when he signs himself 'E. K.' on his review of Godwin's novel *Mandeville* published in the *Examiner* on 28 December 1817; or when, in the Dedication to *Laon and Cythna* (published in the same month), Shelley compares himself to 'some victor Knight of Faëry, / Earning bright spoils for her enchanted dome'. Mary herself, the recipient of this compliment, contributed a somewhat more sceptical assessment of Shelley's chivalric prowess by suggesting, in a letter of 7 January 1817, that he was a descendant, or reincarnation, of Don Quixote: 'if that celebrated personage had ever existed except in the brain of Cervantes', she writes, 'I should certainly form a theory of transmigration to prove that you lived in Spain some hundred years before & fought with Windmills'.[56] As we can infer from his letter to Peacock, quoted above, this is a characterisation that evidently appealed to Shelley.

Shelley also liked to imagine himself in the role of chivalric knight in his personal relations with women. The imaginative attraction here was not so much the idea of courtly love itself (although this phenomenon was certainly of interest to Shelley, particularly in its Dantean variety) as the chivalric notion of *service*. Both in his life and writing, there are many manifestations of this recurrent fantasy, beginning with his youthful act of succour for the distressed in rescuing Harriet Westbrook from boarding school, but it finds clearest expression in a letter Shelley wrote in August 1821 during a visit to Ravenna. The letter is addressed to Mary, who remained in Pisa, but the passage in question concerns Teresa Guiccioli, who had extracted from Shelley a promise not to depart from Ravenna until he had persuaded Byron to move with her to Tuscany. In an exuberant piece of self-dramatisation, Shelley interprets this promise as a binding obligation of the kind familiar to the knights of the middle ages:

> Of course being now, by all the laws of knighthood, captive to a ladys request, I shall only be at liberty on *my parole* until Lord Byron is settled at Pisa. I shall reply of course that the *boon* is granted, and that if her lover is reluctant to quit Ravenna after I have made arrangements for receiving him at Pisa, I am bound to place myself in the same situation as now, to assail him with importunities to rejoin her. – Of this there is fortunately no need: and I need not tell you that there is no fear that this chivalric submission of mine to the great general laws of antique courtesy, against which I never rebel, and which is my religion, should interfere with my soon returning & long remaining with you, dear girl. (*Letters*, II, 335)

Again the tone is playful, but there is an element of moral earnestness in Shelley's vow of commitment to 'the general laws of antique courtesy'; for, in effect, this is another version of the claim he made to Elizabeth Hitchener ten years earlier, when he described his own '*true* Religion' to be 'Devotion to Virtue' (*Letters*, I, 186).

According to Hogg's *Life of Shelley* (1851), it was when he and Shelley were reading Ariosto together in the summer of 1813 that Shelley 'discovered that the realms of romance and the intercourse of

Paladins were his own proper, peculiar element'.[57] If Hogg's account
of Shelley's first rapturous response to *Orlando Furioso* is an accurate
one, then we know from one of his own letters that he later came to
revise his opinion when re-reading the poem with Mary soon after
their arrival in Italy in 1818: 'Where is the gentle seriousness', he
asks, 'the delicate sensibility, the calm & sustained energy without
which true greatness cannot be?' (*Letters*, 1, 20). Still, as we have seen,
his admiration for chivalry – a code of behaviour which he often
looked upon as an *embodiment* of 'delicate sensibility' and 'calm &
sustained energy' – was undiminished. It is appropriate, then, that
Hogg in his *Life* should assign to him the fictitious ancestor 'Sir
Guyon de Shelley', 'one of the most famous of the Paladins' and 'the
personal friend, as well as the companion in arms, of Orlando'. For
Sir Guyon de Shelley is evidently a portrait of Percy Bysshe himself:
a very ingenious portrait, inspired as much by Shelley's own poetry
– and, no doubt, by the frequent references to chivalry in his letters
and conversation – as by the chivalric literature to which the
description alludes:

he carried about with him at all times three conchs fastened to the inside of
his shield, tipt respectively with brass, with silver, and with gold. When he
blew the first shell, all giants, however huge, fled before him. When he put
the second to his lips, all spells were broken, all enchantments dissolved; and
when he made the third conch, the golden one, vocal, the law of God was
immediately exalted, and the law of the Devil annulled and abrogated,
wherever the potent sound reached. Some historians affirm, that the third
shell had a still more remarkable effect; that its melting notes instantly
softened the heart of every female, gentle or simple, who heard them, to such
an extent, that it was impossible for her to refuse whatever its owner might
ask. This power was dangerous indeed; but a knight *sans peur* could find
delight only in the society of a lady *sans tache*; in the pure ages of chivalry,
therefore, nothing derogatory to the limpid honour of knights or dames
would ever be required. It is certain that history has not recorded that the
good Sir Guyon ever abused the irresistible potency of his golden horn.
These wondrous conches, or shells, are still remembered in the name, and
borne in the arms, of the several branches of the house of Shelley. Sir Guyon,
we are told, was the personal friend, as well as the companion in arms, of
Orlando, notwithstanding the well-known attachment of the fair Angelica
for the lord of shells; but if the beauty of Sir Guyon was transcendent,
superhuman, and indeed divine, his continence, chastity, purity, and
unsullied, knight-like honour, as the Archbishop of Rheims, Turpin, (who
is never in error) affirms, were such that there could be no place for jealousy
between the gallant friends.[58]

The passage is largely made up of literary references, not only to Spenser and Ariosto, but also, more interestingly, to Wordsworth's recently published *Prelude*, in particular the chivalric passages about Beaupuis in Book IX, and the earlier description of the 'Transcendent, superhuman' strain of Pitt's oratory, to which Wordsworth had applied the metaphor of a 'hero of romance' blowing a magical horn (VII, 536–43). Yet, for all its allusions to other authors, many of the characteristics of Shelley himself, as both man and poet, are encoded in Hogg's description: notably his willingness to confront unjust authority ('giants, however huge'); his power to dispel illusions and to expose the deceptions of his opponents ('all spells were broken, enchantments dissolved'); his Manichean vision of the moral and political world (the 'law of God' versus 'the law of the Devil' – though for Shelley 'God' and 'Devil' were not entities but metaphors); his attractiveness to women; his supposedly angelic countenance, much remarked on by his friends, especially after his death; and finally his 'chastity, purity, and unsullied, knight-like honour', qualities not conventionally associated with Shelley, though repeatedly attested by Hogg, and confirmed by a much finer judge of Shelley's character, Leigh Hunt.[59] However, the playful irony of the passage leaves open other interpretations, and in this it is close to the spirit of Shelley's own, often self-deprecating humour when in knightly role. Indeed it is quite possible that Shelley himself invented Sir Guyon, or that the fictitious ancestor grew out of one of the many nicknames he used during his lifetime; for it is in the playful self-characterisation of the letters, especially after 1817, rather than in his more philosophical contemplation of the theme, that Shelley shows real mastery of the imagery of chivalry and becomes creative within that idiom.

Even more revealing, with regard both to Shelley's chivalrous inclinations and to the whole question of the role of chivalry among the Shelley circle, is Peacock's novel *Melincourt*. Published in early March 1817, just before the Shelleys came to settle at Marlow, it predates the literary scene at Albion House which Peacock went on to satirise in *Nightmare Abbey* (1818). But Shelley was a regular visitor to Peacock's house at Marlow in the preceding months during which *Melincourt* was being written, and it has long been recognised that this novel reflects the intense literary and political dialogue which had existed between the two since 1815 (they had been friends since 1812, having first met through the publisher Thomas Hookham). Although set in modern times and modelled on the novel of manners, its controlling idiom is chivalric romance and the narrative is constructed in the form of a quest, or rather a series of intertwined quests. The question of how chivalry translates into modern terms is thus implicit in the very idea of the novel, but it is also explicitly and repeatedly voiced by the heroine, Anthelia Melincourt, who we are told has been brought up in 'romantic seclusion' by her father, and nourished by the 'splendid visions of chivalry and enchantment' encountered in her reading of the Italian poets of the Renaissance. The first occasion on which this theme is directly addressed is during a conversation between Anthelia and the Honourable Mrs Pinmoney on the subject of a suitable partner for marriage:

ANTHELIA. I would require him to be free in all his thoughts, true in all his words, generous in all his actions – ardent in friendship, enthusiastic in love, disinterested in both – prompt in the conception, and constant in the execution, of benevolent enterprise – the friend of the friendless, the champion of the feeble, the firm opponent of the powerful oppressor – not to be enervated by luxury, nor corrupted by avarice, nor intimidated by tyranny, nor enthralled by superstition – more desirous to distribute wealth than to possess it, to disseminate liberty than to appropriate power, to cheer the heart of sorrow than to dazzle the eyes of folly.

THE HONOURABLE MRS PINMONEY. And do you really expect to find such a knight-errant? The age of chivalry is gone.

ANTHELIA. It is, but its spirit survives. Disinterested benevolence, the mainspring of all that is really admirable in the days of chivalry, will never perish for want of some minds calculated to feel its influence, still less for want of a proper field of exertion. To protect the feeble – to raise the fallen – to liberate the captive – to be the persevering foe of tyrants (whether the great tyrant of an overwhelming empire, the petty tyrant of the fields, or the 'little tyrant of a little corporation'), it is not necessary to wind the bugle before enchanted castles, or to seek adventures in the depths of mountain-caverns and forests of pine: there is no human life but presents sufficient scope to energetic generosity: the field of action, though less splendid in its accompaniments, is not less useful in its results, nor less attractive to a liberal spirit: and I believe it possible to find as true a knight-errant in a brown coat in the nineteenth century, as in a suit of golden armour in the days of Charlemagne.[60]

Though implored by the worldly Mrs Pinmoney to get rid of her 'chivalrous whimsies' and choose a more up-to-date partner (namely her nephew Sir Telegraph Paxarett), Anthelia holds out for a suitable knight-errant, whom Peacock duly provides for her in the person of Mr Sylvan Forester, the hero of the novel – and a barely disguised portrait of Shelley.

In her book *Peacock Displayed: A Satirist in his Context*, Marilyn Butler draws attention to this exchange, and notes that Mrs Pinmoney's remark 'The age of chivalry is gone' is both an allusion to Burke and 'one of the key sentences in *Melincourt*', for the word chivalry 'functions on two quite separate levels' for Peacock, 'as a positive ideal about which he is serious, and as a satiric tool which undercuts his enemies'. This is certainly true, but the evidence of this chapter must qualify her claim that, since Burke, the word 'was naturally part of the vocabulary of conservatives', and that liberals 'were liable to approach the term with scepticism, even ribaldry'.[61] By 1817 the term was as much part of the vocabulary of *liberals* and *radicals* as of that of conservatives, and this had not just been a battle for possession of the *word*, for a debate had taken place over what the notion of 'chivalry' actually entailed. The 'positive ideal' which Peacock describes here is thus hardly the same as the one painted by Burke or Scott; it is much closer to the conception of chivalry expressed in Leigh Hunt's 'Round Table' essays, or to the notion of the chivalric character developed by Shelley. Indeed, the passage brings into focus many of the ideas about a modernised, radicalised chivalry that have been the subject of the preceding pages.

But Peacock does not let the matter rest there. As if to underline the centrality of this theme in the ideological enquiry of the novel, the eighth chapter actually consists of an impromptu symposium on 'The Spirit of Chivalry'. Once again, Anthelia has informed the assembled company of suitors (and supporting cast) that 'the spirit of the age of chivalry, manifested in the forms of modern life, would constitute the only character on which she could fix her affections'. This causes Lord Anophel some consternation (the aristocrats in the novel being the *least* chivalrous characters), and he has to ask his advisers 'what is the spirit of the age of chivalry?' This question elicits a number of answers, including Mr O'Scarum's ridiculous sketch of duelling (an illustration of the *worst* sense of the term 'modern honour'), and Mr Derrydown's fanciful outpouring about being 'a love-lorn minstrel' writing ballads for his 'lady of the lake'. For one of his advisers, however, the 'celebrated poet' Mr Feathernest, sometime author of 'Odes to Truth and Liberty' but now an ardent monarchist on the payroll of the Marquis, the question is a somewhat painful one:

Mr Feathernest was taken by surprise. Since his profitable metamorphosis into an *ami du prince*, he had never dreamed of such a question. It burst upon him like the spectre of his youthful integrity, and he mumbled a half-intelligible reply, about truth and liberty – disinterested benevolence – self-oblivion – heroic devotion to love and honour – protection of the feeble, and subversion of tyranny.

'All the ingredients of a rank Jacobin, Feathernest, 'pon honour!' exclaimed his Lordship.[62]

With panache and humour, Peacock brings together what, for Burke and others, were the two great opposites of the Revolution debate, that of chivalry and that of Jacobinism. This itself is a brilliant satirical move, exposing but also completing an ambiguous train of associations that goes right to the heart of the radical politics of romance. But the satire is even more pointed, because Mr Feathernest, the character who unwittingly reveals the similarity between a chivalric hero and a 'rank Jacobin', is in fact a caricature of Robert Southey, in 1817 the reactionary poet laureate, but in the 1790s the author of poems which themselves radicalised, if they did not quite Jacobinise, the notion of chivalry.

I have said that *Melincourt* was the product of an on-going dialogue between Peacock and Shelley – a dialogue in which we can reasonably infer that the subject of the politics of romance and chivalry must have figured very largely. During the later stages of composition it is probable that Peacock also came into contact with Leigh Hunt, whose great friendship with Shelley dates from December 1816, and whose 'Round Table' series and wide-ranging interests in romance and politics had certainly contributed to the development of Shelley's thoughts on the subject. Hunt's own Italian romance, *The Story of Rimini*, was published in 1816; and under Hunt's influence, Keats had also recently written a number of poems on chivalric themes, including his fragment 'Calidore', based on the Legend of Courtesy in Book VI of *The Faerie Queene*, and his 'Specimen of an Induction to a Poem', which opens with the line 'Lo! I must tell a tale of chivalry.'[63] This signals the compulsion of the theme, imaginative or even literal, since it is known that the group often wrote pieces to each others' specifications, as a form of knightly 'wager' (see *Endymion* versus *Laon and Cythna*). Whether or not Hunt can also be said to have influenced *Melincourt*, or the two other chivalric texts Peacock wrote in 1817 (a poem called *The Round Table, or King Arthur's Feast*,[64] and his unfinished prose satire 'Calidore'), all this points to the existence in 1816–17 of a Romantic cult of chivalry, focused initially on Hunt's circle at Hampstead, and subsequently spreading to the literary scene at Albion House in Marlow, to which not only Peacock and Hunt, but also other chivalric enthusiasts such as Hogg and Godwin were frequent visitors.

1817 was also the year in which Shelley wrote *Laon and Cythna*. Although completely freed from its association with medieval romance, and transformed into a brand of idealism which is explicitly political and philosophical in character, the notion of chivalry is, as we shall see, highly relevant to Shelley's poem, which, like *Melincourt* and *The Story of Rimini*, is partly modelled on the great chivalric narratives of Ariosto, Tasso and Spenser, as well as more recent romances. In this respect, it stands in contrast to *Queen Mab*, which contains no direct reference – except the one already quoted from the Notes – either to the idea of chivalry or to the 'chivalric age'. Nevertheless, the portrait of the 'virtuous man' which is assembled in *Queen Mab*, the man who is taintless, fearless, independent, and resolute even to the point of martyrdom, bears a marked similarity to the notion of the chivalrous character which emerges in Shelley's prose. Just as the author conceives of 'an aristocracy of chivalry, & refinement' approaching close to 'what man ought to be', Mab's vision of the condition of man in a regenerated world highlights his ethical refinement, often in the very language of aristocratic distinction – with words like 'eminent', 'noble', 'lofty', 'glorious', 'privilege'. Moreover, Shelley's image of himself as a chivalrous republican engaged in combat with the forces of unjust authority is paralleled by Mab's picture of 'Some eminent in virtue', the redemptive élite who 'shall start up, / Even in perversest time' (VI, 33–34). One reason why the whole idea of chivalry later became so important for Shelley was that he came to realise that it articulated ethical principles which he had already arrived at by other means.

Finally, with evidence of what I have termed a cult, or counter-cult, of chivalry and romance among the Hampstead–Marlow fraternity in 1816–17, the question arises: how did this combine with what have usually been taken to be the preoccupations of the Hunt–Shelley group at that time, namely Hellenism and Paganism? The romance of *Laon and Cythna*, whose hero and heroine are natives of the North-East Peloponnesus and whose action takes place amidst the ruins of ancient Greece, provides one answer to that question. Another is given, in more amusing fashion, by Peacock's prose fragment 'Calidore'. The setting is a remote tropical island, to which Arthur and the knights of the Round Table are transported by Merlin after being defeated by Mordred, there to await their prophesied return to Britain. Already ensconced on the island, however, is another group of exiles, the pagan gods and goddesses of ancient Greece and Italy, who are also waiting for more auspicious times at home. After some initial confusion, a 'holy alliance' is formed 'between the powers of Olympus and those of Fairyland', in celebration of which 'the whole assembly of Gods, Nymphs, Genii, Fairies, Knights, and Ladies entered at once into the full spirit of festal harmony, feasting, singing and dancing'.[65]

CHAPTER 4

The right road to paradise: Laon and Cythna; or, The Revolution of the Golden City

The wild burst of the French Revolution called out ten thousand corresponding fancies and furies in the human heart; and no department of civil and military life, no branch of science, or region of taste and literature, was untouched or uninfluenced by this general concussion. Not only were politics rhapsodized in the course of that tremendous occurrence, but rhapsodies became political; and in the midst of the gravest ratiocination on the 'universal economy', appeared the strangest vagaries of versification, to answer to the Pindaric flights of some unfledged philosopher in government.

A singular compound of all these qualities is presented in *The Revolt of Islam*.

The Monthly Review, March 1819.

OF ROMANCE AND HISTORY

The most remarkable product of the Romantic cult of chivalry described in the previous chapter was Shelley's revolutionary romance *Laon and Cythna*. Begun in April 1817, it was written, according to Thomas Medwin,[1] as part of a contest between Shelley and Keats by the terms of which each had to produce a narrative poem of four thousand lines within the space of six months. The result, in Keats's case, was *Endymion: A Poetic Romance*, completed by the end of November and published in May of the following year. Shelley's contribution was finished by the end of October and published in December 1817 under the title *Laon and Cythna; or, The Revolution of the Golden City: A Vision of the Nineteenth Century in the Stanza of Spenser*. Because of the publisher's fear of prosecution for seditious or blasphemous libel, it was immediately withdrawn from sale, and reissued two months later in an amended version entitled *The Revolt of Islam: A Poem in Twelve Cantos*.[2]

In neither version does Shelley's poem call itself a 'romance', but the presence of romance is signalled from the start, both by the Spenserian verse form and by the chivalric imagery of the Dedication, where Mary is figured as his 'Queen' and Shelley himself as 'some victor Knight of Faëry, / Earning bright spoils for her inchanted dome'. The 'bright spoils' are the poem itself, the writing of which is compared to a chivalric 'task', an apt metaphor in light of the contest with Keats (a singular impression of the sheer quantity of creative labour involved is given by the numerical calculations that frequently appear in the margins of the manuscript, where Shelley has obviously been working out the number of stanzas he needs to make up the required number of lines[3]). Indeed, Shelley portrays his whole life as a sequence of quests: an idealistic journey along 'the paths of high intent'; a painful search for love and friendship; a succession of struggles against 'tyrants and foes'; an unfinished crusade against 'the Anarch Custom'. In this miniature autobiographical romance, Shelley is at once the minstrel who can 'charm the minds of men to Truth's own sway', and the spiritual warrior who walks forth 'to war among mankind' wearing 'linkèd armour' wrought out of 'forbidden mines of lore'. Above all, his intellectual inspiration has come from Mary's own 'Sire, of an immortal name', William Godwin, whose 'voice came forth' and

> unwonted fears
> Fell on the pale oppressors of our race,
> And Faith, and Custom, and low-thoughted cares,
> Like thunder-stricken dragons, for a space
> Left the torn human heart, their food and dwelling-place.
>
> (Dedication, xiii, lines 5–9)

No longer the dragon but the dragon-slayer, the reviled philosopher of anti-Jacobin polemic has become one of the heroes of Shelley's romance, as has Mary Wollstonecraft, pictured here as the radiant star whose influence ensures that good will prevail. But it is not just the Godwin family to whom the poem is inscribed. During the months that he was composing *Laon and Cythna*, night after night Shelley would read aloud from *The Faerie Queene*;[4] and this prologue, with its 'inchanted dome', its 'Knight of Faëry' and its 'thunder-stricken dragons', is as much an invocation of Spenser as it is a dedication to Mary and her two 'glorious parents'.

Not just the Dedication, but the poem itself is pervaded by the spirit of romance. What Leigh Hunt called 'its air of mysticism and wildness'[5] owes much to the rapid narrative style and exotic texture that it inherits from the romance tradition. 'Wildness' was frequently defined as a hallmark of the genre, in reference both to the tumult of events of which its plots typically consist, and to the characteristic extravagance of its imagery. Such definitions were generally derived from the romances of earlier periods but the formula was equally well illustrated by any number of contemporary works, including the present one. As for Shelley's 'mysticism', there is, as Hunt goes on to stress, a philosophical component to this, but the mystical atmosphere to which he alludes is also partly created by the Oriental setting and the incorporation of Eastern mythology, elements which *Laon and Cythna* also has in common with other Oriental romances of the time.[6] With regard to the plot, *Laon and Cythna* is a romance in the loose sense of being a love story, a 'story of human passion', but also in the more technical sense that it incorporates narrative motifs from earlier romances, either so common as to be conventional to the genre, or deriving from specific precursors. Several of the incidents are clearly based on episodes from *The Faerie Queene*,[7] while others appear to be drawn from Tasso's *Gerusalemme Liberata*,[8] Ariosto's *Orlando Furioso*, Wieland's *Oberon*,[9] and more recent productions such as Landor's *Gebir*, Southey's *Thalaba the Destroyer* and *The Curse of Kehama*,[10] and Byron's *The Corsair*.[11] Most extensive of all are Shelley's borrowings (apparently with the author's consent) from the plot of Peacock's abandoned Oriental romance *Ahrimanes*,[12] in which two lovers endure separation, persecution and imprisonment at the hands of an evil sultan before eventually being reunited in Paradise – the action, as in *Laon and Cythna*, taking place against a backdrop of Zoroastrian mythology.

Yet Shelley has retained much more of the traditional matter of romance than is discernible from the plot. Take, for instance, the theme of enchantment, one of the commonest of all romance motifs. On the face of it, Shelley appears simply to have abandoned the theme: in *Laon and Cythna* there are no enchanters or enchantresses, no spells, no charms, indeed nothing at all, for much the greater part of the narrative, that is obviously magical in character (in a letter, Shelley described the poem, 'with the exception of the first canto & part of the last', as 'a mere human story without the smallest intermixture of supernatural interference'[13]). At a *figurative* level, however, far from being excluded, the theme occurs again and again in the poem. From the start, Cythna is invested, metaphorically, with the power to enchant: we are told how, as a child, she used to sing hymns of Freedom to 'the enchanted waves' (II, xxviii, 9); and how, when she was older, the 'armèd slaves' of tyrants would 'bend beneath the spell / Of that young maiden's speech' (IV, xx, 6–9), her voice being like that of a 'wizard' according to one of Shelley's drafts (Ryan, p. 179), though in the final version this is altered to 'Like music of some minstrel heavenly gifted' (V, xlvi, 1–2). No less potent, in Cythna's eyes at least, is the magic (or anti-magic) power of Laon's voice: his command, she believes, will 'dissolve the world's unquiet trance' (II, xlv, 6); and his egalitarian ideas and freedom songs are 'sweet spells' with which to 'disenchant' the enslaved women of Greece (II, xlii, 5–6). Even the Hermit is, as one reviewer[14] sneeringly observed, 'a sort of good stupid Archimago', his ministrations to Laon being described at one point as 'enchantments' (IV, vii, 3). The same motif also functions as a metaphor for the power of evil; 'Panic' is personified as 'the pale fiend who charms / Strength to forswear her right' (VI, iii, 5–6); and 'Faith' is 'the inchanter's word' which can 'bind all human hearts in its repose abhorred' (IX, xxiii, 8–9). Whether or not, then, Shelley succeeded in eliminating 'supernatural interference' from the action of the poem, the whole spectrum of romantic magic has been displaced into the imagery, and it is here that we see some of the clearest signs of Shelley's deep involvement with the imaginative materials of romance.

Unlike Scott, Southey, Keats and other contemporary romancers, Shelley does not set his story in the remote past or in some fictional land. *Laon and Cythna* is 'A Vision of the Nineteenth Century', and the events take place in Constantinople and modern Greece. There is an important precedent, both for this choice of setting and for the treatment of the theme of Greek nationalism, in the fashionable 'romaunt' of *Childe Harold's Pilgrimage*, and there can be little doubt that Shelley was consciously exploiting the popularity of these themes, and of the Spenserian stanza,[15] as part of his own engagement with the 'public mind' of 1817. But Byron's celebration of the Spanish rebellion against the French (in Canto I of *Childe Harold*), and his appeal to the Greeks to revolt against their Turkish oppressors (in Canto II), are merely single episodes within a much larger narrative, whereas a political revolution is the central action of Shelley's poem, its advent and aftermath occupying eleven of the twelve cantos; and the hero and heroine are not spectators but instigators of that revolution. *Laon and Cythna*, in other words, is a modern quest romance in which political revolution is actually the goal of the quest (although not, as we shall discover, the only or the final goal).

Moreover, although set in the nineteenth century in part of the Ottoman Empire, and plainly intended to reflect and comment on the new spirit of revolutionary nationalism that was spreading through the occupied countries of Europe, the Revolution of the Golden City also bears an unmistakable resemblance to the French Revolution. The very word 'revolution' would automatically have brought to mind the momentous events in France at the end of the previous century – events which, as Ronald Paulson has stated,[16] largely 'created the paradigm of revolution'. A decisive factor in the Revolution of the Golden City is the influence of political theory: this too would have immediately identified it with the French Revolution, 'the only match that ever took place between philosophy and experience' according to Hazlitt's *Life of Holcroft*;[17] or, in the more circumspect formulation of Shelley's Preface, 'one of those manifest-ations of a general state of feeling among civilized mankind, produced by a defect of correspondence between the knowledge existing in society and the improvement, or gradual abolition of political institutions'. Needless to say, many of the theories themselves, the 'Doctrines of human power' (IV, xii, 7) expounded by Laon and Cythna, are also ones specifically associated with the French Revolution (though if we attend to them closely we will see that there are some crucial modifications of the revolutionary philosophy). Even the personal circumstances of the hero and heroine – brother and sister, orphans, and lovers – can be read as an extreme fictional implementation of the revolutionary ideal of *fraternité*, one that has all sorts of parallels in popular French literature of the late eighteenth century[18] (though again Shelley makes careful amendments on the question of sexual equality).

In fact there are numerous allusions to the French Revolution throughout the first half of the poem, ranging from single words and phrases to whole scenes such as the revolutionary festival in Canto v, a poetic reconstruction of the *fêtes de fédération* held on the anniversary of the fall of the Bastille.[19] Yet if there are obvious similarities between the Revolution in France and the Revolution of the Golden City, the differences are equally manifest. The latter is a bloodless revolution created by two individuals, whereas the former arose out of 'a general state of feeling' and was anything but bloodless (in the poem all the violence is transferred to the *counter*-revolutionaries). The revolution in *Laon and Cythna* lasts for just one day, at which point it is overturned by foreign mercenaries acting on behalf of the deposed king. In France, the honeymoon period of the Revolution is generally reckoned to have lasted for two years, from the summer of 1789 until the King's attempted flight to Austria in June 1791; what happened subsequently has been the subject of much controversy, but the French Republic was not suddenly destroyed in a counter-revolutionary coup, and few would now maintain that the Revolution foundered merely because of foreign intervention. Similarly, although there are suggestive parallels between the dark phase of the poem's plot after the counter-revolution and the troubled course of French history in the years that followed the early successes of the Revolution,[20] none of the 'successive tyrannies' that were re-established in France (again, Shelley's formulation) was that of Louis XVI, who, unlike the fictional King Othman, was of course executed, in 1793.

What is at issue, then, is not the fact but the nature of the poem's relation to history. In a letter to a prospective publisher, Shelley describes the poem thus:

> It is in fact a tale illustrative of such a Revolution as might be supposed to take place in an European nation, acted upon by the opinions of what has been called (erroneously as I think) the modern philosophy, & contending with antient notions & the supposed advantage derived from them to those who support them. It is a Revolution of this kind, that is, the *beau ideal* as it were of the French Revolution, but produced by the influence of individual genius, & out of general knowledge. The authors of it are supposed to be my hero & heroine whose names appear in the title. (*Letters*, I, 563–64)

Several critics have discussed this passage, in particular Shelley's claim that *Laon and Cythna* illustrates the *beau idéal* of the French Revolution. Kenneth Cameron[21] saw it as 'an apparent weakness in the logic of the poem' that a revolution which is supposed to be 'the beautiful ideal' should fail half way through it. Paul Dawson[22] raises the same problem, arriving at the view – in line with his general thesis about Shelley's gradualist politics – that 'the conclusions of the poem are, in fact, profoundly anti-revolutonary'. Richard Cronin,[23] however, takes a different tack by arguing that Shelley is using the word 'ideal' in its philosophical sense, and that the poem recreates the *idea* or mental conception of the French Revolution which had existed in the minds of the English radicals of the 1790s. Cronin's argument seems to me broadly correct: the ideal revolution of *Laon and Cythna* begins, at least, with the vision of revolution that Shelley found in the radical literature of the 1790s, notably in the early writings of Southey, Coleridge and Wordsworth. The truth of this will be underlined by the comparisons I shall be making later in this chapter. But the argument needs to be extended to answer Cameron's objection without requiring Dawson's conclusion. For it is in the manner of its failure as well as its initial success that the Revolution of the Golden City reflects what sympathisers believed, or imagined, about the Revolution in France. What made possible the *continued support* of the English radicals for the French Revolution, until late in the 1790s in many cases – that is, despite the September massacres, the declaration of war against Austria, the Terror, and a succession of other disturbing episodes – was the belief that the Revolution was indeed being subverted, as its leaders repeatedly claimed, by counter-revolutionary forces at home and abroad; and that this threat, summed up in the title of Joel Barlow's poem *The Conspiracy of Kings*, justified, or at least explained, France's actions in the Revolutionary War and much of its domestic policy.

This half-truth concerning the conduct of France during the Revolutionary decade becomes the whole truth about the revolution in Shelley's poem, which ends in failure for no other reason than that it falls victim to 'the confederacy of the Rulers of the World'. Similarly, the treacherous behaviour of Shelley's King Othman, who conspires to betray the revolution having just been granted its mercy, presents an image of what many English people believed were the real intentions of Louis XVI, although these were thwarted by his capture at Varennes. Seen in this light, the fact that the Revolution of the Golden City fails almost as soon as it succeeds does not contradict Shelley's claim to have produced an 'ideal' version of the French Revolution, although we will need to look in more detail at the logic of the poem to understand why, and how, it confronts the subject of revolutionary failure.

Let us stay for a moment, however, with Shelley's phrase 'the *beau ideal*'. Translated, this was a term that he was later to use to characterise the whole nature of his poetry as 'beautiful idealisms of moral excellence'.[24] It is also a term that brings us back once again to the notion of *romance*. It is now a central element in our understanding of romance that it presents us with images of the ideal,[25] but this notion was also present in many contemporary definitions of the genre. Walter Scott, for example, used that very phrase when reviewing *Emma* in 1815, in order to differentiate the kind of novel that Jane Austen writes, offering 'a correct and striking representation of all which is daily taking place around', from earlier novels and romances wherein the author 'paints from *le beau idéal*' and presents 'splendid scenes of an imaginary world'.[26] Of all the early romance scholars, Scott seems to have been the most alert to the idealising tendencies of romance, and his account of the evolution of the genre in his 'Essay on Romance' (1824) includes a highly perceptive discussion of the process by which 'real history' was imaginatively transformed into ideal or 'fabulous' history.[27]

Godwin makes a similar distinction the subject of his unpublished essay 'Of Romance & History' (1797), taking the argument one step further to make the point that, paradoxical as it may sound, romance is in many respects more 'real' than history itself:

> The historian is confined to individual incident & individual man, & must hang upon that his invention or conjecture as he can. The writer of romance collects his materials from all sources, experience, report, & the records of human affairs; he then generalizes them; & finally selects, from the various elements & various combinations they afford, those incidents he is best able to portray, & which he judges most calculated to impress the heart & improve the faculties of his readers.[28]

Since historical evidence is often dubious and fragmentary, Godwin concludes that the man of discrimination is more likely to prefer the 'reality of romance' to the 'falseness & impossibility of history'.

It is an argument which would have appealed to Shelley, closely anticipating his own claims about the respective powers of history and poetry in *A Defence of Poetry*, and finding ready illustration in his own poetic practice. For as we have seen, *Laon and Cythna* is not a literal representation of the French Revolution; Shelley has selected and generalised from the facts of history, and turned the 'actual' into the 'ideal'. Instead of writing a history of the Revolution, he has consciously transformed its history into romance. This is not to suggest that the poem was written in accordance with some abstract generic prescription (as the Preface makes clear, Shelley was no respecter of 'the rules of criticism'); nor that Shelley, like Scott, was simply imitating the manner of the old romances. The point is that *Laon and Cythna* is a romance – a *revolutionary* romance – by virtue of its subject-matter as well as its form. Shelley has both revolutionised the structure of romance and romanticised the paradigm of revolution.

REVIVING THE MYTHOLOGY OF REVOLUTION

Childe Harold's Pilgrimage has already been cited as a precedent for *Laon and Cythna* in its conjunction of the form of romance with the theme of political revolution. Shelley's poem may also have been partly inspired by Louvet de Couvray's *Mémoires sur la Révolution Française* (1793), an autobiographical account of the author's precarious life as a fugitive from the Jacobins during the Girondist proscription, and one that, like *Laon and Cythna*, specifically unites the themes of separated lovers and political revolution.[29] Another Girondin autobiography containing a strong element of romance was Honoré Riouffe's *Mémoires d'un détenu, pour servir à l'Histoire de la tyrannie de Robespierre* (1795), which Shelley is listed as having read in 1816.[30]

Even more important, however, is the relationship between *Laon and Cythna* and the 'revolutionary romance' we encountered in the first chapter of this book, for in depicting the '*beau ideal*' of the French Revolution, Shelley was deliberately reviving the political mythology of the 1790s, recreating in numerous ways the figurative association between the notion of romance and the phenomenon of revolution. Indeed, one could say that Shelley's whole poem, both in its action and its imagery, is born of the suggestion that the revolutionary world is a 'country in Romance': an enchanted land of heroes and villains, of transcendent good and supernatural evil, of paradisal bowers and barren wastelands. In Burke's political fairyland it was Burke himself – the defender of kings (or rather queens) and the *ancien régime* – who was the chivalric hero, and the revolutionaries who represented the forces of darkness. But in Shelley's the poles have been reversed, and it is the revolutionaries who are the hero and heroine, and kings and priests who are the evil antagonists.

The significance of this imaginative connection can be seen at once if we compare Wordsworth's description of the 'French Revolution, As It Appeared to Enthusiasts at Its Commencement' (a text which Shelley would almost certainly have known, either from Wordsworth's *Poems* of 1815, or from Coleridge's *Friend*[31]) with Shelley's portrayal of the Revolution of the Golden City as perceived by Laon:

> To hear, to see, to live, was on that morn
> Lethean joy! so that all those assembled
> Cast off their memories of the past outworn;
> Two only bosoms with their own life trembled,

> And mine was one, – and we had both dissembled;
> So with a beating heart I went, and one,
> Who having much, covets yet more, resembled;
> A lost and dear possession, which not won,
> He walks in lonely gloom beneath the noonday sun.   (v, xlii)

The first point to note is that the exultant opening of this stanza is undoubtedly an echo of Wordsworth's famous proclamation 'Bliss was it in that dawn to be alive, / But to be young was very heaven!' Notice too that Wordsworth's metaphorical dawn has become an actual dawn in the chronology of Shelley's poem, underlining the point that what Shelley is imitating is not so much the actual as the imaginative history of the French Revolution. But the comparison can be pressed further. We established earlier that Wordsworth's description is in fact ambivalent: while appearing to celebrate, and to participate in, the 'hope and joy' occasioned by the events in France, the passage carries too the disturbing suggestion that the 'pleasant exercise' of the enthusiasts was a delusion, and that the earthly paradise promised by the Revolution and its 'prime enchanter' Reason was a *false* paradise – one whose bliss, like Acrasia's in *The Faerie Queene*, would be 'turn'd to balefulnesse'.

Interestingly, the description of the revolutionary dawn in *Laon and Cythna* is also double-edged. Take, for instance, the phrase 'Lethean joy'. In classical mythology, those who drank the waters of Lethe would forget whatever they had done, seen, or heard (the Greek word means 'oblivion'). For Shelley, 'Lethean joy' is thus a strikingly apt metaphor for the rapturous excitement (in Wordsworth's term, 'enthusiasm') of revolution, for a transformational joy so powerful 'that all those assembled / Cast off their memories of the past outworn'. The image assumes a very different complexion, however, as soon as we recall that the river of Lethe was in fact one of the rivers of *Hell*. When Shelley alludes to Lethe for a second time in the same poem, it is to describe the 'hell on earth' that was created by the counter-revolution, a time of 'Faith, and Plague, and Slaughter, / A ghastly brood; conceived of Lethe's sullen water' (x, xvii, 8–9). Lurking within the phrase 'Lethean joy', then, is the suggestion that there is something ominous in the delirious joy of the Greek revolutionaries.[32]

More worrying still is another discordant note which is sustained throughout the whole scene. On the eve of the great Festival of Equality, far from resting peacefully in the knowledge that the revolution he had long sought had now come to fruition, Laon recalls that he spent a sleepless night thinking of Laone 'with hopes that make / The flood recede from which their thirst they seek to slake' (v, xxxvii, 8–9), a bizarre metaphor of frustrated desire probably derived from Southey's *Curse of Kehama* (the ultimate source being the classical myth of Tantalus). If such resonances are largely relieved by the subsequent image of drinking hopes from the 'purple fountains' of dawn, a troubling undertone remains in that they are hopes 'which make the spirit quail' (v, xxxviii, 1–2). This anxiety is restated in the stanza already quoted, which contrasts the all-consuming joy of the rest of the crowd with the trembling bosom and heavy heart of Laon, ending with a line almost antithetical in mood to its opening: 'He walks in lonely gloom beneath the noonday sun' (v, xlii, 9). Even more alarming is the contrast presented a few stanzas later during the festival rites, between the rapturous acclamations of the crowd and the 'fevered cheeks' and 'troubled mind' of Laon, who 'blind / And silent, as a breathing corpse did fare' (v, xlv, 6–9).

The immediate explanation in the plot for these odd discrepancies of mood is that, although the revolution has at last been achieved, Laon has not yet been reunited with Cythna: the political narrative has reached its climax, but the love story has not. Indeed Laon is still uncertain at this stage whether the young revolutionary named Laone of whom the Hermit had often spoken during his convalescence is one and the same as his sister Cythna, whom he had previously believed to be dead. But why should Shelley have so structured his poem as to counterpoint, at this decisive moment, its two principal themes, the progress of love and the progress of revolution? The issue may perhaps be clarified if we return to the comparison with Wordsworth's description of the French Revolution. Wordsworth, writing in 1804, was able to express both the early aspirations of his generation and the subsequent disillusionment by adopting the ambivalent language of romance. As we see, Shelley's version is also ambivalent, but for a different reason: because it reveals an anxious 'hope' in excess of the present 'joy', Laon's tense anticipation of a personal fulfilment in love beyond the communal fulfilment in revolution. The full significance of the difference between the two accounts will emerge later; what one can say already is that Shelley, by offsetting the private against the public plot, and deferring the climax of the former whilst celebrating that of the latter, manages to avoid the unwelcome implication of Wordsworth's poem that the enthusiasts' bliss was as specious as it was complete.

This is not to suggest that Laon, who 'having much, covets yet more', is by his inordinate desire somehow responsible for the ensuing collapse of the Revolution of the Golden City; rather that Shelley wants to direct the reader's attention towards a goal beyond the outcome of the Revolution. With that qualification, there is meanwhile an exuberant celebration of the revolution both in the action and in the poetic language of Canto v. First there is the 'glorious pageant' of the crowds swarming from their encampment on the plain into the liberated city (a scene which combines the pageantry of chivalric romance with that of the French Revolution). Then there is the marvellous spectacle next morning of the festivities beneath the Altar of the Federation. The lyrical energies of the canto are finally gathered in Laone's ceremonial Ode to Equality, which scorns the religious frauds of the overthrown monarchy and praises the moral and political ideals that have replaced them. In a characteristically Shelleyan phrase, the dawn of the revolution is proclaimed 'The dawn of mind' (4, 13).

The triumph, however, is short-lived. That very evening 'none knew whence or why, / Disquiet on the multitudes did fall' (vi, ii, 2–3). Amidst the general panic, it soon emerges that a massive counter-attack has been mounted by Othman's allies. Though abrupt, this reversal in the fortunes of the revolution is perhaps not entirely unexpected after the fitful progress to victory in Canto v. After all, the revolution had almost failed two nights before, during the clandestine assault by the 'false murderers' of the *ancien régime* to whom the insurgents had earlier granted mercy; and the subsequent acts of revenge by the insurgents themselves had also threatened the moral victory of the revolution, as Laon points out when he intervenes to uphold the principles of fraternity and peace. What *is* surprising, however, is that the deferred climax of the love story should now take place, immediately after the most ghastly battle scenes in which the 'despot's bloodhounds' not only succeed in crushing the revolution, but, with a 'gluttony of death', in steadily slaughtering almost all the revolutionaries, including the Hermit and the childhood friend with whom Laon has been recently reunited. Laon alone survives, thanks to the timely intervention of Laone, who appears 'like to an Angel, robed in white' (vi, xix, 6) on a gigantic black horse, plucks him out of 'the grasp of bloody hands', and rushes him off to a lonely, lovely

ruin in the hills by the sea. And before the corpses are cold on the
battlefield, Laon and Cythna (for yes, it *is* her) are hot in one
another's arms on a bed of leaves. This, I say, is surprising. Yet it does
not offend the logic of Shelley's poem, and to understand why, this
pivotal sequence must be carefully situated within the design of the
whole.

AN EXPERIMENT ON THE PUBLIC MIND

Before we can make sense of the deferred climax in Canto VI, we must
therefore ask the question: why in the first place is there a love story
in this political poem? A preliminary answer to that question can in
fact be found in the Preface, where Shelley implies a number of
connections between the *purpose* of the poem and the *plot*. *Laon and
Cythna* is introduced as

> an experiment on the temper of the public mind, as to how far a thirst for a
> happier condition of moral and political society survives, among the
> enlightened and refined, the tempests which have shaken the age in which
> we live. I have sought to enlist the harmony of metrical language, the
> etherial combinations of the fancy, the rapid and subtle transitions of
> human passion, all those elements which essentially compose a Poem, in the
> cause of a liberal and comprehensive morality, and in the view of kindling
> within the bosoms of my readers a virtuous enthusiasm for those doctrines of
> liberty and justice, that faith and hope in something good, which neither
> violence, nor misrepresentation, nor prejudice, can ever totally extinguish
> among mankind.

As becomes clear from the remarks that follow, Shelley's 'experiment'
is directed at a generation and class of readers whose political faith
had been first raised and then shattered by the events of the French
Revolution, and who, in his opinion, had been 'morally ruined' as a
result of having witnessed what appeared to be 'the melancholy
desolation of all their cherished hopes'. Yet it is those very events that
are mirrored – in an intensified and fictionalised form – in the story
of the Revolution of the Golden City. Obviously Shelley could not
expect to achieve his professed aim of rekindling the 'virtuous
enthusiasm' of his readers simply by telling the story of how another
idealistic revolution was defeated. The poem requires a dynamic of
redemption or transcendence. A 'story of human passion' is therefore
superimposed upon the revolutionary narrative, with the intention of
shifting the reader's sympathies from the public events themselves
onto the fate of the hero and heroine, whose own political faith is *not*

extinguished by the disasters they encounter, and whose love for one another triumphs at the very point at which the revolution fails. The idea of Shelley's 'experiment' is that a similar psychological uplift is achieved through the experience of *reading the poem*.[33] The disillusioned enthusiast of 1817 is supposed to be able to overcome the trauma of the French Revolution by confronting the catastrophe of the Revolution of the Golden City while identifying primarily with the fortunes and feelings of Laon and Cythna.

This much can be readily deduced. A more subtle point, however, is made by the Preface, indicating a much closer interaction of the two main themes. Shelley begins his abstract of the plot by stating that the poem is 'a succession of pictures illustrating the growth and progress of individual mind aspiring after excellence, and devoted to the love of mankind; its influence in refining and making pure the most daring and uncommon impulses of the imagination, the understanding, and the senses'. The individuals in question are clearly Laon and Cythna; what these 'daring and uncommon impulses' are is not specified, but we can take it that they include the thoughts and feelings associated with their incestuous love affair. One implication of Shelley's statement, then, is that Laon and Cythna's political idealism purifies the love between them. But the interaction is genuinely reciprocal, for is it not equally the case that their love for one another helps to refine (and define) their political ideals? And, moreover, that their actions as well as their aspirations play a part in this process of development?

This allows us to identify the essential structure of the poem as a sequence of episodes designed to test and refine the desires and ideals of the central characters. The 'moving and romantic adventures' that diversify the plot do so not merely to vary and prolong its excitements, but also to purify and perfect the hero and heroine. Such a description has two implications for our understanding of Shelley's composition. Firstly, in assigning priority to the story of Laon and Cythna, and regarding the Revolution of the Golden City as an episode within this story, it highlights an underlying unity to the poem which cannot be fully visualised through a model which separates the love story from the political narrative, however useful that model may be in other respects. An analogy can be drawn here with the design of *The Prelude*, which is in part a history of the French Revolution, but, as Karl Kroeber observes, one that Wordsworth subordinates to his autobiography:

The mighty events of contemporary history are presented only as they appear to, and exert influence upon, the life of a private individual ... the organization of the poem is founded on a continuous and systematic dialectic between public and private affairs, between social developments and personal growth, between the objective drama of political events and the subjective drama of psychological change.[34]

Laon and Cythna is neither an historical poem nor an autobiography, but at times it displays a very similar dialectic, and Wordsworth's more sustained achievement in this mode can help us to appreciate Shelley's attempt at comparable effects.

It is highly significant, therefore, that the very phrase in the Preface by which Shelley draws attention to the psychological drama in *Laon and Cythna* – his claim that the poem is to illustrate 'the growth and progress of individual mind aspiring after excellence' – actually echoes Wordsworth's reference to his unpublished auto-biography in the Preface to *The Excursion* (1814). Although, according to Mary,[35] 'much disappointed' by *The Excursion* itself, Shelley seems to have been profoundly impressed by Wordsworth's allusion to the existence of a 'preparatory poem' in which he had undertaken 'to record, in verse, the origin and progress of his own powers', to 'take a review of his own mind, and examine how far Nature and Education had qualified him for such employment'.[36] The extent to which *Laon and Cythna* itself is a self-examination of this kind remains a matter for conjecture,[37] but it is clear that Shelley's own 'preparatory poem', the Dedication, is a sort of *Prelude*-in-miniature, charting the origin and progress of the poet's powers. So too Shelley's prose Preface, which contains, in addition to the passages already quoted, a long paragraph about the 'education peculiarly fitted for a Poet' in which Shelley endeavours to show that the circumstances of his own 'accidental education', although very different to Wordsworth's, had been equally 'favourable to this ambition'.

We should also be aware of the parallels between *Laon and Cythna* and *The Excursion* itself. For the latter too is an experiment on the temper of the public mind, in which Wordsworth confronts the trauma of the French Revolution and proposes a remedy for the 'languor and depression of mind'[38] that had succeeeded the joyous optimism of the early 1790s. It was partly in response to *The Excursion*, with its sombre reflections on the Revolutionary experience, and its pious endorsement of 'the great truths of Religion' as the only adequate foundation for a life of peace and happiness, that Shelley wrote his own 'Vision of the Nineteenth Century';[39] and the 'liberal and comprehensive morality' enshrined in *Laon and Cythna* may be understood as a progressive alternative to Wordsworth's reactionary prescription for correcting the despondency of those who had lived through the 'tempests' of the last twenty-five years.

The second major implication of my description of the design of *Laon and Cythna* is that it reveals the teleological core of the poem to be that of Spenserian romance. In the statement from Shelley's Preface which I have just linked with Wordsworth, there is, in addition, an echo of Spenser's famous remark that the purpose of *The Faerie Queene* was 'to fashion a gentleman or noble person in vertuous and gentle discipline',[40] an aim that can be identified with the vision of an ideal prince which extends over the whole poem and provides its allegorical structure.[41] The Romantic revival of romance is concerned at its deepest level with the recreation, and modification, of Spenser's vision of the ideal man. This is manifestly true of, say, Blake's visionary romances or Wordsworth's *Prelude*, but even Byron has been credited with similar ambitions in his 'romaunt' of *Childe Harold's Pilgrimage*, whose ethos, according to Michael Vicario,[42] is explained by two lines from one of the poem's acknowledged forebears, *The Castle of Indolence*: 'Through endless states of being, still more near / To bliss approaching, and perfection clear'. What distinguishes Romantic transformations of romance is their internalisation of the quest for 'bliss'. The search for a perfect state of being, or a restored paradise, may begin in the external world, but it ends within 'the individual Mind': such is the implicit claim of poems like *Childe Harold's Pilgrimage* and *The Prelude*, and the explicit argument of Wordsworth's great 'Prospectus' to *The Recluse*. What I will attempt to demonstrate is that *Laon and Cythna* too is a visionary, internalised romance of this kind; indeed one that contains, in a crude form, an entire paradigm of the generic phenomenon outlined by Harold Bloom, the very theme of the poem being the fate of apocalyptic hope, and its plot a delineation of both the external and the internal phases of the paradisal quest.

In *The Faerie Queene*, it is not through the quest of any single knight but through the allegory as a whole that the total vision of the virtuous man emerges, Spenser having originally intended to devote one book to each of the twelve 'private moral vertues' treated in Aristotle's *Ethics*. Shelley modifies this ethical scheme in two important ways. Firstly, while not entirely dispensing with the device of allegory, he represents the fashioning of this ideal man more naturalistically, as 'the growth and progress of individual mind aspiring after excellence'. Laon resembles the knights in *The Faerie Queene* and the old romances of chivalry in that he aspires to excellence of conduct, to personal perfection; but in other respects he is unmistakably a hero of modern, internalised romance. If lacking the full 'burden of consciousness' that is the hallmark of the true Romantic poet-hero,[43] Laon has a psychological fullness, a complexity of interior life, that means he is far removed from the two-dimensional heroes of medieval romance or Spenserian allegory.

Secondly, Shelley secularises and politicises Spenser's ethical system. The 'vertuous and gentle discipline' exercised in *Laon and Cythna* is essentially the same as the one propounded by *Queen Mab*, and the presiding vision is again not of an ideal prince but of an ideal revolutionary. The fact that Shelley's phrase 'a liberal and comprehensive morality' comes more or less straight out of *Political Justice*[44] underlines the point that his conception of virtue is still fundamentally Godwinian, although there is an important new emphasis on the notion of *trial* (as in Milton's famous argument in *Areopagitica* that 'that which purifies us is triall, and triall is by what is contrary'[45]). Laon and Cythna, then, do not only aspire to *private* excellence: they are 'devoted to the love of mankind', consciously striving to make their own revolutionary ideals prevail in the public world. Shelley's remodelling of chivalry, in other words, entails a commitment to perfectibility in the political as well as the personal sphere.

A third major point about the ethical scheme of *Laon and Cythna* – representing another crucial extension of the politics of romance – is that Shelley assigns equal importance to the two sexes. In *Queen Mab*, we hear only of 'the *man* of virtuous soul' (despite the fact that the two main characters in the poem are female), but the 'liberal and comprehensive morality' of *Laon and Cythna* emphatically includes the *woman* of virtue. There are indeed *two* quests for perfection, *two* narratives of moral and psychological growth: that of Laon and that of Cythna. Although analogous in many respects, and closely intertwined by the circumstances of the plot, the two narratives are clearly differentiated from one another, and the poem cannot be properly interpreted without taking those differences into account. I will therefore deal with the two quests separately, in the order in which we encounter them in the poem itself.

LAON'S QUEST: POLITICS, LOVE, VIRTUE

The focus of the first half of the poem is on Laon's quest. The vision that initiates it occurs early in Canto II when his idealistic 'impulses' take the form of a messianic vocation to deliver from tyranny the 'withered' land of Argolis, and to restore the just and free state so compellingly described in Greek tradition as 'the wondrous fame / Of the past world', whose power is imprinted upon the ancient fragments and ruins that surround him. In a typical Shelleyan scene, Laon learns to read the 'language' of the ruins, and is filled not with nostalgia for the glory of the past but with a sense of possibility for the future:

> Such man has been, and such may yet become!
> Aye, wiser, greater, gentler, even than they
> Who on the fragments of yon shattered dome
> Have stamped the sign of power ...   (II, xii, lines 1–4)

These idealistic longings rapidly translate into revolutionary intentions, as Laon sets himself the task of rousing his kinsmen to rebel against their Turkish oppressors:

> It must be so – I will arise and waken
> The multitude, and like a sulphurous hill,
> Which on a sudden from its snows has shaken
> The swoon of ages, it shall burst and fill
> The world with cleansing fire: it must, it will –
> It may not be restrained! – and who shall stand
> Amid the rocking earthquake steadfast still,
> But Laon? on high Freedom's desart land
> A tower whose marble walls the leaguèd storms withstand! (II, xiv)

Shelley's application of the revolutionary metaphor of the volcano, here and elsewhere, has been justly admired.[46] There is, however, something unsettling about this stanza. Dawson comments that 'we are meant to detect a certain overweening excess of optimism in Laon's volcanic utterance'.[47] But the problem is perhaps not so much a matter of optimism as of self-confidence: there is *too much self* in Laon's confidence, an element even of self-glorification. At any rate, Laon is immediately chastened by what he recalls almost as a moment of conversion from this state of unbridled heroic yearning into one of steady determination:

> One summer night, in commune with the hope
> Thus deeply fed, amid those ruins grey

I watched, beneath the dark sky's starry cope;
And ever from that hour upon me lay
The burthen of this hope, and night or day,
In vision or in dream, clove to my breast:
Among mankind, or when gone far away
To the lone shores and mountains, 'twas a guest
Which followed where I fled, and watched when I did rest. (II, xv)

That Laon *has* been chastened by the experience is not explicit – as it would be in a Wordsworthian 'admonishment' scene – but the transitions of tone and thought between stanzas xiv and xv surely imply this. Laon's sense of his mission is appreciably deepened and refined by his perception of the 'burthen of hope', his recognition that hope is a responsibility, indeed an unyielding obligation that is like some mysterious presence always watching over him (or even, as the wording permits, like some inescapable pursuer 'Which followed where I fled'). Chastened or not, Laon's confidence is soon afterwards put directly to the test by the apostasy and deceit of his best friend (the person whom he calls 'my own heart's brother'), and by the consequent temptation to cynicism or to the ultimate 'dark respite' of suicide (II, xvii–xix). This latter episode is left largely unexplained – deliberately, since it is later revealed to be a misunderstanding rather than a betrayal – but it is obviously supposed to represent an important trial for Laon, which he survives with renewed faith in his 'great aim'. Already, then, a pattern is emerging of psychological growth based on the principle of testing and refining.

Having instigated Laon's political quest, by envisioning its revolutionary goal and equipping his hero 'With words which were weapons' (stanza xx being a reworking of a traditional arming scene from romance or epic), Shelley then starts to develop the love story. The details concerning the growing relationship between Laon and Cythna need no rehearsal here, but it is important to realise the relationship that is set up between the private and the public themes. In conventional romances, erotic love is usually presented as a diversion from the object of the quest, and there is a constant tension between active duty and passive pleasure. But here that tension does not exist: Shelley makes it clear from the start that sexual love is to be a central element in the utopia which the Revolution of the Golden City is intended to create. Within the actual story, Cythna is a solace, a soul-mate, a sounding-board, and then an accomplice for Laon, before her brother comes to feel for her as a lover. Their intimacy grows out of empathy and shared political commitment. It is because, as Laon recalls, 'communion with this purest being / Kindled intenser zeal' (II, xxxii, 1–2) that the communion itself became more intense: Laon's millenarian zeal enriches and is enriched by his love for his sister. In this respect, the political motif and the erotic motif are closely interdependent, and point towards the same goal.

Already by the end of Canto II, however, Cythna has a premonition of a very different union, or reunion, that might take place between her and Laon:

> 'We part to meet again – but yon blue waste,
> Yon desert wide and deep holds no recess,
> Within whose happy silence, thus embraced
> We might survive all ills in one caress:
> Nor doth yon grave – I fear 'tis passionless –
> Nor yon cold vacant Heaven: – we meet again
> Within the minds of men, whose lips shall bless
> Our memory, and whose hopes its light retain
> When these dissevered bones are trodden in the plain.' (II, xlviii)

In the event, after the public defeat in Canto VI, it will be in just such a 'recess' that Laon and Cythna 'survive all ills in one caress'; and then again, after their death in Canto XII, in a 'Heaven' which is anything but 'cold' and 'vacant'. The prophecy is inaccurate, but Cythna's remarks do foreshadow, in some degree, the misfortunes that are to follow. What is more, they proclaim a confidence in the ability of the lovers to transcend ('Within the minds of men', at least) the worst possible outcome of their political venture. To this extent, the dynamic of the love story is signalled as independent from that of the revolutionary narrative.

The separation Cythna expects does, almost immediately, take place: not in the way she foresees, with Laon departing from her to carry out his political mission, but with her own sudden abduction. Cythna is seized by Turkish soldiers and taken off to Othman's seraglio, and Laon is arrested for putting up a violent resistance. The two are not properly reunited until after the revolution. Before their separation, however, Laon has a 'strange vision' in a dream of 'Cythna's pure and radiant self', a sight 'so divine to me, / That, if I loved before, now love was agony' (III, iii, 7–9). Laon's vision is indeed 'strange', raising problems of interpretation that will apply to the whole sequence of dreams in Canto III. What is indisputable is that its *effect* is to create a level of anticipation within the love story that corresponds to the one produced within the political story by Laon's vision of revolution. In terms of the functional structure of the poem, the episode can therefore be said to complete a basic alignment of expectations, requiring, and preparing for, the consummation scene which will occur in Canto vi.

If we seek in the rest of Canto iii (that is, after Laon's arrest) the moral and psychological dynamic that we have discerned in Canto ii, we are immediately faced with the question: how is Laon's mind 'refined' and 'purified' by the experience of imprisonment and madness, and by the macabre visions that punctuate that experience? This question is a difficult one, not only because the material presents direct problems of interpretation, but also because it raises the more fundamental issue: why is Laon in need of improvement? One answer often given is that Laon's suffering is of a penitential nature, resulting from his actions during the dawn raid when he killed three of the Turkish soldiers who had come to take Cythna away. This reading is certainly consistent with Shelley's pacifist inclinations, and can be supported by an analogy with *Prometheus Unbound*, where Prometheus's sufferings in Act i are partly intended to redeem the hatred he had once displayed in his 'sufferer's curse'. Yet the same analogy could also be used to make the case that Laon's suffering is largely innocent and vicarious, an argument that is reinforced by the notion of martyrdom which is explicitly developed later in *Laon and Cythna*. A third possibility, which acknowledges the irrelevance of a theology of sin and expiation, is to read Laon's life story as a kind of *Bildungsroman* in which the passage from innocence to experience involves a subjection to undeserved but inevitable suffering.

A similar divergence of opinion exists about the meaning of particular aspects of Laon's experience, such as his vision of the four corpses in stanzas xxv and xxvi. Most critics have accepted E. B. Murray's suggestion[48] that the three 'Swarthy' corpses represent the three soldiers Laon has killed. More questionable is his claim that the significance of the fourth corpse – Cythna's – lies in the notion that 'Laon had, in effect, murdered her by murdering them', and that the explanation for his eating her flesh is that killing is itself 'a kind of cannibalism, a manifestation of primitive instincts'. After all, the fact that the killings are being turned over in Laon's unconscious does not automatically prove that they are to be construed as a crime. Moreover, such a reading signally fails to account for Cythna's corresponding dream of cannibalism involving Laon's 'mangled limbs' (VII, xv), since she has certainly committed no murder. In Richard Cronin's reading,[49] cannibalism is a metaphor for 'the complex association of lust, sadism and selfishness on which tyranny is based', the idea being that Laon and Cythna are able to confront actual depravity in the grim times ahead – after the revolution – because they have already experienced it within themselves. Stuart Sperry, on the other hand, invokes Freud to argue that Shelley is dealing directly with his sexual theme at this point, interpreting Laon's dream of cannibalism as an elaborate symbol of his 'consuming desire' for Cythna.[50] This psychoanalytic reading has been elaborated by John Donovan, who applies Freud's theory of infantile neurosis, whereby the mother's breast is an object of both nutritional and sexual urges, to relate the theme of cannibalism specifically to that of incest, and therefore to interpret the dream in question (and Cythna's likewise) as a 'symbolic act of incest' which must be accomplished before the actual union can take place.[51]

The juxtaposition of different readings of the canto might appear to yield only one firm conclusion: that the meaning of these episodes is unclear. But the very fact that they have provoked a variety of interpretations is instructive. Whereas only the most determined exegete would wish, for example, to 'interpret' the sufferings of Verezzi in Shelley's gothic novel *Zastrozzi* (Verezzi suffers simply because Matilda causes him to suffer), Laon's ordeal seems to demand interpretation. This is no doubt partly due to what Sperry calls the 'phantasmagoric' quality of the experience;[52] also, perhaps, to the long shadow of authorial intent cast by the Preface. But beyond that there seems to be a pressure of meaning in the very form of the poem, reflecting yet another major transformation of generic convention: namely the transference into the psychological domain of the allegorical stratum of romance. As a result of this transference, the presence of a controlling meaning is felt even as Shelley enters psychological territory whose interpretative codes had not yet been formulated.

The effect is enhanced by Laon's own efforts to comprehend the different phases of his experience. He remembers first 'The darkness of brief frenzy' cast on him by the profound and solemn silence of his prison, a 'madness' in which 'I knew not my own misery' (III, xv); then the agonising sorrow that succeeded, as he regained his senses only to see the ship transporting Cythna to slavery disappear over the horizon; a sorrow that yielded to a suicidal despair for which he now reproves himself. On the fourth morning his 'brain began to fail', as he fell 'far and deep' into the 'caverns dreary and forlorn / Of the riven soul', peopled by dancing devils and phantoms (III, xxii–xxiii). This is when it becomes clear that Laon's nightmares, his descent into the recesses of his own unconscious, are in fact a displaced version of the archetypal *descensus ad infernos*; a connection confirmed in the next stanza when Laon himself refers to 'the realms accursed, / Where then my spirit dwelt' (III, xxiv, 4–5).

The particular form of his terror – 'I descried / All shapes like mine own self, hideously multiplied' (III, xxiii, 8–9) – Laon explains simply as a delirious mental representation of his physical isolation. But the pressure of meaning exerted by the underlying archetype forces us to assign a more exemplary function. What Laon encounters is in fact nothing other than a grotesque manifestation of his own selfhood. Does this mean, then, that Laon needs to be purged of selfishness? One does not have to read far into Shelley's *oeuvre* to discover his belief that man's natural condition is such, a predisposition that can only be relieved, or redeemed, by active virtue, imagination and love. When Laon falls, in a passive trance, into the caverns of his own soul or mind, it is appropriate that he should be exposed to his 'own self, hideously multiplied'. This is a revelation not of his inherent sinfulness, but of the selfish principle within him, in Blakean terms the 'natural man' as opposed to the 'ideal man'. For us to conclude that Laon's experience is purgatorial, there is therefore no need to assume that he is being punished, although this may well be part of the explanation. As to the precise mechanism by which purgation takes place, this remains obscure if only because Laon's encounter with selfhood is passive, and has no immediate outcome. In *Prometheus Unbound*, with its more dramatic presentation of an internalised quest (involving, like Blake's visionary romances, a return to a more directly allegorical mode), such encounters are modelled as *confrontations*, as when Prometheus is confronted by the Furies in Act I.

Of the two visions that 'burst' Laon's 'darkness', the second he can now relate as an actual event, namely the appearance of the Hermit who rescues him from the tower. Regarding the first vision of the four corpses, Laon claims 'I know not yet, was it a dream or no' (III, xxiv, 6), which, if we examine the chronology closely, is not strictly true because by the time Laon is recounting the story he plainly knows that Cythna was at this point alive (the discrepancy can be justified on the artistic ground that it is required in order to maintain narrative suspense). Allowing, then, for the fact that we are left for a while in some doubt as to whether or not the experience was real, we are still faced ultimately with the problem of interpreting a very bizarre dream. Laon himself, simply sickened at the time, accounts for it later much as Cythna does for her dream, by describing it as 'a shade / Such as self-torturing thought from madness breeds' (IV, xxxiv, 6–7). Again, the reader may feel compelled to assign a more exemplary function; at least, to discover a *reason* for Laon's self-torture. This takes us back to my original point about this passage, for what is significant is that each of the interpretations cited above posits a meaning for the dream *beneath* the plane of *Laon*'s consciousness, but within the sphere of *Shelley*'s imaginative control. Unlike Wordsworth's autobiographical romance, Shelley's representation of 'the growth and progress of individual mind' is composed of two levels, only one of which is linked to the hero's own understanding of his experiences. The distinction between these two levels is not always important, but at certain points it becomes crucial. Canto III has this kind of complexity, although its basic function of advancing Laon's moral and psychological development need no longer be disputed.

The convalescence sequence in Canto IV is more straightforward. According to Mary Shelley's editorial note, the figure of the Hermit is based on Shelley's old teacher Dr Lind. Another possible model – as noted by one of the reviewers[53] – is William Godwin. There may also be an element of self-projection involved, insofar as Shelley was in the habit of styling himself 'The Hermit of Marlow' (the pseudonym appears on his two political pamphlets of 1817, *A Proposal for Putting Reform to the Vote* and *An Address to the People on the Death of the Princess Charlotte*). But more important than naming the biographical source is to recognise the literary convention on which Shelley is drawing. Like the various hermits in *The Faerie Queene* and other more recent romances of chivalry, Shelley's 'gentle Hermit' is a descendant of the hermits of medieval romance. Instructing knights in the order of chivalry, and nursing them back to sanity after a crisis, were two of the hermit's traditional roles in romance; and in assigning him the role of psychological nurse to Laon, Shelley's characterisation of the Hermit is very much in keeping with generic tradition. In other respects, however, there is a decisive break with convention. Firstly, Shelley's Hermit abandons his 'lonely peace' in order to go to Argolis to rescue Laon from his prison tower. Secondly,

and more importantly, a role-reversal has occurred in that the
Hermit's inspiration has come from the hero, instead of the other way
round. Indeed during Laon's illness he takes it upon himself to
continue propagating Laon's revolutionary doctrines through his
own writings (IV, xi–xiii). Illustrating once more how Shelley invokes
and then inverts the conventions of romance, the story of the Hermit
thus also forms an interesting subplot concerning the transmission of
revolutionary feelings, bringing to mind Wordsworth's story of the
Solitary in *The Excursion*[54] – another hermit figure – and also his
description of how those 'of gentle mood' were affected by the French
Revolution in the lines from *The Prelude* that were first published in
The Friend.

   Shelley's Hermit lives in the basement of a tower on the edge of a
beautiful lake surrounded by trees, and Laon's recovery is aided by
the restorative effects of this serene setting, 'The wonders of his sylvan
solitude' (IV, v, 8). If not physically rejuvenated by the experience
(he does not omit to mention that his hair had gone prematurely
grey), Laon comes away from this mountain retreat in a state of
strong mental health:

> From the green earth lightly I did arise,
> As one out of dim dreams that doth awake ...
>
> (IV, xxviii, lines 7–8)

His spirits continue to revive as he makes his way across the moors
and dales to the Golden City, revelling in the sensations of spring. If
such details at first seem only incidental, we should think ahead to the
vital part played by the energies of 'the green world' in *Prometheus
Unbound*, and recognise too the Wordsworthian pastoral motifs that
are present here and at other points in *Laon and Cythna*. The
regenerative powers of nature are, in fact, an indispensable element
in this poem of psychological growth, for both Laon and Cythna.

   Although the scene functions as a kind of pastoral interlude, in the
special sense I have mentioned, we do not lose sight of the main plot.
The Hermit reports at length on the progress of the revolution,
revealing that it is now poised on the verge of success, awaiting the
final impetus that Laon is to provide. The rebellious crowd, latterly
inspired by the as-yet-unidentified Laone, is now encamped outside
the walls of the Golden City, trying 'with words of human love' to
win over the tyrant's guards (IV, xxvi). The concluding emphasis in
the canto, however, is upon the love story, and this is at a similar

point of suspense. As a result of his cadaverous vision, Laon still believes – or rather, believed – that Cythna 'slumbered with the dead'; yet not only does she now appear alive in his dreams, he also cannot help entertaining the hope that it is she who is the 'maiden who had reared / The torch of Truth afar'. In the last five stanzas Laon agonises over the two possibilities, ending on a note of nervous optimism:

> Aye as I went, that maiden who had reared
> The torch of Truth afar, of whose high deeds
> The Hermit in his pilgrimage had heard,
> Haunted my thoughts. – Ah, Hope its sickness feeds
> With whatsoe'er it finds, or flowers or weeds!
> Could she be Cythna? – Was that corpse a shade
> Such as self-torturing thought from madness breeds?
> Why was this hope not torture? yet it made
> A light around my steps which would never fade.   (IV, xxxiv)

It is, of course, the light of this private hope that is continually breaking through during the public scenes that follow.

We are now at last in a position to understand more fully the contrapuntal effects that we observed earlier in Cantos V and VI. On the glorious morning of the revolution, Laon likens himself to one who 'walks in lonely gloom beneath the noonday sun'. The very next day, with the revolution crushed, and immediately after a most gruesome bloodbath, Laon is in 'a deep / And speechless swoon of joy'. Viewed out of context, the former would seem at best the affectation of singularity, at worst morose self-absorption; and the latter, an affront to both plausibility and decency. It is only when we consider the internal logic of the narrative that these discrepancies are fully explained. The importance of the goal which Laon 'having much, covets yet more' has been declared almost from the start, complementing his revolutionary aspirations because representing his personal ideal – the focus, as it were, of his utopian vision of an earthly paradise. He has suffered imprisonment, torture and madness as a result of his effort to defend Cythna; and in suffering, been prepared and purified so as to deserve her. When Laon is finally reunited with his sister and lover, the political revolution has failed, but the emotional revolution can now take place; and the climax that occurs satisfies, with energy and precision, both the immediate demands of the plot, and the deeper patterns of meaning by which the first half of *Laon and Cythna* is structured. This is a major achievement for Shelley, which has justified, I hope, my prolonged attempt to analyse the thematic organisation of the poem. It now also warrants a close attention to the consummation scene itself.

THE CONSUMMATION SCENE

In his essay on the internalisation of romance, Bloom writes of the critical moment at which the revolutionary activism of the 'Promethean stage' of the quest is renounced, and the 'Real Man' begins to emerge from the crisis, in the form of a vision of 'self-transcendent' love:

It is, to use Shelley's phrasing, a total going-out from our own natures, total because the force moving out is not only the Promethean libido but rather a fusion between the libido and the active or imaginative element in the ego; or simply, desire wholly taken up into the imagination.[55]

Laon and Cythna does not in all respects conform to Bloom's schema for internalised romance. As we have seen, Laon's purgatorial crisis *precedes* the renunciation of the 'Promethean stage' of his quest, and the renunciation of revolutionary activism is only a temporary one. Moreover, it is not until later in the poem that 'desire' can be said to be 'wholly taken up into the imagination': the love scene in Canto VI is essentially physical in nature. But Bloom's basic claim about the Shelleyan vision of love is graphically illustrated by the erotic climax in *Laon and Cythna*, and it is only by thinking in terms of a psychology and poetics of transcendence that we can adequately account for the great leap of consciousness that occurs at this point in the poem, and for the shift in poetic mode that accompanies it.

Yet paradoxically Shelley's transcendent love scene is another reworking of the topos of the Bower of Bliss, a topos that in Spenser and most of his imitators serves to define limits for the libido and to deny the possibility of human transcendence. What identifies Laon and Cythna's 'green / And lone recess' as a version of Acrasia's Bower in *The Faerie Queene* is not just the fact that it is a scene of sensual pleasure. It is also a place of enchantment, from where can be heard

> the murmur of the motion
> Of waters, as in spots forever haunted
> By the choicest winds of Heaven, which are inchanted
> To music, by the wand of Solitude,
> That wizard wild ...   (VI, xxiii, lines 3–7)

Again and again we are made to feel the 'spell-bound' quality of the
setting, its 'strangest sounds' and 'wondrous light'. Literally, the
location is natural rather than supernatural, but this is nature at its
most magical: 'Nature inchanted', in a telling phrase from the draft
of stanza xxxii (Ryan, p. 226). The presence of the 'marble ruin' is
reminiscent of Spenser's 'Pallace brave' (II, xii, 83, 1), its ruined
condition making the point that Shelley, like Keats, was a belated
visitor to the landscape of romance. The bower itself is inside the ruin,
and it is here that Laon and Cythna make their bed upon a 'natural
couch of leaves' in the remains of the hall, beneath a 'verdurous
woof' of 'clinging weeds' and 'ivy pale', 'a canopy moon-proof' (VI,
xxvii, 7–9).

Once again, the difference between Spenser's Bower of Bliss and
Shelley's is that the latter is not a scene of temptation and deception.
Just as there was no tension for the Hermit between the active and the
contemplative life, here there is no tension between love and duty, or
reason and passion. Laon is not being diverted from his quest, and
Cythna is no 'false enchaunteresse' or fairy mistress. The sexual
encounter is for both of them a transforming experience, but neither
ends up as a pig. Their bliss was not 'turn'd to balefulnesse', like that
of Acrasia's lovers.

To compare *Laon and Cythna* directly with *The Faerie Queene* in this
way is perhaps misleading, although it does serve to highlight
Shelley's revolutionary treament of the motif. We know from a
previous chapter that Shelley was also acquainted with a number of
other adaptations of the Bower of Bliss, and that in *Queen Mab* he had
already done much to reclaim the sexuality of the Bower by
vindicating man's 'blissful impulses'. Shelley was also familiar with
the Italian romances which had supplied Spenser's principal models
for Acrasia's Bower, the Garden of Armida in Tasso's *Gerusalemme
Liberata* and the Garden of Alcina in Ariosto's *Orlando Furioso*;[56] and
with Milton's 'blissful bower' of Adam and Eve in *Paradise Lost*,
which may well have provided a model for Shelley's site of sexual
union without sin (and of which there appear to be verbal echoes[57]).
However, there is strong evidence that the most powerful influence
– albeit of an antithetical kind – upon Shelley's conception of this
scene came once again from Southey, whose metrical romances were
still among Shelley's favourite poems, despite his having largely
outgrown 'the Thalaba style' and contracted a powerful dislike of
the author.

I have already discussed the Bower of Bliss in Book VI of *Thalaba the Destroyer*. The Bower in Book X of *The Curse of Kehama* is rather different. Situated in the Hindu heaven known as Mount Meru, it is a true rather than a false paradise; and there is no danger of sexual temptation because the wicked enchantress Lorrinite and her son Arvalan are specifically excluded from this joyful domain, its main function in the plot being as a place of refuge from the perils of the quest. Though mortal, Ladurlad and his daughter Kailyal are able to gain admission to Mount Meru with the help of the 'glendoveer' Ereenia, who has just rescued Ladurlad from the clutches of Arvalan. They are joined there by the spirit of Ladurlad's dead wife Yedillian, Kailyal's mother, resulting in a passionate and tearful family reunion:

> A blessed family is this
> Assembled in the Bower of Bliss!
> Strange woe, Ladurlad, hath been thine,
>   And pangs beyond all human measure,
>   And thy reward is now divine,
>   A foretaste of eternal pleasure.
>   He knew indeed there was a day
> When all these joys would pass away,
>   And he must quit this blest abode;
>   And, taking up again the spell,
>   Groan underneath the baleful load,
>   And wander o'er the world again
>   Most wretched of the sons of men:
>   Yet was this brief repose, as when
>   A traveller in the Arabian sands,
> Half-fainting on his sultry road,
>   Hath reach'd the water-place at last;
> And resting there beside the well,
>   Thinks of the perils he has past,
> And gazes o'er the unbounded plain,
> The plain which must be traversed still,
> And drinks, ... yet cannot drink his fill;
>   Then girds his patient loins again.
>   So to Ladurlad now was given
> New strength, and confidence in heaven,
>   And hope, and faith invincible.   (x, lines 172–97)

As in *Thalaba*, the 'blest abode' is conceived as both a 'reward' for heroic labours done, and 'A foretaste of eternal pleasure'. But now the ambivalence has been removed. This is not enchanted ground, and Ladurlad is being neither deceived, nor tempted to sin, nor led astray from his quest. Here the Bower of Bliss is a legitimate place of repose and refreshment, from which Ladurlad emerges with 'New strength, and confidence in heaven, / And hope, and faith invincible'. As if this were not a bold enough break with the traditions of romance, by permitting the embrace with Yedillian, Southey contravenes a convention at least as old as the *Odyssey*[58] forbidding the living to embrace the spirits of the dead – an innovation that is justified by the argument that here love is 'tried and purified' (x, 162).

Both of Southey's adaptations of the theme of the Bower of Bliss contribute to the love scene in *Laon and Cythna*, furnishing suggestions that cannot be found in Spenser's original. But to recognise the similarities is also to be aware of how much more unorthodox and complex is Shelley's treatment of the theme. Like those in *Thalaba* and *Kehama*, the bower in *Laon and Cythna* is situated at the top of a mountain, and the episode features a reunion of the hero and heroine. In Shelley's case, however, the meeting is between brother and sister, and it does not consist merely of an embrace. The portrayal of Laon and Cythna's sexual consummation is a breach of generic decorum far greater than Southey's. Shelley's justification is provided by the declaration that 'To the pure all things are pure!' (VI, xxx, 1), an Orphic precept from St Paul's Epistle to Titus (chapter 1, verse 15) which he would also have encountered in the rather more congenial contexts of Godwin's *Enquirer*[59] or Milton's *Areopagitica*,[60] where in each case the apostle's words are cited – somewhat subversively – as part of an argument against censorship. The use of the quotation in *Laon and Cythna* is even more subversive in that 'all things' is now taken to include an act of incestuous love-making, something that St Paul would certainly not have countenanced. Yet the validity of Laon's claim for purity has been carefully established throughout the preceding cantos, the notion of progressive virtue being the pervading rationale of Shelley's poem. By substituting a secular idealism for Southey's 'faith', Shelley has revealed a different means by which love can be 'tried and purified'; and the bliss of his lovers both rewards and completes a process of purification that has been the guiding principle of much of the plot.

For Southey, such joy is a 'foretaste of heaven', and in each of his poems, the Bower of Bliss represents an intermediate or provisional paradise (a false one in the case of *Thalaba*) which is distinguished from the true or permanent heaven attained by the hero and heroine

at the end of the poem. In *Laon and Cythna* the idea of transcendence
has been largely naturalised or humanised (I shall elaborate on this),
and Shelley's bower is not supernatural, but the correspondence
remains in that Laon and Cythna's mountain retreat *is* pictured as a
kind of temporary paradise, offering a foretaste of the bliss that awaits
them after their death. In one sense, then, the bower scene can be said
to serve the same structural function in Shelley's poem as in
Southey's.

There are other correspondences too. As in *Thalaba*, a meteor
appears overhead, which has no particular meaning in Southey's
poem but is used by Shelley to symbolise the dissemination of sexual
energies that occurs beneath it (according to contemporary science,
meteors were formed by exhalations from the earth as a result of
biological processes in plant life[61]). The horse or 'courser' upon
which Shelley's protagonists ascend the mountain is too common a
motif in romance to indicate any particular debt to Southey, and
there are more obvious precedents for the striking portrayal of Laone
on horseback, although it is not often in romance that a man in
distress is rescued by a woman, as happens here. We have already
noted Shelley's ingenious use in Canto v of an image derived from the
curse of perpetual thirst that supplies the title of *The Curse of Kehama*.
We have also just learned that in the Bower of Bliss, Kehama's curse
has no hold over Ladurlad, hence the simile, in the passage quoted
above, of the 'traveller in the Arabian sands' arriving at an oasis. In
Shelley's rescue scene, we find the very same analogy:

> the Tartar horse
> Paused, and I saw the shape its might which swayed,
> And heard her musical pants, like the sweet source
> Of waters in the desert, as she said,
> 'Mount with me Laon, now!' – I rapidly obeyed.
>
> (VI, xx, lines 5–9)

The image of 'the sweet source / Of waters in the desert' not only
conveys the lovely quality of Laone's voice and Laon's overwhelming
sense of relief at hearing that voice; it also implicitly endorses Laon's
surmise that 'Laone' is 'Cythna' by answering the earlier image of
'hopes that make / The flood recede from which their thirst they seek
to slake' (v, xxxvii, 8–9). It thus heralds, before the recognition
proper, the forthcoming climax to the love story. This is only a detail,
but it points to an almost systematic precision of metaphor that is

characteristic of Shelley's mature work. What in *The Curse of Kehama* is an effective but clumsy device to keep the plot turning, becomes part of a subliminal emotional subplot within the imagery of *Laon and Cythna*.

Although revealing in various ways, this comparison should not be pressed too far. Southey's romances are pitched at a very different level to Shelley's, and there is much that separates *Laon and Cythna* from *Thalaba* and *Kehama*, most notably psychological depth. *Thalaba* may be the first proper quest romance of the Romantic period, but, as Curran points out,[62] the quest is never internalised. This is also true of *Kehama*, as De Quincey noted when he remarked that Southey's poems are 'too intensely *objective* – too much reflect the mind, as spreading itself out upon external things – too little exhibit the mind as introverting itself upon its own thoughts and feelings'.[63] In *Laon and Cythna* (a poem which interested De Quincey enough for him to quote it both in his *Confessions of an English Opium-Eater* and in his essay on 'Murder Considered as One of the Fine Arts') the quest *is* internalised, and the scene in question marks a pivotal stage in the process of internalisation. I will try to explain this is more detail.

Amidst the public events of Cantos v and vi, the world of private consciousness is only glimpsed by the reader in Laon's anxieties concerning the identity of Laone and the fate of his sister. Now, as the lovers arrive at their mountain bower, this interior dimension suddenly opens out before us in the passage that begins:

> We know not where we go, or what sweet dream
> May pilot us thro' caverns strange and fair
> Of far and pathless passion, while the stream
> Of life, our bark doth on its whirlpools bear,
> Spreading swift wings as sails to the dim air;
> Nor should we seek to know, so the devotion
> Of love and gentle thoughts be heard still there
> Louder and louder from the utmost Ocean
> Of universal life, attuning its commotion.   (vi, xxix)

An expansive and exotic landscape of the mind is revealed, at once a symbolic summation of experiences already undergone, 'whirlpools' upon 'the stream / Of life', and an act of thought by which the individual can harmonise with the 'universal life'. The stanza has both the generalising force of philosophic statement and an exact dramatic propriety in the story: just as Asia's acceptance of Demogorgon's pronouncement that 'the deep truth is imageless' will permit the 'destined hour' to arrive in Act II of *Prometheus Unbound*, it is the admission that 'We know not where we go' – that destiny is ultimately unknowable – which allows Laon and Cythna to transcend the catastrophe with which they have just been confronted.

If this moment of release has something of the impetus of a tragic 'discovery', the nature of the transcendence itself exactly satisfies Frye's definition of the goal of quest romance: 'a fulfilment that will deliver [the libido or desiring self] from the anxieties of reality but will still contain that reality'.[64] 'Oblivion wrapped / Our spirits', says Laon, 'and the fearful overthrow / Of public hope was from our being snapt, / Tho' linkèd years had bound it there' (VI, xxx, 1–4). But unlike the 'Lethean joy' of the revolutionary dawn, this moment of oblivion is succeeded by a revelation of the entire content of their past:

> for now
> A power, a thirst, a knowledge, which below
> All thoughts, like light beyond the atmosphere,
> Clothing its clouds with grace, doth ever flow,
> Came on us, as we sate in silence there,
> Beneath the golden stars of the clear azure air.
>
> In silence which doth follow talk that causes
> The baffled heart to speak with sighs and tears,
> When wildering passion swalloweth up the pauses
> Of inexpressive speech: – the youthful years
> Which we together passed, their hopes and fears,
> The common blood which ran within our frames,
> That likeness of the features which endears
> The thoughts expressed by them, our very names,
> And all the wingèd hours which speechless memory claims,
>
> Had found a voice...   (VI, xxx–xxxii)

The 'voice' is metaphorical – Laon and Cythna are sitting in silence – but it is the expression of a reality contained not forgotten, a fulfilment rather than an escape.

Yet this moment of heightened perception is only a prelude to the erotic climax itself. Here is Laon's description of what follows:

> The meteor to its far morass returned:
> The beating of our veins one interval
> Made still; and then I felt the blood that burned
> Within her frame, mingle with mine, and fall
> Around my heart like fire; and over all

A mist was spread, the sickness of a deep
And speechless swoon of joy, as might befall
Two disunited spirits when they leap
In union from this earth's obscure and fading sleep.

Was it one moment that confounded thus
All thought, all sense, all feeling, into one
Unutterable power, which shielded us
Even from our own cold looks, when we had gone
Into a wide and wild oblivion
Of tumult and tenderness? or now
Had ages, such as make the moon and sun,
The seasons, and mankind their changes know,
Left fear and time unfelt by us alone below?

I know not. What are kisses whose fire clasps
The failing heart in languishment, or limb
Twined within limb? or the quick dying gasps
Of the life meeting, when the faint eyes swim
Thro' tears of a wide mist boundless and dim,
In one caress? What is the strong controul
Which leads the heart that dizzy steep to climb,
Where far over the world those vapours roll,
Which blend two restless frames in one reposing soul?

(VI, xxxiv–xxxvi)

There is no precedent for such an explicit portrayal of the sexual act among earlier versions of the Bower of Bliss, not least because the traditional imperative had been prohibitive rather than – as here – celebratory. Yet Shelley's real theme is the phenomenon of desire, the 'Unutterable power' that draws Laon and Cythna into one another's arms and then plunges them into 'a deep / And speechless swoon of joy'. One notable feature of the description is that most of it consists of questions. As early as 1810 he had posed similar questions in his 'Fragment. Supposed to be an Epithalamion of Francis Ravaillac and Charlotte Cordé', an erotic dream vision with political overtones which is also the first of his unorthodox reconstructions of the Bower of Bliss (again the immediate model, or counter-model, for the scene appears to have been Southey):

Spirits! when raptures move,
Say what it is to love,
When passion's tear stands on the cheek,
When bursts the unconscious sigh;
And the tremulous lips dare not speak

What is told by the soul-felt eye.
But what is sweeter to revenge's ear
Than the fell tyrant's last expiring yell?
Yes! than love's sweetest blisses 'tis more dear
To drink the floatings of a despot's knell.

                              (*Poems*, I, 123; lines 103–12)

Laon and Cythna as a whole, with its intricate interplay of the erotic
and the political, can be read as a somewhat more complex answer to
that last question, one that does not involve the glorification of
revenge. To the first question, 'what it is to love' 'when raptures
move', the 'Epithalamion' gives no reply. In effect it is this same
question that Laon is asking in the passage above; or rather, a series
of more detailed questions on the same theme.

In answer to Laon's final question, we are told that 'the strong
controul / Which leads the heart that dizzy steep to climb' is 'the
shadow which doth float unseen, / But not unfelt, o'er blind
mortality' (VI, xxxvii, 1–2). This, as many critics have observed, is an
echo of the opening lines of Shelley's 'Hymn to Intellectual Beauty',
whose theme has already been invoked by Laon's earlier mention of
'A power, a thirst, a knowledge, which below / All thoughts... doth
ever flow' (VI, xxx, 5–7). Commenting on the difference between the
notion of Intellectual Beauty expounded in the 'Hymn' and the
notion of Ideal Beauty in Plato's *Symposium*, James Notopoulos writes
that the former is 'emotional and mystic rather than intellectual and
objective', and that Shelley is making 'an imaginative leap with little
distinction between emotion and idea'.[65] The version of Intellectual
Beauty that we meet in *Laon and Cythna* is even further removed from
the original doctrine. The Platonic ladder has, so to speak, been
turned upside down, or thrown away in favour of some other means
of spiritual ascent. The climactic experience is still radically one of
transcendence, but now it is a fusion of sensation, emotion and idea,
a confounding of 'All thought, all sense, all feeling, into one /
Unutterable power'. For the consummation sequence in *Laon and
Cythna*, Shelley merges into one the physical rapture of the lovers of
the 'Epithalamion' and the spiritual ecstasy of the young poet in the
'Hymn'.

Yet there is also a political dimension to this scene, notwithstanding
our earlier distinction between the sexual and the political theme,
and the obvious shift of focus that has taken place from the one to the
other in Canto VI. In the 'Hymn', Shelley vows to the Spirit of

Beauty that 'never joy illumed my brow / Unlinked with hope that thou wouldst free / This world from its dark slavery' (68–70). A similar affirmation follows the *ekstasis* in the present poem, during the 'rite / Of faith' that follows the love-making. But the fact that the relationship between Laon and Cythna has been born of a shared commitment to revolutionary ideals ('high and solemn hopes, … and all the thoughts which smother / Cold Evil's power' (VI, xxxix, 7–9)) is not the only reason why the love scene can be said to have political undertones, nor is Shelley, by vindicating the bliss of the lovers, simply flouting the conventions of romance. According to Stephen Greenblatt's analysis of the original Bower of Bliss in *The Faerie Queene*,[66] the fact that Sir Guyon 'does not merely depart from the place of temptation, but reduces it to ruins' is explained not by Spenser's Puritan disposition but by Freud's 'repressive hypothesis' that civilisation is always built upon a renunciation of instinct – that it requires and presupposes the nonsatisfaction (by suppression, repression, or some other means) of powerful instincts. The violence directed against Acrasia's sensual paradise is Guyon's pledge of loyal service to Gloriana, and thus Spenser's to Queen Elizabeth, 'the autocratic ruler of the English state' to whose political ideology the repressive morality of *The Faerie Queene* is inseparably linked.

That Freud's thesis is relevant to the England of Shelley's day is suggested at once by the existence of The Society for the Suppression of Vice, an organisation with a membership that included the entire bench of bishops, members of both Houses of Parliament, and wealthy bankers, whose purview extended from obscene publications to Sabbath-breaking, and whose zealous concern with public morality coincided perfectly with its practical function of guarding the political and economic *status quo*.[67] Palpably aware of such ideological links, Shelley speaks openly in the Preface to *Laon and Cythna* of wanting 'to break through the crust of those outworn opinions on which established institutions depend'. His celebration of sexual pleasure in Canto VI, in defiance of the conventions of the Bower of Bliss, therefore can be – and was – read as an implicit attack on the ideological foundations of the English establishment.

Shelley's move should not be viewed in isolation. The symbolic connection between the act of love and the act of revolution was a very common one in the revolutionary literature of the 1790s.[68] Negatively, the connection had persisted in the verse romances that flourished in the era of the Napoleonic Wars, where sexuality was

usually portrayed as a disruptive force, often associated with the demonic forces of revolt: Southey's romances contain many examples,
as do Scott's.[69] It was partly in reaction to this, and in a conscious
effort to renew the challenge to 'an institutionalized Christianity that
was part of the apparatus of State', that writers such as Keats, Hunt,
Shelley and Peacock formed around 1816 what Marilyn Butler has
called a literary 'cult of sexuality',[70] but which was known at the time
by the disparaging label 'the Cockney School'.

Laon and Cythna is far more sexually explicit than any of the other
writings of this group. An added provocation is that the sexuality it
depicts (in the original version of the poem) is incestuous. Critics
have tended to interpret this fact symbolically,[71] but it is is worth
remembering that Shelley's stated intention was that it should
'startle the reader from the trance of ordinary life'. At one level, then,
the incest motif can be interpreted as a rhetorical strategy intended
to shock the reader out of his assumptions and conformities, and thus
make him receptive to an alternative set of ethical doctrines.
Unfortunately, as Shelley later acknowledged,[72] this strategy turned
out to have precisely the opposite effect, alienating even those who
might otherwise have been inclined to sympathise with his general
views. Given that when he wrote the poem he had just lost the
custody of his children in the Chancery Court on the grounds – as he
saw them – of his being 'a REVOLUTIONIST, and an *Atheist*' (*Letters*, I,
530), one would think that he could have foreseen this reaction, and
recognised the sociological fallacy contained in his claim that the
'circumstance' of incest was introduced 'merely to accustom men to
that charity and toleration which the exhibition of a practice widely
differing from their own has a tendency to promote'. However, we
need not doubt that, at a conscious level at least, the incest theme was
designed to contribute to the revolutionary dynamic of the poem,
and to help promote a 'liberal and comprehensive morality'.

Returning to the narrative, we are told that by now the 'liquid
ecstasies' have subsided into a 'sweet peace of joy', and that one
night 'and still another day' had elapsed since Laon and Cythna's
retreat to the mountains (VI, xxxvii, 6). The difference between this
measurement of time passed – narrative time, as it were – and the
one intimated by Laon in the midst of his love-making, makes the
point that the consummation scene has entailed a major shift of
poetic mode. The logic of narrative, with its demands of sequence
and its claims to verisimilitude, has been overturned by the logic of

subjective vision. To convey the notion of transcendence Shelley has created a kind of visionary lyric within the narrative, making this another example of the phenomenon explored by Karl Kroeber in his book on Romantic verse narrative.[73] In effecting this transition, Shelley stretches the form of romance to its limits. Nonetheless, the poem manages to contain itself. What ultimately makes this scene so successful is precisely its balancing of opposites – the physical with the spiritual, the objective with the subjective, the descriptive with the symbolic.

Nowhere, moreover, does Shelley handle his chosen verse form so finely as in this section. G. Wilson Knight has remarked upon the differences between Shelley's handling of the Spenserian stanza and Spenser's own:

There is [in Shelley] a high-pitched speed, a rush of language. The Spenserian stanza here serves effects utterly alien to Spenser's langorousness … lines are not units, each end is at once hitched by a passionate syntax to a new beginning.[74]

Of the ordinary narrative parts of *Laon and Cythna*, this is a fair description. But here we sense a different rhythm:

> We know not where we go, or what sweet dream
> May pilot us thro' caverns strange and fair
> Of far and pathless passion, while the stream
> Of life, our bark doth on its whirlpools bear,
> Spreading swift wings as sails to the dim air;
> Nor should we seek to know, so the devotion
> Of love and gentle thoughts be heard still there
> Louder and louder from the utmost Ocean
> Of universal life, attuning its commotion.   (VI, xxix)

The lyrical section opens in a circling, meditative rhythm. There is energy and movement, but not the forward rush of language: the inversion, across a line break, 'while the stream / Of life, our bark doth on its whirlpools bear' reverses the forward motion of the long unbroken phrase that precedes it, and this itself meanders rather than rushes, reinforcing the sense of 'We know not where we go.' This is still not quite 'Spenser's langorousness', but one can see the pertinence of Shelley's admission in the Preface that he had been enticed 'by the brilliancy and magnificence of sound' that can be produced 'by a just and harmonious arrangement of the pauses of this measure'. Later the stanza builds up through the long and powerful phrase beginning 'so the devotion / Of love and gentle thoughts' to the final, lofty, latinate line, using double-syllable rhymes ('devotion' / 'Ocean' / 'commotion') to express through the very sound of the poetry the idea of a developing harmony between the individual and the 'universal life'.

Besides making the transition from narrative to lyrical time, and opening up within the poem a corresponding imaginative space, stanza xxix also provides an abstract, in the symbolical figure of a voyage, of the emotional and spiritual progression to be described in the following seven or eight stanzas: the visionary sequence that begins with the abrupt release from the anxiety of political defeat in stanza xxx, proceeds to the sexual climax of stanzas xxxiv to xxxvi, and ends with the mystical perception of the 'divine darkness' in stanza xxxvii. This is neither the first nor the last lyrical section in *Laon and Cythna*. There has already been Cythna's revolutionary Ode to Equality in Canto v, written in a high oratorical style which recalls the addresses to the 'Spirit of Nature' in *Queen Mab*, as well as pointing forward to later and greater political lyrics like the 'Ode to Liberty' and 'Ode to Naples' (it is also, of course, an imitation of the ceremonial odes sung at the French Revolutionary *fêtes de fédération*). In the next part of this chapter we will encounter the slightly different kind of lyricism contained in the prophetic passage at the end of Cythna's flashback in Canto ix, a passage which shows a more distinct promise of Shelley's future achievements as a lyricist, being a kind of draft for the 'Ode to the West Wind'. But it is in the present scene that Shelley begins to approach the exquisite music of Asia's lyric 'My soul is an enchanted boat', and the rhapsodic harmonies of the fourth act of *Prometheus Unbound*.

CYTHNA'S QUEST: THE PARADISE OF THE HEART

Had the poem ended at Canto vi, it would not have seemed incomplete. Shelley has told the story of the Revolution of the Golden City, the 'ideal' but failed revolution that originated in the mind of his hero, became a momentary reality seven years later, and ended with its suppression by the allies of the deposed king. He has also told the story of the love between Laon and Cythna, of their prolonged separation and persecution, and of their eventual reunion in the dying moments of the revolution. Because of the manner in which these two themes are interwoven, and because of the nature of the final scene, the first half ends not on a note of despair, but on one of transcendent hope and joy, this being exactly the impression with which Shelley wished the poem to leave his contemporary readers. Why, then, did he choose to add another six cantos?

The simplest answer to this question is that he wished to develop the character of the heroine. Had the poem ended at Canto vi, it could only really have justified the title *Laon; or, The Revolution of the Golden City*. In the first half, Cythna is a subsidiary character. Not that her status is like that of the 'veiled maid' in *Alastor*, an abstract and imaginary figure who exists only in the hero's own mind. Nor is she like the pure but passive heroines of other Regency romances, a stereotype that Shelley had not altogether avoided in his characterisation of Ianthe in *Queen Mab*. From the start, Cythna has a real and independent existence in the narrative, and she proceeds to make a contribution to the revolutionary action that is as great if not greater than Laon's. Moreover, sexual equality is an explicit theme in the poem, and an integral part of the social philosophy that the revolution is intended to put into practice. While still a child, Cythna takes upon herself the task of carrying to women the revolutionary message of liberty and equality, having witnessed all around her 'the servitude / In which the half of humankind were mewed / Victims of lust and hate' (ii, xxxvi, 4–6). But we only learn of these early aspirations of hers in the course of Laon's account of his own youth and political awakening. In Canto iv we get further glimpses of Cythna several years later as the eloquent young maid who, according to the Hermit's report, has taught her sex 'equal laws and justice' and brought the country to the verge of revolution; but these are no more than glimpses, and at second hand. Similarly, when she reappears in Canto v as the high priestess at the revolutionary festival, Cythna is a largely symbolic figure, of whose true identity the reader is still uncertain. Although the same is clearly not the case in Canto vi, even the great consummation scene, for all its shared pleasures, is seen very much through Laon's eyes, as the fulfilment of *his* hopes and desires about which we have heard so much.

It is not until Canto vii that the character of Cythna starts to acquire the psychological fullness that has been accorded to Laon – to receive equal treatment *from the poem*, as it were. Not until then do we start to learn about Cythna's formative experiences after her abduction, and about the details of her subsequent involvement in

the revolutionary struggle. What begins in Canto VII, and lasts until
Canto IX, is a flashback (or rather, a flashback within a flashback,
since the whole saga of Laon and Cythna's earthly lives is narrated
retrospectively by the spirit of Laon): this is accommodated in the
plot as part of a conversation in which the reunited lovers, still on
their 'bridal-couch', recount to one another what has happened to
them since their separation. By this point, however, we already know
about Laon's adventures, so he now proceeds rapidly to Cythna's
'strange tale of strange endurance' (VII, iii, 1), beginning it in his own
words but soon (from stanza x onwards) repeating it exactly as he
had it from her.

Cythna's progress through the narrative has been aptly defined as
an 'allegory of the awakening of the female intellect and will to their
real powers and capabilities'.[75] It is, in fact, both literal *and*
allegorical: a literal representation of the enlightenment of an
individual female mind, and an allegorical projection of an ideal
woman. The latter may be said to combine with Shelley's vision of
the ideal man – projected through Laon – to give a total image of
what Blake termed 'the human form divine', the primordial or
transcendent state of undivided being glimpsed during the consummation scene in Canto VI. The point to stress is that, both literally
and allegorically, the character of Cythna does 'develop' in the
course of the narrative, a feature which further differentiates her from
the conventional heroines of Regency romance. The logic of the
narrative is similar to that of Spenserian, or Wordsworthian,
romance; and like Laon's, Cythna's progress is nothing less than a
quest for perfection, in both the private and the public sphere.

Rather than attempting to examine all the different stages in her
quest, I propose instead to make some general observations about
Cythna's role in the poem, and to concentrate on particular elements
in her story, emphasising first the significance of the positioning of the
flashback in which the majority of it is related. This needs careful
attention because the ordering of the material is of vital importance
in a poem conceived according to an affective poetics. The fact that
Cythna's quest mostly follows that of Laon's – though in 'historical'
time the two lives are of course simultaneous – affects the whole way
we read and interpret it, in much the same way as our interpretation
of, say, the legend of Britomart in Book III of *The Faerie Queene* is
conditioned by our understanding of the legend of Sir Guyon in Book
II and of the Knight of the Red Cross in Book I. We cannot therefore

analyse the psychology, or decipher the allegory, of Cythna's 'strange tale' as if it existed in isolation.

The importance of this will be apparent if we turn to the events surrounding the episode in the sea cavern in Canto VII. Like Laon's experience in the prison tower in Canto III, and for similar reasons, this episode has attracted a wide variety of interpretations. The question of how Cythna's physical and mental suffering contributes to her moral and psychological development is made all the more perplexing by the fact that she seems to have done nothing whatsoever to deserve it – except incur the displeasure of the tyrannical king who rapes her. Richard Haswell, however, insists that Cythna has indeed transgressed, just as surely as Laon did in using force against Cythna's abductors: her moral error consists in having 'repulsed' Othman at the moment when 'he cast off the tyrant and accepted love'. Her subsequent imprisonment and madness are 'a form of punishment in which she suffers from the consciousness of the irrationality of her old values'.[76]

Though Haswell is able to find some support for this interpretation by drawing analogies with Shelley's early poem 'Zeinab and Kathema' and with *The Cenci*, it is based on a patent misreading of the passage concerned (VII, iv–vi): when Othman sees Cythna's 'wondrous loveliness', he does for a moment succumb 'to great Nature's sacred power' and 'accept love'; but as soon as 'he bade her to his secret bower / Be borne, a loveless victim', Shelley makes it clear that he became once again 'A king, a heartless beast, a pageant and a name'. Cythna did not repulse Othman in his moment of genuine passion, she repulsed him – or rather 'tore / Her locks in agony' and attempted unsuccessfully to dissuade him – after he had returned to his normal brutish self and given the order for her to be taken to his room to be raped. In the circumstances, the suggestion that Cythna is in some way guilty is simply perverse, and it is not surprising that Haswell's interpretation has been decisively rejected by the poem's female critics. Deborah Gutschera argues instead that the point of this incident, and of the mental crisis that follows, is that 'Cythna learns to maintain her revolutionary zeal in the face of violation and loss.' She is 'matured' by her suffering rather than redeemed by it, the latter being unnecessary, for Cythna is 'shown as a near-perfect heroine with less to learn than Laon'.[77]

This is surely the correct interpretation. From the evidence of the poem, there are no good grounds for imputing to Cythna a 'flaw of

moral character', nor for assuming that she has committed a
reprehensible error in the sense that Laon could be deemed to have
done in killing three of the tyrant's soldiers. Cythna's eminence in
virtue is impressed upon us from the start: one of Laon's earliest
references to her is as 'A second self, far dearer and more fair' (II,
xxiv, 2) – the original draft has 'far purer' (Ryan, p. 149) – and a
little later he speaks of her 'pure and radiant self' (III, iii, 7). It does
not follow, however, that Cythna has 'less to learn' than Laon, or
that she is 'near-perfect' from the start. On the contrary, she has *more*
to learn than Laon *because she is capable of more*. The standard of
perfection towards which she approaches is higher than that of Laon.
Setting Cantos VII to IX against Cantos II to V, it is easy to see that in
terms of consciousness, if not of virtuousness, Cythna advances well
beyond the point that Laon is shown to have reached.

This is not to suggest that Shelley wants his readers to make a
direct comparison between the respective attainments of his hero and
heroine. In any case it would not occur to us to do so for the very
reason that the two narratives are separated from one another.
Rather, that inequivalence reflects the fact that by Canto VII the
reader has already acquired some understanding of the moral and
psychological virtues which the poem is an attempt to inculcate. In
terms of both the ordering of the narratives and the unfolding of
ideas, Cythna's quest effectively begins where Laon's ends; and it is
this that enables Shelley to maintain the teleological momentum of
the poem. *Prometheus Unbound* is structured in a similar way, insofar as
Asia's quest in Act II both follows and presupposes the completion of
Prometheus's trial in Act I, each act being part of a cumulative
process of regeneration.

The point, then, is not that Cythna is seen to be superior to her
brother, but that she represents a further refinement of the aspiration
after excellence, a further step towards the Shelleyan ideal. The
difference begins to be felt when Cythna talks of the philosophical
enlightenment she achieved during her imprisonment:

> My mind became the book through which I grew
> Wise in all human wisdom, and its cave,
> Which like a mine I rifled through and through,
> To me the keeping of its secrets gave –
> One mind, the type of all, the moveless wave
> Whose calm reflects all moving things that are,
> Necessity, and love, and life, the grave,

And sympathy, fountains of hope and fear;
      Justice, and truth, and time, and the world's natural sphere.

(VII, xxxi)

E. B. Murray writes that Cythna's reveries 'teach her the sort of lore
Queen Mab had taught Ianthe – the secrets of the human world,
past, present, and future'.[78] This is of course true, but there is an
aspect to Cythna's lore which is not found in *Queen Mab*. This is the
metaphysical notion of the 'One mind, the type of all', derived
ultimately from the Platonic concept of the World Soul, but most
familiar to Shelley as the cornerstone of what was known as 'the
intellectual system', a blend of Platonic idealism and modern
empiricism that had found its fullest expression in Sir William
Drummond's *Academical Questions* (1805). Shelley actually cites
Drummond's work, as 'a volume of very acute and powerful
metaphysical criticism', in a footnote to the Preface; and Cythna's
reference to the doctrine of the 'One mind' should alert us to the fact
that she is, in effect, giving voice to Shelley's own philosophical
convictions.

   Laon's brief glimpse of intellectual beauty during the love scene
offers a hope of transcendence after the failure of the revolution.
Cythna's initiation into the 'intellectual system' occurs much earlier
in her life, and its doctrines become the basis of her revolutionary
philosophy:

> For, with strong speech I tore the veil that hid
> Nature, and Truth, and Liberty, and Love, –
> As one who from some mountain's pyramid
> Points to the unrisen sun! – the shades approve
> His truth, and flee from every stream and grove.
> Thus, gentle thoughts did many a bosom fill, –
> Wisdom, the mail of tried affections wove
> For many a heart, and tameless scorn of ill,
> Thrice steeped in molten steel the unconquerable will.   (IX, vii)

As we can see, Cythna is no mere theorist. Metaphysical contemplation translates directly into political action. The existence of
an 'intellectual' realm, the realm of Plato's forms, is to her an
argument for changing the world. Having been rescued from the
cavern and returned to the mainland, she therefore confronts the
people of the Golden City with what has been aptly termed[79] a
'revolutionary Platonism': 'I *tore* the veil that hid / Nature, and

Truth, and Liberty, and Love.' It is as though Shelley had finally purified the language of revolutionary politics by transforming the notion of 'unmasking' (a key term in the Jacobin rhetoric of denunciation) into that of Platonic unveiling.

It is not just in its content but also in its form that Cythna's 'strong speech' reveals itself to be more advanced than her brother's. It is significant that in the stanza above the suggestion of strength is immediately followed by that of gentleness, since this combination seems to be the secret of Cythna's spell-binding oratory. The Hermit had implied as much when he spoke first of her 'adamantine eloquence' (IV, xix, 6) and then of the 'awful sweetness' of her voice (IV, xxii, 7). In Cythna's long speech to the mariners in Canto VIII we hear this combination for ourselves: first the polemical vigour of her treatment of the question of God (on this subject, she retains something of the Voltairean spirit of *Queen Mab*), and afterwards the calm assurance of her apostrophe to Love (here she begins to sound like Asia in the second act of *Prometheus Unbound*; or indeed like Demogorgon in the concluding speech of the lyrical drama – a further measure of the authority which Cythna's pronouncements are accorded in *Laon and Cythna*). A similar mixture of sweetness and strength is heard in her Ode to Equality in Canto V; and again, in a less formal context, in the lyrical passage that ends her flashback in Canto IX.

To be sure, Laon too seems to be striving for this potent rhetorical mix (and there is evidence that Shelley himself aspired to such a goal[80]). But one need only juxtapose Cythna's speech to the mariners with, say, Laon's first address to the patriots in Canto V to realise how much more *subtle*, both stylistically and conceptually, is the sister's discourse. Even before we witness it for ourselves in her first public speech, our attention is alerted to this in the account of her incarceration in the cave:

> And on the sand would I make signs to range
> These woofs, as they were woven, of my thought;
> Clear, elemental shapes, whose smallest change
> A subtler language within language wrought:
>
> (VII, xxxii, lines 1–4).

Although it is not entirely clear what this 'subtler language' is (the passage can be read with equal plausibility as an allegory of the discovery of poetry, or of metaphor, or indeed of writing[81]), the essential point is that it is during her forced seclusion in the cave – a setting with obvious allegorical resonances – that Cythna learns to articulate her 'revolutionary Platonism': articulate both in this sense of to organise (to 'range' or 'frame') her ideas, and to give expression to them.

Such is the revolutionary education that Cythna acquires in the sea cavern, a process of mental liberation and self-enlightenment whose successful completion is mirrored, or allegorised, in the plot by the advent of an earthquake which cracks the cavern and transforms it into an island. But this still leaves unexplained the actual sufferings that lead to her growth of consciousness. It also leaves unanswered the question of how this whole episode relates to Shelley's original project, his 'experiment on the temper of the public mind'. Both these issues can be broached by considering what is probably the most traumatic part of her ordeal, namely the loss of the baby that results from her rape. The identity of this child – who reappears at various places in the story – has been the subject of some dis-agreement among critics, but none of the accounts so far offered has really explained the mysterious circumstances of her birth, nor adequately dealt with the crucial fact that the child is forcibly taken away from Cythna.

So mysterious are the circumstances as to shed doubt on whether Cythna was ever pregnant at all. At least, that is the conclusion which Cythna herself has reluctantly reached when she recounts the story to Laon; and it is not until near the end of the poem, when the three of them are reunited in Paradise, that Cythna learns that the birth of her child was not a 'vision wrought from my despair' but a real event. Even as she voices her doubts, however, she looks at Laon as though pleading with him to confirm the truth of her dream of motherhood, for if it was no more than 'the death of brainless phantasy', the disappearance of the child afflicted Cythna with 'more than all misery' (VII, xxii, 8–9). 'I was changed', she says,

> the very life was gone
> Out of my heart – I wasted more and more,
> Day after day, and sitting there alone,
> Vexed the inconstant waves with my perpetual moan.
> (VII, xxiii, lines 6–9)

Even after she has regained her sanity and decided – against the evidence of her swollen breasts – that the birth was a fantasy, the agony is renewed by the recurrence of her dream about the child, and by the associations of the cave.

The eventual uplift in her spirits comes not through the mere passage of time, nor, as in Laon's case, through the intervention of a benign hermit; but, more fortuitously, as a result of seeing an eagle forbear at her request from attacking a nautilus that had come to her for protection. 'This wakened me, it gave me human strength', she recalls (VII, xxviii, 1). Slight as the incident might seem, this is the experience that precipitates the epiphany we have already examined, a fact that is confirmed by the transition of mood in the next stanza, which begins with the ringing affirmation 'We live in our own world', echoing Satan's famous lines in *Paradise Lost* (later used in *A Defence of Poetry* as a motto to encapsulate the 'intellectual philosophy' and Shelley's own poetics[82]): 'The mind is its own place, and in itself / Can make a heaven of hell, a hell of heaven' (I, 54–55). Given that Cythna seems to operate as an Eve figure as well, Shelley may have effected here a synthesis of the liberated Eve and the purified Satan, an imaginative move that is in keeping with other Romantic readings of the Satanic rebellion, but also entails an element of Romantic Miltonism less often remarked, namely the redemption of Eve.

That *Cythna*'s world is made 'From glorious fantasies of hope departed'; that she is able, as Timothy Clark explains,[83] 'to substitute for the loss of a baby born during imprisonment objects of memory or desire conjured up by her own mind', certainly serves to demonstrate the power of her own imagination and will. The fact that her ordeal makes her aware of the creative resources of the mind might seem to be a sufficient explanation of the episode in terms of Cythna's private psychological development. But the momentous sense of loss caused by her separation from the child, together with the theme of 'glorious fantasies of hope departed', are also, I suggest, linked with the fate of the revolution. At this stage in her life the revolution has not yet occurred, but in the *poem* it *has* occurred, and at some level the reader is intended to make a psychological link between the predicament described in Canto VII and the political calamity in Canto VI. The point is that having dealt with the experience of revolutionary *failure* in Canto VI, the reader must now deal with the subsequent and separate trauma of *loss*.

On the face of it there would seem to be no connection between the theme of maternal bereavement and that of failed revolution; a more obvious, biographical explanation for the episode was the death of Mary's first child in March 1815. Yet the way in which the episode is developed suggests that there *is* a thematic association, in the idea of a lost paradise. According to Cythna's own metaphysic, 'We live in our own world'; and though imprisoned at the time, the brief period that she spent with her child is remembered as an Edenic world of love, laughter and play. As described by Shelley, this private paradise of Cythna's is indeed equivalent, in some sense, to that glorious utopian moment of the Revolution of the Golden City. Her shock at losing this private paradise does therefore correspond in some way to the desolation caused by the defeat of the revolution. Given what we already know about the internal dynamics of the poem, it is possible that Cythna's efforts to deal with the experience in Canto VII are designed to help the reader to come to terms with with the experience in Canto VI; in other words, with the trauma of revolutionary failure. Cythna's suspicion that she had imagined the whole episode, that her pregnancy and motherhood were but a 'wondrous vision', a 'dream divine', reinforces this imaginative association, since from the perspective of 1817 the sense of unlimited human possibility associated with of the early years of the French Revolution must indeed have seemed to many like a distant dream, belonging to fantasy rather than history. In fact, that very perception is Shelley's starting point in *Laon and Cythna*, for the first lines of the poem actually compare 'the last hope of trampled France' to 'a brief dream of unremaining glory'.

Also of interest in this connection are the literary allusions in Canto VII. The most obvious is the parallel between the incident with the nautilus and the pivotal scene in 'The Rime of the Ancient Mariner' where the mariner blesses the water-snakes. There are also interesting similarities between Cythna's delightful description of her child and the lines in Coleridge's 'The Nightingale' where his baby son responds to the stars and moon. More pertinent still are the parallels between that same episode in *Laon and Cythna* and two poems by Wordsworth: his little-known ballad 'The Emigrant Mother', published in his *Poems in Two Volumes* (1807), and the celebrated lyric 'A Slumber Did My Spirit Seal' from *Lyrical Ballads*. The first of these poems has as its theme the anguish of a mother who, like Cythna, has been separated from her infant child, having been forced to leave him behind when she was driven into exile from Revolutionary France. The thematic parallel with the second poem is less obvious, but

Cythna's statement 'I had no mortal fears' (VII, xix, 7) is clearly an allusion to Wordsworth's line 'I had no human fears' (2); and having noted this verbal correspondence, we may be alerted to an underlying similarity of theme. For like the other 'Lucy' poems, 'A Slumber Did My Spirit Seal' is essentially about the experience of human loss, which is the precisely the theme of the episode of Cythna and her child. Moreover, the circumstance of Cythna's madness, and the attendant doubt as to whether the child ever really existed, create an atmosphere of mental uncertainty and mystery which is very similar to that of the 'Lucy' poems, just as the fact that Cythna's lost object of love is the product of her own womb allows Shelley to recapture and, as it were, objectify that sense of an *inward* alteration which gives such force to Wordsworth's curious elegies.[84]

'Allusions' may be the wrong word here. Judging from his remarks on the question of 'imitation' in the Preface, Shelley's intention was not to make direct, public reference to other literary texts in the manner of, say, Dryden or Pope. Yet an engagement of some kind with the literature of his contemporaries, as well as being (by his own admission) inescapable, was clearly an integral part of his 'experiment on the temper of the public mind'. Conscious or not, his practice seems to be to assimilate representative ideas and images (or whole episodes and characters) from the works of his contemporaries, and to turn them to his own purposes – without necessarily wanting to draw attention to his source. Thus, in the first of the examples above, Shelley models Cythna's encounter with the eagle and the nautilus on the incident with the water-snakes in 'The Rime of the Ancient Mariner' not because he wants to *allude* as such to the earlier poem, but because he wants to produce a similar effect in his own poem – that is, to include a comparable moment of redemption in Cythna's 'strange tale'. Similarly, he combines the theme of the forlorn mother from 'The Emigrant Mother' with the language of loss from the 'Lucy' poems to create his own scene of separation and loss. The resulting impression made on the reader is supposed to be comparable to the one exerted by Wordsworth's poems, the difference being that Shelley's aim is to provide a *resolution* to the suffering he depicts. The scene in question thus forms part of an ongoing narrative in which Cythna is seen to recover from her trauma.

What I am suggesting, in short, is that *Laon and Cythna* contains, in its constant borrowings from contemporary authors, a kind of record of significant moments in the literature of the period: a record in which many disparate images of grief and joy, of loss and redemption, have been subsumed into a coherent psychological narrative whose function is to enable the reader to relive his imaginative experiences of the past twenty-five years, and to emerge from them with a renewed sense of hope and possibility. A clue to this remarkable compositional technique is given by Laon's remark that Cythna's tale is 'Like broken memories of many a heart / Woven into one' (VII, iii, 2–3).

In terms of actual events, the climax of Cythna's narrative is, of course, the revolution. This she describes in the first half of Canto IX, filling us in on the story up to the point at which Laon joined the insurgents outside the Golden City as already related by him in Canto V. Rhetorically, however, the high point is the prophetic passage with which her speech ends, the long lyrical section that begins in the middle of Canto IX with the words 'The blasts of Autumn drive the wingèd seeds / Over the earth' (IX, xxi, 1–2). Besides being the emotional climax of her speech, this is the point at which the metaphorical power of Cythna's discourse is most vividly demonstrated, and also the place where the lyrical qualities of the poetry are most in evidence. Indeed, what we experience as Cythna turns her attention from the concerns of the past to the question of the future is a shift of emotional mood and poetic mode in every way comparable to the one which took place in the second half of Canto VI. As if to signal this correspondence, and to effect once again the transition from narrative to lyrical time, the stanza that immediately precedes the 'blasts of Autumn' sequence opens with an echo of Laon's 'We know not where we go' (VI, xxix, 1):

> We know not what will come – yet Laon, dearest,
> Cythna shall be the prophetess of Love,
> Her lips shall rob thee of the grace thou wearest,
> To hide thy heart, and clothe the shapes which rove
> Within the homeless Future's wintry grove;
> For I now, sitting thus beside thee, seem
> Even with thy breath and blood to live and move,
> And violence and wrong are as a dream
> Which rolls from steadfast truth an unreturning stream.   (IX, xx)

Within Cythna's quest, as narrated in Cantos VII to IX, what follows occupies exactly the same position as does the earlier passage in Laon's. And like the lyrical sequence in Canto VI, its primary purpose is to proclaim a transcendence over external circumstances, over the 'violence and wrong' of the counter-revolution, and what Laon referred to as 'the fearful overthrow / Of public hope'.

In the earlier passage, the inspiration was essentially erotic in nature, Laon's apprehension of the mystery of intellectual beauty being also the moment of physical consummation of his love for Cythna. Although we are reminded by the stanza just quoted that this is, chronologically, part of the same scene (the lovers are still sitting in their marble ruin, relating to one another the story of their experiences), and although Cythna now styles herself 'the prophetess of Love', the kind of transcendence which is intimated here is not the same as Laon's. Were it so, this climax would merely be a repetition of the earlier one, belying the progress of the previous three cantos, and hardly likely in any case to equal the passionate intensity of the original bower scene.

Yet this scene too is organised around the motif of the Bower of Bliss, not by virtue of its setting or action, but because this is one of the explicit themes of Cythna's speech. The actual phrase 'bower of bliss' appears in the original draft of stanza xxvi (Ryan, p. 322), the only occasion in the poem where we find Shelley using those exact words. Although the phrase does not appear in the published version, the basic metaphor is retained, and the lines that stand reveal the purpose of its application:

> O dearest love! we shall be dead and cold
> Before this morn may on the world arise;
> Wouldst thou the glory of its dawn behold?
> Alas! gaze not on me, but turn thine eyes
> On thine own heart – it is a Paradise
> Which everlasting spring has made its own,
> And while drear winter fills the naked skies,
> Sweet streams of sunny thought, and flowers fresh blown,
> Are there, and weave their sounds and odours into one. (IX, xxvi)

It is now 'thine own heart' that is the 'bower of bliss', or as the published version has it, 'a Paradise / Which everlasting spring has made its own'. So Cythna tells Laon, echoing her earlier injunction to the mariners to look into their own souls, 'And in the inmost bowers of sense and thought, / Until life's sunny day is quite gone down, / To sit and smile with Joy' (VIII, xii, 3–5). The motif of the Bower of Bliss, freed as before from its Spenserian ambivalence, has now been fully internalised so as to become a metaphor for a purely psychological transcendence – a transcendence that is available in the here-and-now. This, in essence, is the message of hope that has been the underlying theme of Cythna's whole speech, an encapsulation of the redemptive creed that she constructed during her imprisonment. Again reminiscent of the Miltonic aphorism that 'The mind is its own place', Cythna's words recall even more distinctly the lines from Book XII of *Paradise Lost* in which the angel Michael explains to Adam how, although excluded from Eden, he may yet possess a 'paradise within thee ... happier far' (586–87).

Cythna's reason for wanting to impress this message upon Laon is not difficult to determine. Laon, too, has suffered a lost paradise, the destruction of a revolutionary world in which 'To hear, to see, to live, was ... / Lethean joy!' The erotic bliss of Canto VI was compensation for this loss, allowing Laon to experience in another form the joy he had not been able fully to share in before. But it is the heroine who discovers the way to complete personal transcendence, the means by which paradise – a 'paradise within' – may be regained and preserved. It is Cythna who proposes to Laon the act of self-knowledge that will enable him to attain to her own state of 'mighty calmness' (IX, xix, 7), to the condition of mind that Shelley holds up to his readers as the ideal towards which post-lapsarian man, that is *post-revolutionary* man, must ultimately aspire.

Cythna's appeal to Laon to 'turn thine eyes / On thine own heart', to find in himself the bliss he has previously found in her, thus extends and completes the movement of ideas that began in Canto VI, the dialectic of self-transcendence through love. Generically, it represents the ultimate stage in the internalisation of romance: the point at which, in Bloomian terms, the 'liberating dream' is 'taken up into the self'. Yet it would be wrong to interpret Cythna's argument for subjective transcendence as a rejection of the external goals of the revolution. Just as Milton's depiction of a 'paradise within' – derived from an allegorical or 'spiritual' reading of the apocalyptic promises of Christianity – does not preclude his literal acceptance in *Paradise Lost* of the millenarian prophecy of a future dispensation where 'the earth / Shall all be paradise, far happier place / Than this of Eden, and far happier days' (XII, 461–3),[85] Cythna's revelation of the paradise of the heart does not negate her earlier vision of a world in which 'mankind was free, / Equal, and pure, and wise in Wisdom's prophecy' (VII, xxxiii, 8–9). It could be argued that the latter was simply a premonition of the Revolution of the Golden City, which has subsequently failed; and that her advice to Laon to try to achieve a utopian state of mind therefore displays a loss of confidence in the idea of *political* revolution. But her remarks about the paradise of the heart actually form part of a larger discussion whose main theme is a restatement (modified to take into account changed circumstances, but not fundamentally altered) of her earlier prophecy. The continuity between the two themes is enhanced by the fact that she breaks off her narrative of events before she reaches the moment at which the revolution finally triumphs, so that the reader's gaze is brought to rest on a future revolution rather than the past one.

Cythna's argument, then, does not stop, as Wordsworth's does in the 'Prospectus' to *The Recluse*, at the notion of a private paradise in the realm of the mind. This is merely a pledge of better things, 'the earnest of the hope' that makes good people great. Stanza xxvii is concerned with the *effect* of that hope, its realisation. As in *Queen Mab*, appeal is now made to the doctrine of Necessity. Cythna does not, however, make the straightforward assertion that a future heaven upon earth is historically inevitable. What she claims is that

> Evil with evil, good with good must wind
> In bands of union, which no power may sever:
> They must bring forth their kind, and be divided never!
>
> (IX, xxvii, lines 7–9)

The argument turns not on the Godwinian theory of 'an un-interrupted chain of causes and effects' (to quote Shelley's footnote on Necessity from *Queen Mab*), but on a belief in the unbroken transmission of human ideals, a belief which is underpinned here by the Platonic theory of transcendent forms. The next stanza makes this clearer:

> The good and mighty of departed ages
> Are in their graves, the innocent and free,
> Heroes, and Poets, and prevailing Sages,
> Who leave the vesture of their majesty
> To adorn and clothe this naked world; – and we
> Are like to them – such perish, but they leave
> All hope, or love, or truth, or liberty,
> Whose forms their mighty spirits could conceive,
> To be a rule and law to ages that survive.   (IX, xxviii)

It is in the knowledge that they have assisted in the propagation of hope, love, truth and liberty, that she and Laon can go to their graves in peace, despite the evident failure of their efforts to make those ideals prevail in their own time and place (Shelley's claim in the

Defence that 'Poets are the unacknowledged legislators of the World'
is a more extreme version of the same argument). For not only does
the law of Necessity – in this interpretation – guarantee the survival
of the ideals for which they have fought, it also ensures for them
personally a kind of immortality: 'the world has seen / A type of
peace', she tells Laon, and 'man shall remember thee' (IX, xxx, 4–9).

   In Shelley's poetry there are many metaphors for the accumulation
of knowledge and the transmission of ideals from one mind or
generation to another, this being one of his most cherished themes. In
this passage, the primary metaphor is of dissemination: it does not
appear in the lines quoted above but in the highly figurative stanzas
that precede them. Initially, then, Cythna's dialectic of revolutionary
change is presented in metaphorical form, through a remarkable
symbolism of the natural cycles which may have been partly inspired
by the paragraph at the end of *Rights of Man* where Paine looks
forward in images of buds and blossom to 'the political summer':

> The blasts of Autumn drive the wingèd seeds
> Over the earth, – next come the snows, and rain,
> And frost, and storms, which dreary Winter leads
> Out of his Scythian cave, a savage train;
> Behold! Spring sweeps over the world again,
> Shedding soft dews from her aethereal wings;
> Flowers on the mountains, fruits over the plain,
> And music on the waves and woods she flings,
> And love on all that lives, and calm on lifeless things.
>
> O Spring, of hope, and love, and youth, and gladness
> Wind-wingèd emblem! brightest, best and fairest!
> Whence comest thou, when, with dark Winter's sadness
> The tears that fade in sunny smiles thou sharest?
> Sister of joy, thou art the child who wearest
> Thy mother's dying smile, tender and sweet;
> Thy mother Autumn, for whose grave thou bearest
> Fresh flowers, and beams like flowers, with gentle feet,
> Disturbing not the leaves which are her winding-sheet.
>
> (IX, xxi–xxii)

So it continues for five stanzas, generating the most powerful
metaphorical sequence in the whole poem, and displaying, as
Richard Holmes has observed, an 'extraordinarily free and forceful
command of the metric pattern and cross-rhythms of the difficult
Spenserian stanza'.[86] The meaning of these five stanzas needs no
elucidation here since that is precisely what is provided by Cythna's

own ensuing remarks. The logic, in any case, will be familiar to anyone who has understood Shelley's 'Ode to the West Wind' (1819), which uses the same imagery to make a very similar argument. Anticipating the 'Ode' not only in its brilliant handling of metaphor but also in its sustained lyrical power, the present passage provides strong evidence – generally overlooked in modern criticism of Shelley – that it is in *Laon and Cythna* that Shelley develops his mature lyrical style, and discovers the prophetic voice that is the mark of his great lyrics of the future.

Two features are present in Cythna's speech that are not found, or at least not in the same form, in the 'Ode to the West Wind'. The first is the depiction of 'the winter of the world':

> Lo, Winter comes! – the grief of many graves,
> The frost of death, the tempest of the sword,
> The flood of tyranny, whose sanguine waves
> Stagnate like ice at Faith, the inchanter's word,
> And bind all human hearts in its repose abhorred.
>
> (IX, xxiii, lines 5–9)

In the tighter metaphorical structure of the 'Ode', these lines are compressed into the single image in the third stanza of the 'dark wintry bed' in which the 'wingèd seeds ... lie cold and low, / Each like a corpse within its grave' (the metaphor of the enchanter also reappears, separately, in the first stanza of the 'Ode'). The more elaborate figuration of winter in *Laon and Cythna* is made necessary by the circumstances of the plot: anything less would hardly convince us that Cythna was seriously confronting the calamities which have already occurred and the others which lie ahead. Being the demonstrable source of much of that oppression, it is appropriate that 'Faith' should be portrayed as the dominant ideology of the political winter, 'the inchanter's word' at which the 'waves' of tyranny 'Stagnate like ice'. In Shelley's resolutely secular romance, orthodox religion has been reduced to the status of black magic, in polar opposition to 'Sense and Reason, those inchanters fair, / Whose wand of power is hope' (IX, xxxii, 2).

The other element missing from the 'Ode' is the notion of the internal paradise. Having already considered its significance in the larger context of the poem, we should now observe how deftly this theme is incorporated into the metaphorical structure of the passage in which it actually appears. The main theme of 'the blasts of Autumn' sequence is the prophecy of regeneration, Cythna's forecast of a political spring that will eventually succeed the encroaching winter. Her personal advice to Laon about the paradise of the heart is in effect a corollary to this argument, albeit one of cardinal importance to the logic of the poem as a whole. What is interesting is how, to extend the argument, she extends the metaphor. Whereas the political prophecy turns on the image of the cycle of seasons, the personal revelation is expressed by the metaphor of an '*everlasting spring*' – this being, of course, a traditional attribute of the earthly paradise, or the Bower of Bliss. By extending the image of spring, Shelley thus manages to create a perfect link between his public and private themes, between the prophecy of revolution and the doctrine of individual transcendence.

CONTEMPORARY REACTIONS

Hazlitt concludes his notorious sketch of Shelley in his essay 'Of Paradox and Commonplace' with the following thoughts:

> Of all people the most tormenting are those who bid you hope in the midst of despair, who, by never caring about any thing but their own sanguine, hare-brained Utopian schemes, have at no time any particular cause for embarrassment and despondency because they have never the least chance of success, and who by including whatever does not hit their idle fancy, kings, priests, religion, government, public abuses or private morals, in the same sweeping clause of ban and anathema, do all they can to combine all parties in a common cause against them, and to prevent every one else from advancing one step farther in the career of practical improvement than they do in that of imaginary and unattainable perfection.[87]

Published in 1822 in the second volume of his *Table Talk*, Hazlitt's remarks may have been partly prompted by the recent appearance of *Queen Mab*, which, as we have seen, attracted considerable attention in the London literary world because of the unusual circumstances of its publication and its politically provocative nature. Whether or not this is the case (Hazlitt makes reference only to *Prometheus Unbound*), the argument could certainly be applied to Shelley's 'philosophical poem', a work notable both for its unrestrained optimism and its relentless polemic against kings, priests, religion, government, public abuses and conventional morality.

The argument seems less applicable to *Laon and Cythna*. Although written, according to Shelley, 'in the same style and for the same object as "Queen Mab",' (*Letters*, I, 557), the later poem is a very different kind of work. It reasserts the revolutionary utopianism of *Queen Mab*, but addresses its own historical moment, and the psychological condition of its intended readership. It urges its readers to hope, but only by making them come to terms with their despair, for Shelley's 'experiment on the temper of the public mind' proceeds from the assumption that the English political psyche had sustained a major trauma as a result of the disappointments of the French Revolution. If the 'liberal and comprehensive morality' to which the poem is dedicated is essentially the same as the one advocated in *Queen Mab*, the whole purpose of the narrative is to test, to put on trial, the ideals which that morality enshrines.

The similarities and differences between the two poems are signalled by the choice of epigraphs. Although omitted from *The Revolt of Islam*, the title page of *Laon and Cythna* carries the famous saying of Archimedes used for *Queen Mab* as a formula linking Shelley's poem to other projects for reforming the world. In this case, however, Archimedes is accompanied not by Voltaire and Lucretius but by four lines from the tenth Pythian Ode of Pindar, which translate as follows:

But as for all things that we, the mortal race, attain he reaches the utmost limits of the voyage. Neither by ships nor by land can you find the wondrous road to the festival place of the Hyperboreans.

The Hyperboreans were a legendary people from the northern parts of Europe and Asia (the word means 'Men-beyond-the-North-Wind') who were said by the Greeks to live up to a thousand years, and, in the words of Peacock, who alludes to the legend in *Calidore*, to lead 'a life eternally diversified by songs and festal dances, the breathing of pipes and the resonance of lyres, and banquets of protracted felicity'.[88] Like the Elysian Islands, the Fortunate Fields, and the Isles of the Blessed, the legend is a classical equivalent of the Christian myth of Paradise. The significance of the particular description chosen by Shelley is that it raises the issue of *how to reach* the happy land of the Hyperboreans, for 'Neither by ships nor by land can you find the wondrous road.' Figuratively, then, one might say that the epigraph serves to indicate that *Laon and Cythna* will *problematise* the search for an earthly paradise; and that the matters on which *Queen Mab* is silent – namely *how* and *when* this world will be transformed into a 'paradise of peace', and what it means to harbour that apocalyptic hope in the aftermath of the French Revolution –

are to be central concerns of Shelley's new 'Vision of the Nineteenth Century'.

I have highlighted these concerns in my own reading of the poem,[89] by charting the progress of the two quests by which the romance is structured, and attempting to explain its teleology in terms of the interplay between the love theme and the political. In particular, I have drawn attention to a sequence of climaxes in the narrative, each of which represents the accession to some kind of paradise, and each of which is, at some level, a reworking of the topos of the Bower of Bliss. The first such moment is the joyous morning of the revolution, described in a passage that recreates the blissful dawn of Wordsworth's 'French Revolution, As It Appeared to Enthusiasts at Its Commencement'. The second is the love scene in Canto VI, a reworking of the Bower of Bliss that reverses the connotations of Spenser's original, and extends the innovations of Southey's adaptations of the motif. The third climax is at the end of Cythna's flashback in Canto IX, where Shelley introduces the notion of the 'paradise of the heart', which is both a reformulation of the Miltonic 'paradise within' and an internalised version of the blissful bower of Canto VI.

In fact Cythna's is not the final image of paradise in the poem. Having fallen victim to the counter-revolution and suffered martyrs' deaths on the pyre, Laon and Cythna are translated to a supernatural realm. Once again, the scene is initially centred around the description of a bower, but Shelley extends his visionary landscape by drawing on many other literary sources, including Coleridge's 'Kubla Khan' and Thomas Moore's 'A Grecian Girl Dreams of the Blessed Islands'.[90] This, however, 'is Paradise / And not a dream', as Cythna says (XII, xxii, 5–6), affirming that it is an actual elysium to which she and Laon have at last been transported, not an imaginary one such as she inhabited during her imprisonment, nor a metaphorical one such as is found in the hearts of the good and free. For the reader, though, these distinctions hardly matter, because this scene, like the visionary narrative in Canto I, plainly needs to be interpreted allegorically – as a symbolic representation of 'the eternity of genius and virtue'.[91] In terms of what I have called the redemptive dynamic, the last scene of the poem is therefore supposed to mark the final stage in the process whereby the 'gloom and misanthropy' of the contemporary reader is transformed into a 'virtuous enthusiasm' for a better world.

Such was the aim of *Laon and Cythna*, announced in the Preface as Shelley's 'first serious appeal to the Public'. The public response was frankly disappointing. First, there was the trouble with the publisher, Ollier, who, fearing prosecution, insisted that *Laon and Cythna* be withdrawn from sale and reissued in a modified, and moderated, version. In either or both of its forms, the poem was then reviewed by several major periodicals, each of which – with the exception of Leigh Hunt's *Examiner* – poured scorn and abuse on Shelley's project, while generally allowing that it had some literary merit. By far the most hostile of the reviews was an anonymous piece by John Taylor Coleridge in the *Quarterly Review* (April 1819), which uses every possible argument to prove that Shelley's attempt to inculcate his ideas was a failure, maintaining at one moment that his indictment of Turkish despotism and Mohammedan fanaticism is inapplicable to the case of 'Englishmen' and 'Christians', but objecting at the next to Shelley's manifest desire to 'pull down our churches, level our Establishment, and burn our bibles'. As for the Revolution of the Golden City, the reviewer notes that it is mostly borrowed from 'that store-house of cast-off mummeries and abominations, the French revolution', but adds that if we are really to believe that 'the hopes of mankind must depend upon the exertion of super-eminent eloquence', the poem is calculated to have the opposite effect to the one intended, since 'they could scarcely depend upon anything of more rare occurrence'.[92]

The success or failure of Shelley's experiment, however, is not to be judged by the reaction of so unsympathetic an organ as the *Quarterly Review*. More pertinent are the criticisms that were made by his friends: by Peacock, for example, who while condemning the review in the *Quarterly*, expressed the view that Shelley 'had carried the expression of his opinions, moral, political, and theological, beyond the bounds of discretion';[93] or by Godwin, who seems to have been even more critical, if we may judge from Shelley's pained response in his letter of 11 December 1817;[94] or by Byron, who remarked to John Murray that had it not been for the publicity which the poem had received in the *Quarterly*, 'nobody would have thought of reading [it], and few who read can understand – I for one'.[95] Even Leigh Hunt, who wrote two long reviews of the poem in the *Examiner* (the second in reply to the attack in the *Quarterly*), rejected Shelley's claim to have appealed 'to the common sympathies of every human breast', and pointed out that, although 'full of humanity', the poem was too remote from ordinary experience and too idiosyncratic in its style to have any chance of achieving its desired object.[96]

Hunt's prediction that 'the work cannot possibly become popular' turned out to be an accurate one. The poem sold very slowly, and never reached a second edition, although Shelley continued to wish for one. However, if we attend more closely to the terms of Shelley's 'experiment', we see that the real question is not whether the poem achieved a large readership, or whether it gained the approval of Tory reviewers, or even whether it satisfied fellow liberals such as Peacock, Godwin and Hunt, who already shared many of Shelley's ideals. The task that the poem sets itself is to restore the political faith of *lapsed* liberals, those erstwhile 'enthusiasts' who had, in Shelley's eyes, been 'morally ruined' by the failure of the French Revolution. It is to these people – the disenchanted liberal intelligentsia – that *Laon and Cythna* is addressed, and at times, in its repeated allusions to contemporary literature, it reads almost like an argument – or rather a psychological counselling session – with their most illustrious representatives, Wordworth, Coleridge and Southey. Unfortunately there is no record of any of these individuals having shown the slightest interest in the poem (though Shelley erroneously believed for a long time that Southey had written the review in the *Quarterly*[97]); and, besides, Hunt may well have been right in supposing that the Lake poets were now 'as dogmatic in their despair as they used to be in their hope'.[98]

There are historical reasons too why the poem was unlikely to succeed. 1817 was a year of reaction and repression in England. Following the revival of the reform movement after the ending of the Napoleonic Wars, a revival which had culminated with the 'riot' at Spa Fields on 2 December 1816, February saw the announcement of a national state of alarm. By the beginning of March, Habeas Corpus had been suspended, and on the 29th the Seditious Meetings Act was passed, which, besides restricting the right of assembly, empowered magistrates to arrest and detain any person suspected of the public sale of blasphemous or seditious literature.[99] Numerous people were imprisoned, and in that year alone there were twenty-one King's Bench prosecutions for seditious libel (of which seven led to convictions).[100]

The situation had somewhat eased by the end of the year, when *Laon and Cythna* was published (December). Yet this was clearly not the most auspicious moment to ask the 'enlightened and refined' to confront the trauma of the French Revolution. Southey was not alone in interpreting the revival of democratic radicalism as a reawakening of 'the Spirit of Jacobinism',[101] and many people had been terrified by the scenes at Spa Fields, where some of the 'rioters' had brandished tricolour flags and liberty caps. Similar fears were raised by the march of the Lancashire 'Blanketeers' in March of 1817, and by the 'Pentridge Rising' in June.[102] Could they be expected to respond differently to the revolutionary scenes in *Laon and Cythna*, a work that made no secret of its support for fundamental political change? Godwin once wrote[103] that David Hume might have been hanged, drawn and quartered for publishing his 'Idea of a Perfect Commonwealth' in the England or Scotland of the 1790s. The 'counter-revolutionary terror' of 1817[104] was a comparable moment in British history, one at which even Spenser's ambition 'to fashion a perfect gentleman' might have been interpreted as revolutionary 'man-mending'.[105] In such circumstances, it is hardly surprising that *Laon and Cythna* failed to meet with an enthusiastic response.

The poem did eventually find a sympathetic readership, but not until after Shelley's death, and not among the people at whom it was aimed. With the benefit of hindsight, it is easy to explain why it did not find favour among the middle classes, but 'I see no reason', wrote a correspondent to Richard Carlisle's *Republican* in December 1826, 'why *The Revolt of Islam* should not follow *Queen Mab* into the hands of the mechanic and labourer'.[106] And follow it did, albeit on a more modest scale than *Queen Mab*. There were to be no cheap pirated editions of *The Revolt of Islam*, but the poem was often cited in the working-class radical press in the 1820s and 30s, in such organs as *The Republican*, *The Lion*, *The Newgate Magazine* and *The Poor Man's Guardian*.[107] It was a favourite too of the Owenites, discussed on more than one occasion in Robert Owen's journal *The New Moral World*.[108] Among the Chartists, in the 1840s and 1850s, the poem appears to have acquired a similar reputation, being included, for example, in the roll call of sacred texts in Thomas Cooper's political epic *The Purgatory of Suicides* (1845).[109] It also influenced the young Benjamin Disraeli's poem *The Revolutionary Epick* (1834), notwithstanding Disraeli's disingenuous claim in the Preface that his epic on the French Revolution was entirely without precedent.[110]

Modern criticism has tended to share Hunt's estimate rather than Cooper's – to see *Laon and Cythna* as a misguided and flawed work rather than as an exemplary piece of political poetry. The politics of the poem is undoubtedly still a problem for many readers, a problem difficult to circumvent in that, unlike some others of Shelley's poems, it is not susceptible to a depoliticised reading. Hard to circumvent too (though this is less true of the revised version) is the unorthodox psychological content, which seems all the more challenging in light of Shelley's startling claim that this tale of incest and insurrection is 'in many respects a genuine picture of my own mind' (*Letters*, I, 577). Another deterrent has been a stylistic one, what Cameron has described as its incongruous mixture of realism and fantasy,[111] a feature that has often frustrated attempts to find a coherent reading of the poem. The stylistic problem diminishes when we identify the generic tradition to which it belongs: that is, when we realise that charges similar to Cameron's have been levelled at romance, and answered by its defenders, almost since the genre began.

Yet *Laon and Cythna* remains a uniquely challenging text. This is a fact I have tried to emphasise in my own treatment of the poem, highlighting its thematic complexities and attempting to comprehend its workings by reference to Shelley's extraordinary 'experiment on the temper of the public mind'. If this interpretation is correct, it is a more coherent and impressive poem than has been previously realised, despite the rapid speed of its composition and despite the fact that the author's intentions sometimes exceeded his powers of execution. This last seems hardly surprising given that *Laon and Cythna* aims at nothing less than to alter the spirit of the age, an ambition it shares with that other large Romantic construction *The Excursion*. With works like *The Prelude* and *Prometheus Unbound* to compare them with, no amount of critical discussion is going to make these two poems look like masterpieces, but both deserve more attention than they have so far received, and *Laon and Cythna* may be the more deserving case in that it is the work of a poet whose imaginative and linguistic powers were increasing rather than declining.

Some of the continuities between this and later Shelley poems such as the 'Ode to the West Wind' and *Prometheus Unbound* have been suggested in the preceding pages, but generally I have taken *Laon and Cythna* on its own terms, or tried to indicate ways in which it refashions earlier and contemporary imaginative literature for its own purposes, notably in its complete recasting of the materials of romance. The poem has been called 'the most ambitious neo-

Spenserian romance in the period, perhaps in all of English literature'.[112] That it is also the poem that addresses in the most sustained way what Shelley termed 'the master theme of the epoch – the French Revolution' (*Letters*, I, 504) may perhaps also be taken as confirmation of the paradoxical but seemingly irresistible convergence between the literary form of romance and the phenomenon of revolution.

Notes

INTRODUCTION

1 Northrop Frye, *The Secular Scripture: A Study of the Structure of Romance* (Cambridge, Mass.: Harvard University Press, 1976), p. 163.

2 Fredric Jameson, 'Magical Narratives: Romance as Genre', *New Literary History*, 7 (1975), 135–63 (p. 142). A modified version of the essay appears in Jameson, *The Political Unconscious: Narrative as a Socially Symbolic Act* (1981; London: Routledge, 1989).

3 Patricia Parker, *Inescapable Romance: Studies in the Poetics of a Mode* (Princeton University Press, 1979).

4 See, for instance, Karen Swann, '"Christabel": The Wandering Mother and the Enigma of Form', *Studies in Romanticism*, 23 (1984), 533–53; Swann, 'Harrassing the Muse' in *Romanticism and Feminism*, ed. Anne K. Mellor (Bloomington: Indiana University Press, 1988); Janice A. Radway, *Reading the Romance: Women, Patriarchy, and Popular Literature* (Chapel Hill: University of North Carolina Press, 1984); Laurie Langbauer, *Women and Romance: The Consolations of Gender in the English Novel* (Ithaca: Cornell University Press, 1990); Laurie Finke, 'Towards a Cultural Poetics of the Romance', *Genre*, 22 (1989), 109–27; Jean Radford, ed., *The Progress of Romance: The Politics of Popular Fiction* (London: Routledge & Kegan Paul, 1986).

5 In Harold Bloom, ed., *Romanticism and Consciousness: Essays in Criticism* (New York: Norton, 1970).

6 Gillian Beer, *The Romance*, Critical Idiom series (London: Methuen, 1970), p. 24.

7 Indicative of this expansion of the category of 'genre' is the recent adoption by the journal *Genre* of the subtitle 'Forms of Discourse and Culture', a change intended, as the editors state, to 'emphasize more fully the intricate relations between genre and the social, institutional, cultural and political texts that constitute its discursive and cultural forms' (*Genre*, 24 (1991), 221).

I. THE FRENCH REVOLUTION AND THE POLITICS OF ROMANCE

1 Samuel P. Huntington, 'Modernization by Revolution' in *Revolution and Political Change*, ed. Claude E. Welch, Jr, and Mavis B. Taintor (1972), p. 23, cited by Ronald Paulson, *Representations of Revolution (1789–1820)* (New Haven: Yale University Press, 1983), p. 2.

2 George Steiner, *In Bluebeard's Castle: Some Notes Towards the Re-definition of Culture* (London: Faber & Faber, 1971), p. 19.

3 Erich Auerbach, *Mimesis: The Representation of Reality in Western Literature*, trans. Willard R. Trask (1953; Princeton University Press, 1971), p. 133.

4 See below, pp. 10–12.

5 What follows is a somewhat simplified account, which will be modified in the course of the book. For more detailed information about the status of romance in the eighteenth century, see Arthur Johnston, *Enchanted Ground: The Study of Medieval Romance in the Eighteenth Century* (London: Athlone Press, 1964); Ioan Williams, ed., *Novel and Romance 1700–1800: A Documentary Record* (New York: Barnes & Noble, 1970); Michael McKeon, *The Origins of the English Novel 1600–1740* (London: Radius, 1987), esp. ch. 1; John Simons, 'Romance in the Eighteenth-Century Chapbook' in *From Medieval to Medievalism*, ed. John Simons (Basingstoke: Macmillan, 1992); and Eithne Henson, '*The Fictions of Romantick Chivalry': Samuel Johnson and Romance* (Cranbury, NJ: Fairleigh Dickinson University Press, 1992).

6 See Vernon Hall, Jr, 'Opposition to the Medieval Romances', *Renaissance Literary Criticism: A Study of Its Social Context* (New York: Columbia University Press, 1945), pp. 203–7.

7 See Donald M. Foerster, *The Fortunes of Epic Poetry: A Study in English and American Criticism 1750–1950* (Washington: Catholic University of America Press, 1962), ch. 1; H. T. Swedenberg, Jr, *The Theory of the Epic in England 1650–1800* (Los Angeles: University of California Press, 1944); and Johnston, *Enchanted Ground*, pp. 1–59.

8 For the influence of *Don Quixote* on the rise of the novel, see McKeon, *Origins of the English Novel*, ch. 7; and Beer, *The Romance*, ch. 3.

9 Logan Pearsall Smith, *Four Words: Romantic, Originality, Creative, Genius* (1924; Oxford: Clarendon Press, 1972), p. 7. Other important studies of the history of the word 'romantic' are René Wellek, 'The Concept of Romanticism in Literary History' (1949) in his *Concepts of Criticism*, ed. Stephen G. Nichols (New Haven: Yale University Press, 1963), pp. 128–98; Hans Eichner, ed., '*Romantic' and Its Cognates: The European History of a Word* (Manchester University Press, 1972); the entry for 'romantic' in Raymond Williams, *Keywords*, 2nd edn. (Glasgow: Fontana, 1976); and, of particular relevance here, the final chapter of Johnston, *Enchanted Ground*, entitled 'What Then Was Romantic?'

10 John Foster, 'On the Application of the Epithet Romantic', *Essays in a Series of Letters to a Friend* (1806; 11th edn, London, 1835), p. 175.

11 Quoted from Ernest Campbell Mossner, 'David Hume's "An Historical Essay on Chivalry and Modern Honour"', *Modern Philology* (August 1947), 54–60 (p. 57). Probably written in 1727, when Hume was only fourteen, this essay remained unpublished until long after his death, and is reprinted in full for the first time in Mossner's article.

12 See M. H. Abrams, *The Mirror and the Lamp: Romantic Theory and the Critical Tradition* (1953; Oxford University Press, 1971), esp. ch. x.

13 See Herbert Weisinger, 'The Middle Ages and the Late Eighteenth-Century Historians', *Philological Quarterly*, 27 (1948), 63–79, and Johnston, *Enchanted Ground, passim*.

14 Thomas Warton, *The History of English Poetry from the Close of the Eleventh Century to the Commencement of the Eighteenth Century to which are Prefixed Three Dissertations*, 3 vols. (London, 1840), I, lvi.

15 *The Works of Richard Hurd, D. D., Lord Bishop of Worcester*, 8 vols. (London, 1811), IV, 323.

16 Sir Walter Scott, *Essays on Chivalry, Romance and the Drama* (London: Frederick Warne, n.d.), pp. 65–68, 76. The 'Essay on Romance', written in 1823, was published in the *Encyclopaedia Britannica* (vol. 6, 2nd part, 1824), as was the 'Essay on Chivalry' (vol. 3, 1st part, 1818) which he wrote in 1814.

17 In a MS fragment from the 1850s, quoted by R. R. Palmer, *The Age of Democratic Revolution: A Political History of Europe and America 1760–1800*, 2 vols. (Princeton University Press, 1959, 1964), II, 130.

18 Edward Dowden, ed., *The Correspondence of Robert Southey with Caroline Bowles* (Dublin, 1881), p. 52, quoted by M. H. Abrams, 'English Romanticism: The Spirit of the Age' in *Romanticism and Consciousness*, ed. Bloom, p. 94.

19 F. W. Raffety, ed., *The Works of the Right Honorable Edmund Burke*, 6 vols. (Oxford University Press, 1906–7), VI, 320. The title of the pamphlet to which he took exception (on the grounds that it flaunted, in the fashionable manner, the 'instability' of the author's opinions, and the 'transitory life' of the production) was *Remarks on the Apparent Circumstances of the War in the Fourth Week of October*, 1795.

20 John Bunyan, *The Pilgrim's Progress from this World to That which is to Come*, ed. J. B. Wharey, 2nd edn. rev. Roger Sharrock (Oxford: Clarendon Press, 1960), pp. 135 ff. On Bunyan's debt to romance, see H. Golder, 'Bunyan's Valley of the Shadow', *Journal of English and Germanic Philology*, 30 (1931), 55–72; Nick Shrimpton, 'Bunyan's Military Metaphor', and Nick Davis, 'The Problem of Misfortune in *The Pilgrim's Progress*', in *The Pilgrim's Progress: Critical and Historical Views*, ed. Vincent Newey (Liverpool University Press, 1980); and McKeon, *Origins of the English Novel*, pp. 295–314.

21 See Johnston, *Enchanted Ground*, pp. 4–9.

22 Addison, *The Spectator*, ed. Donald F. Bond, 5 vols. (Oxford: Clarendon Press, 1965), III, 564–65 (No. 417, 28 June 1712).

23 Edmund Burke, *Reflections on the Revolution in France, and on the Proceedings*

in Certain Societies in London Relative to that Event, ed. Conor Cruise O'Brien (Harmondsworth: Penguin, 1968), p. 130. This and several of the examples that follow are cited by O'Brien in his introduction to illustrate 'how often Burke's references to the Revolution use supernatural or fantastic terms' (p. 31n.).

24 *Reflections*, p. 194.

25 *Reflections*, p. 138.

26 In a letter of 26 September 1791, Burke describes the French Revolution as 'this vile chimera, and sick man's dream of Government' (Alfred Cobban and Robert A. Smith, eds., *The Correspondence of Edmund Burke*, 10 vols. (Cambridge University Press; University of Chicago Press, 1958–78), VI, 414).

27 Burke, *Works*, VI, 46–47.

28 See, for example, Gerald W. Chapman, *Edmund Burke: The Practical Imagination* (Cambridge, Mass.: Harvard University Press, 1967), p. 237; and Isaac Kramnick, *The Rage of Edmund Burke: Portrait of an Ambivalent Conservative* (New York: Basic Books, 1977), ch. 8. Coleridge seems to have been the first to make this diagnosis, in a review of the *Letter to a Noble Lord* in the first issue of his periodical *The Watchman*, where he speaks of Burke's 'phrenetic extravagance' and quotes this passage as an illustration of Hartley's theory of madness (Kathleen Coburn, ed., *The Collected Works of Samuel Taylor Coleridge*, No. 4: *The Watchman*, ed. Lewis Patton (London: Routledge & Kegan Paul, 1970), 32–33).

29 It is worth noting that the image of the harpy had already been used by the French revolutionists themselves to caricature Marie-Antoinette: see Ernest F. Henderson, *Symbol and Satire in the French Revolution* (New York and London: Knickerbocker Press, 1912), pp. 157–58.

30 *Reflections*, p. 238.

31 *Reflections*, p. 125.

32 *Reflections*, pp. 283–84.

33 Speech on Mr Flood's Motion, 4 March 1790, in Alfred Cobban, ed., *The Debate on the French Revolution 1789–1800*, 2nd edn. (London: A. & C. Black, 1960), p. 106.

34 Paulson, *Representations of Revolution*, p. 67.

35 Details of these and other contemporary journals are given in Stanley Harrison, *Poor Men's Guardians: A Record of the Struggles for a Democratic Newspaper Press, 1763–1973* (London: Lawrence & Wishart, 1974), ch. 3.

36 Graham Pechey makes a similar claim for Blake's use of demonic imagery in his article '*The Marriage of Heaven and Hell*: A Text and Its Conjuncture', *Oxford Literary Review*, 3 (Spring 1979), 52–77. In much the same way, Burke's reference to the common people as a 'swinish multitude' (*Reflections*, p. 176) gave rise in the 1790s to a large number of pamphlets and periodicals with titles like *Hog's Wash*, *Pig's Meat*, *Rights of Swine*, and *Twopence Worth of Pig's Bristles*: on which, see R. K. Webb, *The British Working Class Reader 1790–1848: Literacy and Social*

Tension (1955; New York: Augustus M. Kelley, 1971), pp. 36–45. Shelley's chorus of pigs in *Oedipus Tyrannus or Swellfoot the Tyrant* (1820) is a late addition to the theme, analysed by Newman Ivey White in 'Shelley's Swellfoot the Tyrant in Relation to Contemporary Political Satire', *Publications of the Modern Language Association*, 36 (1921), 332–46.

37 [Mary Burges], *The Progress of the Pilgrim Good-Intent, in Jacobinical Times* (5th edn, London, 1800), Preface, pp. iii–iv.

38 See Steven Blakemore, *Burke and the Fall of Language* (Hanover: University Press of New England, 1988).

39 *Reflections*, pp. 169–70.

40 James Boulton, *The Language of Politics in the Age of Wilkes and Burke* (London: Routledge & Kegan Paul, 1963), p. 98.

41 *Reflections*, p. 171.

42 *Reflections*, p. 172. Burke's quotation here is from Horace's *Ars Poetica*.

43 See William C. Dowling, 'Burke and the Age of Chivalry', *Yearbook of English Studies*, 12 (1982), 109–24; and Alfred Cobban, *Edmund Burke and the Revolt against the Eighteenth Century: A Study of the Political and Social Thinking of Burke, Wordsworth, Coleridge and Southey*, 2nd edn. (London: Allen & Unwin, 1960). For a more circumspect account of the place of chivalry in Burke's analysis of the French Revolution, see J. G. A. Pocock, 'The Political Economy of Burke's Analysis of the French Revolution' in his *Virtue, Commerce, and History: Essays on Political Thought and History, Chiefly in the Eighteenth Century* (Cambridge University Press, 1985), pp. 197–99; and his earlier essay 'Burke and the Ancient Constitution: A Problem in the History of Ideas' in his *Politics, Language and Time: Essays on Political Thought and History* (London: Methuen, 1972). See also below, pp. 68–69.

44 According to Marx, in a footnote to *Capital* quoted by John Bowle, *Politics and Opinion in the Nineteenth Century: An Historical Introduction* (London: Jonathan Cape, 1954), p. 339, Burke was 'a sycophant who, in the pay of the English oligarchy played the romanticist against the French Revolution', although 'to the very marrow he was a commonplace bourgeois'. Note, however, that Marx himself echoes Burke in *The Communist Manifesto* when he writes that the bourgeoisie 'has drowned the most heavenly ecstasies of religious fervour, of chivalrous enthusiasm, of philistine sentimentalism, in the icy water of egotistical calculation'; see Marx and Engels, *Collected Works*, 50 vols. in progress (London: Lawrence and Wishart, 1975–), VI, 487. For other examples of Marx's use of chivalric and romantic imagery, see S. S. Prawer, *Karl Marx and World Literature* (Oxford University Press, 1976).

45 Hurd, *Works*, IV, 344–48.

46 Boulton's estimate, in *Language of Politics*, ch. 6. This figure is increased if one includes the reviews in periodicals, on which see F. P. Lock, *Burke's Reflections on the Revolution in France* (London: Allen & Unwin, 1985), ch. 5; and Derek Roper, *Reviewing Before the 'Edinburgh' 1788–1802* (London: Methuen, 1978), ch. 4.

47 Thomas Christie, *Letters on the Revolution in France* (Part I, 1791), pp. 6–7, cited by Boulton, *Language of Politics*, p. 190.

48 The Rev. W. Field, *Memoirs of the Life, Writings and Opinions of the Revd. Samuel Parr, LL.D.* (1828), I, 310–11, in Cobban, ed., *Debate on the French Revolution*, p. 82.

49 As reported in the *Morning Chronicle* on 12 May 1791. Burke's ironic acceptance of this 'sentence' (as he calls it) is the opening theme of his *Appeal from the New to the Old Whigs* (1791).

50 J. Sharpe, *A Rhapsody to E ---- B ---- Esq.* (Sheffield, 1792), p. 4, quoted by Boulton, *Language of Politics*, p. 200.

51 Mary Wollstonecraft, *A Vindication of the Rights of Men* (1790), pp. 65, 108, quoted by Boulton, *Language of Politics*, p. 170.

52 Thomas Paine, *Rights of Man*, ed. Henry Collins (Harmondsworth: Penguin, 1969), p. 62.

53 *Rights of Man*, p. 74.

54 *Rights of Man*, pp. 102–4.

55 Quoted by Hoxie Neale Fairchild, *The Romantic Quest* (New York: Columbia University Press, 1931), p. 2. Reference untraced.

56 *Reflections*, p. 90.

57 *Rights of Man*, p. 72.

58 Paine's representation of Burke as Don Quixote was almost certainly suggested by contemporary caricature, several political cartoons having already made use of the Quixote theme to satirise Burke: see plates 1 to 3. Full explanatory descriptions of these engravings can be found in M. Dorothy George, *Catalogue of Political and Personal Satires Preserved at the Department of Prints and Drawings in the British Museum*, Vol. VI: 1784–92 (London: British Museum, 1938), nos. 7678, 7679, 7824.

59 Quoted from Marilyn Butler, ed., *Burke, Paine, Godwin, and the Revolution Controversy* (Cambridge University Press, 1984), pp. 196–97.

60 William Godwin, *Enquiry Concerning Political Justice and Its Influence on Modern Morals and Happiness*, 3rd edn. (1798), ed. with intro. by Isaac Kramnick (Harmondsworth: Penguin, 1976), p. 471.

61 *Political Justice*, pp. 725–26.

62 James Mackintosh, *Vindiciae Gallicae: Defence of the French Revolution and Its English Admirers against the Accusations of the Right Hon. Edmund Burke; including Some Strictures on the Late Production of Mons. de Calonne* (London, 1791), p. xiii.

63 *Vindiciae Gallicae*, p. xi.

64 *Vindiciae Gallicae*, pp. xi–xiii.

65 Entry for 13 June 1799 in Thomas Green, *Diary of a Lover of Literature*, quoted by M. Ray Adams, *Studies in the Literary Backgrounds of English Radicalism; With Special Reference to the French Revolution* (1947; Westport, Conn.: Greenwood Press, 1968), p. 175.

66 Reprinted in Burton R. Pollin, 'Verse Satires on William Godwin in the Anti-Jacobin Period', *Satire Newsletter*, 2 (1964), 31–40. While drawing attention to the Spenserian idiom of the poem, Pollin overlooks the witty

allusion to Chatterton's *Goddwyn; A Tragedie*, one of the 'Rowley' poems, in *The Works of Thomas Chatterton*, 3 vols. (London, 1803), III, 323–50.

67 Thomas Warton, *Observations on the Fairy Queen of Spenser*, 2 vols. (2nd edn. London, 1762), II, 267.

68 Hurd, *Works*, IV, 246.

69 [Catherine M. Graham], *Observations on the Reflections of the Right Hon. Edmund Burke, on the Revolution in France, in a Letter to the Right Hon. the Earl of Stanhope* (London, 1790), p. 52.

70 Anon., *Temperate Comments upon Intemperate Reflections: or, A Review of Mr. Burke's Letter* (London, 1791), pp. 35–36.

71 *Vindiciae Gallicae*, p. 196.

72 See, for example, William Robertson, *A View of the Progress of Society in Europe* (1769); John Millar, *The Origin of Ranks* (1771); Gilbert Stuart, *A View of Society in Europe* (1778); and Adam Ferguson, *An Essay on the History of Civil Society* (1778). These and other relevant texts are discussed by Weisinger, 'Middle Ages and the Late Eighteenth-Century Historians', pp. 69–70; and Pocock, *Virtue, Commerce, and History*, pp. 198–99. See also Pocock's introduction to his recent edition of Burke's *Reflections on the Revolution in France* (Indianapolis: Hackett, 1987), esp. pp. xxxi–xxxiii.

73 *Vindiciae Gallicae*, p. 198 (wrongly numbered p. 180).

74 See *Political Justice*, p. 757.

75 William Godwin, *Thoughts Occasioned by the Perusal of Dr. Parr's Spital Sermon, Preached at Christ Church, April 15, 1800; Being a Reply to the Attacks of Dr. Parr, Mr. Mackintosh, The Author of An Essay on Population, and Others* (1801) in Godwin, *Uncollected Writings (1785–1822): Articles in Periodicals and Six Pamphlets*, facsimile reproductions, with intro. by J. W. Marken and B. R. Pollin (Gainesville, Fla.: Scholars' Facsimiles and Reprints, 1968), p. 351.

76 Robert Lovell and Robert Southey, *Poems: containing The Retrospect, Odes, Elegies, Sonnets, &c.* (Bath, 1795 [1794]), p. 20.

77 Helen Maria Williams, *Letters from France*, vol. 1 (1790), 192–96, reprinted in Butler, ed., *Burke, Paine, Godwin, and the Revolution Controversy*, p. 82.

78 For many other examples of this kind of imagery, see Neale Robert Reinitz, 'The French Revolution in London Newspaper Verse of the 1790s', unpublished Ph.D. thesis, University of California, 1958.

79 Quoted here from George Dyer, *Poems* (London, 1792), p. 32.

80 Unless otherwise indicated, quotations from Coleridge's poetry are from *The Complete Poetical Works of S. T. Coleridge*, ed. E. H. Coleridge (Oxford: Clarendon Press, 1969).

81 See *Prometheus Unbound*, I, 567. 'France: An Ode' was a favourite poem of Shelley's, and an important source of imagery for his own revolutionary romances, especially *Laon and Cythna*.

82 Except where indicated, all references are to the 1805 text presented in

William Wordsworth, *The Prelude 1799, 1805, 1850*, ed. Jonathan Wordsworth, M. H. Abrams and Stephen Gill (New York: Norton, 1979).

83 Thomas De Quincey, *Recollections of the Lakes and the Lake Poets*, ed. David Wright (Harmondsworth: Penguin, 1970), p. 181.

84 See James K. Chandler, *Wordsworth's Second Nature: A Study of the Poetry and Politics* (University of Chicago Press, 1984), pp. 203–6; Alan Liu, *Wordsworth: The Sense of History* (Stanford University Press, 1989), pp. 373–80; Stuart Curran, *Poetic Form and British Romanticism* (Oxford University Press, 1986), pp. 187–89; Theresa M. Kelley, *Wordsworth's Revisionary Aesthetics* (Cambridge University Press, 1988), p. 116. Liu's notion of the 'conflict of genres' in the Revolution books is especially helpful here, though my own account differs in claiming that the romance model is able to comprehend both positive and negative aspects of the revolutionary experience, as is suggested by the 'Bliss' passage in Book x, discussed below.

85 Lynn Hunt, *Politics, Culture, and Class in the French Revolution* (London: Methuen, 1986), p. 37–38. These ideas are extended in Hunt's recent book *The Family Romance of the French Revolution* (Berkeley: University of California Press, 1992), and in her essay 'The Political Psychology of Revolutionary Caricatures' in *French Caricature and the French Revolution 1789–1799*, Exhibition Catalogue (Los Angeles: Grunwald Centre for the Graphic Arts, University of California, 1988), pp. 33–40.

86 On this crucial aspect of the revolutionary (and counter-revolutionary) psychology, see also François Furet, *Interpreting the French Revolution*, trans. Elborg Forster (Cambridge University Press, 1981), pp. 66–77; and Hannah Arendt, *On Revolution* (1963; Harmondsworth: Penguin, 1973), ch. 3.

87 *The Fall of Robespierre* is quoted here from the second volume of *The Complete Poetical Works of S. T. Coleridge*, ed. E. H. Coleridge.

88 For the exact sources, see Carl R. Woodring, *Politics in the Poetry of Coleridge* (Madison: University of Wisconsin Press, 1961), p. 195.

89 Milton, *Paradise Lost*, ed. Alastair Fowler, corrected edn. (Harlow: Longman, 1971), Book iv, lines 393 ff. All subsequent quotations from the poem are from this edition.

90 Quoted from H. T. Dickinson, ed., *The Political Works of Thomas Spence*, (Newcastle-upon-Tyne: Avero Publications, 1982), p. 52.

91 M. H. Abrams, *Natural Supernaturalism: Tradition and Revolution in Romantic Literature* (New York: Norton, 1971), p. 64 and *passim*. See also Clarke Garrett, *Respectable Folly: Millenarianism and the French Revolution* (Baltimore: Johns Hopkins University Press, 1975); J. F. C. Harrison, *The Second Coming: Popular Millenarianism 1780–1850* (London: Routledge & Kegan Paul, 1979); and Ernest R. Sandeen, *The Roots of Fundamentalism: British and American Millenarianism 1800–1930* (University of Chicago Press, 1970), ch. 1.

92 Thomas Paine, *Common Sense*, ed. with intro. by Isaac Kramnick (Harmondsworth: Penguin, 1976), p. 65.

93 Gwyn Williams, *Artisans and Sans-Culottes: Popular Movements in France and Britain during the French Revolution* (London: Edward Arnold, 1968), p. 70.

94 *Collected Works of Samuel Taylor Coleridge*, No. 4: *The Friend*, ed. Barbara E. Rooke, 2 vols. (1969), II, 147–48. The 1815 text cited below is from Wordsworth, *Poems*, 2 vols., facsimile reprint, Revolution and Romanticism series (Oxford: Woodstock Books, 1989), II, 69–71.

95 Quotations are from the Arden edition of *Antony and Cleopatra*, ed. M. R. Ridley (London: Methuen, 1965).

96 For suggesting this possible allusion, I am grateful to John Birtwhistle.

97 It is significant that when Wordsworth revised the Vaudracour and Julia story for separate publication in 1820, he introduced a passage which contained the phrase 'momentous but uneasy bliss' (see *Vaudracour and Julia*, lines 94–101, replacing *Prelude*, IX, lines 642–46). The interpolated lines emphasise the precarious and temporary ('momentous' but also momentary) nature of the lovers' happiness during the early period of Julia's pregnancy, but the phrase in question could equally be said to characterise the 'bliss' of the early years of the Revolution: Wordsworth certainly plays with the analogy between love and revolution in the 1805 *Prelude*, and the passage from Book x picks up in a wider sense on the language of the Vaudracour and Julia episode.

98 All references are to Spenser, *The Faerie Queene*, ed. A. C. Hamilton, corrected edn. (London: Longman, 1980).

99 Pitt often attracted such metaphors by virtue of his astonishing powers of oratory. See, for example, Charles Pigott's *Political Dictionary* (London, 1795), where he appears under the entry for 'Necromancer' as the political magician 'who, by means of charms and spells, conjures up the House of Commons and the Privy Council to his opinions'. In his 'Character of the Late Mr. Pitt' (1806), Hazlitt makes a similar judgment upon Pitt's rhetorical abilities, unfavourably comparing his eloquence (and intelligence) with those of Burke, Fox and Sheridan, but allowing that Pitt carried 'correctness' of speech 'to a degree which, in an extemporaneous speaker, was almost miraculous' (P. P. Howe, ed., *The Complete Works of William Hazlitt*, 21 vols. (London: Dent, 1930–34), IV, 128).

100 Again, there are specific precedents for Wordsworth's choice of imagery. In his *Essay on the Principle of Population* (1798), Thomas Malthus alludes to the very same speech in *The Tempest* when dismissing the Godwinian system as 'little better than a dream, a beautiful phantom of the imagination. These "gorgeous palaces" of happiness and immortality, these "solemn temples" of truth and virtue will dissolve "like the baseless fabric of a vision", when we awaken to real life and contemplate the true and genuine situation of man on earth' (Malthus, *An Essay on the Principle of Population and A Summary View of the*

Principle of Population, ed. Antony Flew (Harmondsworth: Penguin, 1970), pp. 132–33).

101 The word 'enthusiast', which dates in English from the beginning of the seventeenth century, originally meant someone who erroneously believes himself to be divinely inspired, and was subsequently applied to persons displaying excessive emotion of any kind. In the era of the French Revolution, as in earlier periods of disturbance, it often denoted strong *political* feelings, generally (though not always) being used as a term of abuse, and usually in reference to someone of radical tendencies – Burke, for instance, talks of 'enthusiasts' when warning against 'the philosophical fanatics' in France (*Reflections*, p. 256). Wordsworth's 1815 title may have been suggested by Coleridge's use of the term 'enthusiast' in the 1809 essay in *The Friend* to which the poem was first appended – an essay partly inspired in turn by Wordsworth's poem. Stephen Prickett, *England and the French Revolution* (London: Macmillan, 1989), pp. 105–11, discusses the political application of the word 'enthusiasm' by Wordsworth and Coleridge, but does not mention either of the above texts. For a comprehensive history of the word, see Susie I. Tucker, *Enthusiasm: A Study in Semantic Change* (Cambridge University Press, 1972).

102 The Burkean influence is forcefully argued by Chandler, *Wordsworth's Second Nature*, pp. 31–61. Karina Williamson arrives at a similar, ironic reading of the passage by contextualising the image of the enchanter ('Wordsworth and the Enchanters', *Review of English Studies*, 26 (1985), 355–74). The allusion to the Bower of Bliss is examined by George Richard Pitts, 'Romantic Spenserianism: *The Faerie Queene* and the English Romantics', unpublished Ph.D. thesis, University of Pennsylvania, 1977, pp. 260–62.

103 Pitts, 'Romantic Spenserianism', p. 262.

104 In the Preface to *Alastor*, a poem which offers its own interpretation of Wordsworth's former revolutionary idealism.

105 *The Friend*, II, 146.

106 Direct evidence of Wordsworth's knowledge of 'the master pamphlets of the day' (referred to in the 1805 *Prelude*, Book IX, lines 96–97) can be found in his own unpublished contribution to the pamphlet war, *A Letter to the Bishop of Llandaff* (1793), in W. J. B. Owen and Jane Worthington Smyser, eds., *The Prose Works of William Wordsworth*, 3 vols. (Oxford: Clarendon Press, 1974), I, 19–66. Owen and Smyser's useful bibliographical annotation can be supplemented by Duncan Wu, *Wordsworth's Reading 1770–1799* (Cambridge University Press, 1993). Valuable commentaries on the *Letter to Llandaff* can be found in Chandler, *Wordsworth's Second Nature*, pp. 15–30; Nicholas Roe, *Wordsworth and Coleridge: The Radical Years* (Oxford: Clarendon Press, 1988); John Williams, *Wordsworth: Romantic Poetry and Revolution Politics* (Manchester University Press, 1989); and Kenneth R. Johnston, 'Wordsworth's Revolutions, 1793–1798' in *Revolution and English*

Romanticism: Politics and Rhetoric, ed. Keith Hanley and Raman Selden (Hemel Hempstead: Harvester Wheatsheaf, 1990).

107 The edition cited here is Edward Young, *Night Thoughts*, ed. Stephen Cornford (Cambridge University Press, 1989).

108 The first reader to appreciate the skilful ambiguity of Wordsworth's poem was William Hazlitt, in his *Memoirs of the late Thomas Holcroft*, which was published in 1816 but substantially written in the months after Wordsworth's poem first appeared in *The Friend*. This is revealed by Hazlitt's brilliant imitation of Wordsworth's lines in the passage quoted as an epigraph to this chapter, which recalls how the French Revolution 'seemed' to people of Holcroft's liberal disposition, while at the same time hinting at how things really were, or were to become. References to 'bliss' that 'lulled the senses', to the deceptively easy-looking road to Paradise in *Pilgrim's Progress*, to the giant reason and the 'endless gradations' of Jacob's ladder, are an attempt in the manner of Wordsworth to convey the irony of the 'romantic prospects' opened by the Revolution. The suspended meaning of the passage is made all too clear in the paragraph that follows, which contains a brutal domestic recoding of the plight of a victim of a romance enchantress:

> The French revolution was the only match that ever took place between philosophy and experience: and waking from the trance of theory to the sense of reality, we hear the words, *truth, reason, virtue, liberty*, with the same indifference or contempt, that a cynic who has married a jilt or a termagant, listens to the rhapsodies of lovers. (Hazlitt, *Complete Works*, III, 155–56)

2. ROMANCE AND REVOLUTION IN *QUEEN MAB*

1 Quoted here from Byron, *The Vision of Judgment with Southey's 'Vision of Judgment' as an Appendix*, ed. E. M. Earl (Oxford University Press, 1929), p. 5.

2 The circumstances of *Mab*'s unauthorised republication are summarised in Lewis M. Schwartz, 'Two New Contemporary Reviews of Shelley's *Queen Mab*', *KSJ*, 19 (1970), 77–86.

3 Newman Ivey White, *The Unextinguished Hearth: Shelley and His Contemporary Critics* (Durham, NC: Duke University Press, 1938), pp. 55–56. A further attack on the 'Satanic School' is made in the belated review of Shelley's *Declaration of Rights* (1812) and *The Necessity of Atheism* (1811) in the *Brighton Magazine* (May 1822), reprinted in White, *The Unextinguished Hearth*, pp. 39–44.

4 H. T. Dickinson, *British Radicalism and the French Revolution 1789–1815* (Oxford: Blackwell, 1985), pp. 76–77.

5 Marie Catherine le Jumel de Berneville [Countess of Aulnoy], *Queen Mab; containing A Select Collection of only the Best, Most Instructive, and Entertaining Tales of the Fairies … To which are added A Fairy Tale, in the ancient English Style, by Dr. Parnell: and Queen Mab's Song* (1752; 5th edn,

London, 1799), Preface, p. iv. This precedent was first noted by Donald Reiman in *Shelley and His Circle*, v, 284n.

6 See Arthur E. Waite, ed., *Fairy Music: An Anthology of English Fairy Poetry*, (London: Walter Scott Ltd, n.d.). Charlotte Dacre's poem 'Queen Mab and Her Fays', from her *Hours of Idleness* (1805), is cited by Stuart Curran, 'Women readers, women writers' in *The Cambridge Companion to British Romanticism*, ed. Curran (Cambridge University Press, 1993), p. 188n., where he makes an interesting claim about the 'transgressive potentiality of the realm of fairy for women writers'. This may partly explain why the Mab figure appealed to Shelley, for whom the erotic and the political were always closely connected. For the background to the Mab legend, see Minor White Latham, *The Elizabethan Fairies: The Fairies of Folklore and the Fairies of Shakespeare* (New York: Columbia University Press, 1930).

7 All subsequent quotations from the poem are from the first volume of Geoffrey Matthews and Kelvin Everest, eds., *The Poems of Shelley* (London: Longman, 1989).

8 Four such works are listed in D. F. Foxon, *English Verse 1701–1750. A Catalogue of Separately Printed Poems with Notes on Contemporary Collected Editions*, 2 vols. (Cambridge University Press, 1975), the two I have not mentioned in the text being Charles Leslie, *A Philosophical Poem (Design and Beauty)* (1748) and John Reynolds, *Death's Vision Represented in a Philosophical, Sacred Poem* (1709). For the period 1770–1813, Heming's and Shelley's are the only 'philosophical poems' listed in J. R. de J. Jackson, *Annals of Enlish Verse 1770–1835. A Preliminary Survey of the Volumes Published* (New York: Garland, 1985), but there are two other works which bear a related classification: John Courtenay, *A Poetical and Philosophical Essay on the French Revolution* (1793) and [Thomas Moore], *The Sceptic; A Philosophical Satire* (1809). Not included by Jackson, but cited by Curran, *Poetic Form and British Romanticism*, p. 248n., is George Sanon, *The Causes of the French Revolution; and the Science of Governing an Empire: An Epic and Philosophical Poem* (1806), a poem which bears some striking formal and thematic similarities with *Queen Mab*, though there is no evidence that it was read by Shelley.

9 *The Spectator*, III, 261 (No. 339, 29 March 1812).

10 'On the Application of the Epithet Romantic', p. 231.

11 Chapman, *Burke: The Practical Imagination*, p. 237.

12 Quoted in Prickett, *England and the French Revolution*, p. 103. For a pertinent discussion of this and other tracts by Hannah More, see Robert Hole, 'British Counter-revolutionary Propaganda in the 1790s' in Colin Jones, ed., *Britain and Revolutionary France: Conflict, Subversion and Propaganda* (University of Exeter Publications, 1983), pp. 53–69.

13 Sir William Drummond, *Academical Questions* (1805), facsimile reprint with intro. by Terence Allan Hoagwood (Delmar, NY: Scholars' Facsimiles & Reprints, 1984), pp. xiii–xiv.

14 H. F. B. Smith and C. E. Jones, eds., *The Works of Thomas Love Peacock*,

10 vols. (1924–34; New York: A. M. S. Press, 1967), III, 50. All subsequent quotations from Peacock are from this edition.

15 Cited by Peter H. Marshall, *William Godwin* (New Haven: Yale University Press), p. 221. The author was William Proby.

16 First published in the *Morning Post* in 1801, the poem is reprinted in Coleridge's *Complete Poetical Works*, II, 979.

17 Hazlitt, *Complete Works*, XI, 21.

18 The first of these translations was by John Mason Good, the second by T. Busby: both are listed under the entry for Lucretius in *The British Museum Catalogue of Printed Books* (London, 1965).

19 Erasmus Darwin, *The Botanic Garden; A Poem, in Two Parts. Part I. Containing the Economy of Vegetation. Part II. The Loves of the Plants. With Philosophical Notes* (1791), facsimile edn., with intro. by Desmond King-Hele (Menston, Yorkshire: Scolar Press, 1973), p. v. Darwin's *The Temple of Nature* (1803) also describes itself as 'A Poem, with Philosophical Notes'.

20 On the contemporary fashion for poems with footnotes, see Marilyn Butler, 'Culture's Medium: The Role of the Review' in *The Cambridge Companion to British Romanticism*, pp. 129–30.

21 Quoted from L. Rice-Oxley, ed., *Poetry of the Anti-Jacobin*, Percy Reprints (Oxford: Blackwell, 1924), p. 89.

22 For Shelley's knowledge of Darwin, see Desmond King-Hele, *Erasmus Darwin and the Romantic Poets* (London: Macmillan, 1986). Shelley's knowledge of the other texts discussed here remains conjectural.

23 Paul Ricoeur, *Lectures on Ideology and Utopia*, ed. George H. Taylor (New York: Columbia University Press, 1986), pp. 297–98.

24 Sir Walter Scott, *The Visionary Nos. I. II. III.* (1819), facsimile edn., with intro. by Peter Garside, Regency Reprints (University College, Cardiff Press, 1984), pp. 10–11. For a summary and discussion of the pamphlet, see Crane Brinton, *The Political Ideas of the English Romanticists* (1926; New York: Russell & Russell, 1962), pp. 112–14.

25 See also *Letters*, I, 28–29, 35. Voltaire's slogan was a favourite of Shelley's, which he may have first encountered in Abbé Barruel's *Memoirs Illustrating the History of Jacobinism*, trans. Robert Clifford, 4 vols. (1797–98), I, 116–17, as noted by Gerald McNeice, *Shelley and the Revolutionary Idea* (Cambridge, Mass.: Harvard University Press, 1969), p. 106.

26 It is worth noting that the passage immediately following the lines quoted by Shelley contains Lucretius's classic defence of the genre of the philosophical poem: Lucretius, *On the Nature of the Universe*, trans. Ronald Latham (1951; Harmondsworth: Penguin, 1961), p. 130. See also Paul Turner, 'Shelley and Lucretius', *Review of English Studies*, 10 (1959), 269–82.

27 'On the Application of the Epithet Romantic', p. 217.

28 Extracts from Hébert's news-sheets are reprinted in J. M. Roberts and John Hardman, eds., *French Revolution Documents*, 2 vols. (Oxford:

Blackwell, 1973), II, 131–32, 218–19, 234–35; and, in translation, in P. Beik, ed. and trans., *The French Revolution*, Documentary History of Western Civilization series (London: Macmillan, 1971), pp. 271–76. Other French revolutionary publications that used the 'Père Duchesne' label are noted by J. Gilchrist and W. J. Murray, eds., *The Press in the French Revolution: A Selection of Documents taken from the Press of the Revolution for the Years 1789–1794* (London: Ginn, 1971), pp. 20–21.

29 Roland Barthes, *Writing Degree Zero*, trans Annette Lavers and Colin Smith (1968; New York: Hill and Wang, 1981), pp. 21–27. See also the special section on the 'revolutionary style' in *French Revolution Documents*, II, 35–36; and Emmet Kennedy, *A Cultural History of the French Revolution* (New Haven: Yale University Press, 1989), ch. 10.

30 Howard Mumford Jones, *Revolution & Romanticism* (Cambridge, Mass.: Harvard University Press, 1974), p. 341.

31 P. M. S. Dawson, *The Unacknowledged Legislator: Shelley and Politics* (Oxford: Clarendon Press, 1980), p. 3.

32 Coleridge, for example, observed how at the commencement of the French Revolution, even 'in the remotest villages every tongue was employed in echoing and enforcing the almost geometrical abstractions of the physiocratic politicians and economists' (*The Statesman's Manual* (1816), in Coleridge, *Collected Works*, VI, 15–16; an earlier version of the passage had appeared in *The Friend* on 28 September 1809).

33 See above, p. 38.

34 For Paine's influence on Shelley, see Kenneth Cameron, *The Young Shelley: Genesis of a Radical* (1950; New York: Collier, 1962), p. 277; and Dawson, *The Unacknowledged Legislator*, pp. 54–68.

35 *Political Justice*, pp. 791–92.

36 *Rights of Man*, pp. 234–35.

37 For the background to this debate, see J. G. A. Pocock, 'The Eighteenth Century Debate: Virtue, Passion and Commerce', *The Machiavellian Moment: Florentine Political Thought and the Atlantic Republican Tradition* (Princeton University Press, 1975). Some of the relevant primary texts can be found in Stephen Copley, ed., *Literature and the Social Order: Eighteenth-Century England* (London: Croom Helm, 1984).

38 The history of the word 'enterprise' provides perfect confirmation of Burke's thesis about the fate of chivalry. In its chivalric sense of a bold or arduous undertaking, the word (originally both noun and transitive verb) dates in English from the early fifteenth century, and was first applied explicitly to chivalry in Malory's *Morte D'Arthur* (1475): 'How Trystram enterprysed the Bataylle to fyght for the trewage of Cornwayl'. It was not until the nineteenth century that the word came to be associated with commerce, the first such usage recorded by *OED* being an article by James Beresford in the *London Gazette* (13 September 1806): 'Some of the existing Duties bear too hard on the Enterprize of Commerce'. By 1844, when the phrase 'private enterprise' appears, commerce and enterprise are virtually synonomous. Resisting this

semantic shift, Shelley (following Burke) was using the word 'enterprise' in its old sense at precisely the moment when the chivalric meaning was being superseded by the commercial.

39 Adam Smith, *An Inquiry into the Nature and Causes of the Wealth of Nations*, ed. R. H. Campbell and A. S. Skinner, text ed. W. B. Todd, 2 vols. (Oxford: Clarendon Press, 1976), I, 418–19.

40 For instance, in his *Thoughts on Scarcity* (1795), where he claims that 'the laws of commerce ... are the laws of nature, and consequently the laws of God' (*Works*, VI, 22). For a persuasive account of the 'bourgeois political economist' in Burke, see C. B. Macpherson, *Burke*, Past Masters series (Oxford University Press, 1980), ch. 5.

41 *Common Sense*, p. 65.

42 The text quoted here and in subsequent chapters is J. Logie Robertson, ed., *The Poetical Works of Sir Walter Scott* (1904; Oxford University Press, 1960).

43 Thelwall, *The Rights of Nature* (London, 1796), II, 10–11, quoted by Philip Cox, '"Unnatural Refuge": Aspects of Pastoral in William Blake's Epic Poetry', unpublished Ph.D. thesis, University of York, 1988, p. 141.

44 Cited by Geoffrey Carnall, *Robert Southey and His Age: The Development of a Conservative Mind* (Oxford: Clarendon Press, 1960), p. 112.

45 Cameron, *The Young Shelley*, p. 301.

46 Olwen Campbell, *Shelley and the Unromantics* (London, 1924), p. 114.

47 Michel Beaujour, 'Flight Out of Time: Poetic Language and the Revolution', *Yale French Studies*, Literature and Revolution Special Issue, ed. Jacques Ehrmann, No. 39 (1967), 29–49.

48 David Masson, ed., *The Collected Writings of Thomas De Quincey*, 14 vols. (London: A. & C. Black, 1897), XI, 88–94. These remarks form part of De Quincey's discussion of the distinction between 'the literature of knowledge' and 'the literature of power', a distinction which he elsewhere (e.g. X, 48n.) acknowledges to have originated in conversations with Wordsworth.

49 *Poetry and Prose*, pp. 486–88.

50 Thomas Medwin, *The Life of Percy Bysshe Shelley*, rev. edn., with intro. by H. Buxton Forman (Oxford University Press, 1913), p. 100; G. B. Shaw, 'Shaming the Devil about Shelley' (1892), *Pen Portraits and Reviews* (London: Constable, 1949), p. 244. For further information about the role of *Queen Mab* in nineteenth-century radicalism, see H. Buxton Forman, *The Vicissitudes of Shelley's 'Queen Mab'* (London, 1887); Newman Ivey White, 'Literature and the Law of Libel: Shelley and the Radicals of 1840–42', *Studies in Philology*, 22 (1925), 34–47; White, *Shelley*, 2 vols. (London: Secker & Warburg, 1947), II, 404–10; William Wickwar, *The Struggle for the Freedom of the Press 1819–1832* (1928; New York: Johnson Reprint Corporation, 1972), pp. 260–63; Kenneth Muir, 'Shelley's Heirs', *Penguin New Writing*, 26 (1945), 117–32; Richard Altick, *The English Common Reader: A Social History of the Mass Reading*

Public 1800–1900 (University of Chicago Press, 1963), p. 197; M. Siddiq Kalim, *The Social Orpheus: Shelley and the Owenites*, Research Council Publications (Lahore, 1973); Paul Foot, *Red Shelley* (1980; London: Bookmarks, 1984), pp. 229–41; Bouthaina Shaaban, 'Shelley in the Chartist Press', *KSMB*, 34 (1983), 41–60; and Iain McCalman, *Radical Underworld: Prophets, Revolutionaries and Pornographers in London 1798–1840* (Cambridge University Press, 1988), pp. 81, 155, 189, 193, 211–21.

51 *Letters*, II, 305. Not all of Shelley's retrospective comments on *Queen Mab* are in this vein, however, and there is a noticeable difference between the line he took in public and the views he expressed in private. For a discussion of his shifting attitude to the poem and to the issue of didacticism, see Timothy Webb, *Shelley: A Voice Not Understood* (Manchester University Press, 1977), pp. 85–87.

52 For the literary background to this, see Arthur Melville Clark, 'Milton and the Renaissance Revolt Against Rhyme', *Studies in Literary Modes* (Edinburgh: Oliver & Boyd, 1946).

53 *Paradise Lost*, ed. Fowler, pp. 38–39.

54 See White, *The Unextinguished Hearth*, pp. 60, 59.

55 Curran, *Poetic Form and British Romanticism*, pp. 134–35.

56 For the following account of the origins of 'the Thalaba style', I am indebted to William Haller, *The Early Life of Robert Southey 1774–1803* (New York: Columbia University Press, 1917), pp. 76–88, 250–66.

57 Lionel Madden, ed., *Robert Southey: The Critical Heritage* (London: Routledge & Kegan Paul, 1972), p. 63.

58 Letter to Southey, 8 May 1808, in Charles L. Proudfit, ed., *Landor as Critic* (London: Routledge & Kegan Paul, 1979), p. 66. Landor's remarks are in response to a draft of *The Curse of Kehama*, which employs a similar verse form to *Thalaba*. Southey responded to Landor's criticism by increasing the number of rhymed passages.

59 *Southey: The Critical Heritage*, p. 92.

60 For instance, in the Preface to the fourth volume of his *Collected Poems* of 1838.

61 *Southey: The Critical Heritage*, pp. 78–81.

62 See Bernard Weinberg, *A History of Literary Criticism in the Italian Renaissance*, 2 vols. (University of Chicago Press, 1961); and Parker, *Inescapable Romance*, pp. 16–31.

63 Warton, *History of English Poetry*, I, xlviii. For a survey of contemporary theories concerning the origin of romance, see Johnston, *Enchanted Ground*, pp. 13–27.

64 The critical debate over the 'Thalaba style' may thus be seen as an extension of the controversy surrounding the Pindaric ode, a genre often associated with disorder and excess because of its abrupt transitions of mood and theme, and apparent irregularity of metre, in contrast with the regularity and sobriety of the Horatian ode. See David Trotter, *The Poetry of Abraham Cowley* (London: Macmillan, 1979), ch. 6.

65 Carnall, *Robert Southey and His Age*, p. 58.

66 Hazlitt, *Complete Works*, XI, 81.

67 It has been argued that Southey's superimposition of a Christian morality on an Islamic fable is itself a political move, expressing his commitment (stated explicitly elsewhere) to a new form of 'revolution' that was spreading through the Oriental world: the liberating force of individualistic Christianity – otherwise known as British imperialism. See Marilyn Butler, 'Byron and the Empire in the East' in *Byron: Augustan and Romantic*, ed. Andrew Rutherford (London: Macmillan, 1990); also the same author's 'Plotting the Revolution: The Political Narrative of Romantic Poetry and Criticism' in *Romantic Revolutions: Criticism and Theory*, ed. Kenneth R. Johnston et al. (Bloomington: Indiana University Press, 1990). For a full discussion of the political and literary contexts of Romantic 'Orientalism', see Nigel Leask, *British Romantic Writers and the East: Anxieties of Empire* (Cambridge University Press, 1992).

68 Cameron, *The Young Shelley*, p. 271.

69 Southey's poem, entitled 'July Thirteenth. Charlotte Corday Executed For Putting Marat to Death', was first published in the *Morning Post* in 1798, and is reprinted in Kenneth Curry, ed., *The Contributions of Robert Southey to the 'Morning Post'* (University of Alabama Press, 1984), pp. 74–75.

70 See Kenneth Neill Cameron, 'Shelley vs Southey: New Light on an Old Quarrel', *Publications of the Modern Language Association*, 67 (1942), 489–512.

71 Unless otherwise indicated, all quotations are from Maurice H. Fitzgerald, ed., *Poems of Southey* (Oxford University Press, 1909).

72 Kalim, *The Social Orpheus*, pp. 78–79.

73 Cited by Hermann Fischer, *Romantic Verse Narrative: The History of a Genre*, trans. Sue Bollans (Cambridge University Press, 1991), p. 264n.

74 Carlos Baker, *Shelley's Major Poetry: The Fabric of a Vision* (1948; Princeton University Press, 1970), pp. 24–25. See also Baker, 'Spenser, the Eighteenth Century, and Shelley's *Queen Mab*', *Modern Language Quarterly*, 2 (1941), 81–98. Earlier surveys of eighteenth-century allegory include Henry A. Beers, *A History of English Romanticism in the Eighteenth Century* (1898; New York: Gordian Press, 1966), ch. 2; William Lyon Phelps, *The Beginnings of the English Romantic Movement: A Study in Eighteenth-Century Literature* (Boston: Ginn, 1899), ch. 4; Harko G. de Maar, *A History of Modern English Romanticism: Elizabethan and Modern Romanticism in the Eighteenth Century* (1924; New York: Haskell House, 1970), ch. 7; Eric Partridge, *Eighteenth-Century English Romantic Poetry* (Paris: Edouard Champion, 1924), ch. 6; and Earl R. Wasserman, *Elizabethan Poetry in the Eighteenth Century* (University of Illinois Press, 1947).

75 Gilbert West, 'Education: A Poem, Written in Imitation of the Style and Manner of Spenser's Fairy Queen' (1751) quoted here from Alexander Chalmers, ed., *The Works of the English Poets, from Chaucer to*

Cowper; Including the Series Edited with Prefaces, Biographical and Critical, by Dr. Samuel Johnson: and the Most Approved Translations, 21 vols. (London, 1810), XIII, 180–87.

76 See White, *The Unextinguished Hearth*, pp. 45–46. For the identity of the reviewer, a subject of long dispute among Shelley scholars, see McCalman, *Radical Underworld*, pp. 79–82; and William St Clair, *The Godwins and the Shelleys: The Biography of a Family* (London: Faber & Faber, 1989), Appendix 3: 'Shelley and the Pirates'.

77 E. P. Thompson, *The Making of the English Working Class* (1963; Harmondsworth: Penguin, 1984), p. 107. For a useful analysis of Volney's tract, see Brian Rigby, 'Volney's Rationalist Apocalypse: *Les Ruines ou Méditations sur les Révolutions des Empires*', in Francis Barker *et al.*, eds., *1789; Reading Writing Revolution*, Proceedings of the Essex Conference on the Sociology of Literature, July 1981 (Colchester: University of Essex, 1982).

78 Aldolphe Bossange, ed., *Oeuvres complètes de Volney* (Paris, 1876), pp. 36–37.

79 Subtitled 'An allegorical poem in the manner of Spenser', the text is quoted here from J. H. L. Hunt, *Juvenilia; or, A Collection of Poems Written Between the Ages of Twelve and Sixteen* (2nd edn. London, 1801).

80 *The Faerie Queene*, II, xii, 83 and II, ii, 41.

81 Long recognised as one of Shelley's sources for *Queen Mab*, 'The Palace of Fortune: An Indian Tale' was first published in Jones's *Poems, Consisting Chiefly of Translations from the Asiatick Languages* (1772), and reprinted in his *Works* of 1807, which Shelley ordered on 24 December 1812 (*Letters*, I, 344). The text quoted here is from Chalmers, ed., *Works of the English Poets*, XVIII, 491–994.

82 Quoted here from James Thomson, *The Seasons and The Castle of Indolence*, ed. James Sambrook (Oxford: Clarendon Press, 1972).

83 Patricia Parker, 'The Progress of Phaedria's Bower: Spenser to Coleridge', *English Literary History*, 40 (1973), 372–97 (p. 380).

84 See the entry for 'industry' in Raymond Williams, *Keywords: A Vocabulary of Culture and Society*, 2nd edn. (London: Fontana, 1983), pp. 165–68.

85 Although Southey often acknowledged his general debt to Spenser, there is no mention of *The Faerie Queene* in the copious footnotes to this scene (not reprinted in Fitzgerald's Oxford edition, but found in most earlier collections of Southey's poems, and in the first two editions of *Thalaba* itself). Instead, he cites an impressive range of Orientalist sources, the most important being the description of Aloadin's mountain paradise in *Purchas His Pilgrims*, on which see my comments below.

86 *Poems*, I, 372. As Matthews and Everest point out in their editorial note, Shelley's comments about 'natural temperance' echo James Lawrence's discussion of 'natural chastity' in *The Empire of the Nairs* (1811), an argument in turn derived from Mary Wollstonecraft's *Vindication of the Rights of Woman* (1792).

87 White, *The Unextinguished Hearth*, p. 56.
88 *The Curse of Kehama*, X, 119. The same phrase appears in *Queen Mab*, VI, 40.
89 See A. Bartlett Giamatti, *The Earthly Paradise and the Renaissance Epic* (Princeton University Press, 1966), pp. 358–59.
90 See Cameron, *The Young Shelley*, pp. 133–34.
91 *Letters*, I, 186.
92 Edmund Blunden, *Shelley: A Life Story* (1946; London: Readers Union, 1948), p. 97.
93 The following page references cited in the text are to the third edition of *Political Justice*, ed. Kramnick. See note 108 below.
94 William Godwin, *The Enquirer: Reflections on Education, Manners and Literature: In a Series of Essays* (1797), Reprints of Economics Classics (New York: Augustus M. Kelley, 1965), pp. 10–11.
95 Niccolò Machiavelli, *The Discourses*, trans. Leslie Walker with revisions by Brian Richardson, ed. with intro. by Bernard Crick (Harmondsworth: Penguin, 1970), p. 159.
96 Machiavelli, *Discourses*, editorial introduction, pp. 58–59.
97 For Rousseau's conception of virtue and its influence on the French Revolution, see Carol Blum, *Rousseau and the Republic of Virtue: The Language of Politics in the French Revolution* (Ithaca: Cornell University Press, 1986), and Crane Brinton, *A Decade of Revolution 1789–1799* (1934; New York: Harper & Row, 1963), ch. 6.
98 Hunt, *Politics, Culture and Class in the French Revolution*, p. 3.
99 From his speech 'Sur les Principes de Morale Politique', 18 Pluviôse, An II, in Robespierre, *Textes Choisis*, ed. Jean Poperen, 3 vols. (Paris: Editions Sociales, 1958), III, 119.
100 Arendt, *On Revolution*, pp. 96–99.
101 *Political Justice*, p. 496. Godwin touches here on what has been called 'the Machiavellian element in Rousseau's political thinking': see Maurice Cranston, *Philosophers and Pamphleteers: Political Theorists of the Enlightenment* (Oxford University Press, 1986), pp. 94–95.
102 *Political Justice*, p. 335.
103 See Godwin's own account in his *Thoughts Occasioned by the Perusal of Dr Parr's Spital Sermon* (1801) in Godwin, *Uncollected Writings*, pp. 281–374.
104 *The Tribune*, ii, p. vii, quoted by Roe, *Wordsworth and Coleridge: The Radical Years*, p. 167.
105 William Godwin, *Caleb Williams: or Things As They Are*, ed. Maurice Hindley (Harmondsworth: Penguin, 1988), Preface to the Second Edition, p. 4.
106 For an overview, see Clive Emsley, 'An Aspect of Pitt's "Terror": Prosecutions for Sedition during the 1790s', *Social History*, 6 (1981), 155–84.
107 Godwin, *Uncollected Writings*, p. 284.
108 Godwin in fact modified his theory of virtue between the first (1793) and second (1796) editions of *Political Justice*. The chapter entitled 'Of

the Tendency of Virtue' in 1793 (Bk. IV, ch. ix) was removed in 1796, and replaced by one entitled 'Of Good and Evil' (Bk. IV, ch. xi). Godwin rewrote too the chapter 'Of Personal Virtue and Duty' (Bk. II, ch. iv), laying greater stress on the consequences of an action rather than the motive or intention; and the chapter 'Of Obedience' (Bk. III, ch. vi) was also completely rewritten, Godwin adopting a much more moderate position. The claim I make below is that Shelley was quarrelling with the *revised* version of *Political Justice* (for confirmation that he was familiar with both versions and strongly preferred the first, see *Letters*, I, 124). As indicated previously, my quotations in this chapter are from the Penguin reprint of the third edition (1798), which is essentially the same as the second edition, except for minor verbal alterations. Chapters from the first edition which are omitted from the third, or which undergo substantial alteration, are reproduced in the third volume of F. E. L. Priestley's edition of *Political Justice*, 3 vols. (University of Toronto Press, 1946).

109 Again, I am referring to the revised version of *Political Justice*. In the much shorter version of the chapter that appears in the first edition, Godwin expresses views that are closer to Shelley's own, claiming for example that 'No truth can be more simple ... than that one man can in no case be bound to yield obedience to any other man or set of men upon earth' (Priestley edition, vol. III, p. 266). Yet Godwin immediately goes on to qualify – or contradict – this statement, by discussing cases in which 'limited obedience' would prove mutually beneficial. If this is indeed a contradiction, it seems reasonable to conclude that one of Godwin's motives for revising the chapter was to remove it, as he does by modifying the original assertion and introducing the notion of a 'scale of obedience'.

110 See *Letters*, I, 200: '*Obedience* (were society as I wish it) is a word which ought to be without meaning. – If virtue depended on duty then would prudence be virtue, and imprudence vice, and the only difference between the Marquis Wellesley and William Godwin, would be that the latter had more cunningly devised the means of his own benefit.'

111 Marshall, *William Godwin*, pp. 102–3.

112 Hazlitt, *Complete Works*, XI, 20.

113 See Godwin, *Uncollected Writings*, pp. 314–15.

114 *Le Nouveau monde amoureux* is the title of a work that remained unpublished in Fourier's lifetime (1772–1837), but has recently been rediscovered and printed. Publication details in my bibliography.

115 Important studies of this literature include Carl Becker, *The Heavenly City of the Eighteenth-Century Philosophers* (1932; New Haven: Yale University Press, 1967); Ernest Lee Tuveson, *Millennium and Utopia: A Study in the Background of the Idea of Progress* (1949; New York: Harper & Row, 1964); Frank E. Manuel and F. P. Manuel, *Utopian Thought in the Western World* (Oxford: Blackwell, 1979); Franco Venturi, *Utopia and Reform in the Enlightenment* (Cambridge University Press, 1971); and

Theodore Olsen, *Millennialism, Utopianism and Progress* (University of Toronto Press, 1982). For a full listing of the primary texts, see Glenn Negley, *Utopian Literature: A Bibliography with a Supplementary Listing of Works Influential in Utopian Thought* (Kansas: Regent's Press, 1977).

116 Steiner, *In Bluebeard's Castle*, p. 20.

117 Hazlitt, *Complete Works*, VII, 99.

118 White, *The Unextinguished Hearth*, p. 51.

119 Cameron, *The Young Shelley*, p. 289.

120 *Shelley and his Circle*, VI, 1064. Paul Foot draws attention to this break in the manuscript in *Red Shelley*, p. 189.

121 *Wooler's British Gazette*, 6 May 1821, reprinted in Schwartz, 'New Contemporary Reviews', p. 83.

122 Schwartz, 'New Contemporary Reviews', p. 83; Curran, *Shelley's Annus Mirabilis: The Maturing of an Epic Vision* (San Marino, Calif.: Huntingdon Library, 1975), p. 26; Curran, *Poetic Form and British Romanticism*, p. 172.

123 White, *The Unextinguished Hearth*, pp. 52, 59.

124 Cameron, *The Young Shelley*, p. 267.

125 *Queen Mab* is listed under the entry for 'romance' in J. A. Cuddons, *A Dictionary of Literary Terms* 2nd edn. (London: André Deutsch, 1979), p. 581.

126 Frye, *Secular Scripture*, p. 163.

127 Gerald McNeice, *Shelley and the Revolutionary Idea* (Cambridge, Mass.: Harvard University Press, 1969), p. 152; Ross Greig Woodman, *The Apocalyptic Vision in the Poetry of Shelley* (University of Toronto Press, 1964), p. 81.

128 Curran, *Shelley's Annus Mirabilis*, p. 30.

129 Recent discussions of this vexed issue include Barbara Goodwin and Keith Taylor, *The Politics of Utopia: A Study in Theory and Practice* (London: Hutchinson, 1982); Ricoeur, *Lectures on Ideology and Utopia*; Vincent Geoghegan, *Utopianism and Marxism* (New York: Methuen, 1987); and Krishan Kumar, *Utopia and Anti-Utopia in Modern Times* (Oxford: Blackwell, 1987).

130 Marx and Engels, *Collected Works*, VI, 514–16.

131 The term 'utopian romance' was actually used as the generic subtitle of a prose work which strongly influenced *Queen Mab*: James Lawrence's *The Empire of the Nairs; or, The Rights of Woman: An Utopian Romance, in Twelve Books* (1811).

3. SIR GUYON DE SHELLEY AND FRIENDS: NEW LIGHT ON THE CHIVALRIC REVIVAL

1 A phrase from Samuel Waddington's ironic address of sympathy to the King after the death of Caroline in September 1821; quoted by McCalman, *Radical Underworld*, p. 175. McCalman also discusses the cartoon 'The Rival Champion' (pp. 174–75).

2 'On the "Braziers' Address – To be presented in *Armour* by the Company &c. &c." – as stated in the Newspapers', in Byron's letter to John Murray of 6 January 1821, quoted here from Lord Byron, *The Complete Poetical Works*, ed. Jerome J. McGann, 7 vols. (Oxford: Clarendon Press, 1980–93), VI, 1. All subsequent quotations from Byron's poetry are from this edition.

3 Mark Girouard, *The Return to Camelot: Chivalry and the English Gentleman* (New Haven: Yale University Press, 1981), ch. 6: 'Radical Chivalry'.

4 See Alice Chandler, *A Dream of Order: The Medieval Ideal in Nineteenth-Century English Literature* (London: Routledge & Kegan Paul, 1971); James D. Merriman, *The Flower of Kings: A Study of the Arthurian Legend in England Between 1485 and 1835* (Lawrence: University Press of Kansas, 1973), ch. 6; Kevin L. Morris, *The Image of the Middle Ages in Romantic and Victorian Literature* (London: Croom Helm, 1984); Roger Simpson, *Camelot Regained: The Arthurian Revival and Tennyson, 1800–1849* (Cambridge: D. S. Brewer, 1990); and John Simons, ed., *From Medieval to Medievalism* (Basingstoke: Macmillan, 1992).

5 See Weisinger, 'The Middle Ages and the Late Eighteenth-Century Historians'; and Pocock, *Virtue, Commerce and History*, pp. 198–99.

6 Hurd, *Works*, IV, 345–50.

7 For the following examples, I am indebted to Girouard, *Return to Camelot*, ch. 2.

8 Nathaniel Wraxhall, *Memoirs* (1844), V, 378–89, quoted by Girouard, *Return to Camelot*, p. 25. For other examples of contemporary pseudo-medieval architecture, see James Macaulay, *The Gothic Revival, 1745–1845* (Glasgow: Blackie, 1975).

9 N. H. Nicolas, *History of the Order of Knighthood of the British Empire* (1842), II, xx, quoted by Girouard, *Return to Camelot*, p. 24.

10 Nicolas, *History of the Orders of Knighthood*, p. xxi, quoted by Girouard, *Return to Camelot*, p. 24.

11 Girouard, *Return to Camelot*, pp. 26–27. See also Valerie Cumming, 'Pantomime and Pageantry: The Coronation of George IV' in Celina Fox, ed., *London-World City* (New Haven: Yale University Press, 1992).

12 John O. Hayden, ed., *Scott: The Critical Heritage* (London: Routledge & Kegan Paul, 1970), p. 47.

13 These figures, and the following list of Scott's imitators, are taken from A. D. Harvey, *English Poetry in a Changing Society 1780–1825* (London: Allison & Busby, 1980), p. 100.

14 Scott's debt to medieval romance is examined in detail by Jerome Mitchell, *Scott, Chaucer and Medieval Romance: A Study in Sir Walter Scott's Indebtedness to the Literature of the Middle Ages* (Lexington: University Press of Kentucky, 1987).

15 Marlon Ross, 'Scott's Chivalric Pose: The Function of Metrical Romance in the Romantic Period', *Genre*, 18 (1986), 267–97 (p. 290).

16 For some of the following observations, I am indebted to Ross, 'Scott's

Chivalric Pose', pp. 289–91, and to Anne-Julie Crozier, 'The Influence and Concept of Romance in Scott's Early Narrative Poetry', unpublished M. A. dissertation, University of York, 1989.

17 Ross, 'Scott's Chivalric Pose', pp. 277–78. See also David Hewitt, 'Scott's Art and Politics' in *Sir Walter Scott: The Long Forgotten Melody*, ed. Alan Bold (London: Vision Press, 1983).

18 For a quantitative analysis, see William St Clair, 'The Impact of Byron's Writings: An Evaluative Approach' in *Byron: Augustan and Romantic*, ed. Rutherford, pp. 1–25.

19 On Byron's relation to Scott as metrical romancer, see Harvey, *English Poetry in a Changing Society*, pp. 103, 118; Curran, *Poetic Form and British Romanticism*, pp. 135, 151–57; and Fischer, *Romantic Verse Narrative*, pp. 148–62.

20 A similar case is argued in relation to Byron's Turkish tales by Caroline Franklin, '"At Once Above – Beneath Her Sex": The Heroine in Regency Verse Romance', *Modern Languages Quarterly*, 84 (1989), 273–88.

21 See Ronald A. Schroeder, 'Ellis, Sainte-Palaye, and Byron's "Addition" to the "Preface" of *Childe Harold's Pilgrimage I–II*', *KSJ*, 32 (1983), 25–30. Ellis's review is reprinted in Andrew Rutherford, ed., *Byron: The Critical Heritage* (London: Routledge & Kegan Paul, 1970), pp. 42–51.

22 The reference to Sainte-Palaye, and other aspects of Byron's 'romaunt', are explored by Michael Vicario, 'The Implications of Form in *Childe Harold's Pilgrimage I–II*', *KSJ*, 33 (1984), 103–29.

23 See Fani Maria Tsigakou, *The Rediscovery of Greece: Travellers and Painters of the Romantic Era* (London: Thames & Hudson, 1981), p. 234.

24 Noted by George Rudé, *Revolutionary Europe 1783–1815* (1964; London: Fontana, 1982), p. 266.

25 As long ago as 1690, Sir William Temple was claiming that *Don Quixote* 'had ruined the Spanish Monarchy', for 'before that time, Love and Valour were all Romance among them', but after Cervantes's work appeared, 'and with that inimitable Wit and Humor, turned all this Romantick Honor into Ridicule, the Spaniards began to grow ashamed of both', which was 'a great cause of the ruin of Spain, or of its Greatness and Power' (Sir William Temple, *Miscellanea: The Second Part* (2nd edn. 1690), p. 73, quoted by Anthony Close, *The Romantic Approach to 'Don Quixote'* (Cambridge University Press, 1977), p. 69).

26 For directing my attention to this series, and to relevant passages in Leigh Hunt's *Autobiography*, I am indebted to Timothy Webb, a number of whose ideas I have incorporated in this section.

27 William Hazlitt [and Leigh Hunt], *The Round Table: A Collection of Essays on Literature, Men and Manners*, 2 vols. (Edinburgh, 1817), p. 4.

28 Robert Gittings, ed., *Letters of John Keats*, corrected edn. (Oxford University Press, 1979), p. 13.

29 *Blackwood's Edinburgh Magazine*, 7 (October 1817), 38–41.

30 *The Round Table*, I, 8.

31 'On Pedantry', *The Round Table*, II, 43–44.

32 See Hazlitt's 'On the Causes of Methodism', Hunt's 'On the Poetical Character', and Hazlitt's 'On Poetic Versatility', all reprinted in the book version of *The Round Table*. Many of the themes touched on in these passages are brought together in Hazlitt's critique of the politics of the imagination in his essay on Coriolanus from *Characters of Shakespeare's Plays* (1817), originally a theatrical review which appeared in the *Examiner* on December 15, 1816.

33 All subsequent quotations are from *The Autobiography of Leigh Hunt*, rev. edn. (1860), with intro. by Edmund Blunden (Oxford University Press, 1928), ch. 14.

34 For an intriguing reversal of this motif, see Hunt's poem 'Politics and Poetics; or, The Desperate Situation of a Journalist Unhappily Smitten with the Love of Rhyme' (1810) in Thornton Hunt, ed., *The Poetical Works of Leigh Hunt* (London and New York, 1860), pp. 190–94. As the title suggests, the poem describes the tensions Hunt experiences between the imaginative claims of poetry and the demands of political journalism, tensions encapsulated in the (here purely metaphorical) reference to his 'Bower of Bliss' being 'turned into a jail'.

35 Quoted from Jack Stillinger, ed., *The Poems of John Keats* (London: Heinmann, 1978), p. 32. Richard Lovelace's lines are from his poem 'To Althea, from Prison' (1646–49).

36 For a detailed discussion of Hunt's interest in Spenser, which also touches on other topics addressed in this section, see Greg Kucich, 'Leigh Hunt and Romantic Spenserianism', *KSJ*, 37 (1988), 110–35.

37 'An Offer of Service to the Knights of the Round Table', The *Examiner*, 29 January 1815. This article, which comprises a letter 'To the President of the Round Table' and the President's reply (both probably written by Hunt), is not included in the book version of *The Round Table*.

38 Hurd, *Works*, IV, 246.

39 In his *Autobiography*, p. 285, Hunt himself uses the word 'romantic' to describe his high-principled behaviour in the matter of the attempted bribery.

40 *The Black Dwarf, A London Weekly Publication*, 14 May 1817.

41 The pamphlet originated as a series of articles in *Shadgett's Weekly Review*.

42 See *Letters*, I, 301 and 307 (quoted below).

43 William Godwin, *Life of Geoffrey Chaucer*, 2 vols. (London, 1803), I, 360–61, quoted by D. H. Munro, *Godwin's Moral Philosophy: An Interpretation of William Godwin* (Oxford University Press, 1953), pp. 122–23. Munro's whole chapter on 'The Insufficiency of Honour' is pertinent here.

44 According to a footnote in Hazlitt's essay on Godwin in *The Spirit of the Age*, Henry Fuseli used to object to 'a want of historical correctness' in *Caleb Williams*, 'inasmuch as the animating principle of the true

chivalrous character was the sense of honour, not the mere regard to, or saving of, appearances' (Hazlitt, *Complete Works*, XI, 24n.). Hazlitt considered this a 'hypercriticism', but in light of Godwin's subsequent thinking on this question there is some force in Fuseli's observation. For more recent discussions of the theme of chivalry in *Caleb Williams*, see David McCracken, 'Godwin's *Caleb Williams*: A Fictional Rebuttal of Burke', *Studies in Burke and His Time*, 11 (1969–70); Marilyn Butler, 'Godwin, Burke and *Caleb Williams*', *Essays in Criticism*, 32 (1982), 237–57; Marshall, *William Godwin*, p. 149; and Richard Cronin, 'Carps and *Caleb Williams*', *KSR*, 1 (1986), 35–48.

45 'Fragment of a Romance', quoted by Marshall, *William Godwin*, pp. 282–83. This text was first published in the *New Monthly Magazine* in 1833.

46 William Godwin, *Letter of Advice to a Young American on the Course of Study it might be Most Advantageous for him to Pursue* (1818) in Godwin, *Uncollected Writings*, p. 343.

47 Godwin, *Uncollected Writings*, p. 346. For this idea Godwin is indebted to A. W. Schlegel's *Course of Lectures on Dramatic Art and Literature* (trans. John Black, 1815), which Godwin refers to here as 'one book of criticism, and perhaps the only one, that I would recommend'. See below for Shelley's elaboration of the argument in his *Defence of Poetry* (1821).

48 Quoted in C. Kegan Paul, *William Godwin: His Friends and Contemporaries*, 2 vols. (London, 1876), II, 205–6.

49 Marshall, *William Godwin*, p. 297.

50 Harriet Shelley to Catherine Nugent; *Letters*, I, 320.

51 *Letters*, I, 132.

52 Shelley's thoughts on this subject were strongly influenced by the arguments of William Cobbett, especially his *Paper on Gold* (1815), previously published as a series of letters in the *Political Register*, 1810–12. See Kenneth Cameron, 'Shelley, Cobbett, and the National Debt', *Journal of English and Germanic Philology*, 42 (1943), 197–209.

53 Michael Scrivener, *Radical Shelley: The Philosophical Anarchism and Utopian Thought of Percy Bysshe Shelley* (Princeton University Press, 1982), p. 136.

54 Holmes, *Shelley: The Pursuit*, pp. 386–87. For a similar reading, see Kenneth Neill Cameron, *Shelley: The Golden Years* (Cambridge, Mass.: Harvard University Press, 1974), pp. 136–39.

55 Donald Reiman, 'Shelley as Agrarian Reactionary', *KSMB*, 30 (1979), 5–15.

56 Betty T. Bennett, ed., *The Letters of Mary Wollstonecraft Shelley*, 3 vols. (Baltimore: Johns Hopkins University Press, 1980–88), I, 27.

57 Thomas Jefferson Hogg, *The Life of Percy Bysshe Shelley*, with intro. by Edward Dowden (London: Routledge, 1906), p. 481.

58 Hogg, *Life of Shelley*, pp. 18–19.

59 See, for example, Hunt's *Autobiography*, pp. 318–27.

60 Peacock, *Works*, II, 23–24.

61 Marilyn Butler, *Peacock Displayed: A Satirist in His Context* (London: Routledge & Kegan Paul, 1979), pp. 82–83.

62 Peacock, *Works*, II, 85–87.

63 See also lines 44–47 of Keats's verse epistle 'To Charles Cowden Clarke' (1816), in which he refers to Leigh Hunt as 'The wronged Libertas – who has told you stories / Of laurel chaplets, and Apollo's glories; / Of troops chivalrous prancing through a city, / And tearful ladies made for love, and pity'.

64 King Arthur was also the nominal subject of another literary work published in 1817: John Hookham Frere's *Prospectus and Specimen of an Intended National Work, by William and Robert Whistlecraft, of Stow-Market, in Suffolk, Harness and Collar-Makers. Intended to Comprise the Most Interesting Particulars Relating to King Arthur and His Round Table*, a burlesque poem that is now mainly remembered as the stylistic model for Byron's *Beppo* (1818). It is possible that Frere, a veteran of the *Anti-Jacobin*, was partly intending to mock the Arthurian pretensions of the Hunt–Shelley circle, though the object of the satire has always remained obscure (see Merriman, *The Flower of Kings*, pp. 139–43).

65 Peacock, *Works*, VIII, 327.

4. THE RIGHT ROAD TO PARADISE: *LAON AND CYTHNA; OR, THE REVOLUTION OF THE GOLDEN CITY*

1 Thomas Medwin, *The Life of Percy Bysshe Shelley*, rev. edn., with intro. by H. Buxton Forman (Oxford University Press, 1913), pp. 178–79. Amongst other things, this would explain Keats's reference to *Endymion* in a letter to his brother George (quoted to Benjamin Bailey on 8 October 1817) as 'a test, a trial of my Powers of Imagination and chiefly of my invention ... by which I must make 4000 Lines of one bare circumstance and fill them with Poetry' (H. E. Rollins, ed., *The Letters of John Keats 1814–1821*, 2 vols. (Cambridge, Mass.: Harvard University Press, 1958), I, 169). Keats's remark in turn suggests that the terms of the contest may have additionally specified that the narrative be constructed around a single 'circumstance': presumably the love of Diana for Endymion in Keats's poem, and in Shelley's – as originally conceived – possibly the incestuous love between Laon and Cythna (the 'one circumstance' mentioned in the Preface 'intended to startle the reader from the trance of ordinary life').

2 On Shelley's revisions, see Donald Reiman, 'The Composition and Publication of *The Revolt of Islam*', *Shelley and his Circle*, V, 141–67; F. L. Jones, 'The Revision of *Laon and Cythna*', *Journal of English and Germanic Philology*, 32 (1933), 366–72; and Charles E. Robinson, 'Percy Bysshe Shelley, Charles Ollier, and William Blackwood: The Contexts of Ninteenth-Century Publishing' in *Shelley Revalued: Essays from the Gregynog Conference*, ed. Kelvin Everest (Leicester University Press, 1983),

pp. 183–226. Unless otherwise indicated, all quotations are from the original version, *Laon and Cythna*, as it appears in H. Buxton Forman, ed., *The Poetical Works of Percy Bysshe Shelley*, 4 vols. (London, 1876), vol. 1.

3 See Donald J. Ryan, 'Percy Bysshe Shelley's *Laon and Cythna*: A Critical Edition of the Manuscripts in the Bodleian Library', unpublished Ph.D. thesis, New York University, 1972. Subsequent references to the manuscript version of the poem will be indicated in the text by the abbreviation Ryan, followed by a page reference to this edition. A more accurate transcription of the manuscripts of *Laon and Cythna* will soon be available in the Garland facsimile edition of the Bodleian Shelley Manuscripts.

4 See Paula R. Feldman and Diana Scott-Kilvert, eds., *The Journals of Mary Shelley*, 2 vols. (Oxford: Clarendon Press, 1987), 1, 167–77.

5 The *Examiner*, February 1818, in *Shelley: The Critical Heritage*, p. 106.

6 The poem's affinities with the popular subgenre of the Oriental romance are noted by Curran, *Poetic Form and British Romanticism*, p. 147, and by Butler, 'Byron and the Empire in the East', p. 68. For the background (and political resonance) to contemporary interest in Oriental themes, see Butler, 'Myth and Mythmaking in the Shelley Circle', in Everest, ed., *Shelley Revalued*, pp. 1–19; Michael Rossington, 'Shelley and the Orient', *KSR*, 7, 18–36; and Leask, *British Romantic Writers and the East*, *passim*.

7 Baker, *Shelley's Major Poetry*, p. 79n.

8 Desmond King-Hele, *Shelley: The Man and the Poet* (New York: Thomas Yoseloff, 1960), pp. 88–89.

9 J. R. de J. Jackson, *Poetry of the Romantic Period* (London: Routledge & Kegan Paul, 1980), p. 246.

10 For Shelley's borrowings from Landor and Southey, see Brian Wilkie, *Romantic Poets and Epic Tradition* (Madison: University of Wisconsin Press, 1965), pp. 112–43; and Francis Brett Curtis, 'Shelley and the Idea of Epic: A Study, with Particular Reference to Three pre-1818 Narratives', unpublished Ph.D. thesis, University of Warwick, 1979. Note, however, that many of the features that Wilkie and Curtis associate with *epic* (dreams, vision, allegory, etc.) are equally connected with contemporary notions of *romance*. On the unstable distinction between the two genres, see Curran, *Poetic Form and British Romanticism*, p. 239n.

11 Shelley acknowledges his 'involuntary imitation' of one of the episodes in *The Corsair* in the marginalia of his manuscript (Ryan, p. 380). See Benjamin W. Griffith, 'Shelley's *The Revolt of Islam* and Byron's *The Corsair*', *Notes and Queries*, 201 (1956), 265.

12 This is no ordinary case of poetic borrowing, for it appears that Peacock, having worked sporadically on *Ahrimanes* between 1812 and 1815, handed over the material wholesale to Shelley, to make what use of it he could. For a detailed comparison of the two poems, see Kenneth

Cameron's article in *Shelley and His Circle*, III, 226–44. *Ahrimanes* itself exists in two unfinished versions, each with a prose outline of how the poem was to continue: both versions are included in vol. 8 of Peacock's *Works*, ed. Brett-Smith and Jones.

13 *Letters*, I, 563. The role of 'supernatural interference' was one of the most frequently debated questions in contemporary theories of epic and romance, on which see Swedenberg, *Theory of the Epic in England*, ch. 2.

14 John Taylor Coleridge, in the *Quarterly Review*, April 1819; *Shelley: The Critical Heritage*, p. 131.

15 On the currency of the Spenserian stanza, see Bernard Beatty, 'Lord Byron: Poetry and Precedent' in R. T. Davies and B. G. Beatty, eds., *Literature of the Romantic Period* (Liverpool University Press, 1976), pp. 114–34; and Philip W. Martin, *Byron: A Poet Before His Public* (Cambridge University Press, 1982), ch. 1.

16 Paulson, *Representations of Revolution*, p. 4.

17 Hazlitt, *Complete Works*, III, 156.

18 On the interesting connections between French revolutionary politics and contemporary fascination with incest, parricide and other inversions of familial order, see Lynn Hunt, *The Family Romance of the French Revolution* (Berkeley: University of California Press, 1992).

19 For a full account of the allusions to the French Revolution, see McNeice, *Shelley and the Revolutionary Idea*, the first chapter of which contains a useful survey, based on Shelley's letters, Mary's journal and other sources, of Shelley's extensive reading of the literature of the French Revolution.

20 Kenneth Neill Cameron, *Shelley: The Golden Years* (Cambridge, Mass.: Harvard University Press, 1974), p. 334, argues convincingly that in the final cantos of the poem Shelley is 'painting an impressionistic picture of the Napoleonic Wars'.

21 Cameron, *The Golden Years*, p. 327.

22 Dawson, *Unacknowledged Legislator*, p. 75.

23 Richard Cronin, *Shelley's Poetic Thoughts* (Basingstoke: Macmillan, 1981), p. 97.

24 Preface to *Prometheus Unbound*, in *Poetry and Prose*, p. 135.

25 See, for example, John Stevens, *Medieval Romance: Themes and Approaches* (London: Hutchinson, 1973).

26 *Quarterly Review*, October 1815, in B. C. Southam, ed., *Jane Austen: The Critical Heritage* (London: Routledge & Kegan Paul, 1968), p. 63.

27 Scott, *Essays on Chivalry, Romance and the Drama*, pp. 67–68.

28 Quoted from the MS by Marshall, *William Godwin*, p. 38. The essay has now been published in full for the first time as an appendix to Maurice Hindley's edition of *Caleb Williams* (Harmondsworth: Penguin, 1988), pp. 359–73.

29 McNeice, *Shelley and the Revolutionary Idea*, p. 27. See also John Rivers, *Louvet: Revolutionist and Romance-Writer* (London: Hurst & Blackett, 1910).

30 McNeice, *Shelley and the Revolutionary Idea*, p. 26.

31 Charles E. Robinson, 'The Shelley Circle and Coleridge's *The Friend*', *English Language Notes*, 8 (1971), 269–74, demonstrates that Shelley almost certainly possessed a copy of Coleridge's journal, probably in the one-volume reprint of 1812.

32 Elizabeth Brocking, in an unpublished Ph.D. thesis ('"Common Sympathies": Shelley's *Revolt of Islam*', Rice University, 1985) also interprets this line as a warning signal, on the rather different ground that Shelley would not have considered 'an ignorance of history beneficial' (p. 46).

33 For a helpful discussion of the 'affective poetics' outlined in the Preface to *Laon and Cythna*, see Ronald Tetreault, *The Poetry of Life: Shelley and Literary Form* (University of Toronto Press, 1987), pp. 95–120. In fact, this poetics is essentially Wordsworthian in origin, as Michael Scrivener points out in *Radical Shelley*, pp. 122–23, where he compares Shelley's Preface with that of *Lyrical Ballads* (1800) and with Wordsworth's 'Essay, Supplementary to the Preface' of 1815. For further discussion of Shelley's imaginative engagement with Wordsworth, see below.

34 Karl Kroeber, *Romantic Narrative Art* (Madison: University of Wisconsin Press, 1966), pp. 88–89.

35 *Journals of Mary Shelley*, 1, 25. For an analysis of Shelley's response to *The Excursion* (though one that ignores the evidence of *Laon and Cythna*), see G. Kim Blank, *Wordsworth's Influence on Shelley: A Study of Poetic Authority* (Basingstoke: Macmillan, 1988), ch. 3.

36 Quotations from *The Excursion* and its Preface are from Wordsworth's *Poetical Works*, ed. Thomas Hutchinson, rev. Ernest de Selincourt (1936; Oxford University Press, 1981).

37 The autobiographical content of the poem is emphasised by Stuart Sperry, *Shelley's Major Verse: The Narrative and Dramatic Poetry* (Cambridge, Mass.: Harvard University Press, 1988), but this matter still needs further investigation.

38 Wordsworth's phrase, from the Argument to Book III.

39 Even the subtitle of Shelley's poem may have been partly suggested by Wordsworth's use of the term 'Vision' in the Propectus to *The Recluse* (line 98). *Laon and Cythna* is certainly full of the apocalypticism which this word denotes in Wordsworth's Prospectus, one of the central themes of Shelley's poem being the fate of apocalyptic hope in the aftermath of the French Revolution. Other works in the period which use the term 'vision' as part of a title or a subtitle include Joel Barlow's *The Vision of Columbus* (1787), Blake's *Visions of the Daughters of Albion* (1793), Coleridge's 'The Destiny of Nations. A Vision' (1796) and 'Kubla Khan or, A Vision in a Dream' (1797/1816), Southey's *The Vision of the Maid of Orleans* (1797), Scott's *The Vision of Don Roderick* (1811), Henry Cary's translation of Dante's *Divina Commedia* as *The Vision* (1814), and the second part of Southey's *The Poet's Pilgrimage to Waterloo* (1816).

40 Letter to Sir Walter Raleigh, in *The Faerie Queene*, ed. Hamilton, p. 737. The echo is noted by Pitts, 'Romantic Spenserianism', p. 143.

41 Northrop Frye, 'The Road of Excess' in *Romanticism and Consciousness*, ed. Bloom, p. 125.

42 Vicario, 'Implications of Form', p. 107.

43 Mark Kipperman, *Beyond Enchantment: German Idealism and English Romantic Poetry* (Philadelphia: University of Pennsylvania Press, 1986), p. 4.

44 In the chapter 'On Good and Evil' (revised version), Godwin argues that the 'true equalization of mankind' is 'to raise those who are abased; to communicate to every man all genuine pleasures, elevate every man to all true wisdom and to make all men participators of a liberal and comprehensive benevolence. This is the path which the reformers of mankind ought to travel' (*Political Justice*, pp. 395–96).

45 Milton, *Selected Prose*, ed. C. A. Patrides (Harmondsworth: Penguin, 1974), p. 21.

46 See Geoffrey M. Matthews, 'A Volcano's Voice in Shelley' (1957) in *Shelley: Modern Judgments*, ed. R. B. Woodings (London: Macmillan, 1968), pp. 162–95.

47 Dawson, *Unacknowledged Legislator*, p. 70.

48 E. B. Murray, "Elective Affinity" in *The Revolt of Islam*', *Journal of English and Germanic Philology*, 67 (1968), 570–85 (p. 573).

49 Cronin, *Shelley's Poetic Thoughts*, pp. 103–4. Cronin's suggestion is given added historical weight by the parallel that can be made with English political caricature, in which the motif of cannibalism was often used to represent French revolutionary violence, as is pointed out by David Bindman, *The Shadow of the Guillotine: Britain and the French Revolution*, exhibition catalogue (London: British Museum, 1989), p. 21.

50 Sperry, *Shelley's Major Verse*, p. 211n.

51 This argument was made in an unpublished lecture on *The Revolt of Islam* delivered at the University of York in 1984.

52 Sperry, *Shelley's Major Verse*, p. 52.

53 *Shelley: The Critical Heritage*, p. 131.

54 This analogy is suggested by Cronin, *Shelley's Poetic Thoughts*, p. 100.

55 Bloom, 'The Internalization of Quest Romance', p. 13.

56 In 1818 Shelley wrote a review of Peacock's poem *Rhododaphne; or The Thessalian Spell* in which he confessed to being 'astonished to discover that any thing can be added to the gardens of Armida and Alcina, and the Bower of Bliss' (*Prose Works*, I, 288), a remark which is itself astonishing in light of his own numerous attempts to improve upon the earthly paradises of Ariosto, Tasso and Spenser.

57 Another passage from *Paradise Lost* of which there are echoes in Shelley's scene describes the shady bower where Eve awakes after her creation, soon to fall in love with her own reflection (IV, 449–65). This parallel is suggestive in the context of the love between Laon and Cythna, his mirror image and 'second self'.

58 In Book XI, during a visit to the underworld, Odysseus attempts to clasp the soul of his dead mother Anticleia, only to find that 'like a shadow or a dream, she slipped through my arms' (Homer, *The Odyssey*, trans. E. V. Rieu (Harmondsworth: Penguin, 1945), p. 181).

59 Godwin, 'Of Choice in Reading', *The Enquirer*, p. 145.

60 Milton, *Selected Prose*, p. 213. Shelley is listed in Mary's journal as having read *Areopagitica* in 1815.

61 Webb, *Shelley: A Voice Not Understood*, pp. 242–43.

62 Curran, *Poetic Form and British Romanticism*, p. 134. For a fuller discussion of Southey's handling of the quest motif, see John Holloway, *The Proud Knowledge: Poetry, Insight and the Self* (London: Routledge & Kegan Paul, 1977), ch. 5: 'The Odyssey and the Quest'.

63 De Quincey, *Recollections of the Lakes and the Lake Poets*, p. 223.

64 Frye, *Anatomy of Criticism*, p. 193.

65 James A. Notopoulos, *The Platonism of Shelley* (Durham, NC: Duke University Press, 1949), p. 206.

66 Stephen Greenblatt, 'To Fashion a Gentleman: Spenser and the Destruction of the Bower of Bliss', *Renaissance Self-Fashioning: From More to Shakespeare* (University of Chicago Press, 1980), pp. 157–92. The Freud text that Greenblatt cites is *Civilisation and Its Discontents* (1930).

67 See Elie Halévy, *A History of the English People in the Nineteenth Century*, 2nd edn., with intro. by R. B. MacCallum, 6 vols. (London: Ernest Benn, 1949), vol. 1: *England in 1815*, trans. E. I. Watkin and D. A. Barker, p. 452.

68 Paulson, *Representations of Revolution*, p. 268.

69 See Caroline Franklin, '"At Once Above – Beneath Her Sex": The Heroine in Regency Verse Romance', *Modern Languages Review*, 84 (1989), 273–88.

70 Butler, *Romantics, Rebels and Reactionaries*, p. 136.

71 See Notopoulos, *The Platonism of Shelley*, p. 214; Earl R. Wasserman, *Shelley: A Critical Reading* (Baltimore: Johns Hopkins University Press, 1971), p. 24; Roy R. Male, Jr, 'Shelley and the Doctrine of Sympathy', *University of Texas Studies in English*, 29 (1950), 183–203; and Nathaniel Brown, *Sexuality and Feminism in Shelley* (Cambridge, Mass.: Harvard University Press, 1979), pp. 216–24. The most detailed and historically sensitive treatment of the incest theme is John Donovan, 'Incest in *Laon and Cythna*: Nature, Custom, Desire', *KSR*, 2 (1987), 49–90.

72 See Shelley's letter to Thomas Moore of 16 December 1817; *Letters*, I, 583.

73 Kroeber, *Romantic Narrative Art, passim*. The same phenomenon is discussed in relation to Romantic epic by Thomas A. Vogler, *Preludes to Vision: The Epic Venture in Blake, Wordsworth, Keats, and Hart Crane* (Berkeley: University of California Press, 1971).

74 G. Wilson Knight, *The Starlit Dome: Studies in the Poetry of Vision* (1941; London: Methuen, 1959), p. 188.

75 Brown, *Sexuality and Feminism in Shelley*, p. 182.

76 Richard Haswell, 'Shelley's *The Revolt of Islam*: "The Connexion of Its Parts"', *KSJ*, 25 (1976), 81–102 (pp. 85–86). An even more glaring error occurs later in the article (p. 99) when Haswell attributes to Cythna Laon's description of the love scene in Canto VI.

77 Deborah Gutschera, 'The Drama of Reenactment in Shelley's *The Revolt of Islam*', *KSJ*, 35 (1986), 111–25 (pp. 120–21).

78 Murray, '"Elective Affinity"', p. 576.

79 By Timothy Webb, in conversation.

80 In his letter to Godwin of 11 December 1817, Shelley calls for advice on the subject of 'the economy of intellectual force', confiding that he is conscious in himself 'of an absence of that tranquillity which is the attribute & the accompaniment of power' (*Letters*, I, 578).

81 For various explanations of this passage, see Andrew Welburn, *Power and Self-Consciousness in the Poetry of Shelley* (Basingstoke: Macmillan, 1986), pp. 104–5; Earl Wasserman, *The Subtler Language: Critical Readings of Neoclassic and Romantic Poems* (Baltimore: Johns Hopkins University Press, 1959); and William Keach, 'Romanticism and Language' in *The Cambridge Companion to British Romanticism*, pp. 118–19.

82 *Poetry and Prose*, p. 505.

83 Timothy Clark, *Embodying Revolution: The Figure of the Poet in Shelley* (Oxford: Clarendon Press, 1989), p. 113.

84 I am indebted here to Geoffrey Hartman's reading of the 'Lucy' poems in *Wordsworth's Poetry 1787–1814* (New Haven: Yale University Press, 1964), pp. 158–59.

85 For a discussion of the relationship in Milton between external and internal conceptions of paradise, see Michael Fixler, *Milton and the Kingdoms of God* (London: Faber & Faber, 1964).

86 Holmes, *Shelley: The Pursuit*, p. 397. Holmes mistakenly attributes the speech to Laon.

87 Hazlitt, *Complete Works*, VIII, 150.

88 Peacock, *Works*, VIII, 238.

89 The phrase taken as the title for this chapter occurs in a letter that Shelley wrote to John Gisborne in 1822, where he makes a playful comparison between the apocalyptic yearnings produced in him by a reading of Goethe's *Faust* with the 'demoniacal' thoughts expressed in the final lines of Wordsworth's 'French Revolution, As It Appeared to Enthusiasts at Its Commencement', assuring Gisborne that 'we admirers of Faust are in the right road to Paradise' (*Letters*, II, 406–7). For what the letter reveals about Shelley's understanding of Goethe, see Timothy Webb, *The Violet in the Crucible: Shelley and Translation* (Oxford: Clarendon Press, 1976), pp. 152–54.

90 For the borrowings from 'Kubla Khan', see Neville Rogers, *Shelley at Work: A Critical Enquiry* (Oxford: Clarendon Press, 1967), pp. 110–14; and Wilson Knight, *The Starlit Dome*, pp. 189–96. The parallels with Moore are noted by James Lynn Ruff, 'Image, Theme and Structure in

The Revolt of Islam', unpublished Ph.D. thesis, Northwestern University, 1976, pp. 45–46.

91 The significance of the supernatural 'frame' in Cantos I and XII is discussed by Baker, *Shelley's Major Poetry*, p. 64. For a more adventurous interpretation, containing important new insights into the imaginative processes of the poem, see Peter Finch, 'Shelley's *Laon and Cythna*: The Bride Stripped Bare ... Almost', *KSR*, 3 (1988), 23–46.

92 *Shelley: The Critical Heritage*, pp. 124–25.

93 Peacock, *Works*, VIII, 107.

94 'I have read & considered all that you say about my general powers, & the particular instance of the Poem in which I have attempted to develope them. Nothing can be more satisfactory than the interest which your admonitions express. But I think you are mistaken in some points with regard to the peculiar nature of my powers, whatever be their amount. I listened with deference and self suspicion to your censures of "Laon & Cythna"; but the productions of mine which you commend hold a very low place in my own esteem; & this reassured me, in some degree at least' (*Letters*, I, 576–78).

95 Leslie A. Marchand, ed., *Byron's Letters and Journals*, 12 vols. (London: John Murray, 1973–82), VI, 83.

96 *Shelley: The Critical Heritage*, p. 114.

97 *Letters*, II, 127, 134, 203–4. See Kenneth Neill Cameron, 'Shelley vs Southey: New Light on an Old Quarrel', *Publications of the Modern Language Association*, 67 (1942), 489–512.

98 *Shelley: The Critical Heritage*, p. 110.

99 See R. J. White, *Waterloo to Peterloo* (London: Mercury, 1963), pp. 152–53.

100 Donald Thomas, 'Press Prosecutions of the Eighteenth and Nineteenth Centuries: The Evidence of King's Bench Indictments', *The Library*, Fifth Series, 32 (December 1977), 324, cited by Donovan, 'Incest in *Laon and Cythna*', p. 50.

101 Letter to Lord Liverpool, 19 March 1817, quoted by Halévy, *A History of the English People*, vol. II: *The Liberal Awakening*, trans. E. I. Watkin, p. 19n.

102 For these and other incidents in 1817, see Thompson, *Making of the English Working Class*, ch. 15.

103 William Godwin, *Considerations on Lord Grenville's and Mr. Pitt's Bills, concerning Treasonable and Seditious Practices, and Unlawful Assemblies. By a Lover of Order* (London, 1794) in Godwin, *Uncollected Writings*, p. 237.

104 Halévy's phrase, *The Liberal Awakening*, p. 25.

105 Southey's fine phrase, from his letter to John May of 26 June 1797, recalling the time 'when I believed in the persuadability of man, and had the mania of man-mending' (quoted in Cobban, ed., *Debate on the French Revolution*, p. 376).

106 Quoted by Foot, *Red Shelley*, p. 324.

107 See Newman Ivey White, *Shelley*, 2 vols. (London: Secker & Warburg, 1947), II, 404–10.
108 For details, see Kalim, *The Social Orpheus*.
109 Cited by Holmes, *Shelley: The Pursuit*, p. 402.
110 Benjamin Disraeli, *The Revolutionary Epick and Other Poems*, ed. W. Davenport Adams (London: Hurst & Blackett, 1904), p. xii.
111 Cameron, *Shelley: The Golden Years*, p. 311.
112 Curran, *Poetic Form and British Romanticism*, p. 147.

Select bibliography

PRIMARY SOURCES

Addison, Joseph. *The Spectator*. Ed. Donald F. Bond. 5 vols. Oxford: Clarendon Press, 1965.

Anon. *Temperate Comments upon Intemperate Reflections: or, A Review of Mr. Burke's Letter*. London, 1791.

The Radical Chiefs, A Mock Heroick Poem. Embellished with a Suitable Caricature by Mr. Cruikshank. London, 1821.

Aulnoy, Countess of. *Queen Mab; containing A Select Collection of only the Best, Most Instructive, and Entertaining Tales of the Faires ... To which are added A Fairy Tale, in the Ancient English Style, by Dr. Parnell: and Queen Mab's Song*. 5th edn. London, 1799.

Barlow, Joel. *The Columbiad: A Poem*. Philadelphia, 1807.

Bennett, Betty T., ed. *British War Poetry in the Age of Romanticism: 1793–1815*. New York: Garland, 1976.

Blake, William. *Complete Writings*. Ed. Geoffrey Keynes. Oxford University Press, 1967.

Bunyan, John. *The Pilgrim's Progress from this World to That which is to Come*. Ed. J. B. Wharey. 2nd edn. rev. Roger Sharrock. Oxford: Clarendon Press, 1960.

[Burges, Mary]. *The Progress of the Pilgrim Good-Intent, in Jacobinical Times*. 5th edn. London, 1800.

Burke, Edmund. *Reflections on the Revolution in France, and on the Proceedings in Certain Societies in London Relative to that Event*. Ed. Conor Cruise O' Brien. Harmondsworth: Penguin, 1969.

The Correspondence of Edmund Burke. Ed. Alfred Cobban and Robert A. Smith. 10 vols. Cambridge University Press; University of Chicago Press, 1958–78.

The Works of the Right Honorable Edmund Burke. Ed. F. W. Raffety. 6 vols. Oxford University Press, 1906.

[Buxton, George]. *The Political Quixote; or, The Adventures of the Renowned Don Blackibo Dwarfino, and His Trusty Squire Seditiono; A Romance, in which are Introduced many Popular and Celebrated Political Characters of the Present Day*. London, 1820.

Byron, Lord. *The Complete Poetical Works*. Ed. Jerome J. McGann. 7 vols. Oxford: Clarendon Press, 1980–93.
   Letters and Journals. Ed. Leslie A. Marchand. 12 vols. London: John Murray, 1973–82.
Cartwright, John. *The Comparison: in which Mock Reform, Half Reform, and Constitutional Reform, Are Considered; or, Who Are the Enlightened and Practical Statesmen of Talent and Integrity to Preserve Our Laws and Liberties? Addressed to the People of England*. London, 1810.
Cervantes. *The Adventures of Don Quixote*. Trans. J. M. Cohen. Harmondsworth: Penguin, 1950.
Chalmers, Alexander, ed. *The Works of the English Poets, from Chaucer to Cowper; Including the Series Edited with Prefaces, Biographical and Critical, by Dr. Samuel Johnson: and the Most Approved Translations*. 21 vols. London, 1810.
Chatterton, Thomas. *The Works of Thomas Chatterton*. 3 vols. London, 1803.
Coleridge, Samuel T. *The Collected Works of Samuel Taylor Coleridge*. Princeton University Press; London: Routledge & Kegan Paul, 1961 – .
   The Complete Poetical Works of Samuel Taylor Coleridge. Ed. E. H. Coleridge. 2 vols. 1912; Oxford: Clarendon Press, 1962.
Condorcet, A.-N. de. *Sketch for a Historical Picture of the Progress of the Human Mind*. Trans. June Barraclough, with intro. by Stuart Hampshire. London: Weidenfeld & Nicolson, 1955.
Darwin, Erasmus. *The Botanic Garden: A Poem, in Two Parts. Part I. Containing the Economy of Vegetation. Part II. The Loves of the Plants. With Philosophical Notes*. 1791. Facsimile edition, with intro. by Desmond King-Hele. Menston, Yorkshire: Scolar Press, 1973.
De Quincey, Thomas. *The Collected Writings of Thomas De Quincey*. Ed. David Masson. 14 vols. London: A. & C. Black, 1897.
   Recollections of the Lakes and the Lake Poets. Ed. David Wright. Harmondsworth: Penguin, 1970.
Disraeli, Benjamin. *The Revolutionary Epick and Other Poems*. Ed. W. Davenport Adams. London: Hurst & Blackett, 1904.
Drummond, Sir William. *Academical Questions*. 1805. Facsimile edn., with intro. by Terence Allan Hoagwood. Delmar, NY: Scholars' Facsimiles and Reprints, 1984.
Dyer, George. *Poems*. London, 1792.
Foster, John. 'On the Application of the Epithet Romantic'. *Essays in a Series of Letters to a Friend*. 1806; 11th edn. London, 1835.
Fourier, Charles. *Le Nouveau monde amoureux: manuscrit inédit, texte intégral*. Ed. Simone Debout-Oleszkiewicz. Paris: Honoré Champion, 1978.
Frere, J. Hookham. *Prospectus and Specimen of an Intended National Work, by William and Robert Whistlecraft, of Stow-Market, in Suffolk, Harness and Collar-Makers. Intended to Comprise the Most Interesting Particulars Relating to King Arthur and His Round Table*. London, 1817.
Godwin, William. *Caleb Williams; or Things As They Are*. Ed. Maurice Hindley. Harmondsworth: Penguin, 1988.

The Enquirer: Reflections on Education, Manners, and Literature. In a Series of Essays. 1797. Facsimile edn. New York: Augustus M. Kelley, 1965.

Enquiry Concerning Political Justice and Its Influence on Morals and Happiness. Facsimile of 3rd edn. (1798), with variant readings of the 1st and 2nd edns. Ed. F. E. L. Priestley. 3 vols. University of Toronto Press, 1946.

Enquiry Concerning Political Justice. Ed. Isaac Kramnick. Harmondsworth: Penguin, 1976.

Uncollected Writings (1785–1822): Articles in Periodicals and Six Pamphlets. Facsimile reproductions, with intro. by J. W. Marken and B. R. Pollin. Gainesville, Fla.: Scholars' Facsimiles and Reprints, 1968.

[Graham, Catherine M.] *Observations on the Reflections of the Right Hon. Edmund Burke, on the Revolution in France, in a Letter to the Right Hon. the Earl of Stanhope.* London, 1790.

[Hamilton, Elizabeth.] *Memoirs of the Modern Philosophers.* 3 vols. London, 1800.

Hazlitt, William. *The Complete Works of William Hazlitt.* Ed. P. P. Howe. 21 vols. London: Dent, 1930–34.

[and Leigh Hunt.] *The Round Table: A Collection of Essays on Literature, Men and Manners.* 2 vols. Edinburgh, 1817.

Hunt, Leigh. *The Autobiography of Leigh Hunt.* Rev. edn. (1860), with intro. by Edmund Blunden. Oxford University Press, 1928.

Juvenilia; or, A Collection of Poems Written Between the Ages of Twelve and Sixteen. 2nd edn. London, 1801.

The Poetical Works of Leigh Hunt. Ed. Thornton Hunt. London and New York, 1860.

Hurd, Richard. *The Works of Richard Hurd, D. D., Lord Bishop of Worcester.* 8 vols. London, 1811.

Keats, John. *Letters of John Keats.* Ed. Robert Gittings. Corrected edn. Oxford University Press, 1979.

The Poems of John Keats. Ed. Jack Stillinger. London: Heinmann, 1978.

Landor, Walter Savage. *Poems.* Ed. Geoffrey Grigson. Fontwell, Sussex: Centaur Press, 1964.

Mackintosh, James. *Vindiciae Gallicae: Defence of the French Revolution and Its Admirers against the Accusations of the Right Hon. Edmund Burke; including Some Strictures on the Late Production of Mons. de Calonne.* London, 1791.

Malthus, Thomas R. *An Essay on the Principle of Population and A Summary View of the Principle of Population.* Ed. Antony Flew. Harmondsworth: Penguin, 1970.

Milton, John. *Paradise Lost.* Ed. Alastair Fowler. Corrected edn. Harlow: Longman, 1971.

Selected Prose. Ed. C. A. Patrides. Harmondsworth: Penguin, 1974.

Moore, Thomas. *The Poetical Works.* Reprinted from the early editions. London and New York, 1881.

Owen, Robert. *A New View of Society and Other Writings.* Ed. G. D. H. Cole. London: Dent; New York: Dutton, 1927.

Paine, Thomas. *The Age of Reason*. Ed. Chapman Cohen. London: Pioneer Press, 1937.
　Common Sense. Ed. Isaac Kramnick. Harmondsworth: Penguin, 1976.
　Rights of Man. Ed. Henry Collins. Harmondsworth: Penguin, 1969.
Peacock, Thomas Love. *The Works of Thomas Love Peacock*. Ed. H. F. B. Smith and C. E. Jones. 10 vols. 1924–34; rpt. New York: A. M. S. Press, 1967.
Pigott, Charles. *A Political Dictionary: Explaining the True Meaning of Words. Illustrated and Exemplified in the Lives, Morals, Character and Conduct of the Following Most Illustrious Personages …* London, 1795.
Reeve, Clara. *The Progress of Romance; and the History of Charoba, Queen of Aegypt*. 1785. Facsimile edition, with bibliographical note by Esther M. McGill. New York: Facsimile Text Society, 1930.
Reynolds, John H. *The Eden of Imagination. A Poem*. London, 1814.
Rice-Oxley, L., ed. *Poetry of the Anti-Jacobin*. Percy Reprints. Oxford: Blackwell, 1924.
Ritson, Joseph, ed. *Ancient English Metrical Romanceës*. 3 vols. London, 1802.
Roberts, J. M. and John Hardman, eds. *French Revolution Documents*. 2 vols. Oxford: Blackwell, 1966–73.
Robespierre, Maximilien. *Textes Choisis*. Ed. Jean Poperen. 3 vols. Paris: Editions Sociales, 1958.
Sanon, George. *The Causes of the French Revolution; and the Science of Governing an Empire: An Epic and Philosophical Poem*. London, 1806.
Schlegel, A. W. *A Course of Lectures on Dramatic Art and Literature*. Trans. John Black, rev. A. J. W. Morrison. London, 1846.
Scott, Walter. *Essays on Chivalry, Romance and the Drama*. London: Frederick Warne, n.d.
　The Poetical Works of Sir Walter Scott. Ed. J. Logie Robertson. 1904; Oxford University Press, 1960.
　The Visionary Nos. I. II. III. 1819. Facsimile edn, with intro. by Peter Garside. Regency Reprints. University College, Cardiff Press, 1984.
Shelley, Percy Bysshe. *Laon and Cythna; or, The Revolution of the Golden City: A Vision of the Nineteenth Century in the Stanza of Spenser*. London, 1818 [issued 1817].
　The Letters of Percy Bysshe Shelley. Ed. Frederick L. Jones. Oxford: Clarendon Press, 1964.
　The Poems of Shelley. Ed. Geoffrey Matthews and Kelvin Everest. 1 vol. so far. London: Longman, 1989.
　Poetical Works. Ed. Thomas Hutchinson. 2nd edn. corr. Geoffrey Matthews. Oxford University Press, 1970.
　The Poetical Works of Percy Bysshe Shelley. Ed. H. Buxton Forman. 4 vols. London, 1876.
　The Prose Works of Percy Bysshe Shelley. Ed. E. B. Murray. 1 vol. so far. Oxford University Press, 1993.
　Queen Mab; A Philosophical Poem: With Notes. 1813. Facsimile edn., with

intro. by Jonathan Wordsworth. Revolution and Romanticism series. Oxford: Woodstock Books, 1990.

The Revolt of Islam: A Poem in Twelve Cantos. London, 1818.

Shelley and His Circle 1773–1822. An edition of the manuscripts of Shelley and others in the Carl H. Pforzheimer Library. Vols. i–iv, ed. Kenneth Neill Cameron. Vols. v–viii, ed. Donald H. Reiman. Cambridge, Mass.: Harvard University Press, 1961–86.

Shelley's Poetry and Prose: Authoritative Texts, Criticism. Ed. Donald H. Reiman and Sharon B. Powers. New York: Norton, 1977.

Shelley's Prose; or The Trumpet of a Prophecy. Ed. with intro. by David Lee Clark. Corrected edn., with pref. by Harold Bloom. London: Fourth Estate, 1988.

Shelley, Mary W. *The Journals of Mary Shelley*. Ed. Paula R. Feldman and Diana Scott-Kilvert. 2 vols. Oxford: Clarendon Press, 1987.

The Letters of Mary Wollstonecraft Shelley. Ed. Betty T. Bennett. 3 vols. Baltimore: Johns Hopkins University Press, 1980–88.

Smith, Adam. *An Inquiry into the Nature and Causes of the Wealth of Nations*. Ed. R. H. Campbell and A. S. Skinner. Textual ed. W. B. Todd. 2 vols. Oxford: Clarendon Press, 1976.

Southey, Robert. *Joan of Arc, Ballads, Lyrics and Minor Poems*. London and New York: Routledge, n.d.

Thalaba the Destroyer: A Metrical Romance. 2 vols. London, 1801.

Poems of Southey. Ed. Maurice H. Fitzgerald. Oxford University Press, 1909.

and Robert Lovell. *Poems: containing The Retrospect, Odes, Elegies, Sonnets, &c*. Bath, 1795 [1794].

Spence, Thomas. *The Political Works of Thomas Spence*. Ed. H. T. Dickinson. Newcastle-upon-Tyne: Avero Publications, 1982.

Spenser, Edmund. *The Faerie Queene*. Ed. A. C. Hamilton. Corrected edn. London: Longman, 1980.

Stephens, H. Morse. *The Principal Speeches of the Statesmen and Orators of the French Revolution 1789–1795*. 2 vols. Oxford: Clarendon Press, 1892.

Thomson, James. *The Seasons and The Castle of Indolence*. Ed. James Sambrook. Oxford: Clarendon Press, 1972.

Volney, Comte de. *Oeuvres complètes de Volney*. Paris, 1876.

Warton, Thomas. *The History of English Poetry from the Close of the Eleventh Century to the Commencement of the Eighteenth Century to which are Prefixed Three Dissertations*. From Richard Price's edn of 1824. 3 vols. London, 1840.

Observations on the Fairy Queen of Spenser. 2nd edn. 2 vols. London, 1762.

Wollstonecraft, Mary. *The Works of Mary Wollstonecraft*. Ed. Janet Todd and Marilyn Butler. 7 vols. London: William Pickering, 1989.

Wordsworth, William. *Poems*. 1815. Facsimile edition, with intro. by Jonathan Wordsworth. Revolution and Romanticism series. 2 vols. Oxford: Woodstock Books, 1989.

Poetical Works. Ed. Thomas Hutchinson, rev. Ernest de Selincourt. 1936;
Oxford University Press, 1981.

*The Prelude 1799, 1805, 1850: Authoritative Texts, Context and Reception, Recent
Critical Essays*. Ed. Jonathan Wordsworth, M. H. Abrams and Stephen
Gill. New York: Norton, 1979.

The Prose Works of William Wordsworth. Ed. W. J. B. Owen and Jane
Worthington Smyser. 3 vols. Oxford: Clarendon Press, 1974.

Young, Edward. *Night Thoughts*. Ed. Stephen Cornford. Cambridge
University Press, 1989.

SECONDARY SOURCES

Abrams, M. H. 'English Romanticism: The Spirit of the Age'. In
Romanticism and Consciousness. Ed. Harold Bloom.

The Mirror and the Lamp: Romantic Theory and the Critical Tradition. 1953;
Oxford University Press, 1971.

Natural Supernaturalism: Tradition and Revolution in Romantic Literature. New
York: Norton, 1971.

Adams, M. Ray. *Studies in the Literary Backgrounds of English Radicalism; With
Special Reference to the French Revolution*. 1947; Westport, Conn.:
Greenwood Press, 1968.

Altick, Richard D. *The English Common Reader: A Social History of the Mass
Reading Public 1800–1900*. University of Chicago Press, 1963.

Arendt, Hannah. *On Revolution*. 1963; Harmondsworth: Penguin, 1973.

Artz, Frederick B. *Reaction and Revolution 1814–1832*. Corr. edn. New York:
Harper & Row, 1963.

Auerbach, Erich. *Mimesis: The Representation of Reality in Western Literature*.
Trans. Willard R. Trask. 1953; Princeton University Press, 1971.

Baker, Carlos. *Shelley's Major Poetry: The Fabric of a Vision*. 1948; Princeton
University Press, 1970.

Barker, Francis *et al*., eds. *1789: Reading Writing Revolution*. Proceedings of
the Essex Conference on the Sociology of Literature, July 1981.
Colchester: University of Essex, 1982.

Barthes, Roland. *Writing Degree Zero*. Trans. Annette Lavers and Colin
Smith. Preface by Susan Sontag. 1968; New York: Hill & Wang, 1981.

Bate, W. Jackson. *From Classic to Romantic: Premises of Taste in Eighteenth-
Century England*. New York: Harper, 1946.

Beaujour, Michel. 'Flight Out of Time: Poetic Language and the
Revolution'. Trans. Richard Klein. *Yale French Studies*. Literature and
Revolution Special Issue. Ed. Jacques Ehrmann. Vol. 39 (1967),
29–49.

Becker, Carl L. *The Heavenly City of the Eighteenth-Century Philosophers*. 1932;
New Haven: Yale University Press, 1967.

Beer, Gillian. *The Romance*. Critical Idiom series. London: Methuen, 1970.

Beers, Henry A. *A History of English Romanticism in the Eighteenth Century*. 1898;
New York: Gordian Press, 1966.

Beyer, Werner W. *The Enchanted Forest*. Oxford: Blackwell, 1963.

Billington, James H. *Fire in the Minds of Men: Origins of the Revolutionary Faith*. London: Temple Smith, 1980.

Bindman, David. *The Shadow of the Guillotine: Britain and the French Revolution*. Exhibition Catalogue. London: British Museum, 1989.

Blakemore, Steven. *Burke and the Fall of Language*. Hanover: University Press of New England, 1988.

Blank, G. Kim. *Wordsworth's Influence on Shelley: A Study of Poetic Authority*. Basingstoke: Macmillan, 1988.

Bloom, Harold, ed. *Romanticism and Consciousness: Essays in Criticism*. New York: Norton, 1970.

Blum, Carol. *Rousseau and the Republic of Virtue: The Language of Politics in the French Revolution*. Ithaca: Cornell University Press, 1986.

Boulton, James T. *The Language of Politics in the Age of Wilkes and Burke*. London: Routledge & Kegan Paul, 1963.

Bowle, John. *Politics and Opinion in the Nineteenth Century: An Historical Introduction*. London: Jonathan Cape, 1954.

Brailsford, H. N. *Shelley, Godwin and Their Circle*. 2nd edn. Oxford University Press, 1963.

Brinton, Crane. *The Political Ideas of the English Romanticists*. 1926; New York: Russell & Russell, 1962.

  A Decade of Revolution 1789–1799. Rise of Modern Europe series. 1934; New York: Harper & Row, 1963.

Brown, Nathaniel. *Sexuality and Feminism in Shelley*. Cambridge, Mass.: Harvard University Press, 1979.

Brownlee, Kevin and Marina Scordilis Brownlee, eds. *Romance: Generic Transformation from Chrétien de Troyes to Cervantes*. Hanover: University Press of New England, 1985.

Butler, Marilyn. 'Byron and the Empire in the East'. In *Byron: Augustan and Romantic*. Ed. Andrew Rutherford.

  Peacock Displayed: A Satirist in His Context. London: Routledge & Kegan Paul, 1979.

  Romantics, Rebels and Reactionaries: English Literature and Its Background 1760–1830. Oxford University Press, 1981.

  'Telling It Like a Story: The French Revolution as Narrative'. *Studies in Romanticism*. English Romanticism and the French Revolution Special Issue. Ed. Robert M. Manniquis. Vol. 28, No. 3 (1989), 345–66.

  ed. *Burke, Paine, Godwin and the Revolution Controversy*. Cambridge University Press, 1984.

Cameron, Kenneth Neill. *Shelley: The Golden Years*. Cambridge, Mass.: Harvard University Press, 1974.

  The Young Shelley: Genesis of a Radical. 1950; New York: Collier, 1962.

Carnall, Geoffrey. *Robert Southey and His Age: The Development of a Conservative Mind*. Oxford: Clarendon Press, 1960.

Chandler, Alice. *A Dream of Order: The Medieval Ideal in Nineteenth-Century English Literature*. London: Routledge & Kegan Paul, 1971.

Chandler, James K. *Wordsworth's Second Nature: A Study of the Poetry and Politics*. University of Chicago Press, 1984.

Chapman, Gerald W. *Edmund Burke: The Practical Imagination*. Cambridge, Mass.: Harvard University Press, 1967.

Clark, John P. *The Philosophical Anarchism of William Godwin*. Princeton University Press, 1977.

Clark, Timothy. *Embodying Revolution: The Figure of the Poet in Shelley*. Oxford: Clarendon Press, 1989.

Close, Anthony. *The Romantic Approach to 'Don Quixote'*. Cambridge University Press, 1977.

Cobban , Alfred. *Edmund Burke and the Revolt against the Eighteenth Century: A Study of the Political and Social Thinking of Burke, Wordsworth, Coleridge and Southey*. 2nd edn. London: Allen & Unwin, 1960.

Cobban, Alfred, ed. *The Debate on the French Revolution 1789–1800*. 2nd edn. London: A. & C. Black, 1960.

Cranston, Maurice. *Philosophers and Pamphleteers: Political Theorists of the Enlightenment*. Oxford University Press, 1986.

Cronin, Richard. *Shelley's Poetic Thoughts*. London: Macmillan, 1981.

Crossley, Ceri and Ian Small, eds. *The French Revolution and British Culture*. Oxford University Press, 1989.

Curran, Stuart. *Poetic Form and British Romanticism*. Oxford University Press, 1986.

   Shelley's Annus Mirabilis: The Maturing of an Epic Vision. San Marino, Calif.: Huntingdon Library, 1975.

Curran, Stuart, ed. *The Cambridge Companion to British Romanticism*. Cambridge University Press, 1993.

Curry, Kenneth. *The Contributions of Robert Southey to the 'Morning Post'*. University of Alabama Press, 1984.

Davies, R. T. and B. G. Beatty, eds. *Literature of the Romantic Period 1750–1850*. Liverpool University Press, 1976.

Dawson, P. M. S. *The Unacknowledged Legislator: Shelley and Politics*. Oxford: Clarendon Press, 1980.

Deane, Seamus. *The French Revolution and Enlightenment in England 1789–1832*. Cambridge, Mass.: Harvard University Press, 1988.

De Maar, Harko. *A History of Modern English Romanticism: Elizabethan and Modern Romanticism in the Eighteenth Century*. 1924; New York: Haskell House, 1970.

Dickinson, H. T. *British Radicalism and the French Revolution 1789–1815*. Oxford: Blackwell, 1985.

Dowden, Edward. *The French Revolution and English Literature*. London, 1897.

Dowling, William C. 'Burke and the Age of Chivalry'. *Yearbook of English Studies*, 12 (1982), 109–24.

Duffy, Edward. *Rousseau in England: The Context for Shelley's Critique of the Enlightenment*. Berkeley and Los Angeles: University of California Press, 1979.

Duncan, Ian. *Modern Romance and the Transformation of the Novel: The Gothic, Scott and Dickens.* Cambridge University Press, 1992.

Duvall, Frank Ongley. *Popular Disturbances and Public Order in Regency England.* Introduction by Angus MacIntyre. 1934; Oxford University Press, 1969.

Edwards, Thomas R. *Imagination and Power: A Study of Poetry on Public Themes.* New York: Oxford University Press, 1971.

Eichner, Hans, ed. *'Romantic' and its Cognates: The European History of a Word.* Manchester University Press, 1972.

Emsley, Clive. *British Society and the French Wars 1793–1815.* Basingstoke: Macmillan, 1979.

Everest, Kelvin, ed. *Shelley Revalued: Essays from the Gregynog Conference.* Leicester University Press, 1983.

Fairchild, Hoxie N. *The Romantic Quest.* New York: Columbia University Press, 1931.

Finke, Laurie. 'Towards a Cultural Poetics of the Romance'. *Genre,* 22 (1989), 109–27.

Fischer, Hermann. *Romantic Verse Narrative: The History of a Genre.* Trans. Sue Bollans. Cambridge University Press, 1991.

Fixler, Michael. *Milton and the Kingdoms of God.* London: Faber & Faber, 1964.

Foerster, Donald M. *The Fortunes of Epic Poetry: A Study in English and American Criticism 1750–1950.* Washington: Catholic University of America Press, 1962.

Foot, Paul. *Red Shelley.* 1980; London: Bookmarks, 1984.

Fowler, Alastair. *Kinds of Literature: An Introduction to the Theory of Genres and Modes.* Oxford: Clarendon Press, 1982.

Foxon, D. F. *English Verse 1701–1750. A Catalogue of Separately Printed Poems with Notes on Contemporary Collected Editions.* 2 vols. Cambridge University Press, 1975.

Franklin, Caroline. '"At Once Above – Beneath Her Sex": The Heroine in Regency Verse Romance'. *Modern Languages Review,* 84 (1989), 273–88.

Frow, John. *Marxism and Literary History.* Oxford: Blackwell, 1986.

Frye, Northrop. *Anatomy of Criticism: Four Essays.* 1957; Princeton University Press, 1971.

  The Secular Scripture: A Study of the Structure of Romance. Cambridge, Mass.: Harvard University Press, 1976.

Furet, François. *Interpreting the French Revolution.* Trans. Elborg Forster. Cambridge University Press, 1981.

Garrett, Clarke. *Respectable Folly: Millenarianism and the French Revolution in France and England.* Baltimore: Johns Hopkins University Press, 1975.

Garside, P. D. 'Scott, the Romantic Past and the Nineteenth Century'. *Review of English Studies,* 23 (1972), 147–61.

George, M. Dorothy. *Catalogue of Political and Personal Satires Preserved at the*

Department of Prints and Drawings in The British Museum. Vols. VI to IX. London: British Museum, 1938–52.

English Political Caricature: A Study of Opinion and Propaganda. Vol. 1: To 1792. Vol 2.: 1793–1815. Oxford University Press, 1959.

Giamatti, A. Bartlett. *The Earthly Paradise and the Renaissance Epic.* Princeton University Press, 1966.

Gilchrist, J. and W. J. Murray, eds. *The Press in the French Revolution: A Selection of Documents Taken from the Press of the Revolution for the Years 1789–1794.* London: Ginn, 1971.

Girouard, Mark. *The Return to Camelot: Chivalry and the English Gentleman.* New Haven: Yale University Press, 1981.

Gleckner, Robert F. *Byron and the Ruins of Paradise.* Baltimore: Johns Hopkins University Press, 1967.

Goldstein, Lawrence. *Ruins and Empire: The Evolution of a Theme in Augustan and Romantic Literature.* University of Pittsburgh Press, 1977.

Goodwin, Albert. *The Friends of Liberty: The English Democratic Movement in the Age of the French Revolution.* London: Hutchinson, 1979.

Goodwin, Barbara and Keith Taylor. *The Politics of Utopia: A Study in Theory and Practice.* London: Hutchinson, 1982.

Greenblatt, Stephen. 'To Fashion a Gentleman: Spenser and the Destruction of the Bower of Bliss'. *Renaissance Self-Fashioning: From More to Shakespeare.* University of Chicago Press, 1980.

Griffin, Dustin. *Regaining Paradise: Milton and the Eighteenth Century.* Cambridge University Press, 1986.

Halévy, Elie. *A History of the English People in the Nineteenth Century.* Trans. E. I. Watkin and D. A. Barker. 2nd edn. Intro. by R. B. MacCallum. 6 vols. London: Ernest Benn, 1949.

Haller, William. *The Early Life of Robert Southey 1774–1803.* New York: Columbia University Press, 1917.

Hampson, Norman. *Will and Circumstance: Montesquieu, Rousseau and the French Revolution.* London: Duckworth, 1983.

Hancock, Albert E. *The French Revolution and the English Poets: A Study in Historical Criticism.* New York, 1899.

Hanley, Keith and Raman Selden, eds. *Revolution and English Romanticism: Politics and Rhetoric.* Hemel Hempstead: Harvester Wheatsheaf, 1990.

Harrison, J. F. C. *The Second Coming: Popular Millenarianism 1780–1850.* London: Routledge & Kegan Paul, 1979.

Harrison, Stanley. *Poor Men's Guardians: A Record of the Struggles for a Democratic Newspaper Press, 1763–1973.* London: Lawrence & Wishart, 1974.

Hartman, Geoffrey H. *Wordsworth's Poetry 1787–1814.* New Haven: Yale University Press, 1964.

Harvey, A. D. *English Poetry in a Changing Society 1780–1825.* London: Allison & Busby, 1980.

Hayden, John O., ed. *Romantic Bards and British Reviewers.* London: Routledge & Kegan Paul, 1971.

ed. *Scott: The Critical Heritage*. London: Routledge & Kegan Paul, 1970.

Henderson, Ernest F. *Symbol and Satire in the French Revolution*. New York and London: Knickerbocker Press, 1912.

Henson, Eithne. *'The Fictions of Romantick Chivalry': Samuel Johnson and Romance*. Cranbury, NJ: Fairleigh Dickinson University Press, 1992.

Hobsbaum, E. J. *The Age of Revolution: Europe 1789–1848*. 1962; London: Sphere, 1980.

Hogg, Thomas Jefferson. *The Life of Percy Bysshe Shelley*. Intro. by Edward Dowden. London: Routledge, 1906.

Hogle, Jerrold E. *Shelley's Process: Radical Transference and the Development of His Major Works*. New York: Oxford University Press, 1988.

Hole, Robert. 'British Counter-Revolutionary Propaganda in the 1790s'. In *Britain and Revolutionary France*. Ed. Colin Jones.
   Pulpits, Politics and Public Order in England 1760–1832. Cambridge University Press, 1989.

Holmes, Richard. *Shelley: The Pursuit*. 1974; London: Quartet Books, 1976.

Hughes, A. M. D. *The Nascent Mind of Shelley*. Oxford: Clarendon Press, 1947.

Hunt, Lynn. *The Family Romance of the French Revolution*. Berkeley: University of California Press, 1992.
   'The Political Psychology of Revolutionary Caricatures'. *French Caricature and the French Revolution, 1789–1799*. Exhibition Catalogue. Los Angeles: Grunwald Centre for the Graphic Arts, University of California, 1988.
   Politics, Culture and Class in the French Revolution. 1984; London: Methuen, 1986.

Jackson, J. R. de J. *Annals of English Verse 1770–1835. A Preliminary Survey of the Volumes Published*. New York: Garland, 1985.
   Poetry of the Romantic Period. London: Routledge & Kegan Paul, 1980.

Jackson, Rosemary. *Fantasy: The Literature of Subversion*. New Accents series. London: Methuen, 1981.

Jameson, Fredric. 'Magical Narratives: Romance as Genre'. *New Literary History*, 7 (1975), 135–63.

Jauss, Hans Robert. *Toward an Aesthetic of Reception*. Trans. Timothy Bahti, with intro. by Paul de Man. Minneapolis: University of Minnesota Press, 1982.

Johnston, Arthur. *Enchanted Ground: The Study of Medieval Romance in the Eighteenth Century*. London: Athlone Press, 1964.

Johnston, Kenneth R. *et al.*, eds. *Romantic Revolutions: Criticism and Theory*. Bloomington: Indiana University Press, 1990.

Jones, Colin, ed. *Britain and Revolutionary France: Conflict, Subversion and Propaganda*. University of Exeter Publications, 1983.

Jones, Howard Mumford. *Revolution & Romanticism*. Cambridge, Mass.: Harvard University Press, 1974.

Kalim, Siddiq. *The Social Orpheus: Shelley and the Owenites*. Lahore: Research Council Publications, 1973.

Keach, William. *Shelley's Style*. London: Methuen, 1984.

Keen, Maurice. *Chivalry*. New Haven: Yale University Press, 1984.

Kelly, Gary. *The English Jacobin Novel 1780–1805*. Oxford: Clarendon Press, 1976.

Kennedy, Emmet. *A Cultural History of the French Revolution*. New Haven: Yale University Press, 1989.

King-Hele, Desmond. *Erasmus Darwin and the Romantic Poets*. London: Macmillan, 1986.

    Shelley: His Thought and Work. 2nd edn. London: Macmillan, 1971.

Kipperman, Mark. *Beyond Enchantment: German Idealism and English Romantic Poetry*. Philadelphia: University of Pennsylvania Press, 1986.

Knight, G. Wilson. *The Starlit Dome: Studies in the Poetry of Vision*. 1941; London, Methuen, 1959.

Kramnick, Isaac. *The Rage of Edmund Burke: Portrait of an Ambivalent Conservative*. New York: Basic Books, 1977.

Kroeber, Karl. *Romantic Narrative Art*. Madison: University of Wisconsin Press, 1966.

Langbauer, Laurie. *Women and Romance: The Consolations of Gender in the English Novel*. Ithaca: Cornell University Press, 1990.

Lasky, Melvin. *Utopia and Revolution*. 1976; London: Macmillan, 1977.

Latham, Minor White. *The Elizabethan Fairies: The Fairies of Folklore and the Fairies of Shakespeare*. New York: Columbia University Press, 1930.

Lea, F. A. *Shelley and the Romantic Revolution*. 1945; Folcroft, Pa.: Folcroft Press, 1969.

Leask, Nigel. *British Romantic Writers and the East: Anxieties of Empire*. Cambridge University Press, 1992.

Leighton, Angela. *Shelley and the Sublime: An Interpretation of the Major Poems*. Cambridge University Press, 1984.

Lincoln, Eleanor T. *Pastoral and Romance: Modern Essays in Criticism*. Englewood Cliffs, NJ: Prentice-Hall, 1969.

Lindenberger, Herbert. *The History in Literature: On Value, Genre, Institutions*. New York: Columbia University Press, 1990.

Liu, Alan. *Wordsworth: The Sense of History*. Stanford University Press, 1989.

Lock, F. P. *Burke's Reflections on the Revolution in France*. London: Allen & Unwin, 1985.

Locke, Don. *A Fantasy of Reason: The Life and Thought of William Godwin*. London: Routledge & Kegan Paul, 1980.

Loughrey, Brian, ed. *The Pastoral Mode: A Casebook*. London: Macmillan, 1984.

Macaulay, James. *The Gothic Revival, 1745–1845*. Glasgow: Blackie, 1975.

Macpherson, C. B. *Burke*. Past Masters series. Oxford University Press, 1980.

McCalman, Iain. *Radical Underworld: Prophets, Revolutionaries and Pornographers in London 1798–1840*. Cambridge University Press, 1988.

McCoy, Richard C. *The Rites of Knighthood: The Literature and Politics of Elizabethan Chivalry*. Berkeley: University of California Press, 1989.

McDannell, Colleen and Bernard Lang. *Heaven: A History*. New Haven: Yale University Press, 1988.

McGann, Jerome. *The Romantic Ideology: A Critical Investigation*. University of Chicago Press, 1983.

McKeon, Michael. *The Origins of the English Novel 1600–1740*. London: Radius, 1987.

McNeice, Gerald. *Shelley and the Revolutionary Idea*. Cambridge, Mass.: Harvard University Press, 1969.

Madden, Lionel, ed. *Robert Southey: The Critical Heritage*. London: Routledge and Kegan Paul, 1972.

Manuel, Frank E., ed. *Utopias and Utopian Thought*. 1965; London: Souvenir Press, 1973.

and Fritzie P. Manuel. *Utopian Thought in the Western World*. Oxford: Blackwell, 1979.

Marshall, Peter H. *William Godwin*. New Haven: Yale University Press, 1984.

Medwin, Thomas. *Life of Percy Bysshe Shelley*. Revised edn. Intro. by H. Buxton Forman. Oxford University Press, 1913.

Merriman, James D. *The Flower of Kings: A Study of the Arthurian Legend in England Between 1485 and 1835*. Lawrence: University Press of Kansas, 1973.

Miller, Victor Clyde. *Joel Barlow: Revolutionist, London 1791–92*. Hamburg: Friederichsen, de Gruyter, 1932.

Mitchell, Jerome. *Scott, Chaucer and Medieval Romance: A Study in Sir Walter Scott's Indebtedness to the Literature of the Middle Ages*. Lexington: University Press of Kentucky, 1987.

Morris, Kevin L. *The Image of the Middle Ages in Romantic and Victorian Literature*. London: Croom Helm, 1984.

Morton, A. L. *The English Utopia*. 1952; London: Lawrence & Wishart, 1978.

Mossner, Ernest Campbell. 'David Hume's "An Historical Essay on Chivalry and Modern Honour"'. *Modern Philology*, (August 1947), 54–60.

Munro, D. H. *Godwin's Moral Philosophy: An Interpretation of William Godwin*. Oxford University Press, 1953.

Negley, Glenn. *Utopian Literature: A Bibliography with a Supplementary Listing of Works Influential in Utopian Thought*. Kansas: Regent's Press, 1977.

Notopoulos, James A. *The Platonism of Shelley: A Study of Platonism and the Poetic Mind*. Durham, NC: Duke University Press, 1949.

Olsen, Theodore. *Millennialism, Utopianism and Progress*. University of Toronto Press, 1982.

O'Neill, Michael. 'A More Hazardous Exercise: Shelley's Revolutionary Imaginings'. *Yearbook of English Studies*. The French Revolution in English Literature and Art Special Number. Ed. J. R. Watson. Vol. 19 (1989), 256–64.

Palmer, R. R. *The Age of Democratic Revolution: A Political History of Europe and America, 1760–1800.* 2 vols. Princeton University Press, 1959, 1964.

Parker, Patricia. *Inescapable Romance: Studies in the Poetics of a Mode.* Princeton University Press, 1979.

'The Progress of Phaedria's Bower: Spenser to Coleridge'. *English Literary History*, 40 (1973), 372–97

Patrides, C. A. and Joseph Wittreich, eds. *The Apocalypse in English Renaissance Thought and Literature: Patterns, Antecedents, Repercussions.* Manchester University Press, 1984.

Passmore, John. *The Perfectibility of Man.* London: Duckworth, 1970.

Patterson, Annabel. *Censorship and Interpretation: The Conditions of Writing and Reading in Early Modern England.* Madison: University of Wisconsin Press, 1984.

Pastoral and Ideology: Virgil to Valery. Oxford: Clarendon Press, 1988.

Paul, C. Kegan. *William Godwin: His Friends and Contemporaries.* 2 vols. London, 1876.

Paulson, Ronald. *Representations of Revolution (1789–1820).* New Haven: Yale University Press, 1983.

Peck, Walter Edwin. *Shelley: His Life and Works.* 2 vols. London: Ernest Benn, 1927.

Phelps, William Lyon. *The Beginnings of the English Romantic Movement: A Study in Eighteenth-Century Literature.* Boston: Ginn, 1899.

Philp, Mark. *Godwin's Political Justice.* London: Duckworth, 1986.

Pocock, J. G. A. *The Machiavellian Moment: Florentine Political Thought and the Atlantic Republican Tradition.* Princeton University Press, 1975.

Politics, Language and Time: Essays on Political Thought and History. London: Methuen, 1972.

Virtue, Commerce and History: Essays on Political Thought and History, Chiefly in the Eighteenth Century. Cambridge University Press, 1985.

Pollin, Burton R. 'Verse Satires on William Godwin in the Anti-Jacobin Period'. *Satire Newsletter*, 2 (1964), 31–40.

Prawer, S. S. *Karl Marx and World Literature.* Oxford University Press, 1976.

Prickett, Stephen. *England and the French Revolution.* Context and Commentary series. London: Macmillan, 1989.

Priestley, J. B. *The Prince of Pleasure and His Regency 1811–1820.* 1969; London: Sphere Books, 1971.

Proudfit, Charles L. *Landor as Critic.* London: Routledge & Kegan Paul, 1979.

Radford, Jean, ed. *The Progress of Romance: The Politics of Popular Fiction.* London: Routledge & Kegan Paul, 1986.

Radway, Janice A. *Reading the Romance: Women, Patriarchy, and Popular Literature.* Chapel Hill: University of North Carolina Press, 1984.

Raimond, Jean. 'Southey's Early Writings and the Revolution'. *Yearbook of English Studies*, 19 (1989), 181–96.

Ramsey, Lee C. *Chivalric Romances: Popular Literature in Medieval England.* Bloomington: Indiana University Press, 1983.

Ricoeur, Paul. *Lectures on Ideology and Utopia*. Ed. George H. Taylor. New York: Columbia University Press, 1986.

Ridenour, George M., ed. *Shelley: A Collection of Critical Essays*. Englewood Cliffs, NJ: Prentice-Hall, 1965.

Rivers, John. *Louvet: Revolutionist and Romance-Writer*. London: Hurst & Blackett, 1910.

Robinson, Charles E. 'Percy Bysshe Shelley, Charles Ollier, and William Blackwood: The Contexts of Early Nineteenth-Century Publishing'. In *Shelley Revalued*. Ed. Kelvin Everest.

Roe, Nicholas. *Wordsworth and Coleridge: The Radical Years*. Oxford: Clarendon Press, 1988.

Rogers, Neville. *Shelley at Work: A Critical Enquiry*. Oxford: Clarendon Press, 1967.

Roper, Derek. *Reviewing before the 'Edinburgh', 1788–1802*. London: Methuen, 1978.

Ross, Marlon B. 'Scott's Chivalric Pose: The Function of Metrical Romance in the Romantic Period'. *Genre*, 18 (1986), 267–97.

Royle, Edward and James Walvin. *English Radicals and Reformers 1760–1848*. Brighton: Harvester Press, 1987.

Rudé, George. *Revolutionary Europe 1783–1815*. 1964; London: Fontana, 1982.

Rutherford, Andrew, ed. *Byron: Augustan and Romantic*. London: Macmillan, 1990.

  ed. *Byron: The Critical Heritage*. London: Routledge & Kegan Paul, 1970.

Sage, Lorna, ed. *Peacock: The Satirical Novels*. Casebook series. London: Macmillan, 1976.

Schultz, Max F. *Paradise Preserved: Recreations of Eden in Eighteenth- and Nineteenth-Century England*. Cambridge University Press, 1986.

Scrivener, Michael H. *Radical Shelley: The Philosophical Anarchism and Utopian Thought of Percy Bysshe Shelley*. Princeton University Press, 1982.

Shklar, Judith N. *After Utopia: The Decline of Political Faith*. Princeton University Press, 1969.

Simons, John, ed. *From Medieval to Medievalism*. Basingstoke: Macmillan, 1992.

Simpson, Roger. *Camelot Regained: The Arthurian Revival and Tennyson, 1800–1849*. Cambridge: D. S. Brewer, 1990.

Siskin, Clifford. *The Historicity of Romantic Discourse*. New York: Oxford University Press, 1988.

Smith, Logan Pearsall. *Four Words: Romantic, Originality, Creative, Genius*. 1924; Oxford: Clarendon Press, 1972.

Smith, Olivia. *The Politics of Language 1791–1819*. Oxford: Clarendon Press, 1984.

Southam, B. C., ed. *Jane Austen: The Critical Heritage*. London: Routledge & Kegan Paul, 1968.

Sperry, Stuart M., Jr. *Shelley's Major Verse: The Narrative and Dramatic Poetry*. Cambridge, Mass.: Harvard University Press, 1988.

St Clair, William. *The Godwins and the Shelleys: The Biography of a Family*. London: Faber & Faber, 1989.

Steiner, George. *In Bluebeard's Castle: Some Notes Towards the Re-definition of Culture*. London: Faber & Faber, 1971.

Stevens, John. *Medieval Romance: Themes and Approaches*. London: Hutchinson, 1973.

Swedenberg, H. T., Jr. *The Theory of the Epic in England 1650–1800*. Los Angeles: University of California Press, 1944.

Tetreault, Ronald. *The Poetry of Life: Shelley and Literary Form*. University of Toronto Press, 1987.

Thompson, E. P. *The Making of the English Working Class*. 1963; Harmondsworth: Penguin, 1984.

'Disenchantment or Default? A Lay Sermon'. In *Power and Consciousness*. Ed. Conor Cruise O'Brien and W. D. Vaneck. University of London Press, 1969.

Tuveson, Ernest Lee. *Millennium and Utopia: A Study in the Background of the Idea of Progress*. 1949; New York: Harper & Row, 1964.

Venturi, Franco. *Utopia and Reform in the Enlightenment*. Cambridge University Press, 1971.

Vicario, Michael. 'The Implications of Form in *Childe Harold's Pilgrimage I–II*'. *KSJ*, 33 (1984), 103–29.

Vinaver, Eugène. *The Rise of Romance*. Oxford: Clarendon Press, 1971.

Vogler, Thomas A. *Preludes to Vision: The Epic Venture in Blake, Wordsworth, Keats and Hart Crane*. Berkeley: University of California Press, 1971.

Wardroper, John. *Kings, Lords and Wicked Libellers: Satire and Protest 1760–1837*. London: John Murray, 1973.

Wasserman, Earl R. *Elizabethan Poetry in the Eighteenth Century*. Urbana: University of Illinois Press, 1947.

Shelley: A Critical Reading. Baltimore: Johns Hopkins University Press, 1971.

Webb, R. K. *The British Working Class Reader 1790–1848: Literacy and Social Tension*. 1955; New York: Augustus M. Kelley, 1971.

Webb, Timothy. *Shelley: A Voice Not Understood*. Manchester University Press, 1977.

The Violet in the Crucible: Shelley and Translation. Oxford: Clarendon Press, 1976.

Weinberg, Bernard. *A History of Literary Criticism in the Italian Renaissance*. 2 vols. University of Chicago Press, 1961.

Weisinger, Herbert. 'The Middle Ages and the Late Eighteenth-Century Historians'. *Philological Quarterly*, 27 (1948), 63–79.

Weiskel, Thomas. *The Romantic Sublime: Studies in the Structure and Psychology of Transcendence*. Baltimore: Johns Hopkins University Press, 1976.

Welburn, Andrew. *Power and Self-Consciousness in the Poetry of Shelley*. Basingstoke: Macmillan, 1986.

Wellek, René. 'The Concept of Romanticism in Literary History'. *Concepts of Criticism*. Ed. Stephen G. Nichols. New Haven: Yale University Press, 1963.

White, G. A. and C. Newman, eds. *Literature in Revolution*. New York: Holt, Rinehart & Winston, 1972.

White, Newman Ivey. *Shelley*. 2 vols. London: Secker & Warburg, 1947.
  The Unextinguished Hearth: Shelley and His Contemporary Critics. Durham, NC: Duke University Press, 1938.

White, R. J. *Waterloo to Peterloo*. 1957; London: Mercury Books, 1963.

Wickwar, William H. *The Struggle for the Freedom of the Press, 1819–1832*. 1928; New York: Johnson Reprint Corporation, 1972.

Wilkie, Brian. *Romantic Poets and Epic Tradition*. Madison: Milwaukee: University of Wisconsin Press, 1965.

Williams, Gwyn A. *Artisans and Sans-Culottes: Popular Movements in France and Britain During the French Revolution*. London: Edward Arnold, 1968.

Williams, Ioan, ed. *Novel and Romance 1700–1800: A Documentary Record*. New York: Barnes & Noble, 1970.

Williams, John. *Wordsworth: Romantic Poetry and Revolution Politics*. Manchester University Press, 1989.

Williams, Raymond. *Culture and Society 1780–1950*. 1958; Harmondsworth: Penguin, 1961.
  Keywords: A Vocabulary of Culture and Society. 2nd edn. London: Fontana, 1983.

Winegarten, Renee. *Writers and Revolution: The Fatal Lure of Action*. New York: New Viewpoints, 1974.

Wood, Charles T. *The Age of Chivalry: Manners and Morals 1000–1450*. London: Weidenfeld & Nicolson, 1970.

Woodcock, George. 'The Meaning of Revolution in Britain 1770–1800'. *French Revolution and British Culture*. Ed. Crossley and Small.

Woodman, Ross Greig. *The Apocalyptic Vision in the Poetry of Shelley*. University of Toronto Press, 1964.

Woodring, Carl. *Politics in English Romantic Poetry*. Cambridge, Mass.: Harvard University Press, 1970.
  Politics in the Poetry of Coleridge. Madison: University of Wisconsin Press, 1961.

Yarrington, Alison and Kelvin Everest, eds. *Reflections of Revolution: Images of Romanticism*. London: Routledge, 1993.

Index

268